Oracle Advanced PL/SQL Developer Professional Guide

Master advanced PL/SQL concepts along with plenty of example questions for 1Z0-146 examination

Saurabh K. Gupta

BIRMINGHAM - MUMBAI

Oracle Advanced PL/SQL Developer Professional Guide

First published: May 2012

Production Reference: 1070512

Published by Packt Publishing Ltd.
Livery Place
35 Livery Street
Birmingham B3 2PB, UK.

ISBN 978-1-84968-722-5

www.packtpub.com

Cover Image by Tina Negus (tina_manthorpe@sky.com)

Credits

Foreword

Many of us learned to use PL/SQL recently; many did this many years ago. At that time simple problems required simple PL/SQL code, with lots of procedural code in it. Isn't the procedural part what PL/SQL is all about? Yes, it is, but this is also a threat because, when it is not used smartly, the procedural looping might become a performance hog.

Pl/SQL has evolved a lot. Bulk collections should be commonly in use now. Many programmers that support multiple vendors have little or no knowledge about Oracle collections. Because of this they write code like we did during v7, leaving the huge performance benefits, that Oracle has, untouched.

For these programmers this book is a very helpful addition to their library of knowledge. It helps them to easily perform the same task, but maybe 70 times faster, without making the code more complex. Using the advanced techniques described in the book you can do that. Don't mix up "advanced" with "complex". The fun about this is that many make their code complex using simple PL/SQL, trying to gain some performance, instead of effectively using advanced constructs in PL/SQL that in the end make the code easier to read and understand.

There is more to find in the book. Being a DBA, performance attracts a certain amount of attention. This is because performance is important. It greatly impacts the scalability of a database and the end user experience of the application. Other things you might find useful are the interfaces with the outside world, where external procedures can do work that does not fit the characteristics of a database.

Security is also something that attracts a DBA. Here you will find implementations of Virtual Private Database and enough remarks to keep the reader learning for quite a while. For example, how to protect against SQL injection? This again is a very interesting topic that should be taken very seriously. These days no network is safe. So scan every input.

I won't mention everything that is covered, just find a keyboard, your local database, and start reading. Try out the code samples and see where you can modify your existing code to take advantage of the new insights that the book will give you.

How advanced are the techniques described here depends on your mileage. For many the contents will be valuable enough to justify the term "advanced". As a reviewer it was a pleasure to read it and to try to push Saurabh Gupta to his limits. For me, I could use this book, even today.

Ronald Rood

Oracle ACE, Oracle DBA, OCM

PL/SQL is a programming language that is not only used by application developers, but also by database administrators in their daily tasks. This book contains information that every developer and even DBAs should know. As you read this book, you'll definitely learn a lot of new facts about PL/SQL programming. This book provides detailed information on general PL/SQL programming language, analyzing, tuning, tracing, and securing your code.

What I like most about the book is that it contains a lot of examples and helpful scripts for each chapter. This book also contains a lot of questions for the 1Z0-146 examination at the end of each chapter and it's one of the best guides for getting ready to pass the exam.

If you're a PL/SQL developer, whether a beginner or an expert, this book is for you.

Kamran Agayev A.

Oracle ACE, Oracle DBA Expert

About the Author

Saurabh K. Gupta got introduced to Oracle database around 5 years ago. Since then, he has been synchronizing his on job and off job interests with Oracle database programming. As an Oracle 11*g* Certified Advanced PL/SQL Professional, he soon moved from programming to database designing, development, and day-to-day database administration activities. He has been an active Oracle blogger and OTN forum member. He has authored and published more than 70 online articles and papers. His work can be seen in RMOUG journal, PSOUG, dbanotes, Exforsys, and Club Oracle. He shares his technical experience through his blog: `http://sbhoracle.wordpress.com/`. He is a member of **All India Oracle Users Group (AIOUG)** and loves to participate in technical meets and conferences.

Besides digging into Oracle, sketching and snooker are other pastimes for him. He can be reached through his blog `SbhOracle` for any comments, suggestions, or feedback regarding this book.

Acknowledgement

On a professional note, I am obliged to Ronald Rood, Kamran Agayev, Mohan Dutta, and Marcel Hoefs who reviewed the book with their own insights and perspectives. I was excited with the fact that the technical reviewers of my book are Oracle ACEs, highly respected, and recognized experts in the industry. I am grateful to Ronald who judged the worth of the book from the DBA perspective and helped me to extend my limits on the administrative aspect as well. Thanks to Kamran Agayev who consistently encouraged my writing styles and gave valuable inputs on the chapters. My obligations to Mohan Dutta and Marcel Hoefs who invested their valuable time in my work and added to the quality of the content. I would also like to express my gratitude for Arup Nanda, who has always been a great source of inspiration for me. His sessions and articles, covering all areas of Oracle database, have always been a great source of knowledge and motivation for me.

I would like to extend the appreciation to Packt Publishing for considering my proposal and accepting to go ahead on this book. My sincere thanks to Rukshana Khambatta, the Acquisition Editor at Packt for coordinating the kick-off activities of the book. I deeply appreciate the efforts of the Project Coordinator, Alka Nayak; the Lead Technical Editor, Pramila Balan; and the Technical Editors Vrinda Amberkar and Prasad Dalvi, whose diligent work and coordination added extra miles to the project. There was great tuning established between us and I am glad we worked parally on the editorial process while abiding by the timelines.

It is correctly said that a man's personal and professional achievements are a showcase of his family's support and encouragement. I dedicate all my efforts and works to my parents, Suresh Chandra Gupta and Swadesh Gupta and family for their inevitable support, motivation, and sacrifices, and nurturing me towards all my achievements. Sincere thanks to my wife, Neha, and Sir J.B. Mall for their love, consistent support, and confidence in my endeavors and for being with me during my tough times.

About the Reviewers

Kamran Agayev A. is an Oracle ACE and Oracle Certified Professional DBA working at Azercell Telecom. He's an author of the book, *Oracle Backup & Recovery: Expert secrets for using RMAN and Data Pump*, and also shares his experience with a lot of step-by-step articles and video tutorials in his blog at `http://kamranagayev.com`. He also presents at Oracle OpenWorld, TROUG, and local events.

Mohan Dutt is an Oracle expert, having presented more than 55 sessions at Oracle conferences worldwide. An Oracle evangelist at large, he was awarded Member of the Year by Oracle Applications User Group (OAUG) in 2007. He authors the world's first blog dedicated entirely to Oracle certification. He has founded and chaired 3 Oracle Special Interest Groups (SIG). He was recognized as an Oracle ACE in 2011.

Marcel Hoefs learned his trade participating in numerous Oracle development projects, as an Oracle developer, since 1997. Being a specialist in SQL and PL/SQL database development, Oracle Forms, Reports, and Designer, Marcel currently works as a Technical Architect, Lead Developer, and Performance Specialist. With the advent of web technologies such as Web Services, ADF, and APEX, he currently specializes in innovative solutions opening up traditional Oracle database systems to the Web. As a senior Oracle Consultant with CIBER, he is also an Oracle competence leader, organizing and participating in knowledge sharing sessions with participants from within and outside CIBER.

Ronald Rood is an innovating Oracle DBA with over 20 years of IT experience. He has built and managed cluster databases on almost each and every platform that Oracle has ever supported, from the famous OPS databases in version 7, until the latest RAC releases, currently being 11*g*. Ronald is constantly looking for ways to get the most value out of the database to make the investment for his customers even more valuable. He knows how to handle the power of the rich Unix environment very well and this is what makes him a first class trouble-shooter and a true Oracle ACE. Next to the spoken languages such as Dutch, English, German, and French, he also writes fluently in many scripting languages.

Currently, Ronald is a principal consultant working for CIBER in The Netherlands where he cooperates in many complex projects for large companies where downtime is not an option. CIBER or CBR is a global full service IT provider and Oracle Platinum Partner.

Ronald often replies in the Oracle forums, writes his own blog (`http://ronr.blogspot.com`) called "From errors we learn" and writes for various Oracle related magazines. He also wrote a book, *Mastering Oracle Scheduler in Oracle 11g Databases*, where he fills the gap between the Oracle documentation and customers' questions. You can find him on Twitter at `http://twitter.com/ik_zelf`.

Ronald has lots of certifications:

- Oracle Certified Master
- Oracle Certified Professional
- Oracle Database 11*g* Tuning Specialist
- Oracle Database 11*g* Data Warehouse Certified Implementation Specialist

Ronald fills his time with Oracle, his family, sky-diving, radio controlled model airplane flying, running a scouting group, and having a lot of fun.

He quotes, "A problem is merely a challenge that might take a little time to be solved".

www.PacktPub.com

Support files, eBooks, discount offers, and more

You might want to visit www.PacktPub.com for support files and downloads related to your book.

Did you know that Packt offers eBook versions of every book published, with PDF and ePub files available? You can upgrade to the eBook version at www.PacktPub.com and as a print book customer, you are entitled to a discount on the eBook copy. Get in touch with us at service@packtpub.com for more details.

At www.PacktPub.com, you can also read a collection of free technical articles, sign up for a range of free newsletters and receive exclusive discounts and offers on Packt books and eBooks.

http://PacktLib.PacktPub.com

Do you need instant solutions to your IT questions? PacktLib is Packt's online digital book library. Here, you can access, read and search across Packt's entire library of books.

Why Subscribe?

- Fully searchable across every book published by Packt
- Copy and paste, print, and bookmark content
- On demand and accessible via web browser

Free Access for Packt account holders

If you have an account with Packt at www.PacktPub.com, you can use this to access PacktLib today and view nine entirely free books. Simply use your login credentials for immediate access.

Instant Updates on New Packt Books

Get notified! Find out when new books are published by following @PacktEnterprise on Twitter, or the *Packt Enterprise* Facebook page.

Table of Contents

Preface

Oracle Database 11*g* brings in a weighted package of new features which takes the database management philosophy from instrumental to self-intelligence level. The new database features, which are more properly called "advanced", rather than "complex", aim either of the two purposes:

- Replacement of a workaround solution with a permanent one (as an enhancement)

- By virtue of routine researches and explorations, introduce a fresh feature to help database administrators and developers with their daily activities

Oracle Advanced PL/SQL Professional Guide focuses on advanced features of Oracle 11*g* PL/SQL. The areas targeted are PL/SQL code design, measuring and optimizing PL/SQL code performance, and analyzing PL/SQL code for reporting purposes and immunizing against attacks. The advanced programming topics such as usage of collections, implementation of VPD, interaction with external procedures in PL/SQL, performance orientation by caching results, tracing and profiling techniques, and protecting against SQL injection will familiarize you with the latest programming findings, trends and recommendations of Oracle. In addition, this book will help you to learn the latest, best practices of PL/SQL programming in terms of code writing, code analyzing for reporting purposes, tracing for performance, and safeguarding the PL/SQL code against hackers.

An investment in knowledge pays the best interest.

-Benjamin Franklin

The fact remains that the technical certifications from Oracle Corporation establish a benchmark of technical expertise and credibility, and set the tone of an improved career path for application developers. With the growing market in database development, Oracle introduced Advanced PL/SQL Professional Certification (1Z0-146) in the year 2008. The OCP (1Z0-146) certification exam tests aspirants on knowledge of advanced PL/SQL concepts (validated up to Oracle 11*g* Release 1). An advanced PL/SQL professional is expected to independently design, develop, and tune the PL/SQL code which can efficiently interface database systems and user applications.

The book, *Oracle Advanced PL/SQL Professional Guide*, is a sure recommendation for the preparation of the OCP certification (1Z0-146) exam. Advanced PL/SQL topics are explained thoroughly with the help of demonstrations, figures, and code examples. The book will not only explain a feature, but will also teach its implementation and application. You can easily pick up the content structure followed in the book. The code examples can be tried on your local database setups to give you a feel of the usage of a specific feature in real time scenarios.

What this book covers

Chapter 1, Overview of PL/SQL Programming Concepts, covers the overview of PL/SQL as the primary database programming language. It describes the characteristics of the language and its strengths in database development. This chapter speeds up with the structure of a PL/SQL block and reviews PL/SQL objects such as procedures, functions, and packages. In this chapter, we will also learn to work with SQL Developer.

Chapter 2, Designing PL/SQL Code, discusses the handling of cursors in a PL/SQL program. This chapter helps you to learn the guidelines for designing a cursor, usage of cursor variables, and cursor life cycle.

Chapter 3, Using Collections, introduces a very important feature of PL/SQL—collections. A collection in a database is very similar to arrays or maps in other programming languages. This chapter compares collection types and makes recommendations for the appropriate selection in a given situation. This chapter also covers the collection methods which are utility APIs for working with collections.

Chapter 4, Using Advanced Interface Methods, teaches how to interact with an external program written in a non-PL/SQL language, within PL/SQL. It demonstrates the execution steps for external procedures in PL/SQL. This steps describe the network configuration on a database server (mounted on Windows OS), library object creation, and publishing of a non-language program as an external routine.

Chapter 5, Implementing VPD with Fine Grained Access Control, introduces the concept of Fine Grained Access in PL/SQL. The working of FGAC as Virtual Private Database is explained in detail along with an insight into its key features. You will find stepwise implementation of VPD with the help of policy function and the DBMS_RLS package. This chapter also describes policy enforcement through application contexts.

Chapter 6, Working with Large Objects, discusses the traditional and conventional way of handling large objects in an Oracle database. This chapter starts with the familiarization of the available LOB data types (BLOB, CLOB, BFILE, and Temporary LOBs) and their significance. You will learn about the creation of LOB types in PL/SQL and their respective handling operations. This chapter demonstrates the management of LOB data types using SQL and the DBMS_LOB package.

Chapter 7, Using SecureFile LOBs, introduces one of the key innovations in Oracle 11*g* — SecureFiles. SecureFiles are upgraded LOBs which work on an improved philosophy of storage and maintenance. The key improvements of SecureFiles — deduplication, compression, and encryption — are licensed features. This chapter discusses and demonstrates the implementation of these three properties. You will learn how to migrate (or rather upgrade) the existing older LOBs into a new scheme — SecureFiles. The migration techniques covered use an online redefinition method and a partition method.

Chapter 8, Compiling and Tuning to Improve Performance, describes fair practices in effective PL/SQL programming. You will be very interested to discover how better code writing impacts code performance. This chapter explains an important aspect of query optimization — the PLSQL_OPTIMIZE_LEVEL parameter. The code behavior and optimization strategy at each level will help you to understand the language internals. Subsequently, the new PRAGMA feature will give you a deeper insight into subprogram inlining concepts.

Chapter 9, Caching to Improve Performance, covers another hot feature of Oracle 11*g* Database — server-side result caching. The newly introduced server-side cache component in SGA holds the results retrieved from SQL query or PL/SQL function. This chapter describes the configuration of a database server for caching feature through related parameters, implementation in SQL through RESULT_CACHE hint and implementation in PL/SQL function through the RESULT_CACHE clause. Besides the implementation section, this chapter teaches the validation and invalidation of result cache, using the DBMS_RESULT_CACHE package.

Chapter 10, Analyzing PL/SQL Code, helps you to understand and learn code diagnostics tricks and code analysis for reporting purposes. You will learn to monitor identifier usage, about compilation settings, and generate the subsequent reports from SQL Developer. This chapter discusses a very important addition in Oracle 11g—PL/Scope. It covers the explanations and illustrations to generate the structural reports through the dictionary views. In addition, this chapter also demonstrates the use of the DBMS_METADATA package to retrieve and extract metadata of database objects from the database in multiple formats.

Chapter 11, Profiling and Tracing PL/SQL Code, aims to demonstrate the tracing and profiling features in PL/SQL. The tracing demonstration uses the DBMS_TRACE package to trace the enabled or all calls in a PL/SQ program. The PL/SQL hierarchical profiler is a new innovation in 11g to identify and report the time consumed at each line of the program. The biggest benefit is that raw profiler data can be reproduced meaningfully into HTML reports.

Chapter 12, Safeguarding PL/SQL Code against SQL Injection Attacks, discusses the SQL injection as a concept and its remedies. The SQL injection is a serious attack on the vulnerable areas of the PL/SQL code which can lead to extraction of confidential information and many fatal results. You will learn the impacts and precautionary recommendations to avoid injective attacks. This chapter discusses the preventive measures such as using invoker's rights, client input validation tips, and using DBMS_ASSERT to sanitize inputs. It concludes on the testing strategies which can be practiced to identify vulnerable areas in SQL.

Appendix, Answers to Practice Questions, contains the answers to the practice questions for all chapters.

What you need for this book

You need to have a sound understanding of SQL and PL/SQL basics. You must have mid-level experience of working with Oracle programming.

Who this book is for

The book is for associate-level developers who are aiming for professional-level certification. This book can also be used to understand and practice advanced PL/SQL features of Oracle.

Conventions

In this book, you will find a number of styles of text that distinguish between different kinds of information. Here are some examples of these styles, and an explanation of their meaning.

Code words in text are shown as follows: "The SERVEROUTPUT parameter is a SQL*Plus variable which enables the printing of block debug messages."

A block of code is set as follows:

```
/*Start the PL/SQL block*/
DECLARE

/*Declare a local variable and initialize with a default value*/
   L_NUM NUMBER := 15;
   L_RES NUMBER;
BEGIN

/*Calculate the double of local variable*/
L_RES := L_NUM *2;

/*Print the result*/
   DBMS_OUTPUT.PUT_LINE('Double of '||TO_CHAR(L_NUM)||' is '||TO_
CHAR(L_RES));
END;
/
Double of 15 is 30

PL/SQL procedure successfully completed.
```

When we wish to draw your attention to a particular part of a code block, the relevant lines or items are set in bold:

```
/*Check if the cursor is already open*/
   IF NOT C_EMP%ISOPEN THEN
      DBMS_OUTPUT.PUT_LINE('Cursor is closed....Cursor has to be
opened');
   END IF;
```

Any command-line input or output is written as follows:

```
SQL> HELP INDEX
```

New terms and **important words** are shown in bold. Words that you see on the screen, in menus or dialog boxes for example, appear in the text like this: "Right-click on the **Connections** node and select **New Connection...** to open the connection wizard".

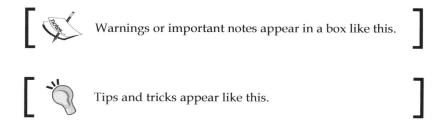

Warnings or important notes appear in a box like this.

Tips and tricks appear like this.

Reader feedback

Feedback from our readers is always welcome. Let us know what you think about this book—what you liked or may have disliked. Reader feedback is important for us to develop titles that you really get the most out of.

To send us general feedback, simply send an e-mail to feedback@packtpub.com, and mention the book title in the subject of your message.

If there is a topic that you have expertise in and you are interested in either writing or contributing to a book, see our author guide on www.packtpub.com/authors.

Customer support

Now that you are the proud owner of a Packt book, we have a number of things to help you to get the most from your purchase.

Downloading the example code

You can download the example code files for all Packt books you have purchased from your account at http://www.packtpub.com. If you purchased this book elsewhere, you can visit http://www.packtpub.com/support and register to have the files e-mailed directly to you.

Errata

Although we have taken every care to ensure the accuracy of our content, mistakes do happen. If you find a mistake in one of our books—maybe a mistake in the text or the code—we would be grateful if you would report this to us. By doing so, you can save other readers from frustration and help us improve subsequent versions of this book. If you find any errata, please report them by visiting http://www.packtpub. com/support, selecting your book, clicking on the **errata submission form** link, and entering the details of your errata. Once your errata are verified, your submission will be accepted and the errata will be uploaded to our website, or added to any list of existing errata, under the Errata section of that title.

Piracy

Piracy of copyright material on the Internet is an ongoing problem across all media. At Packt, we take the protection of our copyright and licenses very seriously. If you come across any illegal copies of our works, in any form, on the Internet, please provide us with the location address or website name immediately so that we can pursue a remedy.

Please contact us at copyright@packtpub.com with a link to the suspected pirated material.

We appreciate your help in protecting our authors, and our ability to bring you valuable content.

Questions

You can contact us at questions@packtpub.com if you are having a problem with any aspect of the book, and we will do our best to address it.

1
Overview of PL/SQL Programming Concepts

In the summer of 1970, Dr. E.F. Codd published his paper, *A Relational Model of Data for Large Shared Data Banks*, for the ACM journal. The projected model was accepted and subsequently an interactive database language, SQL, was developed by IBM Corporation, Inc. In 1979, Relational Software, Inc. stepped into the commercial implementation of SQL as the primary RDBMS language. Later, Relational Software, Inc. transformed into Oracle and since then, its story has been a success.

The **Structured Query Language** or **SQL** (pronounced "Sequel") has been used as the primary interactive language for all data operations such as selection, creation, and manipulation. Besides data operations, the language has administrative and monitoring features which ensure data consistency, integrity, and object controllability. By virtue of its multifaceted and versatile behavior in data centric environments, all major RDBMS support SQL as a database interaction language. The universal acceptance of SQL eases the logical usability across the databases (such as MySQL and SQL Server) with minor syntactical modifications.

Over the initial years of exploration, the procedural limitations of SQL were identified which prevented it from being an efficient programming language amongst the fourth generation languages. The head to head competition and demanding expectations of the industry led to the evolution of a procedural version of SQL in the Oracle database family. The first version of PL/SQL was debuted in Oracle 6.0 (in 1991) as an optional procedural extension in SQL* forms. Since its induction, PL/SQL has emerged as a strong and proven database programming language. With the release of Oracle 11*g* database (in 2007), PL/SQL has successfully stepped into its 11.0 version.

In this chapter, we will tour the Oracle PL/SQL programming concepts to get an overview of PL/SQL block, subprograms, exception handling, and object dependencies. The chapter outlines the benefits and characteristics of the language in the following sections:

- Introduction to PL/SQL
- Oracle development tools—SQL Developer and SQL*Plus
- Recapitulate procedures, functions, packages, and cursors
- Exception handling
- Object dependencies
- Major Oracle supplied packages

PL/SQL—the procedural aspect

PL/SQL stands for **Procedural Language-Structured Query Language**. It is a significant member of the Oracle programming toolset and extensively used to code server-side programs. Some of its major accomplishments are that it:

- Supports programming constructs to design a program unit
- Implements business logic in an Oracle server using cursors and database objects such as packages, subprograms, and many more
- Makes the application portability easier
- Preserves execution privileges and transaction management
- Makes use of advanced PL/SQL features such as collections to process bulk data and enhance performance
- Allows external programs to be executed from PL/SQL

As a language, the different perceptions of PL/SQL are as follows:

- **An interactive and structured language**: The PL/SQL language comprises of a glossary of expressive and explanatory keywords. The self-indenting, structured feature, and ANSI compatibility ensures quick learning and adaptation for an individual.

- **An embedded language**: A PL/SQL program is not environment-dependent but can be easily invoked from any recognized Oracle development environment such as SQL* Plus, SQL Developer, TOAD, reporting tools, and so on.

- **An integral language**: A database manager can easily integrate a PL/SQL server-side program with other client-side programming interfaces such as Java, C++, or .NET. The PL/SQL procedures or subprograms can be invoked from client programs as executable statements.

My first PL/SQL program

A PL/SQL block is the elementary unit of a program which groups a set of executable procedural statements. A block has defined "start" and "end" stages and it has three forms:

- **Anonymous**: This block is an unnamed PL/SQL block which is persistent for single execution only
- **Named**: This block contains named PL/SQL programs which are stored physically in the database as schema objects
- **Nested**: A block within another PL/SQL block forms a nested block structure

The skeleton of a PL/SQL block has four sections:

- **Header**: This is an optional section which is required for the named blocks. It contains block name, block owner's name, parameter specifications, and return type specification (for functions).
- **Declaration**: This is an optional section which is used for declaration of local variables, cursors, and local subprograms. The DECLARE keyword indicates the beginning of the declaration section.
- **Execution**: This is the mandatory section of a PL/SQL block which contains the executable statements. These statements are parsed by the PL/SQL engine and executed on the block invocation. The BEGIN and END keywords indicate the beginning and end of an executable section.
- **Exception**: This is the optional section of the block which contains the exception handlers. The appropriate exception handler is activated upon any exception raised from the executable section to suggest alternate steps. The EXCEPTION keyword indicates the start of the exception section.

The following block diagram shows the structure of a PL/SQL block. The sections marked in red are the mandatory ones with the others being optional:

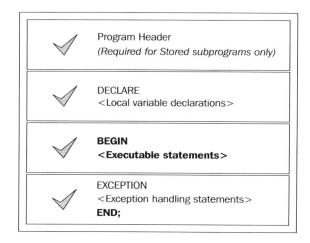

The PL/SQL following program illustrates the declaration and executable sections. The program declares a number variable, calculates its double value, and prints the result.

```
/*Enable the Serveroutput to display block messages*/
SET SERVEROUTPUT ON
```

 The SERVEROUTPUT parameter is a SQL*Plus variable which enables the printing of block debug messages. It is discussed in detail in the *SQL*Plus* section.

```
/*Start the PL/SQL block*/
DECLARE
/*Declare a local variable and initialize with a default value*/
   L_NUM NUMBER := 15;
   L_RES NUMBER;
BEGIN
/*Calculate the double of local variable*/
L_RES := L_NUM *2;
/*Print the result*/
   DBMS_OUTPUT.PUT_LINE('Double of '||TO_CHAR(L_NUM)||' is '||TO_
CHAR(L_RES));
END;
/
Double of 15 is 30

PL/SQL procedure successfully completed.
```

PL/SQL development environments

Oracle provides and recommends the usage of its development tools for SQL writing and code execution. This chapter will cover the two main developer tools from Oracle:

- SQL Developer
- SQL*Plus

However, there are many SQL development interfaces available on the Web such as TOAD from Quest Software, Dreamcoder by Mentat Technologies, and so on.

SQL Developer

SQL Developer is a **Graphical User Interface (GUI)** tool from the Oracle Corporation. It is free to use and includes a wide spectrum of new features with each of its releases. It allows the users to perform database activities such as SQL writing, PL/SQL execution, DBA activities easily, interactively, and considerably within time. Many of the database utilities such as unit testing, profiling, extended search, and SQL monitoring have been implemented as GUI utilities and can be easily used with the PL/SQL programs. The latest version of SQL Developer is 3.1 (3.1.07.42) which has been released on February 7, 2012. SQL Developer can be downloaded from the Oracle Technology Network link:

```
http://www.oracle.com/technetwork/developer-tools/sql-developer/
downloads/index.html
```

The latest release of the database development tool offers new features such as inclusion of RMAN under DBA navigator, support for data pump technology, renovated data copy and difference features, support for migration to Teradata and Sybase, and generation of PDF reports.

The key accomplishments offered by SQL Developer are:

- Authenticating and connecting to multiple Oracle databases
- Allowing creation and maintenance of schema objects packages, procedures, functions, triggers, indexes and views
- Querying and manipulating the data
- Database utilities such as version maintenance, admin activities, migration, and database export
- Support for SQL*Plus commands

The major offerings shown in the preceding list are by virtue of the tool features. The salient features of the SQL Developer tool are:

- Connection browser and Schema browser
- SQL Worksheet and Query Builder
- Database import and export utility wizard
- Database user-defined reports
- Code repository configuration for version control
- Database copy and migration utility wizard
- Third-party databases
- Oracle APEX integration
- TimesTen integration

The following screenshot shows the **Start Page** of Oracle SQL Developer:

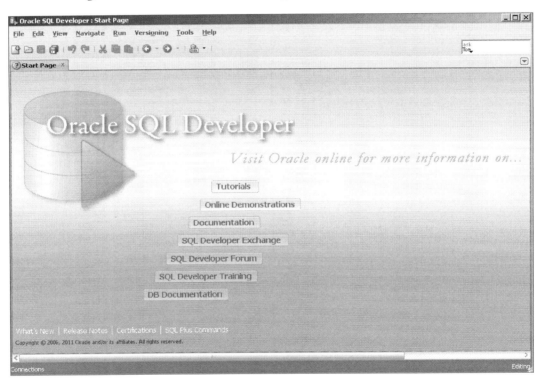

SQL Developer—the history

The following flowchart demonstrates the release history of SQL Developer:

SQL Developer 1.X	• Release with Oracle 11g R1
SQL Developer 1.2.X	• Database Migration introduced in SQL Developer
SQL Developer 1.5.X	• New features such as Version Control and File Management introduced
SQL Developer 1.5.4	• Supported 9 languages
SQL Developer 1.5.5	• Released with Oracle 11g R2
SQL Developer 1.5.6	• Released with Oracle JDeveloper 11g
SQL Developer 2.0	• PL/SQL unit testing and Data Modeler Viewer
SQL Developer 3.0	• Latest Release

Creating a connection

Once the SQL Developer tool is downloaded from the **Oracle Technology Network (OTN)** website (in ZIP format), it is ready for use and does not require any installation. The target server can be Oracle 11*g* database software. For educational and practice purposes, Oracle recommends the usage of the Oracle Database Express edition. It can be downloaded for free from the following URL:

```
http://www.oracle.com/technetwork/database/express-edition/overview/
index.html
```

By default, the database software installation takes care of the Oracle database configuration and Oracle network configuration.

Now, we shall start working with SQL Developer to connect to the database. The first and foremost step is establishing the connection to the target database.

The steps for creating a connection in SQL Developer are as follows:

1. Double-click on **\\sqldeveloper\sqldeveloper.exe**.

2. Go to **Menu | View | Connections**. A tabbed page titled **Connections** will appear at the left-hand side of the page. The top node of the tree is **Connections**.

3. Right-click on the **Connections** node and select **New Connection...** to open the connection wizard.

4. Specify the connection name, username, password, connection type, role (DBA or default), host name, port number, and SID of the target database. Connection type must be **Basic** if you specify the connection parameters. If **TNS**, then select a connection string from the **Network Alias** drop-down list (which is in sync with the TNSNAMES.ORA file)

5. Check the **Save Password** option to allow the Connection wizard to remember the password of this user.

6. Click on the **Test** button to verify the connection. The status (success or error message) will appear in the wizard's console.

7. Click on the **Connect** button to connect to the database. By default, it opens a SQL Worksheet to write and execute queries.

SQL Worksheet

The SQL Worksheet window is the primary editor to perform database activities. It is used to write and execute SQL statements, PL/SQL code, and SQL*Plus commands.

A new worksheet can be opened in two ways:

- Hitting the shortcut key, *Alt + F10*
- Navigating to **Tools | SQL Worksheet**

When a SQL worksheet is opened by following either of the preceding options, a window pops up which prompts the user to select the database connection applicable for the current worksheet. The available database connection to open a new SQL worksheet can be selected from the drop-down option:

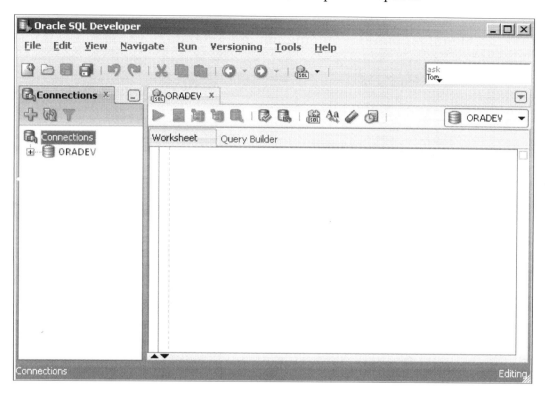

The worksheet contains multiple, quick utility actions as iconized menus. These menus perform a few of the basic activities associated with a script execution; for example, running a script, autotrace, and explain plan. With reference to the preceding screenshot of a sample SQL worksheet, the menu functions are described as follows:

- **Run Statement**: It executes the statement at the current cursor position.
- **Run Script**: It executes a script.
- **Autotrace**: It generates trace information about the statement.

- **Explain Plan**: It generates an execution plan for the query, starting at the current cursor position
- **SQL Tuning Advisor**: It advises the tuning tips for the current user. The user must have ADVISOR system privilege to use this icon.
- **Commit**: It commits the ongoing transaction in the current session.
- **Rollback**: It rollbacks the ongoing transaction in the current session.
- **Unshared SQL Worksheet**: It opens a new SQL worksheet.
- **To Upper/Lower/InitCaps**: It changes the string case of the statement to upper or lower or initial caps.
- **Clear**: It clears all the statements from the current SQL Worksheet.
- **SQL History**: It opens a dialog box with all the SQL statements executed for this user.

Executing a SQL statement

A SQL statement can be executed from the SQL Worksheet in three ways:

- Selecting the SQL statement and clicking on the **Run Statement** or **Run Script** icon from the Worksheet menu
- Selecting the SQL statement and pressing *F9*
- Terminating the SQL statement with a semicolon and pressing *Ctrl + Enter*

The result of the SQL statement execution is displayed in the **Query Result** tab. The following screenshot shows the execution of the SELECT statement using *Ctrl + Enter*:

The SQL Worksheet doesn't supports some SQL*Plus commands such as append, archive, attribute, and break.

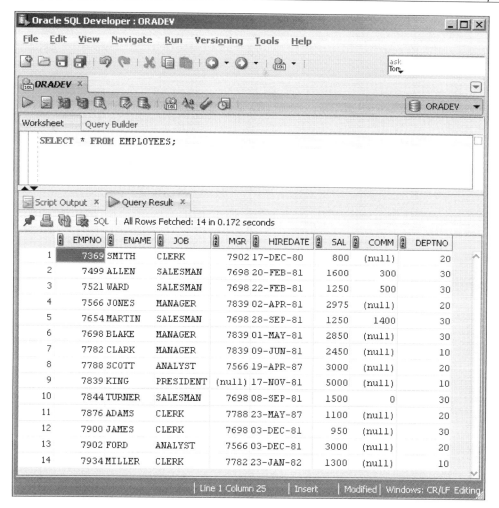

Calling a SQL script from SQL Developer

A SQL script saved on a specific OS location can be invoked from SQL Developer Worksheet. We will cover an overview of the two methods to execute a saved SQL script:

- A saved SQL script from an OS location can be invoked in The SQL Worksheet. It can be executed either by clicking on the **Run Script** (or *F5*) icon, or *Ctrl + Enter* or *F9*. The output of the script is displayed in the **Script Output** tab.

- Another option to invoke a saved script is to open it from the menu path, **File | Open**. Navigate to the script location and open the script. The script code would be opened in a new SQL Worksheet. Note that the worksheet's name is renamed as the actual script name. Now, the code can be executed using the **Run Script** icon.

A SQL script, `Test_Script.sql` at the `C:\Labs\` location contains the following SQL statement:

```
SELECT * FROM EMPLOYEES
/
```

As shown in the following screenshot, the script has been invoked in the SQL Worksheet using SQL*Plus execute command, `@`:

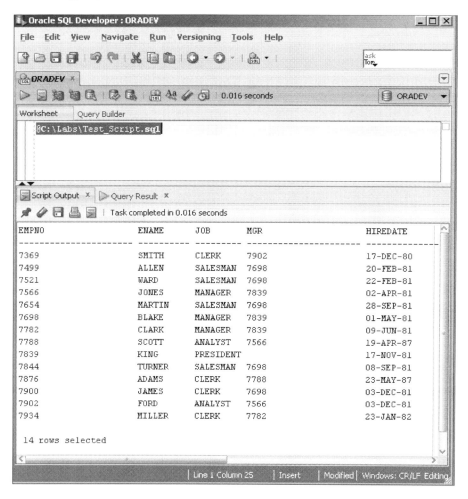

Creating and executing an anonymous PL/SQL block

An anonymous PL/SQL block can be written and executed, as shown in the following screenshot. Note that the PL/SQL block must be terminated with a semicolon. The **Script Output** tab displays the confirmed status of the block execution as **anonymous block completed**.

The block output can be viewed in the **Dbms Output** Tab. This tab remains hidden until it can be enabled and activated by navigating to **Menu | View | Dbms Output**:

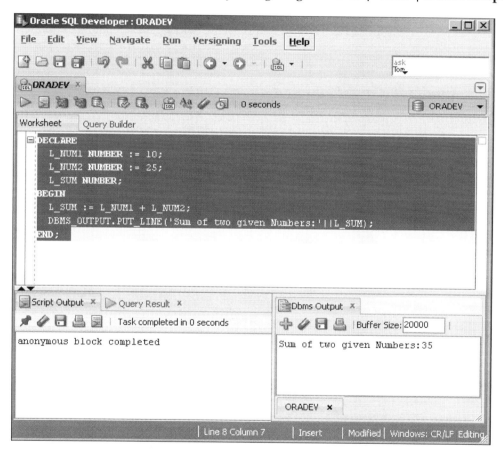

Debugging the PL/SQL code

The PL/SQL code can be debugged to observe the execution flow. The PL/SQL blocks and stored subprograms (procedures, functions, triggers, and packages) can be compiled for debugging.

An anonymous PL/SQL block can be debugged by selecting the block and choosing the **Debug** option from the right-click option list, as shown in the following screenshot:

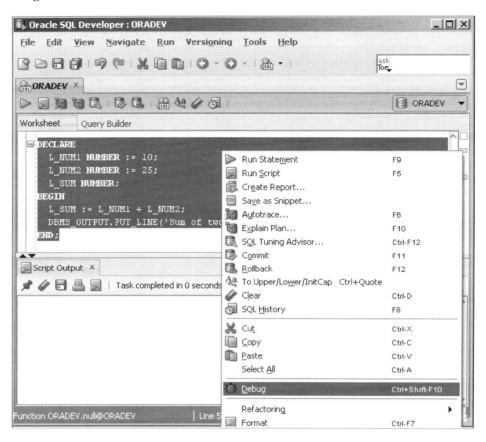

Once the **Debug** option is clicked, the debugging starts and the following output appears in the **Messages** tab:

```
Connecting to the database ORADEV.
Executing PL/SQL: ALTER SESSION SET PLSQL_DEBUG=TRUE
Executing PL/SQL: CALL DBMS_DEBUG_JDWP.CONNECT_TCP
  ( '127.0.0.1', '3953' )
Debugger accepted connection from database on port 3953.
Executing PL/SQL: CALL DBMS_DEBUG_JDWP.DISCONNECT()
Sum of two given Numbers:35
Process exited.
Disconnecting from the database ORADEV.
Debugger disconnected from database.
```

The database user must have DEBUG CREATE SESSION and DEBUG ANY PROCEDURE privileges to debug the PL/SQL code.

Likewise, the stored subprograms can be compiled using **Compile for Debug** to mark them for the debugging process. Henceforth, the execution of the subprograms can be traced line by line using the Oracle supplied package, DBMS_TRACE.

Editing and saving the scripts

SQL Developer provides enhanced editing features while writing the code in the SQL Worksheet. The automated code completion suggestion in the drop-down menu effectively eases the code writing. Besides, the PL/SQL syntax highlights, member method drop-down menu, code folding, and bookmarks are the other code editing features available in the SQL Worksheet.

A stored subprogram in the schema object tree can be opened in the SQL Worksheet for editing.

The following screenshot shows the auto-code completion feature of SQL Developer. You can select any of the available options as suited for the script:

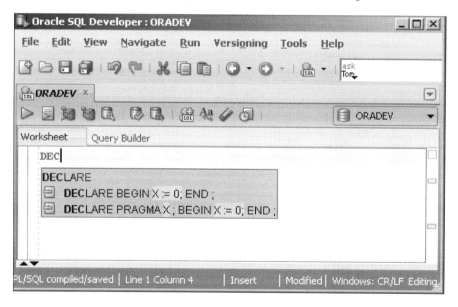

The SQL statements or PL/SQL code in the current SQL Worksheet can be saved as a text or SQL file at any specified location on the OS. Either follow the full navigation path (**File | Save**) or use the quick utility **Save** icon. Once the Windows **Save** dialog box appears, navigate to the target location, specify the filename, and click on the **Save** button.

SQL*Plus

SQL*Plus is a command-line utility interface and has been one of the primitive interfaces used by database professionals for database activities. The SQL*Plus session is similar to the SQL Worksheet of SQL Developer, where you can write and execute SQL statements and PL/SQL code.

Starting from Oracle 5.0, the SQL*Plus interface has been a part of the Oracle development kit. With regular revisions and enhancements in subsequent Oracle releases, it has been deprecated in the Oracle 11*g* release to recommend the use of SQL Developer. However, the SQL*Plus environment can still be established from command prompt.

The evolution cycle of SQL*Plus is shown in the following diagram:

The Oracle SQL*Plus session can be invoked from `sqlplus.exe`. This executable file is located in the `$Oracle_home\bin` folder. Alternatively, it can also be invoked by performing the following steps:

1. Open command prompt.
2. Enter `SQLPLUS`, press *Enter*. Note the SQL*Plus welcome message. The editor will prompt for a username and password.
3. Enter the username, password, and database connection string. Press *Enter*.
4. Connect to the database:

```
C:\>SQLPLUS

SQL*Plus: Release 11.2.0.1.0 Production on Fri Dec 23 14:20:36 2011
Copyright (c) 1982, 2010, Oracle.  All rights reserved.
```

```
Enter user-name: ORADEV/ORADEV


Connected to:

Oracle Database 11g Enterprise Edition Release 11.2.0.1.0 - Production
With the Partitioning, OLAP, Data Mining and Real Application Testing
options


SQL>
```

SQL*Plus has its own set of shell commands which can be used for the execution of scripts, editing the code, and formatting the query output.

The complete set of SQL*Plus commands can be obtained by entering HELP [INDEX |?] after the SQL prompt. The complete list of SQL*Plus commands are as follows:

```
SQL> HELP INDEX


Enter Help [topic] for help.
```

@	COPY	PAUSE	SHUTDOWN
@@	DEFINE	PRINT	SPOOL
/	DEL	PROMPT	SQLPLUS
ACCEPT	DESCRIBE	QUIT	START
APPEND	DISCONNECT	RECOVER	STARTUP
ARCHIVE LOG	EDIT	REMARK	STORE
ATTRIBUTE	EXECUTE	REPFOOTER	TIMING
BREAK	EXIT	REPHEADER	TTITLE
BTITLE	GET	RESERVED WORDS (SQL)	UNDEFINE
CHANGE	HELP	RESERVED WORDS (PL/SQL)	VARIABLE
CLEAR	HOST	RUN	WHENEVER OSERROR
COLUMN	INPUT	SAVE	WHENEVER SQLERROR
COMPUTE	LIST	SET	XQUERY
CONNECT	PASSWORD	SHOW	

Executing a SQL statement in SQL*Plus

A SQL statement can be executed in the SQL*Plus editor, terminated by a semicolon or a forward slash (/). The following screenshot demonstrates the execution of a SELECT statement. The query selects the names of all employees from the EMPLOYEES table:

```
C:\WINNT\system32\cmd.exe - sqlplus / as sysdba

SQL> SELECT ENAME FROM EMPLOYEES;

ENAME
----------
SMITH
ALLEN
WARD
JONES
MARTIN
BLAKE
CLARK
SCOTT
KING
TURNER
ADAMS
JAMES
FORD
MILLER

14 rows selected.

SQL>
```

Executing an anonymous PL/SQL block

Similar to the execution in SQL Developer, a PL/SQL block can be executed in SQL*Plus. The SERVEROUTPUT environment variable has to be set to ON to display the results in the editor.

The following screenshot demonstrates the execution of a PL/SQL block in SQL*Plus:

```
C:\WINNT\system32\cmd.exe - SQLPLUS

SQL> SET SERVEROUTPUT ON
SQL> DECLARE
  2       L_NUM1 NUMBER := 10;
  3       L_NUM2 NUMBER := 35;
  4       L_SUM NUMBER;
  5  BEGIN
  6       L_SUM := L_NUM1 + L_NUM2;
  7       DBMS_OUTPUT.PUT_LINE('Sum of two numbers is:'||L_SUM);
  8  END;
  9  /
Sum of two numbers is:45

PL/SQL procedure successfully completed.

SQL>
```

Procedures

A **procedure** is a derivative of PL/SQL block structure which is identified by its own specific name. It is stored as a schema object in the database and implements business logic in the applications. For this reason, procedures are often referred to as Business Managers of PL/SQL which not only maintain the business logic repository, but also demonstrate solution scalability and a modular way of programming.

The characteristics of procedures are as follows:

- A procedure can neither be called from a SELECT statement nor can it appear as a right-hand operand in an assignment statement. It has to be invoked from the executable section of a PL/SQL block as a procedural statement.

- They can optionally accept parameters in IN, OUT, or IN OUT mode.

- This implies that the only possibility for a procedure to return a value is through OUT parameters, but not through the RETURN [value] statement. The RETURN statement in a procedure is used to exit the procedure and skip the further execution.

For recapitulation, the following table differentiates between the IN, OUT, and IN OUT parameters:

IN	OUT	IN OUT
Default parameter mode	Has to be explicitly defined	Has to be explicitly defined
Parameter's value is passed into the program from the calling environment	Parameter returns a value back to the calling environment	Parameter may pass a value from the calling environment to the program or return a value to the calling environment
Parameters are passed by reference	Parameters are passed by value	Parameters are passed by value
May be constant, literal, or initialized variable	Uninitialized variable	Initialized variable
Can hold the default value	Default value cannot be assigned	Default value cannot be assigned

The syntax for a procedure is as follows:

```
CREATE [OR REPLACE] PROCEDURE [Procedure Name] [Parameter List]
[AUTHID DEFINER | CURRENT_USER]
IS
   [Declaration Statements]
BEGIN
 [Executable Statements]
EXCEPTION
 [Exception handlers]
END [Procedure Name];
```

The following standalone procedure converts the case of the input string from lowercase to uppercase:

```
/*Create a procedure to convert the string from lower case to
upper case*/
CREATE OR REPLACE PROCEDURE P_TO_UPPER (P_STR VARCHAR2)
IS
/*Declare the local variables*/
   L_STR VARCHAR2(50);
BEGIN
/*Convert the case using UPPER function*/
   L_STR := UPPER(P_STR);
/*Display the output with appropriate message*/
   DBMS_OUTPUT.PUT_LINE('Input string in Upper case : '||L_STR);
END;
/

Procedure created.
```

Executing a procedure

A procedure can be either executed from SQL*Plus or from a PL/SQL block. The P_TO_UPPER procedure can be executed from SQL*Plus.

The following illustration shows the execution of the procedure from SQL*Plus (note that the parameter is passed using the bind variable):

```
/*Enable the SERVEROUTPUT parameter to print the results in the
environment*/
SQL> SET SERVEROUTPUT ON

/*Declare a session variable for the input*/
SQL> VARIABLE M_STR VARCHAR2(50);
```

```
/*Assign a test value to the session variable*/
SQL> EXECUTE :M_STR := 'My first PLSQL procedure';

PL/SQL procedure successfully completed.


/*Call the procedure P_TO_UPPER*/
SQL> EXECUTE P_TO_UPPER(:M_STR);
Input string in Upper case : MY FIRST PLSQL PROCEDURE

PL/SQL procedure successfully completed.
```

The P_TO_UPPER procedure can be called as a procedural statement within an anonymous PL/SQL block:

```
/*Enable the SERVEROUTPUT parameter to print the results in the
environment*/
SQL> SET SERVEROUTPUT ON

/*Start a PL/SQL block*/
SQL> BEGIN
        /*Call the P_TO_UPPER procedure*/
          P_TO_UPPER ('My first PLSQL procedure');
      END;
      /

Input string in Upper case : MY FIRST PLSQL PROCEDURE

PL/SQL procedure successfully completed.
```

Functions

Like a procedure, a **function** is also a derivative of a PL/SQL block structure which is physically stored within a database. Unlike procedures, they are the "workforce" in PL/SQL and meant for calculative and computational activities in the applications.

The characteristics of functions are as follows:

- Functions can be called from SQL statements (SELECT and DMLs). Such functions must accept only IN parameters of valid SQL types. Alternatively, a function can also be invoked from SELECT statements if the function body obeys the database purity rules.

- Functions can accept parameters in all three modes (IN, OUT, and IN OUT) and mandatorily return a value. The type of the return value must be a valid SQL data type (not be of BOOLEAN, RECORD, TABLE, or any other PL/SQL data type).

The syntax for a function is as follows:

```
CREATE [OR REPLACE] FUNCTION [Function Name] [Parameter List]
RETURN [Data type]
[AUTHID DEFINER | CURRENT_USER]
[DETERMINISTIC | PARALLEL_ENABLED | PIPELINES]
[RESULT_CACHE [RELIES_ON (table name)]]
IS
   [Declaration Statements]
BEGIN
 [Executable Statements]
   RETURN [Value]
EXCEPTION
 [Exception handlers]
END [Function Name];
```

The standalone function, F_GET_DOUBLE, accepts a single argument and returns its double:

```
/*Create the function F_GET_DOUBLE*/
CREATE OR REPLACE FUNCTION F_GET_DOUBLE (P_NUM NUMBER)
RETURN NUMBER   /*Specify the return data type*/
IS
/*Declare the local variable*/
   L_NUM NUMBER;
BEGIN
/*Calculate the double of the given number*/
   L_NUM := P_NUM * 2;
/*Return the calculated value*/
   RETURN L_NUM;
END;
/

Function created.
```

Function—execution methods

As a common feature shared among the stored subprograms, functions can be invoked from a SQL*Plus environment and called from a PL/SQL as a procedural statement.

The following code snippet demonstrates the execution of a function from a SQL*Plus environment and its return value have been captured in a session bind variable:

```
/*Enable the SERVEROUTPUT parameter to print the results in the
environment*/
SQL> SET SERVEROUTPUT ON

/*Declare a session variable M_NUM to hold the function output*/
SQL> VARIABLE M_NUM NUMBER;

/*Function is executed and output is assigned to the session
variable*/
SQL> EXEC :M_NUM := F_GET_DOUBLE(10);

PL/SQL procedure successfully completed.

/*Print the session variable M_NUM*/
SQL> PRINT M_NUM

M_NUM
----------
20
```

Now, we will see the function execution from an anonymous PL/SQL block as a procedural statement:

```
/*Enable the SERVEROUTPUT parameter to print the results in the
environment*/
SQL> SET SERVEROUTPUT ON

SQL>DECLARE
    M_NUM NUMBER;
  BEGIN
    M_NUM := F_GET_DOUBLE(10);
    DBMS_OUTPUT.PUT_LINE('Doubled the input value as : '||M_NUM);
  END;
  /
Doubled the input value as : 20

PL/SQL procedure successfully completed.
```

Restrictions on calling functions from SQL expressions

Unlike procedures, a stored function can be called from SELECT statements; provided it must not violate the database purity levels. These rules are as follows:

- A function called from a SELECT statement cannot contain DML statements

- A function called from a UPDATE or DELETE statement on a table cannot query (SELECT) or perform transaction (DMLs) on the same table

- A function called from SQL expressions cannot contain the TCL (COMMIT or ROLLBACK) command or the DDL (CREATE or ALTER) command

Besides these rules, a standalone user-defined function must qualify the following conditions:

- The parameters to the stored function, if any, should be passed in "pass by reference" mode that is, IN parameter only. The data type of the parameter must be a valid SQL data type. Also, the parameters must follow positional notation in the list.

- The return type of the function must be a valid SQL data type.

The F_GET_DOUBLE function can easily be embedded within a SELECT statement as it perfectly respects all the preceding rules:

```
/*Invoke the function F_GET_DOUBLE from SELECT statement*/
SQL> SELECT F_GET_DOUBLE(10) FROM DUAL;


F_GET_DOUBLE(10)
----------------
              20
```

In Oracle, DUAL is a table owned by the SYS user, which has a single column, DUMMY, of VARCHAR2 (1) type. It was first designed by Charles Weiss while working with internal views to duplicate a row. The DUAL table is created by default during the creation of data dictionaries with a single row, whose value is X. The users other than SYS, use its public synonym, to select the value of pseudo columns, such as USER, SYSDATE, NEXTVAL, or CURRVAL. Oracle 10g has considerably improved the performance implications of the DUAL table through a "fast dual" access mechanism.

PL/SQL packages

Packages are the database objects which behave as libraries and grounds on the principle of encapsulation and data hiding. A package is privileged to contain a variety of constructs such as subprograms, variables, cursors, exceptions, and variables. In addition, it enjoys multiple add-on features such as subprogram overloading, public and private member constructs, and so on.

> Standalone subprograms cannot be overloaded. Only packaged subprograms can be overloaded by virtue of their signatures.

The following diagram shows the advantages of a package:

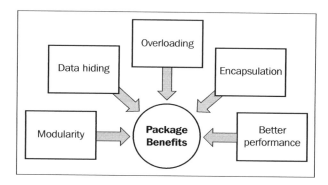

A package has two components—package specification and package body. While package specification contains the prototype of public constructs, the package body contains the definition of public, as well as private (local) constructs.

The characteristics of package specification are as follows:

- Package specification is the mandatory component of the package. A package cannot exist without its specification.

- Package specification contains the prototypes of the constructs. The prototype is the forward declaration of the constructs which would be referenced later in the package body. The subprogram (procedure and function) prototype includes the signature information with a semicolon. The subprograms, once prototyped, must have their definition in the package body section. The package specification cannot contain an executable section.

- These member constructs enjoy their visibility within and outside the package. They can be invoked from outside the package by the privileged users.

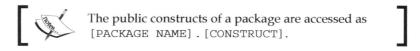

The public constructs of a package are accessed as
[PACKAGE NAME].[CONSTRUCT].

- The valid package constructs can be PL/SQL types, variables, exceptions, procedures, and functions.
- If package specification contains variables, they are implicitly initialized to NULL by Oracle.

The characteristics of the package body are as follows:

- The package body contains the definition of the subprograms which were declared in package specification.
- The package body can optionally contain local constructs. The visibility scope of the local constructs is limited to the package body only.
- The package body is an optional component; a package can exist in a database without its package body.

The syntax for creating a package is as follows:

```
CREATE [OR REPLACE] PACKAGE [NAME] IS
   [PRAGMA]
   [PUBLIC CONSTRUCTS]
END;

CREATE [OR REPLACE] PACKAGE BODY [NAME] IS
   [LOCAL CONSTRUCTS]
   [SUBPROGRAM DEFINITION]
   [BEGIN...END]
END;
```

Note the optional BEGIN-END block in the package body. It is optional, but gets executed only the first time the package is referenced. They are used for initialization of global variables.

A package can be compiled with its specification component alone. In such cases, packaged program units cannot be invoked as their executable logic has not been defined yet.

The compilation of a package with specification and body ensures the concurrency between the program units prototyped in the specification and the program units defined in the package body. All the packaged program units are compiled in the single package compilation. If the package is compiled with errors, it is created as an invalid object in the database. The USER_OBJECTS dictionary view is used to query the status of a schema object. The STATUS column in the view shows the current status as VALID or INVALID.

Cursors—an overview

Cursors make a concrete conceptual ground for database professionals. In simple words, a **cursor** is a memory pointer to a specific private memory location where a SELECT statement is processed. This memory location is known as a **context area**.

Every SQL statement in a PL/SQL block can be realized as a cursor. The context area is the memory location which records the complete information about the SQL statement currently under process. The processing of the SQL statement in this private memory area involves its parsing, data fetch, and retrieval information. The data retrieved should be pulled into local variables and, henceforth, used within the program.

On the basis of their management, cursors are classified as **implicit** and **explicit** cursors.

The Oracle server is fully responsible for the complete execution cycle of an implicit cursor. Oracle implicitly creates a cursor for all SQL statements (such as SELECT, INSERT, UPDATE, and DELETE) within the PL/SQL blocks.

For explicit cursors, the execution cycle is maneuvered by database programmers. Explicit cursors are meant only for the SELECT statements which can fetch one or more rows from the database. The developers have the complete privilege and control to create a cursor, fetch data iteratively, and close the cursor.

Cursor execution cycle

Let us have a quick tour through the cursor management and execution cycle. Note that this execution cycle starts after the cursor has been prototyped in the declarative section:

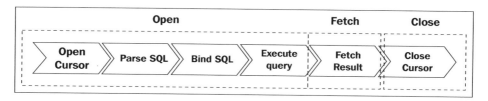

- The OPEN stage allocates the context area in **Process Global Area** (PGA) for carrying out further processing (parsing, binding, and execution) of the SELECT statement associated with the cursor. In addition, the record pointer moves to the first record in the data set.

- The FETCH stage pulls the data from the query result set. If the result set is a multi-record set, the pointer increments with every fetch. The Fetch stage is live until the last record is reached in the result set.

- The CLOSE stage closes the cursor, flushes the context area, and releases the memory back to the PGA.

Cursor attributes

The cursor attributes, which carry important information about the cursor processing at each stage of their execution, are as follows:

- %ROWCOUNT: Number of rows returned/changed in the last executed query. Applicable for SELECT as well as DML statements.

- %ISOPEN: Boolean TRUE if the cursor is still open, else FALSE. For an implicit cursor, it is only FALSE.

- %FOUND: Boolean TRUE, if the fetch operation switches and points to a record, else FALSE.

- %NOTFOUND: Boolean FALSE when the cursor pointer switches but does not point to a record in the result set.

[%ISOPEN is the only cursor attribute which is accessible outside the cursor execution cycle.]

We will illustrate the usage of cursor attributes with a simple PL/SQL program. The following program implements the %ISOPEN, %NOTFOUND, and %ROWCOUNT attributes to iterate the employee data from the EMPLOYEES table and display it:

```
/*Enable the SERVEROUTPUT to display block messages*/
SET SERVEROUTPUT ON

/*Start the PL/SQL Block*/
DECLARE

/*Declare a cursor to select employees data*/
    CURSOR C_EMP IS
        SELECT EMPNO,ENAME
        FROM EMPLOYEES;
```

```
    L_EMPNO EMPLOYEES.EMPNO%TYPE;
    L_ENAME EMPLOYEES.ENAME%TYPE;
BEGIN
/*Check if the cursor is already open*/
IF NOT C_EMP%ISOPEN THEN
     DBMS_OUTPUT.PUT_LINE('Cursor is closed....Cursor has to be
opened');
    END IF;
/*Open the cursor and iterate in a loop*/
    OPEN C_EMP;
    LOOP
/*Fetch the cursor data into local variables*/
    FETCH C_EMP INTO L_EMPNO, L_ENAME;
  EXIT WHEN C_EMP%NOTFOUND;
  /*Display the employee information*/
    DBMS_OUTPUT.PUT_LINE(chr(10)||'Display Information for
employee:'||C_EMP%ROWCOUNT);
       DBMS_OUTPUT.PUT_LINE('Employee Id:'||L_EMPNO);
       DBMS_OUTPUT.PUT_LINE('Employee Name:'||L_ENAME);
    END LOOP;
END;
/


Cursor is closed....Cursor has to be opened

Display Information for employee:1
Employee Id:7369
Employee Name:SMITH

Display Information for employee:2
Employee Id:7499
Employee Name:ALLEN

Display Information for employee:3
Employee Id:7521
Employee Name:WARD

Display Information for employee:4
Employee Id:7566
Employee Name:JONES
....


PL/SQL procedure successfully completed.
```

Cursor FOR loop

The iterative construct, FOR loop, can be aligned to the cursor execution cycle. The benefit is that the cursor can be directly accessed without physically opening, fetching, or closing the cursor. In addition, it reduces the overhead of declaring local identifiers. The stages are handled implicitly by the FOR loop construct.

The cursor FOR loop qualifies for the best programming practices where the cursor carries multi-row set. The following program demonstrates the working of a cursor FOR loop:

```
/*Enable the SERVEROUTPUT parameter to print the results in the
environment*/
SQL> SET SERVEROUTPUT ON
/*Start the PL/SQL block*/
DECLARE
/*Declare an explicit cursor to select employee name and salary*/
    CURSOR CUR_EMP IS
        SELECT ENAME, SAL
        FROM EMPLOYEES;
BEGIN
/*FOR Loop uses the cursor CUR_EMP directly*/
    FOR EMP IN CUR_EMP
    LOOP
/*Display appropriate message*/
    DBMS_OUTPUT.PUT_LINE('Employee '||EMP.ENAME||' earns '||EMP.SAL||'
per month');
    END LOOP;
END;
/

Employee SMITH earns 800 per month
Employee ALLEN earns 1600 per month
Employee WARD earns 1250 per month
Employee JONES earns 2975 per month
Employee MARTIN earns 1250 per month
Employee BLAKE earns 2850 per month
Employee CLARK earns 2450 per month
Employee SCOTT earns 3000 per month
Employee KING earns 5000 per month
Employee TURNER earns 1500 per month
Employee ADAMS earns 1100 per month
Employee JAMES earns 950 per month
Employee FORD earns 3000 per month
Employee MILLER earns 1300 per month

PL/SQL procedure successfully completed.
```

Exception handling in PL/SQL

During runtime, the abnormal program flow which occurs within a precompiled program unit with the actual data is known as an **exception**. Such errors can be trapped in the EXCEPTION section of a PL/SQL block. The exception handlers within the section can capture the appropriate error and redirect the program flow for an alternative or final task. An efficient exception handling ensures safe and secure termination of the program. The situation without exceptions may become serious if the program involves transactions and the program doesn't handle the appropriate exception, thus ending up in abrupt termination of the program.

There are two types of exceptions—system-defined exceptions and user defined exceptions. While system defined exceptions are implicitly raised by the Oracle server, user-defined exceptions follow different ways to be explicitly raised within the program.

In addition, Oracle avails two utility functions, SQLCODE and SQLERRM, to retrieve the error code and message for the last occurred exception.

System-defined exceptions

As the name suggests, the system-defined exceptions are defined and maintained implicitly by the Oracle server. They are defined in the Oracle STANDARD package. Whenever an exception occurs inside the program. The Oracle server matches and identifies the appropriate exception from the available set of exceptions. Majorly, these exceptions have a negative error code associated with it. In addition to the error code and error message, the system-defined exceptions have a short name which is used with the exception handlers.

For example, ORA-01422 is the error code for the TOO_MANY_ROWS exception whose error message is "exact fetch returns more than requested number of rows". But the name is required only in exception handlers.

The PL/SQL block contains a SELECT statement which selects the name and salary of an employee whose employee ID is one of the declared variables. Note that such SELECT statements are more prone to the NO_DATA_FOUND exception.

```
/*Enable the SERVEROUTPUT parameter to print the results in the
environment*/
SQL> SET SERVEROUT ON

/*Start the PL/SQL block*/
SQL> DECLARE
        /*Declare the local variables*/
        L_ENAME VARCHAR2 (100);
```

```
        L_SAL NUMBER;
        L_EMPID NUMBER := 8376;
     BEGIN
     /*SELECT statement to fetch the name and salary details of
the employee*/
        SELECT ENAME, SAL
        INTO L_ENAME, L_SAL
        FROM EMPLOYEES
        WHERE EMPNO = L_EMPID;
     EXCEPTION
     /*Exception Handler when no data is fetched from the
table*/
        WHEN NO_DATA_FOUND THEN
        /*Display an informative message*/
           DBMS_OUTPUT.PUT_LINE ('No Employee exists with the id '||L_
EMPID);
     END;
     /

No Employee exists with the id 837

PL/SQL procedure successfully completed.
```

The following table consolidates some of the common system-defined exceptions along with their ORA error code:

Error	Named exception	Comments (raised when)
ORA-00001	DUP_VAL_ON_INDEX	Duplicate value exists
ORA-01001	INVALID_CURSOR	Cursor is invalid
ORA-01012	NOT_LOGGED_ON	User is not logged in
ORA-01017	LOGIN_DENIED	System error occurred
ORA-01403	NO_DATA_FOUND	The query returns no data
ORA-01422	TOO_MANY_ROWS	A single row query returns multiple rows
ORA-01476	ZERO_DIVIDE	A number is attempted to divide by zero
ORA-01722	INVALID_NUMBER	The number is invalid
ORA-06504	ROWTYPE_MISMATCH	Mismatch occurred in row type
ORA-06511	CURSOR_ALREADY_OPEN	Cursor is already open
ORA-06531	COLLECTION_IS_NULL	Working with NULL collection
ORA-06532	SUBSCRIPT_OUTSIDE_LIMIT	Collection index out of range
ORA-06533	SUBSCRIPT_BEYOND_COUNT	Collection index out of count

User-defined exceptions

Sometimes, the programs are expected to follow agile convention norms of an application. The programs must have standardized error codes and messages. Oracle gives flexibility in declaring and implementing your own exceptions through user-defined exceptions.

Unlike system-defined exceptions, they are raised explicitly in the BEGIN...END section using the RAISE statement.

There are three ways of declaring user-defined exceptions:

- Declare the EXCEPTION type variable in the declaration section. Raise it explicitly in the program body using the RAISE statement. Handle it in the EXCEPTION section. Note that here no error code is involved.

- Declare the EXCEPTION variable and associate it with a standard error number using PRAGMA EXCEPTION_INIT.

A **Pragma** is a clue to the compiler to manipulate the behavior of the program unit during compilation, and not at the time of execution.

PRAGMA EXCEPTION_INIT can also be used to map an exception to a non-predefined exception. These are standard errors from the Oracle server, but not defined as PL/SQL exceptions.

- Use the RAISE_APPLICATION_ERROR to declare own error number and error message.

The following PL/SQL block declares a user-defined exception and raises it in the program body:

```
/*Enable the SERVEROUTPUT parameter to print the results in the
environment*/
SQL> SET SERVEROUTPUT ON

/*Declare a bind variable M_DIVISOR*/
SQL> VARIABLE M_DIVISOR NUMBER;

/*Declare a bind variable M_DIVIDEND*/
SQL> VARIABLE M_DIVIDEND NUMBER;

/*Assign value to M_DIVISOR as zero*/
SQL> EXEC :M_DIVISOR := 0;
```

```
PL/SQL procedure successfully completed.

/*Assign value to M_DIVIDEND as 10/
SQL> EXEC :M_DIVIDEND := 10;

PL/SQL procedure successfully completed.

/*Start the PL/SQL block*/
SQL> DECLARE
        /*Declare the local variables and initialize with the bind
variables*/
        L_DIVISOR NUMBER := :M_DIVISOR;
        L_DIVIDEND NUMBER := :M_DIVIDEND;
        L_QUOT NUMBER;
        /*Declare an exception variable*/
        NOCASE EXCEPTION;
     BEGIN
        /*Raise the exception if Divisor is equal to zero*/
        IF L_DIVISOR = 0 THEN
            RAISE NOCASE;
        END IF;
        L_QUOT := L_DIVIDEND/L_DIVISOR;
        DBMS_OUTPUT.PUT_LINE('The result : '||L_QUOT);
     EXCEPTION
        /*Exception handler for NOCASE exception*/
        WHEN NOCASE THEN
            DBMS_OUTPUT.PUT_LINE('Divisor cannot be equal to zero');
     END;
     /
Divisor cannot be equal to zero

PL/SQL procedure successfully completed.

/*Assign a non zero value to M_DIVISOR and execute the PL/SQL
block again*/
SQL> EXEC :M_DIVISOR := 2;

PL/SQL procedure successfully completed.

SQL> /
The result : 5

PL/SQL procedure successfully completed.
```

The RAISE_APPLICATION_ERROR procedure

Oracle gives privilege to the database programmers to create their own error number and associate an error message, too. These are dynamic user defined exceptions and are done through an Oracle-supplied method, RAISE_APPLICATION_ERROR. It can be implemented either in the executable section to capture specific and logical errors, or it can be used in the exception section to handle errors of a generic nature.

The syntax for the RAISE_APPLICATION_ERROR procedure is as follows:

```
RAISE_APPLICATION_ERROR (error_number, error_message[, {TRUE |
FALSE}])
```

In this syntax, the error_number parameter is a mandatory formal parameter whose value must be in the range of -20000 to -20999. The second parameter, error_message, corresponds to the error number and appears with the exception when raised in the program. The last parameter is the optional parameter which allows the error to be added to the current error stack. By default, its value is FALSE.

The following program rewrites the last program by creating a user-defined exception, dynamically (note that it doesn't have the EXCEPTION type variable):

```
/*Enable the SERVEROUTPUT parameter to print the results in the
environment*/
SQL> SET SERVEROUTPUT ON

/*Declare a bind variable M_DIVISOR*/
SQL> VARIABLE M_DIVISOR NUMBER;

/*Declare a bind variable M_DIVIDEND*/
SQL> VARIABLE M_DIVIDEND NUMBER;

/*Assign value to M_DIVISOR as zero*/
SQL> EXEC :M_DIVISOR := 0;

PL/SQL procedure successfully completed.

/*Assign value to M_DIVIDEND as 10/
SQL> EXEC :M_DIVIDEND := 10;

PL/SQL procedure successfully completed.

/*Start the PL/SQL block*/
SQL> DECLARE
        /*Declare the local variables and initialize them with
bind variables*/
```

```
                    L_DIVISOR NUMBER := :M_DIVISOR;
                    L_DIVIDEND NUMBER := :M_DIVIDEND;
                    L_QUOT NUMBER;
            BEGIN
                /*Raise the exception using RAISE_APPLICATION_ERROR is
        the divisor is zero*/
                    IF L_DIVISOR = 0 THEN
                        RAISE_APPLICATION_ERROR(-20005,'Divisor cannot be equal
        to zero');
                    END IF;
                    L_QUOT := L_DIVIDEND/L_DIVISOR;
                    DBMS_OUTPUT.PUT_LINE('The result : '||L_QUOT);
            EXCEPTION
                /*Print appropriate message in OTHERS exception handler*/
                WHEN OTHERS THEN
                DBMS_OUTPUT.PUT_LINE(SQLERRM);
            END;
            /
```

ORA-20005: Divisor cannot be equal to zero

```
PL/SQL procedure successfully completed.


/*Assign a non zero value to M_DIVISOR and check the output of the
PL/SQL block*/
SQL> EXEC :M_DIVISOR := 2;

PL/SQL procedure successfully completed.

SQL> /
The result : 5

PL/SQL procedure successfully completed.
```

As soon as the exception is raised through RAISE_APPLICATION_ERROR, the program control skips the further execution and jumps to the EXCEPTION section. As there is no exception name mapped against this error code, only OTHERS exception handler can handle the exception.

If a EXCEPTION variable has been declared and mapped to the same user-defined error number, the exception handler can be created with the exception variable. Let us rewrite the preceding program to include an exception variable and suitable exception handler. The following program demonstrates the working of user-defined exceptions and dynamic user-defined exceptions in a single program:

```
/*Enable the SERVEROUTPUT parameter to print the results in the
environment*/
SQL> SET SERVEROUTPUT ON

/*Declare a bind variable M_DIVISOR*/
SQL> VARIABLE M_DIVISOR NUMBER;

/*Declare a bind variable M_DIVIDEND*/
SQL> VARIABLE M_DIVIDEND NUMBER;

/*Assign value to M_DIVISOR as zero*/
SQL> EXEC :M_DIVISOR := 0;

PL/SQL procedure successfully completed.

/*Assign value to M_DIVIDEND as 10/
SQL> EXEC :M_DIVIDEND := 10;

PL/SQL procedure successfully completed.

/*Start the PL/SQL block*/
SQL> DECLARE
        /*Declare an exception variable*/
        NOCASE EXCEPTION;
        /*Declare the local variables and initialize them with
bind variables*/
        L_DIVISOR NUMBER := :M_DIVISOR;
        L_DIVIDEND NUMBER := :M_DIVIDEND;
        L_QUOT NUMBER;
        /*Map the exception with a non predefined error number*/
        PRAGMA EXCEPTION_INIT(NOCASE,-20005);
    BEGIN
        /*Raise the exception using RAISE statement if the
divisor is zero*/
        IF L_DIVISOR = 0 THEN
            RAISE_APPLICATION_ERROR(-20005,'Divisor cannot be equal
to zero');
        END IF;
```

```
            L_QUOT := L_DIVIDEND/L_DIVISOR;
            DBMS_OUTPUT.PUT_LINE('The result : '||L_QUOT);
        EXCEPTION
            /*Include exception handler for NOCASE exception*/
            WHEN NOCASE THEN
            DBMS_OUTPUT.PUT_LINE(SQLERRM);
        END;
        /
    ORA-20005: Divisor cannot be equal to zero

    PL/SQL procedure successfully completed.
```

Exception propagation

Exception propagation is an important concept when dealing with nested blocks. A propagating exception always searches for the appropriate exception handler until its last host. The search starts from the EXCEPTION section of the block, that raised it, and continues abruptly until the host environment is reached. As soon as the exception handler is found, the program control resumes the normal flow.

The following cases demonstrate the propagation of exception which is raised in the innermost block:

- **Case 1**: The following diagram shows the state of a nested PL/SQL block. The inner block raises an exception which is handled in its own EXCEPTION section:

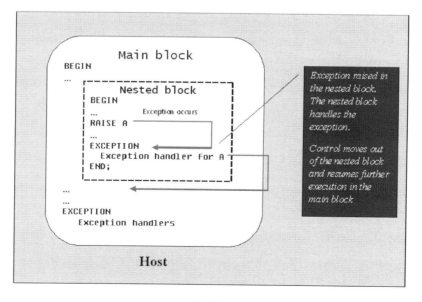

Exception A is raised by the inner block. The inner block handles the exception A within its scope. After the exception is handled, the program control resumes the flow with statements after the inner block in the outer block.

- **Case 2**: The following diagram shows the state of a nested PL/SQL block where the inner block raises an exception but does not handle the same in its own EXCEPTION section. The EXCEPTION section of the outer block handles the raised exception:

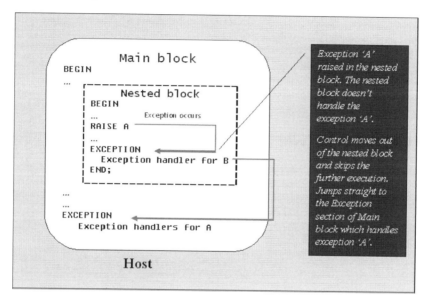

The inner block raises the exception A but does not handle it, so it gets propagated to the EXCEPTION section of the enclosing outer block. Note the abrupt skipping of statements in the outer block.

Now, the outer block handles the exception A. The exception propagated from the inner block is handled in the outer block and is then terminated.

- **Case 3**: The following diagram shows the state of a nested PL/SQL block where both the inner and outer block doesn't handle the exception raised in the inner block:

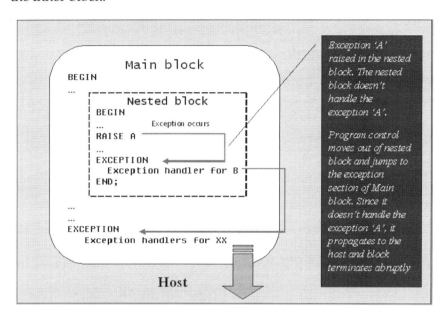

Handling for exception A is missing in the inner as well as the outer block. As a result, the unhandled exception error is raised. The exception is propagated to the host with an error message and the program is terminated abruptly.

Managing database dependencies

Oracle objects which avail the standings and services of other objects are dependent on them. Suppose, a complex view, V, is created on two tables, T1 and T2. The object, V, is dependent on T1 and T2, while T1 and T2 are the referenced objects. Therefore, as a thumb rule of dependency, a valid database object can either be a dependent or a referenced object. The thumb rule of dependency has some exceptions for synonyms and the package body. While synonyms can always be referenced objects, the package body is always a dependent object.

Database dependency can be classified as **direct** or **indirect**. Consider three objects—P, M, and N. If P references M and M references N, then P is directly dependent on M. In the same case, P and N share indirect dependency. Schema objects can refer tables, views, sequences, procedures, functions, packages specification, triggers, and synonyms in their definitions and can behave as both dependent and referenced objects. Out of these, a sequence can appear as a referenced object only, while package body can only be a dependent object.

Displaying the direct and indirect dependencies

The dependency matrix is automatically generated and maintained by the Oracle server. The status of an object is the basis of dependency among the objects. The status of an object can be queried from the USER_OBJECTS view. The following query displays the status of our previously created functions:

```
/*Check the status of the function F_GET_DOUBLE*/
SQL> SELECT STATUS
     FROM USER_OBJECTS
     WHERE OBJECT_NAME='F_GET_DOUBLE';

STATUS
-------
VALID
```

DEPTREE and IDEPTREE are two views which capture and store necessary information about the direct and indirect dependencies, respectively. The views are created by a DBA by running the script from $ORACLE_HOME\RDBMS\ADMIN\utldtree.sql

The execution steps for the script are as follows:

1. Login as SYSDBA in SQL Developer or SQL*Plus.
2. Copy the complete path and script name (prefix with @).
3. Execute the script (with F9).
4. Query the DEPTREE and IDEPTREE views to verify their creation.

The script creates the DEPTREE_TEMPTAB table and the DEPTREE_FILL procedure. The DEPTREE_FILL procedure can be executed as follows, to populate the dependency details of an object:

```
/*Populate the dependency matrix for the function F_GET_DOUBLE*/
SQL> EXEC DEPTREE_FILL('FUNCTION','ORADEV','F_GET_DOUBLE');

PL/SQL procedure successfully completed.
```

Note that the first parameter of the DEPTREE_FILL procedure is the object type, second is the owner and third is the object name.

Then, the DEPTREE and IDEPTREE views can be queried to view the dependency information.

Dependency metadata

Oracle provides the data dictionary views, namely, USER_DEPENDENCIES, ALL_DEPENDENCIES, and DBA_DEPENDENCIES, to view complete dependency metrics shared by an object. Besides the dependent object's list, it also lists its referencing object name and owner.

The following screenshot shows the structure of the dictionary view DBA_DEPENDENCIES:

```
SQL> DESC DBA_DEPENDENCIES
 Name                                      Null?    Type
 ---------------------------------------   -------- ---------------
 OWNER                                     NOT NULL VARCHAR2(30)
 NAME                                      NOT NULL VARCHAR2(30)
 TYPE                                               VARCHAR2(18)
 REFERENCED_OWNER                                   VARCHAR2(30)
 REFERENCED_NAME                                    VARCHAR2(64)
 REFERENCED_TYPE                                    VARCHAR2(18)
 REFERENCED_LINK_NAME                               VARCHAR2(128)
 DEPENDENCY_TYPE                                    VARCHAR2(4)
```

Dependency issues and enhancements

As per the conventional dependency phenomenon, the status validity of the dependent object depends upon the status of the referenced object. So, if the definition of the referenced object is altered, the dependent object is marked INVALID in the USER_OBJECTS view. Though the object recompilation can easily solve the problem, it becomes a serious hindrance in working of the object validations. Dependent objects are used to fall prey to their own dependency matrix. They are rendered invalidated even if the change is not for them.

Oracle 11g brings in a fundamental change in dependency management, known as **Fine Grained Dependency (FGD)**. The FGD concept modifies the dependency principle as *if the alteration in the referenced object does not affect the dependent object, the dependent object would remain in VALID state*. The new principle was received well amongst the community as it shifted the granularity from object level to element level. For instance, if a view is created with selected columns of a table and the table is altered to add a new column, the view shall remain in a valid state.

Reviewing Oracle-supplied packages

Oracle-supplied packages are provided by the Oracle server and inbuilt in the database as a wrapper code. These packages not only facilitate the database programmers to work on extended functionalities but also reduce writing extensive and complex code. Use of Oracle-supplied API is always recommended as it improves the code standardization, too.

The scripts for these packages are available in the `$ORACLE_HOME\RDBMS\ADMIN\` folder. All packages reside on the database server. Public synonyms are available for these packages so that these packages are accessible to all users. Until Oracle 11*g*, more than 1000 packages were available and this count tends to increase with every database release.

Some of the important packages are listed as follows:

- `DBMS_ALERT`: This package is used for notification of database events
- `DBMS_LOCK`: This package is used for managing the lock operations (lock, conversion, release) in PL/SQL applications
- `DBMS_SESSION`: This package is used to set session level preferences from PL/SQL programs (similar to ALTER SESSION)
- `DBMS_OUTPUT`: This package is one of the most frequently used built ins for buffering of data messages and display debug information
- `DBMS_HTTP`: This package is used for HTTP callouts
- `UTL_FILE`: This package is used for reading, writing and other file operations on the server
- `UTL_MAIL`: This package is used to compose and send mails
- `DBMS_SCHEDULER`: This package is used for scheduling execution of stored procedures at a given time

Based on the objective achieved, the packages can be categorized as follows:

- **Standard application development**: `DBMS_OUTPUT` is the most frequently used package to display the required text. It is used for tracing and debugging purposes. Accessing and writing OS files was made possible through `UTL_FILE`. Similarly, system dependent binary files are accessed through the `DBMS_LOB` package.

The Oracle supplied packages often try to access SQL features which is their other big advantage.

- **General usage and application administration**: The Oracle server has many packages to monitor the applications and users. Stats generation, load history, and space management are the key objectives accomplished by these packages

- **Internal support packages**: Oracle maintains these packages for its own use.

- **Transaction processing packages**: Oracle provides utility packages which enables the monitoring of transaction stages. Though they are rarely used, but could efficiently ensure transparent and smooth transactions. For example, DBMS_TRANSACTION.

Among these categories, standard application development packages are the most frequently used ones.

Summary

We toured the fundamentals of PL/SQL programming. Starting with a small flashback on evolution of PL/SQL, we understood its working with Oracle Development tools such as SQL Developer and SQL*Plus.

We had an overview of cursor handling and major Oracle schema objects such as procedures, functions, and packages. Thereafter, we refreshed the error management in PL/SQL through exception handlers using server-defined, user-defined, and dynamic exceptions.

In the upcoming chapters, we will discuss programming guidelines and advanced PL/SQL concepts in details. In the next chapter, we will cover cursor handling in detail and usage guidelines for various types of cursors.

Practice exercise

1. Which of the following features are not available in SQL Developer?

    a. Query builder

    b. Database export and import

    c. Database backup and recovery functions

    d. Code Subversion repository

2. For a function to be called from the SQL expression, which of the following conditions should it obey:

   a. A function in the SELECT statement should not contain DML statements.

   b. The function should return a value.

   c. A function in the UPDATE or DELETE statement should not query the same table.

   d. A function called from SQL expressions cannot contain the TCL (COMMIT or ROLLBACK) command or the DDL (CREATE or ALTER) command.

3. The following query is executed in the ORADEV schema:

   ```
   SELECT NAME, referenced_owner, referenced_name
   FROM all_dependencies
   WHERE owner = USER
   AND referenced_type IN ('TABLE', 'VIEW')
   AND referenced_owner IN ('SYS')
   ORDER BY owner, NAME, referenced_owner, referenced_name;
   ```

   Which statement is true about the output of this query?

   a. It displays the schema objects created by the user ORADEV which use a table or view owned by SYS.

   b. Exception occurs as user ORADEV has insufficient privileges to access ALL_DEPENDENCIES view.

   c. It displays all PL/SQL code objects that reference a table or view directly for all the users in the database.

   d. It displays only those PL/SQL code objects created by the user OE that reference a table or view created by the user SYS.

4. Which of the following is true about PL/SQL blocks?

   a. Exception is a mandatory section without which an anonymous PL/SQL block fails to compile.

   b. Bind variables cannot be referred inside a PL/SQL block.

   c. The scope and visibility of the variables declared in the declarative section of the block is within the current block only.

   d. The RAISE_APPLICATION_ERROR procedure maps a predefined error message to a customized error code.

5. From the following options, identify the ways of defining exceptions:

   a. Declare a EXCEPTION variable and raise it using the RAISE statement.

   b. Use PRAGMA EXCEPTION_INIT to associate a customized exception message to a pre-defined Oracle error number.

   c. Declare a EXCEPTION variable and use it in RAISE_APPLICATION_ERROR.

   d. Use RAISE_APPLICATION_ERROR to create a dynamic exception at any stage within the executable or exception section of a PL/SQL block.

6. Chose the differences between procedures and functions:

   a. A function must mandatorily return a value, while a procedure may or may not.

   b. A function can be called from SQL queries, while a procedure can never be invoked from SQL.

   c. A function can accept parameters passed by value, while a procedure can accept parameters as passed by reference only.

   d. A standalone function can be overloaded but a procedure cannot.

7. Examine the values of the cursor attribute for the following query and pick the attribute with the wrong value:

```
BEGIN
...
SELECT ENAME, SAL
INTO L_ENAME, L_SAL
FROM EMPLOYEES
WHERE EMPID = 7900;
...
END;
```

   a. SQL%ROWCOUNT = 1

   b. SQL%ISOPEN = FALSE

   c. SQL%FOUND = FALSE

   d. SQL%NOTFOUND = FALSE

2
Designing PL/SQL Code

The PL/SQL code construction can accommodate SQL to interact with the Oracle database for transactions or data retrieval. The data operations and activities such as iteration, comparison or manipulation is one of the major accomplishments of PL/SQL control structures. In a PL/SQL block, the data fetch strategy is realized through **cursor structures**. The design and handling of cursor structures forms the basis of the PL/SQL code design. In this chapter, we will understand the cursor structures in detail, their types and implementation along with some best practices. This chapter covers the following topics:

- Cursor fundamentals
  - ○ Cursor execution cycle
  - ○ Cursor design guidelines
  - ○ Cursor attributes
  - ○ Overview of implicit cursor and explicit cursor
- Cursor variables
- Introduction to subtypes

Understanding cursor structures

Cursor structures in PL/SQL allow the data access for a row or set of rows. Every SQL statement executed from PL/SQL is processed as a cursor. For all the SQL statements encountered by the PL/SQL engine, the Oracle server assigns a chunk of memory, privately held in SGA, for processing the statement. A cursor is a constant pointer to this work area in the memory which is also termed as **context area**. This context area contains the complete processing information of the SQL statement. It includes the SQL query, its parsing information, and the data set pulled out from the database tables. Even, the cursor structure captures the relevant information of the context-area activities as cursor attributes.

There are number of methods to act and access upon this work area. These methods are as follows:

- **Implicit cursors**: Every SQL query in the executable section of a PL/SQL block is executed as an implicit cursor by Oracle. The SQL statement can be a SELECT statement or a DML statement.

- **Explicit cursors**: Only the SELECT statements, which are physically named and declared by the user in the declaration section, are explicit cursors. A user has full control on their execution cycle.

- **Cursor variables**: A variable of cursor type allows program units to share data sets as parameters and variables.

- **Cursor expressions**: REF cursors usually make use of cursor expressions to dynamically associate the query to it.

- **Dynamic SQL**: Dynamic SQL provide the execution of all SQL queries during runtime. Unlike explicit cursors or cursor variables, dynamic SQL can work with DML statements, too.

As per the scope of the chapter, we will cover implicit cursor, explicit cursor, and cursor variables.

Cursor execution cycle

The cursor execution cycle involves the stages which describe the processing of the SQL query associated with the cursor. This execution cycle remains common for all types of cursors in PL/SQL. In case of implicit cursors, the Oracle server takes care of these steps. But for explicit cursors, the user has full control on these stages.

 Cursors cannot be stored in the database; instead they enjoy their life within the scope of a session. For this reason, they are often marked as **session cursors**.

The stages of cursor execution cycle are summarized as follows:

- OPEN: The Oracle server allocates a portion of private memory of the server process which is available for this session. The allocated memory would be used for SQL statement processing. It is in this stage when the cursor points to a specific memory location. Prior to this stage, the cursor acts as a null pointer variable.

- PARSE: It is the starting step of SQL processing where the SQL statement is checked for the syntax, object status, and optimization.

- BIND: If the SQL statement requires additional input values, the placeholders created for them are replaced by the actual values (either from the program or from the available bind parameters, if any).

- EXECUTE: The SQL engine executes the SQL statement, fetches the data result set from the database, and sets the record pointer on the first record of the set.

- FETCH: Fetch the record from the result set corresponding to the current position of the record pointer. The record pointer leaps forward by one step after each successful fetch.

- CLOSE: The cursor is closed and the context area is flushed off. The memory is released back to the server and, hence, no reference to the last result set can be made. If you skip this step, the PL/SQL engine implicitly performs the close operation after exiting the block.

Cursor design considerations

The factors to consider for the cursor design are as follows:

- **Data required from the database**: A SELECT query fetching single record should be made an implicit cursor instead of an explicit cursor.

  Steven Feuerstein, a renowned Oracle expert, writes in his book, *Oracle PL/ SQL Programming* (fifth edition) regarding the encapsulation and exposure of implicit cursor queries:

  You should always encapsulate your single-row query, hiding the query behind a function interface, and passing back the data through the RETURN clause.

- **Cursor usability and scalability in the program**: The explicit cursor design depends on the cursor's role in the PL/SQL block. It can be a conventional one, if the role of the cursor is purely a data source in the block. It can be made a parameterized one, if the same data source has to be accessed for varying inputs in the query predicate.

  Parameterized cursors enhance the reusability of the cursor. For example, consider the following code snippet:

```
/*Cursor to select employees who have joined before 01st Jan
1985*/
CURSOR cur IS
SELECT ename, deptno
FROM employees
WHERE hiredate  < TO_DATE('01-01-1985','DD-MM-YYYY');
```

The preceding code can be rewritten as:

```
/*Cursor to select employees who have joined before the input
date parameter*/
CURSOR cur (p_date VARCHAR2) IS
SELECT ename, deptno
FROM employees
WHERE hiredate  < p_date;
```

- **Usage of cursor variables**: If the cursor role has to be of a data source in different scenarios within a single block, ref cursors must be used. As we understood, an explicit cursor is a constant pointer to a view created by the SELECT statement. If the view via the SELECT statement has to be different upon each invocation, ref cursors provide the best solution. Cursor variables act like an actual pointer variable which can refer to different cursor objects. Cursor variables can be well used as arguments to subprograms especially while passing result sets from a database to client environments.

Cursor design—guidelines

We have already seen the multiple ways for framing a SQL statement in a cursor. The same results can be achieved with the use of an explicit or parameterized cursor and even with cursor variables. The appropriate strategy can be followed depending on the usage and application demanding in the program.

Certain recommendations to be followed during cursor design and handling are as follows:

- If the SELECT statement associated with the explicit cursor requires substitutable inputs in the WHERE clause, a parameterized cursor must be preferred over an explicit cursor. It extends the reusability of the cursor and reduces erratic hard coding in the program. It can be opened multiple times in the block or nested blocks for different values of input arguments.

- One must follow the complete execution cycle of the cursor. The cursor must be opened, accessed, and closed. If it is not closed, the allocated memory remains busy and, thus, the program memory reduces. It is released only when the block is terminated.

- Except for %ISOPEN, all the cursor attributes must be addressed within the same cursor execution cycle. Similarly, for implicit cursors, the attributes must be accessed just after the SQL statement as they might reset later for other SQL statements.

- Use of %ROWTYPE must be encouraged to fetch a record from the cursor result set. It not only reduces the overhead of creating and maintaining multiple local variables but also inherits the structure of the SELECT column list. For example, consider the following code snippet:

```
/*Cursor to select employees with its annual salary*/
CURSOR cur_dept IS
  SELECT ename, deptno, (sal*12) annual_sal
  FROM employees;


l_cur_dept cur_dept%ROWTYPE;
```

- Note that the columns which are created virtually for calculative purposes must have an alias name for reference through the record variable.

- A cursor FOR loop associates a cursor with the FOR loop construct. It is one of the strongest features of PL/SQL which simplifies the code writing. It implicitly takes care of all the stages of cursor execution such as OPEN, FETCH, or CLOSE and minimizes the erroneous handling.

```
/*Demonstrate working with cursor FOR loop*/
DECLARE
CURSOR cur_dept IS
   SELECT ename, deptno
   FROM employees;
BEGIN
   FOR c IN cur_dept
   LOOP
   ...
   END LOOP;
END;
```

Cursor attributes

As I stated earlier, the cursor structure retains the relevant information of the context area's processing activities. This information is stored as cursor attributes. These attributes are %ROWCOUNT, %ISOPEN, %FOUND, and %NOTFOUND.

 %BULK_ROWCOUNT and %BULK_EXCEPTIONS are the additional cursor attributes used in bulk processing using the FORALL statement.

These attributes must be accessed by prefixing their respective explicit cursor name. For example, cur_emp%ROWCOUNT returns the rows selected by the cursor cur_emp. As implicit cursors don't have any name, a keyword SQL must be prefixed to access attributes for implicit cursors, as in SQL%FOUND or SQL%NOTFOUND.

The cursor attributes are briefly explained as follows:

- %ROWCOUNT: This attribute answers the question—"how many"—of the cursor processing. It returns the number of rows fetched or affected by the SQL statement in the context area. In the OPEN stage of the cursor, the attribute is initialized with zero. During the FETCH stage, the value of the %ROWCOUNT attribute increments parallel to the record pointer in the result set, that means it increases by one for each forward movement. Once the FETCH stage is over, the attribute holds the final number of rows fetched or affected by the cursor SQL statement.

  Note that the attribute must be addressed within the cursor execution cycle that is within the OPEN and CLOSE stages of a cursor or else it raises the INVALID_CURSOR exception.

- %ISOPEN: This attribute is set to TRUE if the cursor has already entered the OPEN stage, otherwise it is FALSE. It is often used in the programs to make sure that no action should be taken on the cursor without opening it.

  Unlike other attributes, it can be referenced outside the cursor execution cycle.

- %FOUND: This attribute reveals whether the current position of the record pointer points to a valid record or not. If it points to a record in the record set, it returns TRUE. If the last record of the result set is reached and a further request for fetch is made, the attribute returns FALSE.

  Again, the attribute must be addressed within the cursor execution cycle or else it raises a INVALID_CURSOR exception.

- %NOTFOUND: This attribute is just the reverse of the %FOUND attribute. The %NOTFOUND attribute also returns the status of the last fetch request and set to FALSE, if the fetch request returns a record from the data set. It returns TRUE when the last record is reached and a request for fetch is made.

  The attribute must be addressed within the cursor execution cycle or else it raises the INVALID_CURSOR exception.

Implicit cursors

The SQL statements in the executable section of a PL/SQL block are treated as implicit cursors by the Oracle server. The Oracle server takes end to end responsibility of their processing such cursor opening, memory allocation, fetching, and closing the cursor. The SQL statement liable to be an implicit cursor can be SELECT, INSERT, UPDATE, and DELETE.

While the SELECT statement involved in the implicit cursor must return a single row, the DML operations might affect multiple rows of a table.

The executable section of the following block contains a SELECT and a UPDATE statement. Both, the SELECT and UPDATE statements are processed as different implicit cursors by PL/SQL. The programmer has no control over any stage of the cursor execution cycle except the cursor attributes:

```
/*Enable the SERVEROUTPUT parameter to print the results in the
environment*/
SET SERVEROUTPUT ON
/*Demonstrate implicit cursors in PL/SQL execution block*/
DECLARE
    l_ename employees.ename%TYPE;
    l_sal employees.sal%TYPE;
BEGIN
/*Select name and salary of employee 7369. Oracle creates an
implicit cursor to execute it*/
    SELECT ename, sal
    INTO l_ename, l_sal
    FROM employees
    WHERE empno = 7369;
    DBMS_OUTPUT.PUT_LINE('Rows returned from SELECT:'||SQL%ROWCOUNT);
/*Update the salary of employee 7369. Oracle recreates an implicit
cursor to execute it*/
    UPDATE employees
    SET sal = l_sal + 1000
    WHERE empno = 7369;
    DBMS_OUTPUT.PUT_LINE('Rows updated from UPDATE:'||SQL%ROWCOUNT);
END;
/


Rows returned from SELECT:1
Rows updated from UPDATE:1

PL/SQL procedure successfully completed.
```

The information about the last executed SQL statement can be checked by querying the cursor attributes. Let us check out these attributes for implicit cursors:

Cursor attributes	Description
SQL%FOUND	This attribute returns TRUE if SELECT fetches a single record or DML statement affects a minimum one record of the table. Otherwise it is set as FALSE
SQL%NOTFOUND	This attribute returns TRUE if SELECT...INTO fetches no row from the database that is NO_DATA_FOUND exception would be raised.
SQL%ROWCOUNT	This attribute returns 1 for the SELECT statement and the number of rows affected by the DML statement.
SQL%ISOPEN	This is a redundant attribute for implicit cursors. It is always set as FALSE.

Explicit cursors

Explicit cursors go exactly with their name—they are explicitly handled by the user. An explicit cursor requires its prototype declaration and manually operated execution cycle. This authoritative control over the cursor execution cycle has made explicit cursors the hallmark of PL/SQL coding.

Explicit cursors can accommodate only the SELECT statements; no DML statements are allowed. Unlike, an implicit cursor, an explicit cursor prototype has to be given in the DECLARE section with a valid cursor name. During its declaration, the cursor is similar to a pointer. The cursor execution cycle can be observed in the executable section of the PL/SQL block. The steps in the cursor execution cycle involve opening the cursor (OPEN), iterating through the result set and fetching the records (FETCH), and closing the cursor (CLOSE). For each stage, the Oracle server performs the following operations:

- OPEN stage
    - **Open cursor**: Allocate and open a work area in memory for cursor processing
    - **Parse SQL**: Check the SQL query for syntax, object status, and optimization
    - **Bind SQL**: Check for the inputs required by the SQL along with their replacements
    - **Execute query**: Execute the parsed SQL statement to pull the data from the database and move the pointer to the first record of the data set

- FETCH stage
  - ○ **Fetch result**: Iterate the data set for each fetch request. Fetch the data into block variables (or record) and move the result set pointer to the next record.
- CLOSE stage
  - ○ **Close cursor**: Close the cursor and release the memory back to SGA

The following diagram demonstrates a fetch operation in a cursor execution cycle:

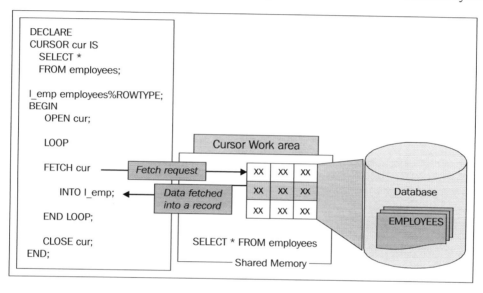

Let us examine the syntax followed for declaring and controlling the execution cycle of an explicit cursor:

```
DECLARE
    CURSOR [Cursor Name] [Parameters]
    RETURN [Return type]
    IS
    [SELECT statement];
BEGIN
    OPEN [Cursor Name];
    FETCH...INTO [Cursor into a ];
    CLOSE [Cursor Name];
END;
```

In the syntax, [Cursor Name] is any valid cursor name. Naming convention for cursors is same as that of identifiers. Thereafter, the cursor shall be referenced with the same name. Parameters are required in parameterized explicit cursors. The argument value would be used as input to the SELECT statement. RETURN is the optional clause for strong cursors, where the return type of the cursor is fixed. [SELECT statement] is any valid SQL SELECT statement. Make sure, no DMLs are allowed.

Here are a few examples for reference. You can observe that the same cursor is rewritten in different formats.

In the following code snippet, the cursor CUR_EMP is the simplest explicit cursor which selects the employees working in department number 10:

```
/*Cursor definition to fetch employee data working in department
10*/
CURSOR CUR_EMP IS
    SELECT *
    FROM employees
    WHERE deptno = 10;
```

The same cursor can be parameterized as follows:

```
/*Cursor definition to fetch employee data working in input
department parameter*/
CURSOR CUR_EMP (P_DEPTNO NUMBER)
IS
    SELECT *
    FROM employees
    WHERE deptno = P_DEPTNO;
```

Even the optional RETURN statement can be added to the above cursor, as shown in the following code snippet:

```
/*Cursor definition to fetch employee data working in input
department parameter and return type as the employee record
structure*/
CURSOR CUR_EMP (P_DEPTNO NUMBER)
RETURN employees%ROWTYPE
IS
    SELECT *
    FROM employees
    WHERE deptno = P_DEPTNO;
```

The following PL/SQL block selects the details for the first two employees, based on their salary (note the usage of cursor attributes in the executable section):

```
/*Enable the SERVEROUTPUT parameter to print the results in the
environment*/
SET SERVEROUTPUT ON
DECLARE
/*Declare a cursor to select top 2 highest paid employees*/
    CURSOR cur_emp
    IS
        SELECT empno, ename, hiredate, sal
        FROM
        (SELECT empno, ename, hiredate, sal,
                ROW_NUMBER() OVER (PARTITION BY 1 ORDER BY sal DESC) RN
         FROM employees)
        WHERE RN < 3;
    l_empno employees.empno%TYPE;
    l_ename employees.ename%TYPE;
    l_doj employees.hiredate%TYPE;
    l_sal employees.sal%TYPE;
BEGIN
/*Open the cursor*/
    OPEN cur_emp;
    LOOP
/*Fetch the cursor select column list into local variables*/
        FETCH cur_emp INTO l_empno, l_ename, l_doj, l_sal;
        EXIT WHEN cur_emp%NOTFOUND;
        DBMS_OUTPUT.PUT_LINE('Employee details for '||l_ename);
        DBMS_OUTPUT.PUT_LINE('Employee Number: '||l_empno);
        DBMS_OUTPUT.PUT_LINE('Date of joining: '||l_doj);
        DBMS_OUTPUT.PUT_LINE('Salary: '||l_sal);
        DBMS_OUTPUT.PUT_LINE(CHR(10));
    END LOOP;
/*Close the cursor*/
    CLOSE cur_emp;
END;
/

Employee details for SMITH
Employee Number: 7369
Date of joining: 17-DEC-80
Salary: 800
```

```
Employee details for ALLEN
Employee Number: 7499
Date of joining: 20-FEB-81
Salary: 1600

PL/SQL procedure successfully completed.
```

Cursor attributes play a vital role while traversing through the explicit cursor execution cycle. The attributes are automatically set at each stage and the following table shows the behavioral flow:

Event	%FOUND	%NOTFOUND	%ISOPEN	%ROWCOUNT
Before OPEN	Exception	Exception	FALSE	Exception
After OPEN	NULL	NULL	TRUE	0
Before first FETCH	NULL	NULL	TRUE	0
After first FETCH	TRUE	FALSE	TRUE	1
Before next FETCH	TRUE	FALSE	TRUE	1
After next FETCH	TRUE	FALSE	TRUE	n + 1
Before last FETCH	TRUE	FALSE	TRUE	n + 1
After last FETCH	FALSE	TRUE	TRUE	n + 1
Before CLOSE	FALSE	TRUE	TRUE	n + 1
After CLOSE	Exception	Exception	FALSE	Exception

Cursor variables

Cursor variables provide a unique service to refer to different context areas in SGA as they can be associated to more than one SELECT statement in the same block. While static cursors remain stuck to a single static SELECT, cursor variables purely act like a pointer variable. At runtime, the pointer can be moved to point to different work areas having different SELECT statements and hence, different result sets.

By virtue of their behavior, a cursor variable differs from a static cursor. Static cursors have the life cycle of only one SQL processing, but cursor variables can live for many SQL statements. Once the processing under a work area is finished, they are ready to move on and point to a different work area. Cursors cannot be passed as arguments, but cursor variables can pass the result sets to other programs and even client environments. These indifferent properties make cursor variables a robust and flexible code feature in PL/SQL.

Cursor variables can be very handy in improving performance while communicating from server to the client. In a single round trip, multiple cursor variables, hence multiple memory references, can be sent to the client environments:

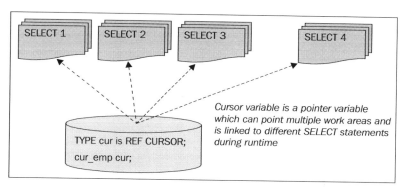

In Oracle, cursor variables exist in the form of ref cursors that is, reference to a cursor. A variable can be declared as the REF CURSOR type to point to a context area in SGA.

 As cursor variables have to be opened explicitly, they are not supported with cursor FOR loops. cursor FOR loops are exclusively supported for explicit cursors only.

A REF CURSOR follows the following syntax:

```
DECLARE
TYPE [CURSOR VARIABLE NAME] IS REF CURSOR [RETURN (return type)]
```

In the preceding syntax, the RETURN type of a cursor variable must be a record type. It is required in strong ref cursors to fix the return type of the result set.

In the example code shown as follows, the PL/SQL block declares a ref cursor as a cursor type and a subsequent cursor variable. Observe the capabilities of a cursor variable to be opened more than once in the program.

```
/*Enable the SERVEROUTPUT parameter to print the results in the
environment*/
SET SERVEROUTPUT ON
DECLARE
/*Declare a REF cursor type*/
  TYPE C_REF IS REF CURSOR;
/*Declare a Cursor variable of REF cursor type*/
  CUR C_REF;
  l_ename employees.ename%TYPE;
  l_sal employees.sal%TYPE;
  l_deptno departments.deptno%TYPE;
  l_dname departments.dname%TYPE;
BEGIN
/*Open the cursor variable for SELECT statement*/
  OPEN cur FOR SELECT ename, sal
        FROM employees
        WHERE ename='JAMES';
  FETCH cur INTO l_ename, l_sal;
  CLOSE cur;
  DBMS_OUTPUT.PUT_LINE('Salary of '||L_ENAME||' is '||L_SAL);
/*Reopen the same cursor variable for second SELECT statement*/
  OPEN cur FOR SELECT deptno, dname
        FROM departments
        WHERE loc='DALLAS';
  FETCH cur INTO l_deptno, l_dname;
  CLOSE cur;

  DBMS_OUTPUT.PUT_LINE('Department name '||l_dname ||' for '||l_
deptno);
END;
/

Salary of JAMES is 950
Department name RESEARCH for 20

PL/SQL procedure successfully completed.
```

Ref cursor types—strong and weak

A ref cursor can be either of a strong or weak type.

A ref cursor can be made strong if its return type is fixed during the prototype. The RETURN clause makes the ref cursor restrictive upon the SQL query statement being associated to it. Additionally, in a large application environment, such cursors are less error prone and set the application standards. The return type of a cursor must always be of a record type only.

The return type of a cursor can be a record structure of the table or a user-defined record structure.

For example, a strong ref cursor having a return type record structure of the employees table:

```
TYPE c_strong_rf IS REF CURSOR OF employees%ROWTYPE;
```

Alternatively, a user-defined record can be declared and assigned as the return type of a strong ref cursor.

For example, the cursor in the following code snippet specifies the structure of the return type as the structure of a local record:

```
/*Demonstrate the strong ref cursor where type is a local record
structure*/
DECLARE
    TYPE myrec IS RECORD
    (myname VARCHAR2(10),
     myclass  VARCHAR2(10));
TYPE mycur IS REF CURSOR RETURN myrec;
cur_var mycur;
```

A ref cursor without the return type makes it weak and open to all SELECT statements. As they provide free-hand association, they are the most frequently used cursor variables. For example, see the following code:

```
TYPE c_weak_rf IS REF CURSOR;
```

SYS_REFCURSOR

SYS_REFCURSOR is an Oracle built-in cursor variable data type which declares a weak ref cursor variable without declaring the ref pointer type. It is used as a generic cursor variable and extensively used as an argument for stored subprograms. It carries data sets across the client environments.

`SYS_REFCURSOR` acts like a cursor variable type, as shown in the following syntax:

```
DECLARE
   [Cursor variable name] SYS_REFCURSOR;
```

As stated, `SYS_REFCURSOR` can also be specified as a parameter type in Oracle subprograms. It appears as follows:

```
PROCEDURE P_DEMO (P_DATA OUT SYS_REFCURSOR)
IS
...
END;
```

Processing a cursor variable

The process and execution life cycle of a cursor variable resembles the same as that of an explicit cursor.

Let us recapitulate the execution cycle with the help of an example.

The following program displays the grades of all employees based on their salary (the highlighted sections represent the DECLARE, OPEN, FETCH, and CLOSE stages):

```
/*Enable the SERVEROUTPUT parameter to print the results in the
environment*/
SET SERVEROUTPUT ON
DECLARE
/*Define a ref cursor type and declare cursor variable*/
  TYPE c_ref IS REF CURSOR;
  cur C_REF;

    l_empno employees.empno%type;
    l_ename employees.ename%type;
    l_deptno employees.deptno%type;
    l_grade salgrade.grade%type;
  BEGIN
/*Open the cursor variable for a SELECT query*/
  OPEN cur FOR SELECT e.empno, e.ename, e.deptno, s.grade
               FROM employees e, salgrade s
               WHERE e.sal between s.losal and s.hisal;

    LOOP
/*Iterate and fetch the records from the result set*/
  FETCH cur INTO l_empno, l_ename, l_deptno, l_grade;
    EXIT WHEN cur%NOTFOUND;
    DBMS_OUTPUT.PUT_LINE('Grade for '||l_ename||'('||l_empno||') is
  '||l_grade);
```

```
      END LOOP;
/*Close the cursor variable*/
  CLOSE cur;
  END;
  /
```

```
  Grade for SMITH(7369) is 1
  Grade for JAMES(7900) is 1
  Grade for ADAMS(7876) is 1
  Grade for WARD(7521) is 2
  Grade for MARTIN(7654) is 2
  Grade for MILLER(7934) is 2
  Grade for TURNER(7844) is 3
  Grade for ALLEN(7499) is 3
  Grade for CLARK(7782) is 4
  Grade for BLAKE(7698) is 4
  Grade for JONES(7566) is 4
  Grade for SCOTT(7788) is 4
  Grade for FORD(7902) is 4
  Grade for KING(7839) is 5

  PL/SQL procedure successfully completed.
```

Cursor variables as arguments

Very often in a client-based application, data sets are required to be passed from database to the client environment such as Oracle forms, C++, or Java. One of the most feasible and easily implementable solutions is the cursor variable. Cursor variables can appear in a formal parameter list of a procedure or as return type of a function. Logically, there is no passing of physical data sets over the client but it is just sharing of a pointer variable. Once an active memory pointer has been shared among the database programs or other clients, the cursor work area in the memory and hence, the containing result set can be accessible to all.

For example, the organization asks for the report showing the employees and their current location. The report has to be shown on the employee portal of the company. Now, our task is to transfer the information from the database to the client. Let us write a program to achieve the purpose:

```
/*Enable the SERVEROUTPUT parameter to print the results in the
environment*/
SET SERVEROUTPUT ON
/*Create the procedure to demonstrate cursor variable in parameter
list*/
CREATE OR REPLACE PROCEDURE
```

```
p_emp_location (p_emp_data OUT SYS_REFCURSOR)
IS
/*Declare a local ref cursor variable*/
   TYPE cur_emp_rf IS REF CURSOR;
   cur_emp_loc cur_emp_rf;
BEGIN
/*Open the local ref cursor variable for the SELECT query*/
   OPEN cur_emp_loc FOR SELECT e.ename, d.loc
                       FROM employees e, departments d
                       WHERE e.deptno = d.deptno;
/*Assign the cursor OUT parameter with the local cursor variable*/
   p_emp_data := cur_emp_loc;
END;
/

Procedure created.

/*Declare a host cursor variable in SQLPLUS*/
SQL> VARIABLE M_EMP_LOC REFCURSOR;

/*Execute the procedure P_EMP_LOCATION using the above host cursor
variable*/
SQL> EXEC P_EMP_LOCATION(:M_EMP_LOC);

PL/SQL procedure successfully completed.

/*Print the host cursor variable*/
SQL> PRINT M_EMP_LOC

ENAME        LOC
----------   -------------
CLARK        NEW YORK
KING         NEW YORK
MILLER       NEW YORK
JONES        DALLAS
FORD         DALLAS
ADAMS        DALLAS
SMITH        DALLAS
SCOTT        DALLAS
WARD         CHICAGO
TURNER       CHICAGO
ALLEN        CHICAGO
JAMES        CHICAGO
BLAKE        CHICAGO
MARTIN       CHICAGO

14 rows selected.
```

Cursor variables—restrictions

The following list shows the restrictions on the usage of cursor variables:

- Cursor variables cannot be declared as a public construct of a package specification. But a ref cursor type can be declared in a package specification:

```
/*Demonstrate the restriction listed above*/
CREATE OR REPLACE PACKAGE pkg_dec_public_cursor IS
    cur_public SYS_REFCURSOR;
END;
/
```

```
Warning: Package created with compilation errors.
```

```
/*List the errors in the last compilation*/
SHOW ERROR
Errors for PACKAGE PKG_DEC_PUBLIC_CURSOR:
```

```
LINE/COL ERROR
-------- ----------------------------------------------------------
2/3      PL/SQL: Declaration ignored
2/3      PLS-00994: Cursor Variables cannot be declared as part of
         a package
```

```
/*Recreate the package with the ref cursor type prototype*/
CREATE OR REPLACE PACKAGE pkg_dec_public_cursor IS
  TYPE cur_public IS REF CURSOR;
END;
/
```

```
Package created.
```

The preceding example also deduces the fact that the cursor and the cursor variables are interoperable and mutually exclusive. They must fit in the code appropriately as per the requirement.

- Cursor variables cannot be shared across the servers through remote procedures.

- The SELECT query associated to a cursor variable during runtime should not lock the rows that is, it must not have the FOR UPDATE clause.

- Cursor variables cannot be used to specify the data type for a database column in a table or collection attribute. It implies that cursor variables cannot be stored in the database. Instead, they are non persistent pointers and are available only within a session's scope.

- Cursor variables cannot be assigned the NULL value.

Subtypes

The Oracle data type is one of the fundamental concepts of the database. Every element, or piece of data in the database, has its own basic behavioral pattern, which is known as **data type**. An element can be numeric, string, periodic, Boolean or large object. Scalar data types are the original data types which are not derivatives of any other types. Scalar data types constitute a family of base types and their subtypes.

PL/SQL is open to all categories of SQL data types. In addition to available SQL data types, PL/SQL maintains its own data types, most of which are subtypes of SQL data types. We will extend our discussion on these subtypes now.

The following table shows the base types and subtypes under each scalar data types:

Number	Character	Date/Time	Boolean
NUMBER	VARCHAR	DATE	BOOLEAN
DECIMAL/DEC	VARCHAR2	INTERVAL	
DOUBLE PRECISION	NVARCHAR2	TIMESTAMP	
FLOAT	CHAR		
INTEGER/INT	NCHAR		
NUMERIC	CHARACTER		
REAL	LONG		
SMALLINT	LONG RAW		
PLS_INTEGER	RAW		
BINARY_DOUBLE	ROWID		
BINARY_FLOAT	STRING		
BINARY_INTEGER	UROWID		
POSITIVE			
POSITIVEN			
NATURAL			
NATURALN			
SIGNTYPE			

A **subtype** is a data type evolved from the existing scalar data types. The purpose of creating subtypes is to customize the primitive data types by constraining some of the other property features such as nullity, range, or sign. A subtype can be an unconstrained one too, which can be often used in place of base types to maintain application standards.

The evolution of subtypes has categorized the scalar data types into super types. The subtype inherits the behavior of its parent base type and extends it by a distinguishing feature. For example, NATURALN is a subtype of BINARY_INTEGER which prevents the entry of nulls and non negative values. Similarly, SIGNTYPE permits only three fixed values as -1, 0, or 1.

Subtype classification

Once again, similar to cursors, subtypes can be classified based on their creator and mentor. The subtypes can be categorized as predefined and user-defined.

Oracle's predefined subtypes

These are built-in subtypes maintained by the Oracle server. They reside within the STANDARD package along with the scalar data types.

The following list of the NUMBER base type and subtypes has been compiled from Oracle's STANDARD package:

```
/*NUMBER family from STANDARD package*/
type NUMBER is NUMBER_BASE;
subtype FLOAT is NUMBER;
subtype INTEGER is NUMBER(38,0);
subtype INT is INTEGER;
subtype SMALLINT is NUMBER(38,0);
subtype DECIMAL is NUMBER(38,0);
subtype NUMERIC is DECIMAL;
subtype DEC is DECIMAL;
subtype BINARY_INTEGER is INTEGER range '-2147483647'..2147483647;
subtype NATURAL is BINARY_INTEGER range 0..2147483647;
subtype NATURALN is NATURAL not null;
subtype POSITIVE is BINARY_INTEGER range 1..2147483647;
subtype POSITIVEN is POSITIVE not null;
subtype SIGNTYPE is BINARY_INTEGER range '-1'..1;
```

 FLOAT is an unconstrained subtype of NUMBER. The constrained subtypes such as NATURAL and NATURALN work mostly on the ranges and nullity.

User-defined subtypes

Oracle allows the users to create a subtype of their own. User-defined subtypes aims to create an alias of predefined types or set certain rules on them in regards to ranges or constraints. It can be created in the DECLARE section of a PL/SQL block or subprogram:

```
SUBTYPE [SUBTYPE NAME] IS [PREDEFINED TYPE] [CONSTRAINT | RANGE (range
specification)]
```

The following PL/SQL block defines a subtype of NUMBER base type which has been constrained in the range of 1 to 10. As soon as the subtype variable is assigned with an out-of-range value, the VALUE_ERROR exception is raised.

```
SQL> DECLARE
/*Create a subtype with value range between 1 to 10*/
    SUBTYPE ID IS BINARY_INTEGER RANGE 1..10;
        L_NUM ID;
    BEGIN
/*Assign a value beyond range*/
        L_NUM := 11;
    END;
    /
DECLARE
*
ERROR at line 1:
ORA-06502: PL/SQL: numeric or value error
ORA-06512: at line 5
```

The PL/SQL block shows the working of a constrained subtype. Note that the variable of a not null subtype must be initialized with a definite default value. Observe the working of a constrained subtype by equating a NULL variable to it. It prevents the action by raising an exception against it.

```
SQL> DECLARE
/*Create a not null constrained subtype with value range between 1 to
10*/
    SUBTYPE ID IS BINARY_INTEGER RANGE 1..10 NOT NULL;
        L_NUM ID := 3;
        L_NULL NUMBER;
    BEGIN
/*Assign NULL to the subtype variable*/
        L_NUM := L_NULL;
    END;
    /
```

```
DECLARE
*
ERROR at line 1:
ORA-06502: PL/SQL: numeric or value error
ORA-06512: at line 6
```

Subtypes are beneficial in setting up the standards of large applications where the data types must be compatible with ANSI/ISO or DB2 data types. They increase code interactivity, readability, and offer code sampling advantages. The programmer defines the subtype at higher level. If any change in the behavior of the data type is identified, changes can be cascaded by modifying the subtype definition at the top level.

Type compatibility with subtypes

This is a quite obvious feature of subtypes that they are interchangeable with their base types under their service conditions. These service conditions are the constraints in the subtype definitions, which must be obeyed during assignment.

In the following program, the SUBTYPE ID is a BINARY_INTEGER whose range is constrained from 1 to 10. If a NUMBER variable with a value greater than 10 is assigned to it, Oracle raises the VALUE_ERROR exception:

```
SQL> DECLARE
/*Create a subtype with value range between 1 to 10. Declare the
subtype variable*/
      SUBTYPE ID IS binary_integer range 1..10;
      L_NUM ID ;
      L_BN BINARY_INTEGER;
    BEGIN
/*Assign a NUMBER variable to SUBTYPE variable*/
      L_NUM := 4;
      L_BN := 15;
      L_NUM := L_BN;
    END;
    /
DECLARE
*
ERROR at line 1:
ORA-06502: PL/SQL: numeric or value error
ORA-06512: at line 8
```

In this case, reverse assignment is possible because BINARY_INTEGER can accept numeric values in range of -2147483647 to 2147483647.

Summary

In this chapter, we discussed the importance of cursor structures in the PL/SQL code. We understood the working of cursor structures, their execution cycle, design considerations, and guidelines. We discussed implicit and explicit cursors and covered the working of cursor variables. Meanwhile, we learnt how cursor variables are superior to static cursors. At the end, we overviewed the working of subtypes in Oracle. Subtypes can be a handy feature in large database systems to provide flexibility and maintenance of data types in a modularized way.

In the next chapter, we shall cover composite data types and understand how collections can boost PL/SQL code performance and perform data caching.

Practice exercise

1. What are the possible reasons that cause the INVALID_CURSOR exception to occur?

    a. The cursor result set has not been fetched.

    b. The cursor does not have parameters.

    c. The value of the %ROWCOUNT attribute has been referenced after closing the cursor.

    d. The cursor result set has been fetched into a non matching variable.

2. Identify the guidelines to be considered when designing cursors in a PL/SQL block:

    a. Explicit cursors must be used irrespective of the number of records returned by the query.

    b. Cursor FOR loops must be used as it implicitly takes care of the OPEN, FETCH, and CLOSE stages.

    c. Cursor data must be fetched as a record.

    d. Use ROWNUM to index the records in the cursor result sets.

3. While processing DMLs as implicit cursors in the PL/SQL executable block, implicit cursor attributes can be used anywhere in the block.

    a. True

    b. False

4. From the following, identify the two correct statements about the REF CURSOR types:

    a. Ref cursors are reference pointers to cursor objects

    b. REF CURSOR types can be declared in package specification

    c. SYS_REFCURSOR is a strong ref cursor type

    d. Cursor variables cannot be used as arguments in stored subprograms

5. The RETURN type for a ref cursor can be declared using %TYPE, %ROWTYPE, or a user-defined record.

    a. True

    b. False

6. Which two statements, among the following, are true about cursor variables?

    a. Cursor variables can process more than one SELECT statement

    b. Cursor variables can be passed as program arguments across subprograms and even to the client end programs

    c. A cursor variable can be declared as a public construct in package specification

    d. Cursor variables can be stored in the database as database columns

7. Similar to static explicit cursors, cursor variables can also be opened in the FOR loop.

    a. True

    b. False

8. Which of the following is true while creating subtypes from a table record structure?

    SUBTYPE [Name] IS [TABLE]%ROWTYPE

    a. The subtype inherits complete column structure of the record structure

    b. The subtype inherits the default values of the database columns in the table

    c. The subtype inherits the index information of the database columns

    d. The subtype inherits none except the NOT NULL constraint information of the database columns

3
Using Collections

Conceptually, "array" has been a colloquial term in programming glossaries. It refers to a list of similar elements. In Oracle, an array is known by the name, collection. A **collection** consists of a list of elements of the same type, where each element can be identified by its index or subscript.

A collection works on the same philosophy as an array, a queue, or a linked list works. Collections provide wide scope of usability and applications in database programming. Besides being a performance booster, collections can also be used for data caching mechanisms in programs. It can also be used as database columns, type attributes or subprogram parameters. In this chapter, we shall perform a detailed study on collections, its types and usage in the following topics:

- Collections—an overview
    ○ Categorization
    ○ Selection of an appropriate collection type
- Associative arrays
- Nested tables
- Varray
- Collections—a comparative study
- PL/SQL collection methods
- Manipulating collection elements
- Collection initialization

Collections—an overview

A collection is a homogeneous single dimensional structure, which constitutes an ordered set of elements of a similar type. Being a homogeneous structure, all elements are of the same data type. The structure of the element contains cells with a subscript. The elements reside in these cells to make the index as their location information. The subscript or cell index becomes identification of an element and is used for its access.

Structure of a collection type, SPORT, is shown in the following diagram. Note the subscript and elements into it. A new element, GOLF, enters at the last empty location and is represented as SPORT [6]:

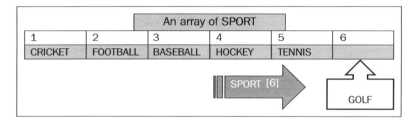

A collection element can be of any valid SQL data type or a user-defined type. An element of the SQL primitive data type is a scalar value while an element of the user-defined type is an object type instance. A collection can be used within a PL/SQL program by declaring a PL/SQL variable of collection type. The local PL/SQL variable can hold the instances of its collection type. Besides, a database column in a table can also be of the schema collection type.

The collections in Oracle are strictly one dimensional. They cannot be realized on two-dimensional coordinates. However, multidimensional arrays can be realized when the collection has an object type or collection type attribute.

A collection can be bounded or unbounded. Bounded collections can accommodate a limited number of elements while unbounded collections have no upper limit for subscripts.

Collections provide an efficient way to organize the data in an array or set format while making the use of object-oriented features. An instance of a nested table or varray collection type is accessed as an object while the data is still stored in database columns. Collections can be used to avail data caching in programs and boost up the performance of SQL operations. On dedicated server connections, a session always uses **User Global Area (UGA)**, a component of PGA, for collection operations. On the other hand, for shared server mode, the collection operations are still carried out in UGA; but UGA is now a part of **System Global Area (SGA)**, thus indirectly in SGA. This is because in shared server connections, multiple server processes can affect a session, thus UGA must be allocated out of the SGA.

Categorization

Collections are of two types—**persistent** and **non-persistent**. A collection is persistent if it stores the collection structure and elements physically in the database. Contrarily, a non-persistent collection is active for a program only that is, maximum up to a session.

Apart from the preceding categories, a collection can be realized in three formats namely, associative array, nested table or varray. This categorization is purely based on their objective and behavioral properties in a PL/SQL program. The following diagram combines the abstract and physical classification of collections:

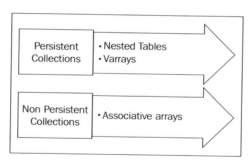

We will take a quick tour of these collection types now and discuss them in detail in the coming sections:

- **Associative array (index-by table)**: This is the simplest form of non-persistent unbounded collections. As a non-persistent collection, it cannot be stored in the database, but they are available within a PL/SQL block only. The collection structure and data of associative array cannot be retained once the program is completed. Initially, during the days of Oracle 7, it was known as PL/SQL tables. Later, Oracle 8 version released it as index-by tables as they used an index to identify an element.

- **Nested table**: This is a persistent form of unbounded collections which can be created in the database as well as in PL/SQL block.
- **Varray (variable-size array)**: This is a persistent but bounded form of collection which can be created in the database as well as in PL/SQL. Similar to a nested table, a varray is also a unidimensional homogeneous collection. The collection size and storage scheme are the factors which differentiate varrays from nested tables. Unlike a nested table, a varray can accommodate only a defined (fixed) number of elements.

Selecting an appropriate collection type

Here are a few guidelines to decide upon the appropriate usage of collection types in programs:

Use of associative arrays is required when:

- You have to temporarily cache the program data in an array format for lookup purpose.
- You need string subscripts for the collection elements. Note that it supports negative subscripts, too.
- Map hash tables from the client to the database.

Use of nested tables is preferred when:

- You have to stores data as sets in the database. Database columns of nested table type can be declared to hold the data persistently.
- Perform major array operations such as insertion and deletion, on a large volume of data.

Use of varrays is preferred when:

- You have to store calculated or predefined volume of data in the database. Varray offers limited and defined storage of rows in a collection.
- Order of the elements has to be preserved.

Associative arrays

Associative arrays are analogous to conventional arrays or lists which can be defined within a PL/SQL program only. Neither the array structure nor the data can be stored in the database. It can hold the elements of a similar type in a key-value structure without any upper bound to the array. Each cell of the array is distinguished by its subscript, index, or cell number. The index can be a number or a string.

Associative arrays were first introduced in Oracle 7 release as PL/SQL tables to signify its usage within the scope of a PL/SQL block. Oracle 8 release identified the PL/SQL table as Index by table due to its structure as an index-value pair. Oracle 10g release recognized the behavior of index by tables as arrays so as to rename it as associative arrays due to association of an index with an array.

The following diagram explains the physical lookup structure of an associative array:

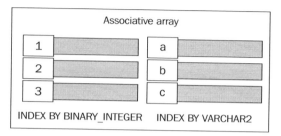

Associative arrays follow the following syntax for declaration in a PL/SQL declare block:

```
TYPE [COLL NAME] IS TABLE OF [ELEMENT DATA TYPE] NOT NULL
    INDEX BY [INDEX DATA TYPE]
```

In the preceding syntax, the index type signifies the data type of the array subscript. RAW, NUMBER, LONG-RAW, ROWID, and CHAR are the unsupported index data types. The suited index types are BINARY_INTEGER, PLS_INTEGER, POSITIVE, NATURAL, SIGNTYPE, or VARCHAR2.

The element's data type can be one of the following:

- **PL/SQL scalar data type**: NUMBER (along with its subtypes), VARCHAR2 (and its subtypes), DATE, BLOB, CLOB, or BOOLEAN
- **Inferred data**: The data type inherited from a table column, cursor expression or predefined package variable
- **User-defined type**: A user defined object type or collection type

For illustration, the following are the valid conditions of the associative array in a PL/SQL block:

```
/*Array of CLOB data*/
TYPE clob_t IS TABLE OF CLOB
INDEX BY PLS_INTEGER;
/*Array of employee ids indexed by the employee names*/
TYPE empno_t IS TABLE OF employees.empno%TYPE NOT NULL
INDEX BY employees.ename%type;
```

The following PL/SQL program declares an associative array type in a PL/SQL block. Note that the subscript of the array is of a string type and it stores the number of days in a quarter. This code demonstrates the declaration of an array and assignment of the element in each cell and printing them. Note that the program uses the FIRST and NEXT collection methods to display the array elements. The collection methods would be covered in detail in the *PL/SQL collection methods* section:

```
/*Enable the SERVEROUTPUT on to display the output*/
SET SERVEROUTPUT ON
/*Start the PL/SQL block*/
DECLARE
/*Declare a collection type associative array and its variable*/
  TYPE string_asc_arr_t IS TABLE OF NUMBER
  INDEX BY VARCHAR2(10);
  l_str string_asc_arr_t;
  l_idx VARCHAR2(50);
BEGIN
/*Assign the total count of days in each quarter against each cell*/
  l_str ('JAN-MAR') := 90;
  l_str ('APR-JUN') := 91;
  l_str ('JUL-SEP') := 92;
  l_str ('OCT-DEC') := 93;
  l_idx := l_str.FIRST;
  WHILE (l_idx IS NOT NULL)
  LOOP
  DBMS_OUTPUT.PUT_LINE('Value at index '||l_idx||' is '||l_str(l_
idx));
    l_idx := l_str.NEXT(l_idx);
  END LOOP;
END;
/

Value at index APR-JUN is 91
Value at index JAN-MAR is 90
Value at index JUL-SEP is 92
Value at index OCT-DEC is 93

PL/SQL procedure successfully completed.
```

In the preceding block, note the string indexed array. A string indexed array considerably improves the performance by using indexed organization of array values. In the last block, we noticed the explicit assignment of data.

In the following program, we will try to populate the array automatically in the program. The following PL/SQL block declares an associative array to hold the ASCII values of number 1 to 100:

```
/*Enable the SERVEROUTPUT on to display the output*/
SET SERVEROUTPUT ON
/*Start the PL/SQL Block*/
DECLARE
/*Declare an array of string indexed by numeric subscripts*/
  TYPE ASCII_VALUE_T IS TABLE OF VARCHAR2(12)
  INDEX BY PLS_INTEGER;
  L_GET_ASCII ASCII_VALUE_T;
BEGIN
/*Insert the values through a FOR loop*/
  FOR I IN 1..100
  LOOP
    L_GET_ASCII(I) := ASCII(I);
  END LOOP;
/*Display the values randomly*/
  DBMS_OUTPUT.PUT_LINE(L_GET_ASCII(5));
  DBMS_OUTPUT.PUT_LINE(L_GET_ASCII(15));
  DBMS_OUTPUT.PUT_LINE(L_GET_ASCII(75));
END;
/

53
49
55

PL/SQL procedure successfully completed.
```

The salient features of associative arrays are as follows:

- An associative array can exist as a sparse or empty collection
- Being a non-persistent collection, it cannot participate in DML transactions
- It can be passed as arguments to other local subprograms within the same block
- Sorting of an associative array depends on the NLS_SORT parameter
- An associative array declared in package specification behaves as a session-persistent array

Nested tables

Nested tables are a persistent form of collections which can be created in the database as well as PL/SQL. It is an unbounded collection where the index or subscript is implicitly maintained by the Oracle server during data retrieval. Oracle automatically marks the minimum subscript as 1 and relatively handles others. As there is no upper limit defined for a nested table, its size can grow dynamically. Though not an index-value pair structure, a nested table can be accessed like an array in a PL/SQL block.

A nested table is initially a dense collection but it might become sparse due to delete operations on the collection cells.

 Dense collection is the one which is tightly populated. That means, there exists no empty cells between the lower and upper indexes of the collection. Sparse collections can have empty cells between the first and the last cell of the collection. A dense collection may get sparse by performing the "delete" operations.

When a nested table is declared in a PL/SQL program, they behave as a one-dimensional array without any index type or upper limit specification.

A nested table defined in a database exists as a valid schema object type. It can be either used in a PL/SQL block to declare a PL/SQL variable for temporarily holding program data or a database column of particular nested table type can be included in a table, which can persistently store the data in the database. A nested table type column in a table resembles a table within a table, but Oracle draws an out-of-line storage table to hold the nested table data. This scenario is illustrated in the following diagram:

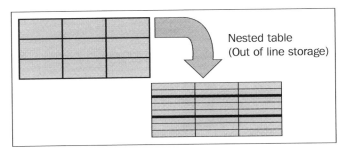

Nested table
(Out of line storage)

Whenever a database column of nested table type is created in a table (referred to as **parent table**), Oracle creates a storage table with the same storage options as that of the parent table. The storage table created by Oracle in the same segment carries the name as specified in the `NESTED TABLE STORE AS` clause during creation of the parent table. Whenever a row is created in the parent table, the following actions are performed by the Oracle server:

- A unique identifier is generated to distinguish the nested table instances of different parent rows, for the parent row
- The instance of the nested table is created in the storage table alongside the unique identifier of the parent row

The Oracle server takes care of these nested table operations. For the programmer or user, the whole process is hidden and appears as a normal "insert" operation.

A nested table definition in PL/SQL follows the following syntax:

```
DECLARE
TYPE type_name IS TABLE OF element_type [NOT NULL];
```

In the preceding syntax, `element_type` is a primitive data type or a user-defined type, but not as a `REF CURSOR` type.

In a database, a nested table can be defined using the following syntax:

```
CREATE [OR REPLACE] TYPE type_name IS TABLE OF [element_type] [NOT
NULL];
/
```

In the preceding syntax, `[element_type]` can be a SQL supported scalar data type, a database object type, or a `REF` object type. Unsupported element types are `BOOLEAN`, `LONG`, `LONG-RAW`, `NATURAL`, `NATURALN`, `POSITIVE`, `POSITIVEN`, `REF CURSOR`, `SIGNTYPE`, `STRING`, `PLS_INTEGER`, `SIMPLE_INTEGER`, `BINARY_INTEGER` and all other non-SQL supported data types.

If the size of the element type of a database collection type has to be increased, follow this syntax:

```
ALTER TYPE [type name] MODIFY ELEMENT TYPE [modified element type]
[CASCADE | INVALIDATE];
```

The keywords, `CASCADE` or `INVALIDATE`, decide whether the collection modification has to invalidate the dependents or the changes that have to be cascaded across the dependents.

The nested table from the database can be dropped using the DROP command, as shown in the following syntax (note that the FORCE keyword drops the type irrespective of its dependents):

```
DROP TYPE [collection name] [FORCE]
```

Nested table collection type as the database object

We will go through the following illustration to understand the behavior of a nested table, when created as a database collection type:

```
/*Create the nested table in the database*/
SQL> CREATE TYPE NUM_NEST_T AS TABLE OF NUMBER;
/

Type created.
```

The nested table type, NUM_NEST_T, is now created in the database. Its metadata information can be queried from the USER_TYPES and USER_COLL_TYPES dictionary views:

```
SELECT type_name, typecode, type_oid
FROM USER_TYPES
WHERE type_name = 'NUM_NEST_T';
```

TYPE_NAME	TYPECODE	TYPE_OID
NUM_NEST_T	COLLECTION	96DE421E47114638A9F5617CE735731A

Note that the TYPECODE value shows the type of the object in the database and differentiates collection types from user-defined object types:

```
SELECT type_name, coll_type, elem_type_name
FROM user_coll_types
WHERE type_name = 'NUM_NEST_T';
```

TYPE_NAME	COLL_TYPE	ELEM_TYPE_NAME
NUM_NEST_T	TABLE	NUMBER

Once the collection type has been successfully created in the database, it can be used to specify the type for a database column in a table. The CREATE TABLE statement in the following code snippet declares a column of the NUM_NEST_T nested table type in the parent table, TAB_USE_NT_COL. The NESTED TABLE [Column] STORE AS [Storage table] clause specifies the storage table for the nested table type column. A separate table for the nested table column, NUM, ensures its out-of-line storage.

```
SQL> CREATE TABLE TAB_USE_NT_COL
        (ID NUMBER,
        NUM NUM_NEST_T)
            NESTED TABLE NUM STORE AS NESTED_NUM_ID;

Table created.
```

DML operations on nested table columns

Let us check out the way we perform DML operations on nested table type columns.

Inserting a nested table instance

The nested table data will be inserted using a collection type constructor. A collection type constructor is a default constructor from Oracle which can be used to provide value of each of its attributes.

```
INSERT INTO TAB_USE_NT_COL (ID, NUM)
VALUES
(1, NUM_NEST_T(10,12,3));
/

1 row created.


INSERT INTO TAB_USE_NT_COL (ID, NUM)
VALUES
(2, NUM_NEST_T(23,43));
/

1 row created.
```

Selecting a nested table column

When a table having a nested table column is queried, the nested table column appears as an instance of the nested table object type:

```
SQL> SELECT *
     FROM tab_use_nt_col;

        ID NUM
---------- ------------------------------
         1 NUM_NEST_T(10, 12, 3)
         2 NUM_NEST_T(23, 43)
```

The TABLE expression can be used to open the instance and display the data in relational format. The TABLE expression is used to access the attributes of the nested table type. Oracle implicitly joins the parent row with the nested table row in the query output.

```
SQL> SELECT T.id, T1.column_value
     FROM tab_use_nt_col T, TABLE (T.num) T1;

        ID COLUMN_VALUE
---------- ------------
         1           10
         1           12
         1            3
         2           23
         2           43
```

In the preceding SELECT query, COLUMN_VALUE is an Oracle pseudo column which is used in the SELECT queries to signify the nested table column with no attribute name.

Updating the nested table instance

Nested table data can be updated either as a "cut and replace" option or through the TABLE expression. Using the UPDATE statement, an instance can be replaced with the new one.

Let us update the collection instance for ID 2 in the TAB_USE_NT_COL table:

```
UPDATE tab_use_nt_col
SET num = num_nest_t(10,12,13)
WHERE id=2
/

1 row updated.
```

Now, query the table data to verify the nested table update:

```
SQL> SELECT * FROM tab_use_nt_col;

        ID NUM
---------- ----------------------------
         1 NUM_NEST_T(10, 12, 3)
         2 NUM_NEST_T(10, 12, 13)
```

The TABLE expression can be used to update a single element in the collection. For example, in the table data shown above, if the collection instance has to be NUM_NEST_T(10, 100, 3) for ID 1 instead of NUM_NEST_T(10, 12, 3), the TABLE expression can be used to update the single element. Let us check out how to do it:

```
UPDATE TABLE (SELECT num FROM tab_use_nt_col WHERE id = 1)   P
SET P.COLUMN_VALUE = 100
WHERE P.COLUMN_VALUE = 12;

1 row updated.
```

In the preceding UPDATE statement, the TABLE expression reads the collection type instance returned by the subquery. It opens up the instance in relational format and the instance values can be accessed and, hence, manipulated. It is to be noted that the subquery must return a single instance only. It implies that the subquery must return a single collection row.

Now query the table to verify the preceding modification:

```
SQL> SELECT * FROM TAB_USE_NT_COL;

        ID NUM
---------- ----------------------------
         1 NUM_NEST_T(10, 100, 3)
         2 NUM_NEST_T(10, 12, 13)
```

A nested table collection type in PL/SQL

In PL/SQL, a nested table can be declared and defined in the declaration section of the block as a local collection type. As a nested table follows object orientation, the PL/SQL variable of the nested table type has to be necessarily initialized. The Oracle server raises the exception ORA-06531: Reference to uninitialized collection if an uninitialized nested table type variable is encountered during block execution.

As the nested table collection type has been declared within the PL/SQL block, its scope, visibility, and life is the execution of the PL/SQL block only.

The following PL/SQL block declares a nested table. Observe the scope and visibility of the collection variable. Note that the COUNT method has been used to display the array elements. It is covered later in this chapter in the *Collections – a comparative study* section:

```
/*Enable the SERVEROUTPUT to display the results*/
SET SERVEROUTPUT ON
/*Start the PL/SQL block*/
DECLARE
/*Declare a local nested table collection type*/
  TYPE LOC_NUM_NEST_T IS TABLE OF NUMBER;
  L_LOCAL_NT LOC_NUM_NEST_T := LOC_NUM_NEST_T (10,20,30);
BEGIN
/*Use FOR loop to parse the array and print the elements*/
  FOR I IN 1..L_LOCAL_NT.COUNT
  LOOP
     DBMS_OUTPUT.PUT_LINE('Printing '||i||' element: '||L_LOCAL_
NT(I));
  END LOOP;
END;
/

Printing 1 element: 10
Printing 2 element: 20
Printing 3 element: 30

PL/SQL procedure successfully completed.
```

Additional features of a nested table

In the earlier sections, we saw the operational methodology of a nested table. We will now focus on the nested table's metadata. Furthermore, we will demonstrate a peculiar behavior of the nested table for the "delete" operations.

Oracle's USER_NESTED_TABLES and USER_NESTED_TABLE_COLS data dictionary views maintain the relationship information of the parent and the nested tables. These dictionary views are populated only when a database of a nested table collection type is included in a table.

The USER_NESTED_TABLES static view maintains the information about the mapping of a nested table collection type with its parent table.

The structure of the dictionary view is as follows:

```
SQL> desc USER_NESTED_TABLES

 Name                           Null?      Type
 ---------------------          --------   ---------------
 TABLE_NAME                                VARCHAR2(30)
 TABLE_TYPE_OWNER                          VARCHAR2(30)
 TABLE_TYPE_NAME                           VARCHAR2(30)
 PARENT_TABLE_NAME                         VARCHAR2(30)
 PARENT_TABLE_COLUMN                       VARCHAR2(4000)
 STORAGE_SPEC                              VARCHAR2(30)
 RETURN_TYPE                               VARCHAR2(20)
 ELEMENT_SUBSTITUTABLE                     VARCHAR2(25)
```

Let us query the nested table relationship properties for the `TAB_USE_NT_COL` table from the preceding view:

```
SELECT parent_table_column, table_name, return_type, storage_spec
FROM user_nested_tables
WHERE parent_table_name='TAB_USE_NT_COL'
/

PARENT_TAB      TABLE_NAME        RETURN_TYPE        STORAGE_SPEC
-------------------------------------------------------------------------
NUM             NESTED_NUM_ID     VALUE              DEFAULT
```

In the preceding view query, `RETURN_TYPE` specifies the return type of the collection. It can be `VALUE` (in this case) or `LOCATOR`. Another column, `STORAGE_SPEC`, signifies the storage scheme used for the storage of a nested table which can be either `USER_SPECIFIED` or `DEFAULT` (in this case).

The `USER_NESTED_TABLE_COLS` view maintains the information about the collection attributes contained in the nested tables:

```
SQL> desc USER_NESTED_TABLE_COLS

 Name                           Null?      Type
 ---------------------          --------   ---------------
 TABLE_NAME                     NOT NULL   VARCHAR2(30)
 COLUMN_NAME                    NOT NULL   VARCHAR2(30)
 DATA_TYPE                                 VARCHAR2(106)
 DATA_TYPE_MOD                             VARCHAR2(3)
 DATA_TYPE_OWNER                           VARCHAR2(30)
 DATA_LENGTH                    NOT NULL   NUMBER
 DATA_PRECISION                            NUMBER
 DATA_SCALE                                NUMBER
 NULLABLE                                  VARCHAR2(1)
```

COLUMN_ID		NUMBER
DEFAULT_LENGTH		NUMBER
DATA_DEFAULT		LONG
NUM_DISTINCT		NUMBER
LOW_VALUE		RAW(32)
HIGH_VALUE		RAW(32)
DENSITY		NUMBER
NUM_NULLS		NUMBER
NUM_BUCKETS		NUMBER
LAST_ANALYZED		DATE
SAMPLE_SIZE		NUMBER
CHARACTER_SET_NAME		VARCHAR2(44)
CHAR_COL_DECL_LENGTH		NUMBER
GLOBAL_STATS		VARCHAR2(3)
USER_STATS		VARCHAR2(3)
AVG_COL_LEN		NUMBER
CHAR_LENGTH		NUMBER
CHAR_USED		VARCHAR2(1)
V80_FMT_IMAGE		VARCHAR2(3)
DATA_UPGRADED		VARCHAR2(3)
HIDDEN_COLUMN		VARCHAR2(3)
VIRTUAL_COLUMN		VARCHAR2(3)
SEGMENT_COLUMN_ID		NUMBER
INTERNAL_COLUMN_ID	NOT NULL	NUMBER
HISTOGRAM		VARCHAR2(15)
QUALIFIED_COL_NAME		VARCHAR2(4000)

We will now query the nested storage table in the preceding dictionary view to list all its attributes:

```
SELECT COLUMN_NAME, DATA_TYPE, DATA_LENGTH, HIDDEN_COLUMN
FROM user_nested_table_cols
where table_name='NESTED_NUM_ID'
/

COLUMN_NAME                     DATA_TYP    DATA_LENGTH    HID
------------------------------- ----------- -------------- ---------
NESTED_TABLE_ID                 RAW                   16    YES
COLUMN_VALUE                    NUMBER                22    NO
```

We observe that though the nested table had only number elements, there is two-columned information in the view. The COLUMN_VALUE attribute is the default pseudo column of the nested table as there are no "named" attributes in the collection structure. The other attribute, NESTED_TABLE_ID, is a hidden unique 16-byte system generated raw hash code which latently stores the parent row identifier alongside the nested table instance to distinguish the parent row association.

If an element is deleted from the nested table, it is rendered as parse. This implies that once an index is deleted from the collection structure, the collection doesn't restructure itself by shifting the cells in a forward direction. Let us check out the sparse behavior in the following example.

The following PL/SQL block declares a local nested table and initializes it with a constructor. We will delete the first element and print it again. The system raises the NO_DATA_FOUND exception when we query the element at the index 1 in the collection:

```
/*Enable the SERVEROUTPUT to display the block messages*/
SQL> SET SERVEROUTPUT ON

/*Start the PL/SQL block*/
SQL> DECLARE

    /*Declare the local nested table collection*/
    TYPE coll_method_demo_t IS TABLE OF NUMBER;

    /*Declare a collection variable and initialize it*/
    L_ARRAY coll_method_demo_t := coll_method_demo_t
(10,20,30,40,50);
    BEGIN

    /*Display element at index 1*/
     DBMS_OUTPUT.PUT_LINE('Element at index 1 before deletion:'||l_
array(1));
    /*Delete the 1st element from the collection*/
     L_ARRAY.DELETE(1);
    /*Display element at index 1*/
     DBMS_OUTPUT.PUT_LINE('Element at index 1 after deletion:'||l_
array(1));
    END;
    /

Element at index 1 before deletion:10
DECLARE
*
ERROR at line 1:
ORA-01403: no data found
ORA-06512: at line 15
```

Varray

Varrays were introduced in Oracle8*i* as a modified format of a nested table. The varray or variable size arrays are bounded and the persistent form of collection whose major operational features resemble nested tables. The varray declaration defines the limit of elements a varray can accommodate. The minimum bound of the index is 1, current bound is the total number of resident elements and maximum bound is the varray size. At any moment, the current bound cannot exceed the maximum bound.

Like nested tables, varrays can be created as database objects and can also be used in PL/SQL. Though the implementation is the same as a nested table, varray follow a different storage orientation than the nested tables. They are stored in line with their parent record as a raw value in the parent table. The inline storage mechanism no more needs a storage clause specification, unique identifier or separate storage table. For some exceptional situations when the varray exceeds 4 K data, Oracle follows the out-of-line storage mechanism and stores varray as an LOB.

The inline storage mechanism of varrays helps Oracle to reduce the number of IOs on the disk. This makes varrays superior and more performance efficient than nested tables.

As a database collection type, varrays can be a valid type for a table column or object type attribute. If declared in a PL/SQL block, varrays are visible only within the block.

The syntax for varrays, when defined as a database collection type, is as follows:

```
CREATE [OR REPLACE] TYPE type_name IS {VARRAY | VARYING ARRAY} (size_
limit) OF element_type
```

In PL/SQL, varrays can be declared as follows:

```
DECLARE
TYPE type_name IS {VARRAY | VARYING ARRAY} (size_limit) OF
element_type [NOT NULL];
```

In the preceding syntax, `size_limit` represents the maximum count of elements in the array.

If the varray size has to be modified after its creation in the database, follow this ALTER TYPE syntax:

```
ALTER TYPE [varray name] MODIFY LIMIT [new size_limit]
[INVALIDATE | CASCADE];
```

The varray size can only be increased by using the ALTER TYPE... MODIFY statement. Even if the current maximum size has not been utilized, Oracle doesn't allow the ripping off a varray size. If a user attempts to reduce the varray size, Oracle raises the PLS-00728: the limit of a VARRAY can only be increased and to a maximum 2147483647 exception and invalidates the varray collection type.

The INVALIDATE and CASCADE options signify the invalidation or propagation effect on the dependent objects as a result of the type alteration.

Use the DROP command to drop a varray type from the database:

```
DROP TYPE [varray type name] [FORCE]
```

Varray in PL/SQL

Similar to the handling of a nested table as PL/SQL construct, varrays also can be declared local to a PL/SQL block. In the following illustrations, observe the scope and visibility of the varray variables.

Similar to nested tables, varrays too follow object orientation. For this reason, varrays require initialization mandatorily before accessing them in the executable section of the PL/SQL block.

```
/*Enable the SERVEROUTPUT to display the results*/
SET SERVEROUTPUT ON
/*Start the PL/SQL block*/
DECLARE
/*Declare a local varray type, define collection variable and
initialize it*/
   TYPE V_COLL_DEMO IS VARRAY(4) OF VARCHAR2(100);
   L_LOCAL_COLL V_COLL_DEMO := V_COLL_DEMO('Oracle 9i',
                'Oracle 10g',
                'Oracle 11g');
BEGIN
/*Use FOR loop to parse the array variable and print the elements*/
   FOR I IN 1..L_LOCAL_COLL.COUNT
   LOOP
      DBMS_OUTPUT.PUT_LINE('Printing Oracle version:' ||L_LOCAL_
COLL(I));
   END LOOP;
END;
/
```

```
Printing Oracle version:Oracle 9i
Printing Oracle version:Oracle 10g
Printing Oracle version:Oracle 11g

PL/SQL procedure successfully completed.
```

Varray as a database collection type

Let us illustrate the creation of a varray as a database collection type. We will see the SELECT and DML operations on varrays:

```
/*Create the nested table in the database*/
SQL> CREATE OR REPLACE TYPE num_varray_t AS VARRAY (5) OF NUMBER;
/

Type created.
```

Oracle maintains the complete information about the newly created varray types in the dictionary views USER_VARRAYS, USER_COLL_TYPES, and USER_TYPES.

Now, we will create a table which has a column of the varray type. Note that it has no NESTED TABLE STORE AS clause as it used in the case of nested tables to specify the name of the storage table.

```
CREATE TABLE tab_use_va_col
  (ID NUMBER,
   NUM num_varray_t);

Table created.

/*Query the USER_VARRAYS to list varray information*/
SELECT parent_table_column, type_name, return_type, storage_spec
FROM user_varrays
WHERE parent_table_name='TAB_USE_VA_COL'
/
```

PARENT_TAB	TYPE_NAME	RETURN_TYPE	STORAGE_SPEC
NUM	NUM_VARRAY_T	VALUE	DEFAULT

DML operations on varray type columns

Being the common behavior of the homogeneous collections, varrays respond affirmatively to the DML operations upon them. Similar to the nested tables, let us demonstrate the DML actions on varray type columns.

Inserting a varray collection type instance

The following code inserts the test data into the table created in the *Varray as a database collection type* section. The INSERT statement uses a collection type constructor and looks similar to that of the nested table:

```
/*Insert the sample data in the varray collection*/
INSERT INTO tab_use_va_col
VALUES
(1, num_varray_t (10,12,13))
/

1 row created.

INSERT INTO tab_use_va_col
VALUES
(2, num_varray_t (32, 23, 76, 27))
/

1 row created.
```

Note that the DML statements on varrays raise exception if elements supplied exceed the defined limit. The following INSERT statement attempts to include six elements in the collection type instance. Note that the maximum limit of a varray collection is five. Exception roars!!

```
INSERT INTO tab_use_va_col
VALUES
(3, num_varray_t (32, 23, 76, 27, 38, 3));
(3, num_varray_t (32, 23, 76, 27, 38, 3))
    *
ERROR at line 3:
ORA-22909: exceeded maximum VARRAY limit
```

Selecting a varray column

The following SELECT query selects the varray in an instance format:

```
SQL> SELECT * FROM tab_use_va_col;

    ID NUM
---------- ------------------------------
     1 NUM_VARRAY_T(10, 12, 13)
     2 NUM_VARRAY_T(32, 23, 76, 27)
```

Like we saw in nested tables, the TABLE expression can open the collection instance and represent the object rows in relational format:

```
SQL> SELECT T.id, T1.column_value
FROM tab_use_va_col T, TABLE(T.num) T1;


        ID COLUMN_VALUE
---------- ------------
         1           10
         1           12
         1           13
         2           32
         2           23
         2           76
         2           27

7 rows selected.
```

Updating the varray instance

Similar to the demonstration shown in the nested tables, varrays can be updated using the instance replacement option. The following UPDATE statement modifies the varray instance for ID 1:

```
UPDATE TAB_USE_VA_COL
SET NUM =  NUM_VARRAY_T(10, 12, 25)
WHERE ID = 1;

1 row updated.
```

Now, the table can be queried to verify the update:

```
SQL> select * from tab_use_va_col;

        ID NUM
---------- ----------------------------
         1 NUM_VARRAY_T(10, 12, 25)
         2 NUM_VARRAY_T(32, 23, 76, 27)
```

In case of varrays, a single element cannot be updated using the TABLE expression. The reason is the different storage philosophy of varrays. A varray is stored in line with the parent row and not as separate storage tables, as in the case of nested tables. Therefore, a single element of a varray can be updated only through a PL/SQL block.

Collections—a comparative study

In this section, we will compare the available collection types and also throw light on the considerable points to select the appropriate collection type in the database.

Common characteristics of collection types

All three forms of collection types oblige to certain characteristics under all situations. Let us check out some of the common properties of collection types:

- Persistent collection types can be passed as a formal argument to database stored subprograms. Local collection types and non-persistent collection types can be used for local subprograms only.

- Collection types can be used as a RETURN type of a function.

- Due to the object-oriented behavior of persistent collection types—nested tables and varrays—the PL/SQL variables must be initialized by either of the following ways:

    ○ Use the default collection constructor during declaration or in the executable section

    ○ Assign a NOT NULL collection to the uninitialized collection variable

    ○ Fetch data from the database to assign to the uninitialized collection variable

- A collection element can always be referenced as [Collection] [index].[Attribute].

- Common collection related exceptions are as follows:

    ○ COLLECTION_IS_NULL: This exception is raised when the collection is NULL

    ○ NO_DATA_FOUND: This exception is raised when the element corresponding to a subscript does not exist

    ○ SUBSCRIPT_BEYOND_COUNT: This exception is raised when the index exceeds the number of elements in the collection.

    ○ SUBSCRIPT_OUTSIDE_LIMIT: This exception is raised when the index is not a legal value

    ○ VALUE_ERROR: This exception is raised when an element is attempted for access without index

The following diagram branches the different places where collections can mark their presence:

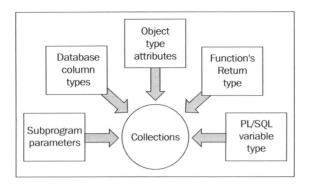

Nested table versus associative arrays

The following table compares the nested table and associative arrays in terms of size, sparse, ordering, and storage:

Factor	Nested table	Associative array
Maximum size	Dynamic	Dynamic
Sparsity	May exist	Exists
Storage	Out-of-line storage	Non-persistent temporary memory storage
Ordering	No retention of index ordering	Retains index order

Nested tables are preferred over associative arrays when the data has to be physically stored in the database. Also, array operations are much more convenient and smoother in nested tables as compared to associative arrays.

Associative arrays are used to temporarily hold the data for lookup or caching purposes.

Nested table versus varrays

Nested tables and varrays resemble each other up to a greater extent. Both store their structures and data persistently in the database as collection types. The upper limit is notably a difference which makes varrays more disciplined and tidy. Varrays are always dense and maintain their subscript order:

Factor	Nested table	Varray
Maximum size	Dynamic	Fixed
Sparsity	May exist	Dense
Storage	Out-of-line storage	In Line storage (up to 4K)
Ordering	No retention of index ordering	Retains index order

Varrays are used in scenarios when the element count is fixed and sequential access of elements is expected. For example, Address of employees is fixed to three lines and must be accessed sequentially to maintain its credibility. Nested tables provide untidy access to all elements where a user can delete or insert elements simultaneously.

PL/SQL collection methods

Oracle provides a set of methods which can be used in conjunction with collections in PL/SQL blocks. These methods access a collection type variable and perform relevant activities such as extension, trimming, and deleting collection elements. Besides these activities, few methods also provide information about the collection such as COUNT and EXISTS. These utilities are known as **collection methods** and they are not a built-in subprogram, because they can be used exclusively in conjunction with collections.

The common syntax for all the collection methods is as follows:

```
[COLLECTION].METHOD (PARAMETERS)
```

EXISTS

The EXISTS function checks the existence of an element in a collection. The general syntax of this function is EXISTS(<index>). It takes the subscript as an input argument and searches it in the collection. If the element corresponding to the index is found, it returns TRUE or else, returns FALSE. It is the only method which doesn't raise any exception during its application with an uninitialized collection.

The following PL/SQL block declares a local nested table collection and its two variables. While one array is uninitialized, the other one is initialized with sample data. We will check the existence of the first element in both arrays:

```
/*Enable the SERVEROUTPUT on to display the output*/
SET SERVEROUTPUT ON

/*Start the PL/SQL block*/
DECLARE
/*Declare a local nested table collection*/
  TYPE coll_method_demo_t IS TABLE OF NUMBER;
/*Declare collection type variables*/
  L_ARRAY1 coll_method_demo_t;
  L_ARRAY2 coll_method_demo_t := coll_method_demo_t (45,87,57);
BEGIN
/*Check if first cell exists in the array 1*/
  IF L_ARRAY1.EXISTS(1) THEN
     DBMS_OUTPUT.PUT_LINE('Element 1 found in Array 1');
  ELSE
     DBMS_OUTPUT.PUT_LINE('Element 1 NOT found in Array 1');
  END IF;
/*Check if first cell exists in the array 2*/
  IF L_ARRAY2.EXISTS(1) THEN
     DBMS_OUTPUT.PUT_LINE('Element 1 found in Array 2');
  ELSE
     DBMS_OUTPUT.PUT_LINE('Element 1 NOT found in Array 2');
  END IF;
END;
/

Element 1 NOT found in Array 1
Element 1 found in Array 2

PL/SQL procedure successfully completed.
```

COUNT

As the name suggests, the COUNT function counts the number of elements in an initialized collection. The COUNT method raises the COLLECTION_IS_NULL exception for uninitialized collections.

> The COUNT function returns zero when:
>
> A nested table or varray collection is initialized with an empty collection
>
> An associative array doesn't have any elements

It can be operated upon all three types of collections.

The following PL/SQL block declares a local nested table collection and its two variables. We will check the element count in both the collection variables:

```
/*Enable the SERVEROUTPUT on to display the output*/
SET SERVEROUTPUT ON

/*Start the PL/SQL block*/
DECLARE
/*Declare the local collection type*/
  TYPE coll_method_demo_t IS TABLE OF NUMBER;

/*Declare the collection variables and initialize them with test
data*/
  l_loc_var coll_method_demo_t := coll_method_demo_t (10,20,30);
BEGIN
  DBMS_OUTPUT.PUT_LINE('The array size is '||l_loc_var.count);
END;
/

The array size is 3

PL/SQL procedure successfully completed.
```

LIMIT

The LIMIT function returns the maximum number of elements that can be accommodated by a VARRAY collection type variable. This method can be used with VARRAY collection types only. The LIMIT method raises the COLLECTION_IS_NULL exception for uninitialized collections.

 For associative arrays and nested tables, the LIMIT method returns NULL.

The following PL/SQL block declares a local varray type and a variable of its type. The varray type variable has been initialized with test data. Observe the difference between the COUNT and LIMIT methods:

```
/*Enable the SERVEROUTPUT on to display the output*/
SET SERVEROUTPUT ON

/*Start the PL/SQL block*/
DECLARE
/*Declare local varray and its variable*/
  TYPE coll_method_demo_v IS VARRAY(10) OF NUMBER;
  L_ARRAY1 coll_method_demo_v := coll_method_demo_v (10,20,30);
```

```
BEGIN
/*Display the current count*/
  DBMS_OUTPUT.PUT_LINE('The varray has '||L_ARRAY1.COUNT||'
elements');

/*Display the maximum limit*/
  DBMS_OUTPUT.PUT_LINE('The varray can hold '||L_ARRAY1.LIMIT||'
elements');
END;
/

The varray has 3 elements
The varray can hold 10 elements

PL/SQL procedure successfully completed.
```

FIRST and LAST

The FIRST and LAST functions return the first and last subscripts of a collection. For an empty collection, these methods return NULL value. These methods can be used with all three types of collections. The FIRST and LAST methods raise exception COLLECTION_IS_NULL for uninitialized collections.

The following PL/SQL block demonstrates the use of the FIRST and LAST methods with an initialized collection:

```
/*Enable the SERVEROUTPUT on to display the output*/
SET SERVEROUTPUT ON

/*Start the PL/SQL bock*/
DECLARE
/*Display a local nested table collection*/
  TYPE coll_method_demo_t IS TABLE OF NUMBER;
  L_ARRAY coll_method_demo_t := coll_method_demo_t (10,20,30);
BEGIN
/*Display the first and last elements*/
  DBMS_OUTPUT.PUT_LINE('First element of the array: '|| L_ARRAY (L_
ARRAY.FIRST));
  DBMS_OUTPUT.PUT_LINE('Last element of the array: '|| L_ARRAY (L_
ARRAY.LAST));
END;
/

Starting Index of the array: 10
Last Index of the array: 30

PL/SQL procedure successfully completed.
```

PRIOR and NEXT

The PRIOR and NEXT functions take an input index and return its previous and next index from the given collection. If the PRIOR and NEXT functions are used with the first and last indexes respectively, the method returns NULL.

Both the methods can be used with all three types of collections. The PRIOR and NEXT methods raise exception COLLECTION_IS_NULL for uninitialized collections.

The following PL/SQL shows the usage of the PRIOR and NEXT methods with a PL/SQL type collection:

```
/*Enable the SERVEROUTPUT on to display the output*/
SET SERVEROUTPUT ON

/*Start the PL/SQL block*/
DECLARE
/*Declare a local nested table collection*/
  TYPE coll_method_demo_t IS TABLE OF NUMBER;
  L_ARRAY coll_method_demo_t := coll_method_demo_t
(10,20,30,100,48,29,28);
BEGIN

/*Display the element which appears before 5th index*/
  DBMS_OUTPUT.PUT_LINE('Element before 5th element: '||L_ARRAY(L_
ARRAY.PRIOR(5)));

/*Display the element which appears after 6th index*/
  DBMS_OUTPUT.PUT_LINE('Element after 6th element: '||L_ARRAY(L_ARRAY.
NEXT(6)));
END;
/

Element before 5th element: 100
Element after 6th element: 28

PL/SQL procedure successfully completed.
```

EXTEND

The EXTEND function is used to append elements to a collection variable of nested table or varray type. It cannot be used with associative arrays.

It is an overloaded function which can be used in three signatures as follows:

- EXTEND: It appends the collection with a NULL element
- EXTEND(x): It appends the collection with x number of NULL elements

- EXTEND(x,y): It appends the collection with x elements and with the value as that of the y element. If the y element doesn't exist, the system raises a SUBSCRIPT_BEYOND_COUNT exception.

The following PL/SQL block demonstrates the extension using all three signatures of the EXTEND method. The first extension appends the fourth NULL element to the array. The second extension appends the fifth and sixth NULL elements to the array. The third extension appends the seventh and eighth elements as 10 (value of the first element) to the array:

```
/*Enable the SERVEROUTPUT on to display the output*/
SET SERVEROUTPUT ON

/*Start the PL/SQL block*/
DECLARE
/*Declare local nested table collection type*/
TYPE coll_method_demo_t IS TABLE OF NUMBER;

/*Declare collection type variable and initialize it*/
L_ARRAY coll_method_demo_t := coll_method_demo_t (10,20,30);
BEGIN

/*Extend the collection. It adds a NULL element to the collection*/
  L_ARRAY.EXTEND;
  DBMS_OUTPUT.PUT_LINE(L_ARRAY.LAST||' element of the array is  =
'||L_ARRAY(L_ARRAY.LAST));

/*Extend the collection. It adds two NULL elements at the end of the
collection*/
  L_ARRAY.EXTEND(2);
  DBMS_OUTPUT.PUT_LINE(L_ARRAY.LAST||' element of the array is  =
'||L_ARRAY(L_ARRAY.LAST));

/*Extend the collection. It adds two NULL elements at the end of the
collection and populates with the 1st element*/
  L_ARRAY.EXTEND(2,1);
  DBMS_OUTPUT.PUT_LINE(L_ARRAY.LAST||' element of the array is  =
'||L_ARRAY(L_ARRAY.LAST));
END;
/

L_ARRAY(4) element of the array is  =
L_ARRAY(6) element of the array is  =
L_ARRAY(8) element of the array is  = 10

PL/SQL procedure successfully completed.
```

The EXTEND method raises the COLLECTION_IS_NULL exception for uninitialized collections. If a varray is attempted for extension beyond its maximum allowed limit, Oracle raises a SUBSCRIPT_BEYOND_LIMIT exception.

TRIM

The TRIM function is used to cut the elements from the specified collection, of the nested table or varray type. It cannot be used with associative array type collections. TRIM is an overloaded method, which can be used in the following two signatures:

- TRIM: It trims one element from the end of the collection
- TRIM(n): It trims n elements from the end of the collection. If n exceeds the total count of elements in the collection, the system raises a SUBSCRIPT_BEYOND_COUNT exception. No action has been defined for NULL value of n.

The following PL/SQL block shows the operation of the TRIM method on an initialized PL/SQL table collection type:

```
/*Enable the SERVEROUTPUT on to display the output*/
SET SERVEROUTPUT ON

/*Start the PL/SQL block*/
DECLARE

/*Declare a local nested table collection type*/
   TYPE coll_method_demo_t IS TABLE OF NUMBER;

/*Declare a collection variable and initialize it*/
   L_ARRAY coll_method_demo_t := coll_method_demo_t (10,20,30,40,50);
BEGIN

/*Trim the last element of the collection*/
   L_ARRAY.TRIM;
   DBMS_OUTPUT.PUT_LINE('L_ARRAY('||L_ARRAY.LAST||') element is  =
'||L_ARRAY(L_ARRAY.LAST));

/*Trim the last 2 elements of the collection*/
   L_ARRAY.TRIM(2);
   DBMS_OUTPUT.PUT_LINE('L_ARRAY('||L_ARRAY.LAST||') element is  =
'||L_ARRAY(L_ARRAY.LAST));
END;
/

L_ARRAY(4) element is  = 40
L_ARRAY(2) element is  = 20

PL/SQL procedure successfully completed.
```

Like other methods, the TRIM method raises a COLLECTION_IS_NULL exception for uninitialized collections.

DELETE

The DELETE function is used to delete elements from a given collection. The DELETE operation leaves the collection sparse. Any reference to the deleted index would raise a NO_DATA_FOUND exception. The DELETE method raises a COLLECTION_IS_NULL exception for uninitialized collections. It can be used with all three types of collections.

The overloaded method can be used in the following signatures:

- DELETE: It flushes out all the elements of a collection
- DELETE(n): It deletes the *nth* index from the collection
- DELETE(n,m): It performs range deletion, where all the elements within the range of the subscripts n and m are deleted.

The following PL/SQL block declares a coll_method_demo_t collection along with its collection variable. This program displays the first element of the collection before and after the deletion of the first subscript:

```
/*Enable the SERVEROUTPUT on to display the output*/
SET SERVEROUTPUT ON
/*Start the PL/SQL block*/
DECLARE

/*Declare the local nested table collection*/
TYPE coll_method_demo_t IS TABLE OF NUMBER;

/*Declare a collection variable and initialize it*/
L_ARRAY coll_method_demo_t := coll_method_demo_t (10,20,30,40,50);
BEGIN
  DBMS_OUTPUT.PUT_LINE('First element before deletion is :L_
ARRAY('||L_ARRAY.FIRST||') = '||L_ARRAY(L_ARRAY.FIRST));

/*Delete the 1st element from the collection*/
  L_ARRAY.DELETE(1);
  DBMS_OUTPUT.PUT_LINE('First element after deletion is : L_
ARRAY('||L_ARRAY.FIRST||') = '||L_ARRAY(L_ARRAY.FIRST));
END;
/

First element before deletion is : L_ARRAY(1) = 10
First element after deletion is : L_ARRAY(2) = 20

PL/SQL procedure successfully completed.
```

Interestingly, Oracle doesn't allow the deletion of individual elements in a varray collection. Either all the elements of the varray have to be removed using the VARRAY.DELETE method or the elements can be trimmed from the end of the varray collection. This scenario is illustrated in the following program:

```
/*Enable the SERVEROUTPUT on to display the output*/
SET SERVEROUTPUT ON
/*Start the PL/SQL block*/
DECLARE
/*Declare the local varray collection*/
TYPE coll_method_demo_t IS VARRAY (10) OF NUMBER;
/*Declare a collection variable and initialize it*/
L_ARRAY coll_method_demo_t := coll_method_demo_t (10,20,30,40,50);
BEGIN
/*Delete the second element of varray*/
  L_ARRAY.DELETE(2);
END;
/

  L_ARRAY.DELETE(2);
  *
ERROR at line 8:
ORA-06550: line 8, column 3:
PLS-00306: wrong number or types of arguments in call to 'DELETE'
ORA-06550: line 8, column 3:
PL/SQL: Statement ignored
```

It is recommended that the TRIM and DELETE methods must not be operated together or simultaneously on a collection. The DELETE method retains a placeholder for the deleted element, while the TRIM method destroys the element from the collection. Therefore, the operation sequence "DELETE(last) followed by TRIM(1)" would result in removal of a single element only.

Manipulating collection elements

A database column of collection type physically stores the data in the database. As part of data operations, the collection type instance held by a column might get updated. There are two approaches to manipulate the collection instance in the database column:

- The complete instance can be replaced with a new one
- The target element can be solely modified

The first approach is feasible when the structure of the collection and the value of other attributes of the instance are known. But it may not be the case every time. However, it has been demonstrated in earlier sections. Therefore, Oracle recommends manipulating the collection element through a PL/SQL program.

Let us demonstrate the collection element update with the following illustration. Check out the latest data in the table TAB_USE_NT_COL:

```
SQL> SELECT * FROM TAB_USE_NT_COL;

        ID NUM
---------- -------------------------
         1 NUM_NEST_T(10, 12, 3)
         2 NUM_NEST_T(10, 12, 13)
```

Now, we will try to add an element (23) at the end of the collection instance for ID 2.

```
/*Enable the SERVEROUTPUT on to display the output*/
SET SERVEROUTPUT ON

/*Start the PL/SQL block*/
DECLARE

/*Declare a local variable of database collection type*/
  L_INS_NUM NUM_NEST_T;
BEGIN

/*Select the collection instance into the local variable for ID = 2*/
  SELECT num INTO L_INS_NUM
  FROM tab_use_nt_col WHERE id=2;

/*Extend the collection variable using EXTEND method. Include the new
element at the end of the collection*/
  L_INS_NUM.EXTEND;
  L_INS_NUM (L_INS_NUM.LAST) := 23;

/*Update the local collection instance in the table for ID = 2*/
  UPDATE tab_use_nt_col
  SET num = L_INS_NUM
  WHERE id=2;
END;
/

PL/SQL procedure successfully completed.
```

Query the table to verify the manipulation in the collection:

```
SQL> SELECT * FROM TAB_USE_NT_COL;

        ID NUM
---------- ---------------------------------
         1 NUM_NEST_T(10, 12, 3)
         2 NUM_NEST_T(10, 12, 13, 23)
```

Collection initialization

The persistent collection types—nested tables and varrays—follow features of object orientation. By virtue of their behavior, PL/SQL variables of collection types must be initialized. Initialization is a mandatory activity before the collection is accessed in the PL/SQL program. An uninitialized exception generates the ORA-06531: Reference to uninitialized collection exception.

Associative arrays are the local non-persistent arrays, so no initialization is required for them.

We will discuss some of the ways to initialize a collection type variable in a PL/SQL block:

- **Using the default collection constructor during declaration or in the executable section:**

  Oracle provides a default constructor (with the same name as the collection type) with every type which can be used to provide attribute values. It can be used to initialize the collection variable either as NULL or with the sample default data:

```
/*Start the PL/SQL block*/
DECLARE
   TYPE coll_nt_t IS TABLE OF NUMBER;
/*A collection variable is initialized with sample data in default
constructor*/
   L_LOCAL_VAR1 coll_nt_t := coll_nt_t (10,20);
/*A collection variable is initialized with an empty collection*/
   L_LOCAL_VAR2 coll_nt_t := coll_nt_t();
BEGIN
  ...
  ...
END;
```

In the preceding PL/SQL block, the L_LOCAL_VAR1 collection variable is initialized with a collection constructor having two rows. Note that this is a default initialization, not the actual assignment. The actual assignment of collection instances is done in the executable section only which overrides the initialized instance. The L_LOCAL_VAR2 collection variable is initialized with an empty collection.

However, the initialization can be made in an executable section also before the collection variable is accessed for any operation:

```
/*Start the PL/SQL block*/
DECLARE
  TYPE coll_nt_t IS TABLE OF NUMBER;
/Uninitialized collection variables*/
  L_LOCAL_VAR1 coll_nt_t;
  L_LOCAL_VAR2 coll_nt_t;
BEGIN
/*Initialization in executable section*/
 L_LOCAL_VAR1:= coll_nt_t (10,20);
 L_LOCAL_VAR2:= coll_nt_t();
END;
```

- **Selecting a collection instance into the local collection variable:**

    In the executable section, a SELECT statement can pull a collection instance (of the same collection type) into the local collection variable. This method is permissible only when the collection type exists as a database type and the PL/SQL collection variable is of that particular collection type.

    In our earlier illustrations, num_nest_t is a nested table in the database. We will use the same type to declare a local collection variable:

```
/*Start the PL/SQL block*/
DECLARE
  l_loc_num num_nest_t;
BEGIN
/*Fetching collection instance from database to initialize a
collection variable*/
  SELECT num INTO l_loc_num
  FROM tab_use_nt_col
  WHERE id = 1;
END;
/

PL/SQL procedure successfully completed.
```

Summary

This chapter covers one of the efficient features of PL/SQL programming—collections. We discussed and learned the three types of collections in PL/SQL. With the help of the illustrations, we understood their handling such as the selections and transactions in the database as well as in PL/SQL. We learned about the various collection methods and discovered the ways of collection initialization. The next chapter brings in a unique feature and one of the strengths of PL/SQL language—external procedures.

Practice exercise

1. Which two statements are true about associative arrays?

    a. Associative arrays can have negative subscripts.

    b. Associative arrays are always dense collections.

    c. Associative arrays don't need initialization in a PL/SQL block.

    d. The upper limit of associative arrays can be dynamically modified.

2. Which of the following statements is true about nested tables?

    a. Nested tables are stored in a segment different from that of the parent table.

    b. Nested table columns can have string subscripts

    c. Nested tables can grow dynamically up to any extent.

    d. A database column of the nested table collection type can be separately queried by its storage name.

3. Only varrays can have sequential numbers as subscripts.

    a. True

    b. False

4. Which of the following associative array declarations is/are correct?

```
DECLARE
TYPE T1 IS TABLE OF NUMBER INDEX BY BOOLEAN;
TYPE T2 IS TABLE OF VARCHAR2(10) INDEX BY NUMBER;
TYPE T3 IS TABLE OF DATE INDEX BY SIGNTYPE;
TYPE T4 IS TABLE OF EMPLOYEES%ROWTYPE INDEX BY POSITIVE;
BEGIN
...
...
END;
```

   a. T1

   b. T2

   c. T3

   d. T4

5. Which of the following statements is/are true about varrays?

   a. The limit of varray elements can be modified during runtime using the ALTER TABLE statement.

   b. A Varray element can be deleted using the DELETE method.

   c. For an empty collection of a varray type, the value of LAST is equal to COUNT.

   d. Varrays can exist as sparse collections.

6. What will be the output of the following PL/SQL block?

```
DECLARE
    TYPE T IS TABLE OF NUMBER;
    L_NUM T := T(1,2);
BEGIN
    DBMS_OUTPUT.PUT_LINE(L_NUM(1));
    L_NUM := T(10,20);
    DBMS_OUTPUT.PUT_LINE(L_NUM(1));
END;
```

   a. 1 and 1.

   b. 1 and 10.

   c. Oracle raises a COLLECTION_IS_NULL exception at line 5.

   d. 10 and 10.

7. The EMPLOYEES table stores the details of 14 employees. Identify the solution of the error in the following PL/SQL program:

```
DECLARE
    TYPE EMP_VARRAY_T IS VARRAY (10) OF EMPLOYEES%ROWTYPE;
    L_EMP EMP_VARRAY_T := EMP_VARRAY_T();
BEGIN
    DBMS_OUTPUT.PUT_LINE(L_EMP.COUNT);
    SELECT *
    BULK COLLECT INTO L_EMP
    FROM EMPLOYEES;
    DBMS_OUTPUT.PUT_LINE(L_EMP.COUNT);
END;
/
0
DECLARE
*
ERROR at line 1:
ORA-22165: given index [11] must be in the range of [1] to [10]
ORA-06512: at line 6
```

a. The varray size must be increased to 14 or a higher limit.

b. The varray variable must be initialized with a define employee data.

c. Data for only 10 employees must be selected into a varray variable.

d. The varray definition is wrong; a record type cannot be made as an element type of a varray collection.

8. Which of the following statements are wrong about the collection methods?

a. EXISTS raises NO_DATA_FOUND exception if the element for the input subscript does not exist.

b. DELETE can be used with varrays.

c. LIMIT returns the current limit of the nested table collection.

d. TRIM removes an element of the collection from the end.

4

Using Advanced Interface Methods

External routines enable the communication between the Oracle database and the programs, which are written in non-database language such as C, C++, Java, or COBOL. The fact is not new that Oracle has emerged as a compatible database manager for application clients. But from the programming and development perspective, every language has its own special features and utilities. Before UTL_MAIL and UTL_SMTP came to the rescue, there was no option for sending an e-mail in Oracle. In some situations, a special logic written on the client side is required to be used on the server side too. The idea is to resolve the situations where a non-PL/SQL program has to be invoked from PL/SQL. To confront such situations, Oracle introduced external routines in its eighth release (Oracle 8) to bridge the gap between the database and non-PL/SQL programs. This chapter covers the external procedures and its implementation in the following topics:

- Understanding external routines
  - Architecture
  - Benefits
- Executing external C programs from PL/SQL
- Executing external Java programs from PL/SQL

Understanding external routines

An external routine allows a program, which is written in a language other than PL/SQL, to be used in PL/SQL. For instance, a program logic written in Java can be invoked and used from PL/SQL. The program in non-PL/SQL language is referred to as external programs. The favorable situations for the use of external routines may arise in an application development environment which follows strict regimentation of the client, API and database layers. On broader terms, an external program has to be stored as a shared library on the server followed by its publishing through call specification. Once the external routine is published, it is ready to be used in PL/SQL.

Within the scope of this chapter, we will discuss the invocation of external programs written in C and Java language from PL/SQL.

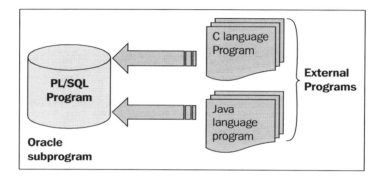

Architecture of external routines

Before we get into the core methodology followed for external routines, we will discuss some of the crucial components of Oracle architectural support to the external routines. These components are

- **The** extproc **process**: The extproc process is the protagonist of the complete architecture. It is a session specific process which receives the request from the Oracle Net listener and kicks off the external program execution. It loads the DLL, takes care of the arguments, receives the required output from the execution of an external program and sends it back through the listener. It is an essential element of the architecture.

- **Shared library of external routine**: An external program has to be executed as a shared library to be accessed in Oracle PL/SQL. Microsoft operating systems identify shared libraries in the form of .dll files (Dynamic Linked Library) while the shared files of operating systems such as Unix, Linux, or Solaris, have .so extension. The external program language must be the one whose shared library can be invoked from C. It can be C, C++, FORTRAN, COBOL, or Visual Basic. The shared libraries may include multiple programs which can be invoked as external programs. Thus, loading a smaller number of libraries can provide access to multiple external programs.

Dynamic linked shared libraries are easy to create and maintain than their statically linked component. A shared library can be shared across the database sessions; thus reducing memory consumption in multisession environments. Spawned by the Oracle listener, the extproc process automatically loads the shared libraries. The external program contained within the shared library is executed and the result is returned back to the extproc process and flows down to the PL/SQL procedure call.

There are two relevant terms—**callout** and **callback**—associated with the external routine handling.

A call is referred to as callout when the PL/SQL procedure invokes an external procedure. On the other hand, if the external procedure invokes a statement, which drives the database engine, the call is known as callback. The statement can be a SQL or a PL/SQL construct, which hits the Oracle server to perform an operation.

The architecture of an external program processing depends a lot on the two components mentioned earlier. Whenever the PL/SQL runtime engine receives the request for the execution of an externally implemented procedure, it directs the call to the TNS service ORACLR_CONNECTION_DATA. Note that the ORACLR_CONNECTION_DATA is the default TNS service for external routine connections, which is configured by the Oracle Net Configuration assistant during database software installation to establish the interaction between the database server and external routine connections. **Oracle Common Language Runtime (ORACLR)** is a host which coordinates the external process to invoke a non-PL/SQL program in PL/SQL. However, the default net configurations can be modified manually to ensure enhanced security standards. From the TNS service address, it picks up the key and verifies the network with the current running active listener. Now, using the specific connection details, it invokes the extproc process. As stated earlier, the extproc process uses the specified DLL path to load the shared library. In addition, the process handles the input arguments (if any) and transfers the output from the execution of the external program through the listener.

The preceding description has been pictorially demonstrated in the following flowchart:

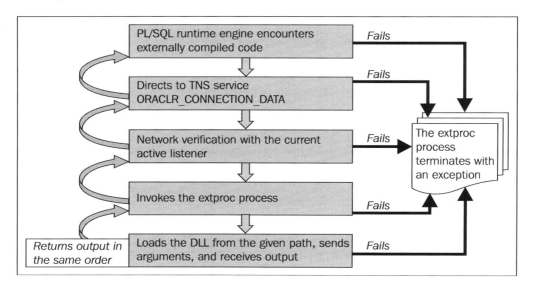

 The processing of the extproc process is carried out separately from the other database process. Even if the extproc process crashes, it does not produce any side effects on the kernel memory.

In the course of the steps shown in the preceding flowchart, failure of any of them results in the termination of the extproc process. Some of the commonly encountered exceptions during the cycle are as follows:

- **ORA-28576: Lost RPC connection to external procedure agent**: The exception is raised when the Oracle listener is not able to establish the connection with the extproc process.

- **ORA-28595: Extproc agent: Invalid DLL path**: The exception is raised when the extproc process is not able to locate the compatible DLL in the specified location. The probable causes of the exception may be:

  - Wrong DLL path specification: DLL has been generated at a different OS location and manually moved to the target location. It is always recommended to move the program file at the target location and natively generate the DLL at the particular location.

- ° The Oracle Net configuration expects a dedicated listener for the `extproc` process. If the mapping of the `TNSNAMES.ora` and `LISTENER.ora` file works perfectly, this step can be overruled. However, it has been a recommended step to maintain concurrencies among the listeners.

- **ORA-06521: PL/SQL Error mapping function**: The external program has been wrongly mapped in the PL/SQL call specification. The reason can be parameter data type mismatch or an incorrect program name reference in the call specification.

Oracle Net Configuration

As we discussed in the previous section, the `extproc` process acts as the communication channel between PL/SQL and the external program. It is started by the Oracle listener and interacts with the external program through the DLL and transmits back the program output through the same passage.

The `extproc` process activation is governed by the Oracle Net services where the `TNSNAMES.ora` and `LISTENER.ora` files are configured by default by the Oracle Net Configuration assistant during database software installation. However, the net configuration can be modified to enforce and ensure high-level security. We will now discuss the requirements of Oracle Net services configuration and management. Both the ORA files can be found under `$ORACLE_HOME\network\admin\` directory. One must keep a hawk eye on the security scheme to modify the files on the server as we will be working with the ORA files in this section.

TNSNAMES.ora

The `TNSNAMES.ora` file provides the database connection aliases or service names to connect to the appropriate listener and, hence, the target database. It takes the requests from the client which is trying to establish the connection with the database.

 The term **TNS** stands for **Transparent Network Substrate**.

In the default `TNSNAMES.ora` file, which is configured during the database software installation, a `ORACLR_CONNECTION_DATA` service is created to support external services. This service is responsible for activating the `extproc` process. It verifies the network connection using the `ADDRESS` parameter value, followed by a connection establishment using the `CONNECT_DATA` parameter value. The service entry in the `TNSNAMES.ora` file looks as follows:

```
ORACLR_CONNECTION_DATA =
  (DESCRIPTION =
    (ADDRESS_LIST =
      (ADDRESS = (PROTOCOL = IPC)(KEY = EXTPROC1521))
    )
    (CONNECT_DATA =
      (SID = CLRExtProc)
      (PRESENTATION = RO)
    )
  )
```

In the preceding entry, the parameters `KEY` and `SID` have variable values while other values are fixed. The values must be concurrent with those of the corresponding listener entries.

The `ADDRESS` parameter value checks for the listeners which can receive `IPC` (Internet Procedure Calls) requests through the `KEY` value `EXTPROC1521`. The `PROTOCOL` parameter has a fixed value `IPC` to establish the interaction between the server and the external service requests. Once the `ADDRESS` setup matches the current active listener, it uses the `CONNECT_DATA` parameter value to shoot the `extproc` process. The `PRESENTATION` parameter is a performance booster parameter which directs the database server to concentrate and respond to the client through a protocol—**Remote-Ops (RO)**.

Note the `CONNECT_DATA` parameter value. It searches for the listener with the same `SID` `CLRExtProc`. The `CLRExtProc` is a listener mode which allows PL/SQL programs to access external programs.

LISTENER.ora

All the database connection requests pass through the listeners. A listener entry in the file contains the network configuration parameters of the server.

A typical `LISTENER.ora` file which is set up during the database installation contains two entries namely `LISTENER` and `SID_LIST_LISTENER`.

The LISTENER entry gives the protocol and key details. From the entry details, we can notice that it can listen to an IPC request, as well as TCP requests:

```
LISTENER =
  (DESCRIPTION_LIST =
    (DESCRIPTION =
      (ADDRESS = (PROTOCOL = IPC)(KEY = EXTPROC1521))
      (ADDRESS = (PROTOCOL = TCP)(HOST = localhost)(PORT = 1521))
    )
  )
```

The SID_LIST_LISTENER contains the SID details of the external services which can interact with the LISTENER listener. It contains the SID_NAME, ORACLE_HOME, and PROGRAM parameters. The SID_NAME parameter must be in sync with the SID value under the CONNECT_DATA parameter of the ORACLR_CONNECTION_DATA service in TNSNAMES.ora. It identifies the extproc process. The PROGRAM parameter value is used for the program identification for extproc.

The SID_LIST_LISTENER entry in the LISTENER.ora is as follows:

```
SID_LIST_LISTENER =
  (SID_LIST =
    (SID_DESC =
      (SID_NAME = CLRExtProc)
      (ORACLE_HOME = <<Oracle Home>>)
      (PROGRAM = EXTPROC1521)
      (ENVS= "EXTPROC_DLLS=[ONLY | ANY | (DLL path)]")
    )
  )
```

The location of the shared library file has to be registered in the preceding SID_LIST_LISTENER entry. From Oracle 9.2 and higher, Oracle has imposed restriction on the default location of shared libraries. By default, it can interpret the shared libraries located in the $ORACLE_HOME\bin\ directory. If the shared library is located at another location on the server, it has to be specified in the EXTPROC_DLLS environment parameter. The permissible value for the environment are ONLY, ANY, or the actual DLL path.

- ONLY: [DLL:DLL...] gives the authority to specify multiple DLL files in varied locations. The DLL file paths are separated by a colon. It offers high-level security as it limits the libraries to be interpreted by extproc.

- [DLL : DLL ...]: One can specify only the DLL path without using the ONLY parameter. In such case, all the DLLs under the $ORACLE_HOME\bin\ directory are accessible by the extproc process.

- ANY allows any DLL on the server to be loaded by the extproc process.

Some of the sample ENVS parameter looks as follows:

- ENVS= "EXTPROC_DLLS=ANY" (allows any DLL on the server to be loaded by the extproc process)

- ENVS= "EXTPROC_DLLS=ONLY:C:\MyDLL\Hello.dll"

- ENVS= "EXTPROC_DLLS=ONLY:C:\MyDLL\Hello.dll:C:\TestDLL\Math.dll"

These specifications allow only the DLLs from the specified locations to be loaded by the extproc process.

In secured production environments, it is advisable to include a separate listener for the extproc process to segregate the handling of the IPC and TCP requests through the SID_LIST entries. In that case, follow the following steps:

1. Take the backup of the existing LISTENER.ora and TNSNAMES.ora files.

2. Modify the existing LISTENER and SID_LIST_LISTENER entries for TCP requests and SID_NAME, respectively.

3. Add the EXTPROC_LISTENER and SID_LIST_EXTPROC_LISTENER entries in the LISTENER.ora file. An example of externally registered LISTENER entries is shown as follows:

```
LISTENER =
  (DESCRIPTION_LIST =
    (DESCRIPTION =
      (ADDRESS = (PROTOCOL = TCP)(HOST = <<host>>)(PORT = 1521))
    )
  )

SID_LIST_LISTENER =
  (SID_LIST =
    (SID_DESC =
      (SID_NAME = <<Database Name>>)
      (ORACLE_HOME = <<Oracle Home>>)
    )
  )

EXTPROC_LISTENER =
  (DESCRIPTION_LIST =
    (DESCRIPTION =
      (ADDRESS = (PROTOCOL = IPC)(KEY = <<extproc key>>))
    )
```

```
    )

SID_LIST_EXTPROC_LISTENER =
  (SID_LIST =
    (SID_DESC =
      (SID_NAME = CLRExtProc)
      (ORACLE_HOME = <<Oracle Home>>)
      (PROGRAM = EXTPROC1521)
      (ENVS= "EXTPROC_DLLS=[ONLY | ANY | (DLL path)]")
    )
  )
```

4. The original service has to be rebuilt to inherit the changes and a new service has to be created for the new listener.

With the default settings, Oracle 11*g* configuration has not been reported for issues in the `extproc` process establishment, activation, or working.

Oracle Net Configuration verification

The Oracle Net Configuration can be verified by testing the ORACLR_CONNECTION_ DATA TNS service in the command-line window. The `tnsping` command verifies only the existence of the service name. Neither does it verify the listener configuration for the external routines nor does it ensure the listener compatibility on the server. The probable responses of the `tnsping` command are as follows:

*   If the result of the `tnsping` command is OK, it means the configuration has been perfectly done

*   If the result of the `tnsping` command is an exception TNS-03505: Failed to resolve name, the service name doesn't exist in the TNSNAMES.ora file

*   If the result of the `tnsping` command is an exception TNS-12541: TNS:no listener, the service is not currently available on the server

The demonstrations for these cases are as follows:

*   **Case 1**: The service exists in the TNSNAMES.ora file:

    ```
    C:\>tnsping ORACLR_CONNECTION_DATA

    TNS Ping Utility for 32-bit Windows: Version 11.2.0.1.0 -
    Production on 05-JAN-2012 14:46:24

    Copyright (c) 1997, 2010, Oracle.  All rights reserved.

    Used parameter files:
    ```

```
C:\ORACLE\product\11.2.0\dbhome_1\network\admin\sqlnet.ora


Used TNSNAMES adapter to resolve the alias
Attempting to contact (DESCRIPTION = (ADDRESS_LIST = (ADDRESS
= (PROTOCOL = IPC)(KEY = EXTPROC1521))) (CONNECT_DATA = (SID =
CLRExtProc)
(PRESENTATION = RO))
OK (20 msec)
```

- **Case 2**: The service does not exist in the TNSNAMES.ora file:

```
C:\>tnsping MYEXT_CONNECTION_DATA


TNS Ping Utility for 32-bit Windows: Version 11.2.0.1.0 -
Production on 05-JAN-2012 14:51:38


Copyright (c) 1997, 2010, Oracle.  All rights reserved.


Used parameter files:
C:\app\INSAGUP\product\11.2.0\dbhome_1\network\admin\sqlnet.ora


TNS-03505: Failed to resolve name
```

Benefits of external procedures

The benefits of external procedures are:

- **Integration of strengths**: The realization of capabilities of a programming language in another one demonstrates flexibility of one and adaptation of the other. Also a program adding up to the features of another language integrates strengths and capabilities of the programming.

- **Reusability of client logic**: As the server-side external program is sharable among all the database users, the logic could be reused by the connecting user.

- **Logical extensibility**: External routines maintain the margin to extend its logic. From the application's perspective, external procedures also avoid logical redundancy.

- **Enhanced performance**: Moving the execution of calculative programs and methods from client to server side improve their execution by reducing the network round trips.

Executing external C programs from PL/SQL

Oracle extends the architectural support to the external programs in C, C++, Java, or the one whose library is interpretable by C. In the external procedure architecture, we saw the processing steps of an external program. Now, we will list the development steps to run a C program from PL/SQL:

1. Write a C program and compile it.

2. Copy the C program's code file in the $ORACLE_HOME\bin\ directory. Generate the DLL using a hardware supported native C compiler.

 For demonstration purposes, we will use the MingW (Minimal GNU for Windows) compiler to compile C program and generate the DLLs. It can be downloaded from http://www.mingw.org/wiki/ Getting_Started.

3. Configure the Oracle Net service.

4. Create a PL/SQL library object for the DLL.

5. Create a call specification in PL/SQL to publish the external program. Specify the external language used in the program (here, it is C), the PL/SQL library name, the method in the external program and the parameters mapped as per the mapping matrix between PL/SQL and external programming language.

6. Execute the call specification to observe the execution of the external program.

We will illustrate these steps in detail in the case study mentioned in the following section.

Executing C program through external procedure—development steps

In a secure application environment, the client team has segregated the string utility methods from the data layer to the client layer. We will take up a small program, which converts the case of a string input to uppercase, as an example. Check it out!

1. Creating and compiling the C program:

   The following C program (`CaseConvert.c`) takes two numeric inputs and returns their sum:

   ```
   #include<stdio.h>
   #include<conio.h>
   char ChangeCase(char *caps)
   {
     int index = 0;
     while (caps[ind])
     {
     caps[index] = toupper(caps[index]);
     index++;
     }
     return caps;
     getch();
   }
   ```

   The file can be placed at any writable OS location on the server. In production environments, the privilege scheme to create or save a file on the operation system is decisive over the security factor on the server. For demonstration purposes, we will place the compiled file in the `C:\Labs\C\` directory.

   Note that compilation is necessary to check the validity of the program.

   `C:\Labs\C> gcc -c CaseConvert.c`

   As a result, the `CaseConvert.o` compiled module got generated at the same location.

2. Generating the shared library for the C program:

   The shared library (DLL) can be generated using the `gcc` command:

   `C:\Labs\C>gcc -shared CaseConvert.c -o CaseConvert.dll`

   Verify the generation of DLL at the same path. Moreover, the DLL path must be included in the `ENVS="EXTPROC_DLLS="` parameter in the `LISTENER.ora` file.

3. Configuring the Oracle Net service:

   Recheck the Oracle Net services configuration based on the recommendations made in the last section. The configuration checklist is as follows:

   ○ The `KEY` value under the `ADDRESS` parameter of the `ORACLR_CONNECTION_DATA` TNS service is same as the `KEY` value under `ADDRESS` parameter of the active listener. Make note of the case sensitiveness.

- ○ The SID value under CONNECT_DATA parameter of TNS service ORACLR_CONNECTION_DATA matches the SID_NAME of the SID_LIST_LISTENER.
- ○ The DLL path has been mapped correctly for the ENVS parameter in the listener file.
- ○ The ORACLR_CONNECTION_DATA pings successfully.

4. Creating a PL/SQL library object for the DLL:

This is the first programming step in the Oracle database. The PL/SQL library object acts as a database alias for the shared library location to be accessed by the PL/SQL subprograms. It is created either by a DBA or a user who enjoys the CREATE LIBRARY or the CREATE ANY LIBRARY privilege. If a DBA creates the library, he must grant the EXECUTE privilege on the library to the user.

A PL/SQL library can be created as per the following syntax:

```
CREATE [OR REPLACE ] LIBRARY  [Library name]  [IS | AS]
[DLL path with the name in single quotes]
AGENT [Agent DB link, if any];
/
```

In the syntax, the DLL path is the OS location of the DLL on the server. Note that the Oracle server never verifies the existence of the file specified in the library syntax.

In our case, we will follow the first method. The DBA or a user with DBA privileges grants the CREATE LIBRARY privilege to the ORADEV user and the ORADEV user creates the library

```
/*Connect as SYSDBA*/
CONN sys/system AS SYSDBA
Connected.

/*Grant the CREATE LIBRARY privilege*/
GRANT CREATE LIBRARY TO ORADEV;

Grant succeeded.
```

Now, the ORADEV user can create the library in its own schema as follows:

```
/*Connect as ORADEV*/
CONN ORADEV/ORADEV
Connected.

/*Connect the library specifying the complete DLL path*/
CREATE OR REPLACE LIBRARY EXTDLL
AS 'C:\Labs\C\CaseConvert.dll'
/

Library created.
```

5. Publishing the external program through call specification:

A PL/SQL wrapper method is created to invoke the external procedure from the database. It uses the library object to refer to the DLL which contains the C program as a linked module. It contains the external program method name which must be exactly the same as the one used in the external program. It maps the parameter based on inter compatibility between PL/SQL and the external program's base language. For example, char will be mapped as VARCHAR2, int will be mapped as NUMBER, and so on.

This PL/SQL wrapper method is known as **call specification** and the process is known as **publishing** the external program. The call specification serves the following objectives:

- Intercommunicates between the database engine and the external base language (C or Java)
- Dispatches the C-language program
- Parameter mode mappings and data type conversions
- Memory management
- Database purity state

The call specification can be a standalone procedure, function, or a package, too. It is the structure of the external C program which categorizes the call specification object type. The general structure of a call specification of function type looks as follows:

```
CREATE OR REPLACE FUNCTION [Name] [Parameters]
RETURN [data type]
[IS | AS]
[call specification]
END;
```

Similarly, call specification when linked to a procedures looks as follows:

```
CREATE OR REPLACE PROCEDURE [Name] [Parameters]
 [IS | AS]
[Call specification]
END;
```

The call specification unites the details of the database library, external programming language, and the external program. It links the complete call to a subprogram such as procedure, function, package, or object type body.

The call specification follows the following syntax:

```
AS LANGUAGE C
[LIBRARY (library name)]
[NAME (external program name)]
[WITH CONTEXT]
[AGENT IN (formal parameters)]
[PARAMETERS (parameter list)];
```

The components in the preceding syntax are listed as follows:

- LANGUAGE C states the base language of the external program. In this case, it is C.

- LIBRARY is the database library object.

- NAME is the external program name. Note that it is case sensitive; it must be the same as specified in the program code.

- The [WITH CONTEXT] clause directs PL/SQL to pass the "context pointer" to the external program being invoked. Such parameters are of the OCIExtProcContext type.

- [AGENT IN (formal parameters)] is a list of formal parameters to the call specification.

- [PARAMETERS (parameter list)] represents the parameter mapping between PL/SQL and C by position.

For our illustration, the call specification can be coded as follows:

```
CREATE OR REPLACE FUNCTION F_CASE_CONVERT (P_STRING VARCHAR2)
/*Specify the RETURN type in compatibility with the external
program*/
RETURN VARCHAR2

/*Specify the external program's base language*/
AS LANGUAGE C

/*Specify the PL/SQL library object name*/
LIBRARY EXTDLL

/*Specify the external function name*/
NAME "ChangeCase"

/*Specify the parameters*/
PARAMETERS (P_STRING STRING);

Function created.
```

Let us verify the working of the preceding call specification with a PL/SQL anonymous block, shown as follows:

```
SQL> DECLARE
        /*Declare a local parameter. Initialize with the test
data*/
        l_str VARCHAR2(1000) := 'oracle pl/sql developer';
     BEGIN
        /*Invoke the function and display he result*/
        l_str := F_CASE_CONVERT (l_str);
        DBMS_OUTPUT.PUT_LINE(l_str);
     END;
     /
ORACLE PL/SQL DEVELOPER

PL/SQL procedure successfully completed.
```

Executing Java programs from PL/SQL

Similar to C programs, Oracle can communicate with Java classes as external procedures, too. Unlike C external programs, the Java classes and Java source files are stored as schema objects in the database. But the caveat here is that the Java classes must be operational in the logical side and not on the user interface. It implies that the Java programs which offer generic utility or data processing operations are the best candidates to be loaded into Oracle.

Invoking Java code from PL/SQL not only reduces the network overhead from the client but it also helps in the distribution of logic across the layers and reduces code redundancy. Under this section, we will discuss how to load a Java class into the database and access it through the call specification.

Unlike C external procedures, calling Java program from PL/SQL is convenient. There is no dependency on the shared library, too. But yes, there is something known as **Libunit** which is like the Java shared library. Upon invocation of a Java external procedure, these shared libraries are loaded automatically by the extproc process and executed.

Java is natively a part of the Oracle database. It doesn't use the extproc agent process for setting up the communication between Java and Oracle. Instead, the channel known as **Java Virtual Machine (JVM)** resides within the Oracle itself. The Java program execution process is carried out in the dedicated portion of SGA known as **Java pool**. For this reason, C programs might be better performers than Java programs when invoked from PL/SQL.

Calling a Java class method from PL/SQL

A Java class must be made available in the database for its access from a PL/SQL program. Oracle provides a command-line utility tool known as `loadjava` to perform the program loading activity. Internally, the `loadjava` utility creates some schema objects such as tables and an index. Then the class files and source files are loaded in PL/SQL as Java objects. The syntax of the utility is as follows:

```
loadjava {-user | -u} username/password[@database] [option ...]
filename [filename ]...
```

Whenever a Java class is loaded into the database through the command link utility, JVM acknowledges the request. It loads the Java binaries and resources from the OS location to the database library units. This operation is similar to the generation of shared library units in an external C program access through PL/SQL.

The help regarding the `loadjava` command-line tool can be found using `loadjava -h | -help`.

Uploading a Java class into the database—development steps

The following steps can be followed to upload a Java class or source file to the database:

1. Prepare a Java class file and place it at an OS location on the server.
2. Load the Java source or class file from the command-line editor with the help of the `loadjava` utility.
3. Create a call specification or a PL/SQL subprogram to publish the Java program.
4. Verify the execution of the Java class' method.

The loadjava utility—an illustration

As discussed earlier, a Java class file can be uploaded into the database using the `loadjava` utility of the command DOS shell. Once the Java program is successfully loaded into the database, its metadata is record in the USER_OBJECTS and USER_SOURCE data dictionary views. Lets us take up a case study to illustrate the whole process.

This is just a case similar to our last case study with C, we have a computational-based utility method to add and multiply two numbers. You need a similar utility in PL/SQL. Instead of rewriting the code again, you decide to use the same program in PL/SQL through external procedures. This is demonstrated in the following steps:

1. Writing a Java class for demo purpose:

    A mathematical utility class has been created to include two methods to add and multiply two given numbers:

    ```
    public class Compute {
      public static int Sum (int x, int y) {
      return x+y;
      }
      public static int Cross (int x, int y) {
      return x*y;
      }
    }
    ```

2. Loading the Java class into the database:

    Save the program in the `C:\Labs\Java\` directory as `ComputeSumCross.java`. Now, run the `loadjava` command-line tool to load the program into the database.

    C:\> CD C:\Labs\Java

    C:\Labs\Java>loadjava -user ORADEV/ORADEV ComputeSumCross.java

    The task completion is not confirmed by any message. Once the Java class is loaded into the database, it is stored as a Java stored object in the schema. A Java object can be queried from the USER_OBJECTS data dictionary view and Java class source code can be viewed from the USER_SOURCE data dictionary view. Let us check the details in the USER_OBJECTS view:

    ```
    /*Query the Java objects in the schema*/
    SELECT object_name, object_type
    FROM USER_OBJECTS
    WHERE  TRUNC(created)=TRUNC(SYSDATE)
    order by timestamp;
    ```

OBJECT_NAME	OBJECT_TYPE
SYS_LOB0000080347C00002$$	LOB
CREATE$JAVA$LOB$TABLE	TABLE
SYS_C0014189	INDEX
JAVA$OPTIONS	TABLE
Compute	JAVA SOURCE
Compute	JAVA CLASS

    ```
    6 rows selected.
    ```

In the preceding query result, note the objects which were created by the `loadjava` utility; a CREATE$JAVA$LOB$TABLE table with an LOB column. And, finally the class name, Compute, appeared as JAVA SOURCE and JAVA CLASS in the query output.

3. Publishing the Java class method:

    Similar to the C external program publishing, a call specification is required to map the Java class to a PL/SQL subprogram along with the parameter mapping. A call specification can be an Oracle stored procedure or a function. The syntax for the call specification looks as follows:

    ```
    {IS | AS} LANGUAGE JAVA
      NAME 'method_fullname (java_type_fullname  [, java_type_
    fullname]...)
      [return java_type_fullname]';
    ```

    Note that it is different from the one we discussed in the *Executing external C programs from PL/SQL* section.

    The following F_COMPUTE function contains a call specification which maps the Sum method of the Compute class to the PL/SQL function:

    ```
    CREATE OR REPLACE FUNCTION F_COMPUTE_SUM (P_X NUMBER, P_Y NUMBER)
    /*Specify the return type as per the method in the java class*/
    RETURN NUMBER
    AS
    /*Specify the external programs base language*/
      LANGUAGE JAVA
      NAME 'Compute.Sum(int,int) return int';
    /

    Function created.
    ```

4. Verifying the Java class execution method:

    As the F_COMPUTE_SUM function maintains the purity level of the database, it can be called from the SELECT statement as follows:

    ```
    SQL> SELECT f_compute_sum(200,482) FROM DUAL;

    F_COMPUTE_SUM(200,482)
    ---------------------
                      682
    ```

Creating packages for Java class methods

If a Java class code has several member methods, creating multiple standalone subprograms would not be a scalable approach. It would be better to follow the Java approach and create a package to encapsulate all Java class methods under one schema object.

The Java class which we used in the illustration, in the *The loadjava utility — an illustration* section, contains two methods Sum and Cross. But we published only one of them for demonstration purposes. Let us see how we can publish both the methods as one package. The Java class has been already loaded into the database.

The package specification prototypes for the Java class methods as follows:

```
CREATE OR REPLACE PACKAGE PKG_ComputeJavaClass
AUTHID DEFINER
AS
/*Declare the functions with similar structure as that of Java
class methods*/
  FUNCTION F_GET_SUM(P_X NUMBER, P_Y NUMBER) RETURN NUMBER;
  FUNCTION F_GET_CROSS (P_X NUMBER, P_Y NUMBER) RETURN NUMBER;
END;
/

Package created.
```

The package body defines the call specification for both the functions:

```
CREATE OR REPLACE PACKAGE BODY PKG_ComputeJavaClass
IS
/*Attach the call specification for each function*/
  FUNCTION F_GET_SUM(P_X NUMBER, P_Y NUMBER) RETURN NUMBER IS
  LANGUAGE JAVA
  NAME 'Compute.Sum(int,int) return int';

  FUNCTION F_GET_CROSS (P_X NUMBER, P_Y NUMBER) RETURN NUMBER IS
  LANGUAGE JAVA
  NAME 'Compute.Cross(int,int) return int';
END;
/

Package body created.
```

Now, we have mapped all the Java class methods with the packaged functions through call specifications:

```
SQL> SELECT PKG_ComputeJavaClass.F_GET_SUM(293,182) FROM DUAL;

PKG_COMPUTEJAVACLASS.F_GET_SUM(293,182)
-------------------------------------
                                   475


SQL> SELECT PKG_ComputeJavaClass.F_GET_CROSS(23,43) FROM DUAL;

PKG_COMPUTEJAVACLASS.F_GET_CROSS(23,43)
-------------------------------------
                                   989
```

Summary

This chapter has covered the philosophy, architecture, and support for external routines in PL/SQL. We learned the external routine concepts from basic to advanced level. We demonstrated the execution of C and Java programs as external procedures.

In the next chapter, we will learn a fresh application data security feature known as Virtual Private Database

Practice exercise

1. Which of the following statements are true about the `extproc` process?
    a. It loads the shared library of the external C program.
    b. It is started by the PL/SQL runtime engine.
    c. It is a session specific process.
    d. The `extproc` process compiles the C program while loading.

2. Oracle 7 introduced the external procedure feature for sending mails from PL/SQL.
    a. True
    b False

3. Determine the effect of dropping the library object which has been used in a PL/SQL call specification and in use:

    a. The PL/SQL wrapper method gets invalidated

    b. The shared library gets corrupted

    c. The PL/SQL wrapper method still works fine as it has been already executed once

    d. The PL/SQL wrapper method gives no output

4. Examine the following TNSNAMES.ora and LISTENER.ora entries and choose the correct option:

```
//TNSNAMES.ora
ORACLR_CONNECTION_DATA =
  (DESCRIPTION =
    (ADDRESS_LIST =
      (ADDRESS = (PROTOCOL = IPC)(KEY = EXTPROC1521))
    )
    (CONNECT_DATA =
      (SID = extproc)
      (PRESENTATION = RO)
    )
  )


//LISTENER.ora
SID_LIST_LISTENER =
(SID_LIST =
 (SID_DESC =
  (SID_NAME = CLRExtProc)
  (ORACLE_HOME = C:\ORCL\11.2.0\dbhome_1)
  (PROGRAM = EXTPROC1521)
  (ENVS= "EXTPROC_DLLS=ONLY:C:\ORCL\product\11.2.0\dbhome_1\BIN\
Ext.dll")
 )
)

LISTENER =
  (DESCRIPTION_LIST =
    (DESCRIPTION =
      (ADDRESS = (PROTOCOL = IPC)(KEY = EXTPROC1521))
      (ADDRESS = (PROTOCOL = TCP)(HOST = localhost)(PORT = 1521))
    )
  )
```

a. The KEY value under ADDRESS of ORACLR_CONNECTION_DATA must be extproc.

b. The SID value under CONNECT_DATA of ORACLR_CONNECTION_DATA must be CLRExtProc.

c. The KEY value under ADDRESS of LISTENER must be extproc.

d. The PROGRAM value of SID_LIST_LISTENER must be extproc.

5. Which of the following are true statements about the loadjava utility?

a. It generates a shared library for Java programs.

b. It loads the Java program into the Oracle database.

c. The loadjava utility requires a Java compiler to run.

d. It loads the Java class file into the Java pool in the database instance.

6. External programs in Java don't require the shared libraries to be executed from PL/SQL.

a. True

b. False

7. An external C program looks like this:

```
#include<stdio.h>
#include<conio.h>
int GetDouble(int num)
{
  return num * 2;
  getch();
}
```

The PL/SQL wrapper method looks like this:

```
CREATE OR REPLACE FUNCTION F_GET_DOUBLE (P_NUM NUMBER)
RETURN NUMBER
AS EXTERNAL LIBRARY NUMLIB
NAME "GETDOUBLE"
LANGUAGE C
PARAMETERS (P_NUM INT);
```

When you call the PL/SQL wrapper, you get the following exception:

```
DECLARE
*
ERROR at line 1:
ORA-06521: PL/SQL: Error mapping function
ORA-06522: Unable to load symbol from DLL
ORA-06512: at "ORADEV.F_GET_DOUBLE", line 1
ORA-06512: at line 4
```

Identify the cause for this exception:

    a.   The NUMLIB library has been incorrectly placed.

    b.   The C program has syntactical errors.

    c.   The C program name in the call specification (PL/SQL wrapper) should be GetDouble instead of GETDOUBLE.

    d.   The extproc process is not working properly

5
Implementing VPD with Fine Grained Access Control

Data security has always been a questionable criterion for a solution which promises data repository. "How much is my data secure or vulnerable?" We make a lot of effort on the concepts of data storage, fetch optimization, and its integrity to ensure and evolve a concrete database philosophy. But the last question hovers every time the database design and security paradigms are planned. The Oracle database offers multiple solutions in variety of areas to enforce best security strategies on the data. Some of the focused areas have been securing user accounts, their authentication, their roles and privileges, data encryption, data audit, and data vaulting.

In this chapter, we will discuss one of the data security features which builds up a protocol or mechanism to impose latent dynamic querying criteria on the data selection. The security feature comes up with the name **Fine Grained Access Control** which is also known as **Virtual Private Database**. The processing of the security scheme in the database appears transparent to the logged in user. Moreover, since the security scheme is implemented at the database level, it cannot be skipped too. Thus, the security scheme is becoming a stringent security channel.

The feature was introduced in Oracle9*i*. Later in Oracle 10*g*, the security feature was extended to include Fine Grained Access Control features. As a result, data restriction could be imposed upon the selection of columns too.

We will understand the concept and walk through its implementation under the following topics:

- Fine Grained Access Control
    - Overview
    - Virtual Private Database — the alias
    - How FGAC or VPD works

- VPD implementation — outline and components
  - Application context
  - Policy function definition and implementation of Row Level Security
  - Associating a policy using the DBMS_RLS package
- VPD implementation — demonstrations
  - Assignment 1: Implement VPD using a simple security policy
  - Assignment 2: Implement VPD using the application context
- VPD policy metadata
- Policy utilities — refresh and drop

Fine Grained Access Control

In this section, we will discuss about Fine Grained Access Control.

Overview

The authoritative rules (as referred to above) enable the security at a table row or a column. This feature limits the access to the secured data only for the users who are authorized for it. The feature is known as **Fine Grained Access Control (FGAC)**. The FGAC security feature imposes row-level and column-level security so that only privileged users can see them. The feature creates a private window of a table for the currently logged in user who can view only the data for which he is authorized.

Prior to FGAC, it used to be a cumbersome activity to decide the data authorization barriers and segregate the schema or the data, as required. Maintenance of multiple users and their multiple schemas used to be a DBA's overhead.

In a multiuser database environment, users are required to access the information authorized for them. One way could be that admin holds the schema and all database objects and creates synonyms for the user who intends to use it. But note that it is an object level security not the data security. FGAC provides the solution to such scenarios by creating virtual data groups of a table. By nature of its implementation, FGAC is also known as **Virtual Private Database (VPD)**.

Virtual Private Database—the alias

Suppose, an organization "ABC" wants its employees to view only those employees' details who are currently working in his/her department. He/she cannot query the employee working in all other departments. One option is to create the employee table (of course, with the same structure) separately for each department. The second option is to always be reminded of appending a WHERE clause in the queries and DML statements. The third option is to automate the second option through FGAC. It is through the implementation of FGAC where the DEPTNO (department number) column of employees table can be secured as a policy. The security on the department number column demonstrates the **Row Level Security** (**RLS**) and the portion of the data authorized and available for a user in a particular department appears apparently as a virtual database. Thus, the name Virtual Private Database, evolves as an alias for FGAC.

Since the VPD protocol restructures the query and affects the query access path, it is important to learn the performance implications of the policy execution. It is true that the VPD implementation affects the query performance by two factors. The first factor is the processing of the security protocol implemented under VPD. The second factor is the predicate clause resulting from the VPD protocol processing. The predicate clause, along with the index(indexes) on the columns, participates in the query optimization. It affects the net query cost and, hence, the query performance. The predicate also appears in the explain plan of the query. We will see the performance implications resulting from the predicate in the demonstrations discussed later in this chapter.

Now, let us understand the working of Row Level Security in VPD.

How FGAC or VPD works?

As per our explanation on VPD, the DEPTNO column in the employees table is secured for RLS. This implies that an employee working in department number 10 can view the employees who are working in department number 10. The users in the respective departments can view only the marked data portions from the following employees' data:

```
SELECT * FROM employees;

    EMPNO ENAME          DEPTNO
---------- ---------- ----------
      7782 CLARK              10
      7839 KING               10
      7934 MILLER             10
      7566 JONES              20
      7902 FORD               20
      7876 ADAMS              20
```

```
7369  SMITH            20
7788  SCOTT            20
7521  WARD             30
7844  TURNER           30
7499  ALLEN            30
7900  JAMES            30
7698  BLAKE            30
7654  MARTIN           30

14 rows selected.
```

FGAC works with policies. A policy can be created for the DEPTNO column in the employees table. This policy would be associated to the employees table and assigned to the users. As soon as the user logs in to the database, the policy gets activated. The activated policy automatically appends a WHERE clause predicate to the SELECT statement on the employees table.

Programmatically, if a VPD protected user from department number 20 fires the following query:

```
SELECT empno, ename, sal
FROM employees;
```

Oracle would implicitly modify this query by appending a WHERE clause to it and it would look like the following:

```
SELECT empno, ename, sal
FROM employees
WHERE deptno = 20
```

The SELECT query, as shown in the previous code snippet, is the one processed by the optimizer. Similar implementation works for the department numbers 10 and 30. This implicit appending of a clause creates a virtual partition of the table for the users. They have access to the restricted data in the tables. This strategy prevents manipulative actions in the data from unauthorized users.

 VPD is unsupported for DDL commands such as TRUNCATE or ALTER.

Salient features of VPD

Some important features of VPD are as follows:

- A VPD security policy is a rule definition which is required to enforce a privacy rule appropriate for the current logged in database user.

- Security policy can be associated to the columns in a table or a view. They can be applied to SELECT, INSERT, UPDATE, INDEX, and DELETE statements.

- Multiple security policies can be enforced on a table or view.

- Policy groups can be created to group multiple policies within them. In this way, multiple policies can be associated to a table or a view in a single attempt.

- VPD objectives are limited only up to data access operations (query and DMLs). It does not operate on **data definitions** (DDL):

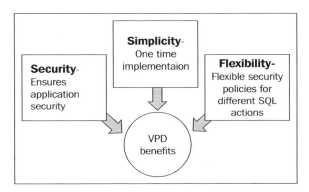

VPD implementation—outline and components

The development steps of VPD implementation is demonstrated in the flowchart as follows:

- **Creation of an application context**: The application context is a collection of variables whose values, once set, remain the same and are available in the same session. The variables are known as attributes. Each session accessing the same application context attributes can have different values.

- **Create the context key and value**: Create the trusted program to set the context using DBMS_SESSION.SET_CONTEXT. During the creation of the context, Oracle does not verify the existence of the program being specified. It relies on the trust of the user to create and use a program with the same name to set the context attributes. Therefore, the program is referred to as trusted.

- **Set the context key explicitly or through a Logon trigger**: The context must be set for the whole session or just before each call. System-level Logon triggers are also capable of scheduling the context key assignment as soon as the user logs in. Performance implication could be a considerable factor to choose the appropriate method of context setting. By method of their processing, the Logon trigger method would yield a better performance since the trigger would be executed once at the database logon only. On the other hand, an explicit assignment would be executed once for each query.

- **Create Policy function**: The policy function prepares the predicate using the context key and value.

- **Associate the policy function to a database table or view**: A policy can be associated using the DBMS_RLS package.

Before moving on to the VPD implementation in the database, let us discuss the crucial components of VPD and their desirable features.

Application context

Oracle VPD policies use the application context to set the WHERE clause predicate for a query. Application contexts are session variables which hold relevant information about a database user and the session. It is recognized as a pair of Name-Value pair under a Namespace (also called label). Namespaces such as USERENV are predefined in the Oracle Server which retain session information such as DB_NAME, SESSION_USER, and so on.

The value of an attribute under an application context can be retrieved through an Oracle built-in function SYS_CONTEXT. The SYS_CONTEXT function accepts the context name and its attribute as the input parameter. The function does not validate the input context name. The function does not raise any exception if the context or attribute specified as the argument does not exist. However, for the USERENV context, the function raises an exception called ORA-02003: invalid USERENV parameter, if a non-existing attribute is specified.

User defined application contexts can be created by the DBA or the user who enjoys the CREATE ANY CONTEXT privilege, using a trusted application package. An application context can be created as local (session specific) or global.

A local context is accessible only within the session of its creator. The attributes along with their values, are stored in **User Global Area (UGA)**. The attributes of a local context can be queried along with their values under SESSION_CONTEXT view.

A global context can be accessed by all the user sessions. The attributes along with their values, are stored in **System Global Area (SGA)**. The attributes of a global context can be queried along with their value in the GLOBAL_CONTEXT view.

Syntactically, creation of a user defined context looks like the following:

```
CREATE CONTEXT [CONTEXT NAME] USING [TRUSTED PACKAGE][CONTEXT TYPE]
```

In the above syntax, the context type can be ACCESSED GLOBALLY or ACCESSED LOCALLY. By default, a context is created as local that is, ACCESSED LOCALLY. For demonstrations, we will work with local contexts.

For example, the context DB_NAME displays the current database name in use as shown in the following code snippet:

```
SQL> SELECT SYS_CONTEXT('USERENV','DB_NAME') FROM DUAL;
SYS_CONTEXT('USERENV','DB_NAME')
--------------------------------------------------------
Orcl
```

 A user is not allowed to update the USERENV application context attribute values except for a few attributes. The modifiable attributes are CLIENT_INFO, CLIENT_IDENTIFIER, CURRENT_SCHEMA_INFO, and NLS_DATE_FORMAT.

Now, let us examine how to create a user defined context.

A DBA or a user with the CREATE ANY CONTEXT privilege creates the context using a trusted package of a trusted user. The trusted package is a database package or a stored procedure which controls the values of context attributes. The value of the attributes in a context can be modified only through this trusted package. At the time of creation of the context, the package is not verified by the server. The context creation is thus, based on the trust that the package exists and is valid.

Creating a context is just creating the namespace. It still does not have any context keys and their values. The trusted package provides the context variables key and its value:

```
/*Connect as DBA*/
SQL> CONN sys/system AS SYSDBA
Connected.

/*Grant CREATE ANY CONTEXT, DROP ANY CONTEXT privileges to ORADEV*/
SQL> GRANT CREATE ANY CONTEXT, DROP ANY CONTEXT TO ORADEV
/
```

```
Grant succeeded.

/*Connect as ORADEV*/
SQL> CONN ORADEV/ORADEV
Connected.

/*Create the context*/
SQL> CREATE CONTEXT demo_context USING P_SET_CONTEXT
/

Context created.
```

Once the context is created, let us create the trusted package. For demonstration, we will create a parameterized standalone procedure to create a context key and assign a value. Observe the use of DBMS_SESSION.SET_CONTEXT to set the values for context attributes:

```
/*Connect as ORADEV*/
SQL> conn ORADEV/ORADEV
Connected.

/*Create the stored procedure to set the context attribute*/
SQL> CREATE OR REPLACE PROCEDURE P_SET_CONTEXT (P_VAL VARCHAR2)
  IS
  BEGIN
  /*Set the context using DBMS_SESSION*/
  DBMS_SESSION.SET_CONTEXT(NAMESPACE => 'DEMO_CONTEXT',
    ATTRIBUTE => 'COUNTRY',
    VALUE     =>  P_VAL);
  END;
/

Procedure created.
```

Now, the context and its controlling program have been created. Query the context key COUNTRY using the SYS_CONTEXT built-in. Ensure that the context and attribute exist in this case:

```
/*Select the value of COUNTRY attribute under DEMO_CONTEXT namespace*/
SQL> SELECT SYS_CONTEXT('DEMO_CONTEXT','COUNTRY') FROM DUAL;
SYS_CONTEXT('DEMO_CONTEXT','COUNTRY')
----------------------------------------------------------------------------
```

It is a NULL value! It is because the context key COUNTRY is still unassigned. Set the value of the context key COUNTRY by executing the context control program:

```
/*Assign value to the COUNTRY attribute through the context
controlling program*/
SQL> EXEC P_SET_CONTEXT('INDIA');

PL/SQL procedure successfully completed.
```

Now, re-query the context key COUNTRY and check its value:

```
/*Select the value of COUNTRY attribute under DEMO_CONTEXT namespace*/
SQL> SELECT SYS_CONTEXT('DEMO_CONTEXT','COUNTRY') FROM DUAL;
SYS_CONTEXT('DEMO_CONTEXT','COUNTRY')
-------------------------------------------------------------
INDIA
```

Verify the context key by modifying its value and querying it again:

```
/*Modify the value of COUNTRY attribute through the context
controlling program*/
SQL> EXEC P_SET_CONTEXT('FINLAND');
PL/SQL procedure successfully completed.
/*Select the value of COUNTRY attribute under DEMO_CONTEXT namespace*/
SQL> SELECT SYS_CONTEXT('DEMO_CONTEXT','COUNTRY') FROM DUAL;
SYS_CONTEXT('DEMO_CONTEXT','COUNTRY')
-------------------------------------------------------------
FINLAND
```

Policy function definition and implementation of row-level security

The policy function creates the WHERE clause predicate using the application context. It is an Oracle stored standalone function which must be created by the user to be protected under VPD. The policy function should posses and follow the following features:

- The function should accept the schema name and database object name as input parameters. Though these parameters are not used in the function body, the parameters are supplied by the DBMS_RLS package while creating the policy. The sequence of parameters must be the schema name followed by the object name.

- The function must return the predicate in a string format that is, the condition to be used in the WHERE clause of a query. For example, [Column name] = [Value]. Note that the condition must be a valid one.

- A policy can be STATIC, DYNAMIC, SHARED_STATIC, CONTEXT_SENSITIVE, or SHARED_CONTEXT_SENSITIVE. The type of policy determines the frequency of modification of predicate clause. It is set while associating a policy to the table, view, or synonym as policy_type parameter in DBMS_RLS.ADD_POLICY. If nothing is specified for the policy type, its behavior is dynamic.

- A dynamic policy uses context information for predicate clause and is evaluated on every execution of the query.

- The function should not perform selection or transaction on the table to be protected under VPD.

The following table shows the differentiation amongst the policy types:

Policy type	Comments	When to Use
STATIC	Oracle caches the predicate clause output in SGA which is used for all further executions of the query.	A static policy is used when the same predicate information can be applied to every query. It yields better performance since it is executed only once.
DYNAMIC (Default)	It is a default policy type. Policy function is executed for each and every query on the VPD protected table.	Dynamic policies are preferred when the different policy function and, hence, a different predicate is required for the SQL statements. Since a dynamic policy type is executed automatically for each execution, it decreases the query performance.
SHARED_STATIC	It is similar to STATIC but a policy can be shared among multiple schema objects (tables).	A shared static policy is preferred over static policies when multiple tables share the same policy function. It is mostly suited for data warehousing environments.
CONTEXT_SENSITIVE	Policy function is executed during SQL parsing, only if the local context has been changed. If the local context remains unchanged, the policy function is not executed.	A context sensitive policy is chosen when the predicate information for a table varies with the user or group.
SHARED_CONTEXT_SENSITIVE	Oracle caches the predicate in UGA during SQL parsing and a policy can be shared among multiple objects.	A shared context sensitive policy is used where the predicate information which varies by user, can be shared by multiple database objects (tables).

Associating a policy using the DBMS_RLS package

The policy operations can be done using the DBMS_RLS package. The DBMS_RLS package is used to add, drop, or refresh a security policy, enable or disable a policy, and handle the policy groups. It is owned by the SYS user who must grant the EXECUTE privilege on the DBMS_RLS package to a user who is intended to implement aVPD policy within it.

The DBMS_RLS package subprograms are shown in the following table:

Subprogram	Description
ADD_POLICY	Adds a fine-grained access control policy to a table, view, or synonym
DROP_POLICY	Drops a fine-grained access control policy from a table, view, or synonym
REFRESH_POLICY	Causes all the cached statements associated with the policy to be reparsed
ENABLE_POLICY	Enables or disables a Fine Grained Access Control policy
CREATE_POLICY_GROUP	Creates a policy group
ADD_GROUPED_POLICY	Adds a policy associated with a policy group
ADD_POLICY_CONTEXT	Adds the context for the active application
DELETE_POLICY_GROUP	Deletes a policy group
DROP_GROUPED_POLICY	Drops a policy associated with a policy group
DROP_POLICY_CONTEXT	Drops a driving context from the object so that it will have one less driving context
ENABLE_GROUPED_POLICY	Enables or disables a row-level group security policy
DISABLE_GROUPED_POLICY	Disables a row-level group security policy
REFRESH_GROUPED_POLICY	Re-parses the SQL statements associated with a refreshed policy

VPD implementation—demonstrations

We will demonstrate two ways of VPD implementation. While the first method is simple association of a policy, the second demonstration uses an application context for the same. Before we get into the actual implementation, let us have a look at the employees table. Notice the explain plan for the SELECT query:

```
/*Select the EMPLOYEES table data*/
SQL> SELECT *
  FROM employees
/
```

```
    EMPNO ENAME      JOB           MGR HIREDATE           SAL      COMM      DEPTNO
     7369 SMITH      CLERK        7902 17-DEC-80         9200                    20
     7499 ALLEN      SALESMAN     7698 20-FEB-81         2000       300          30
     7521 WARD       SALESMAN     7698 22-FEB-81         1650       500          30
     7566 JONES      MANAGER      7839 02-APR-81         3375                    20
     7654 MARTIN     SALESMAN     7698 28-SEP-81         1650      1400          30
     7698 BLAKE      MANAGER      7839 01-MAY-81         3250                    30
     7782 CLARK      MANAGER      7839 09-JUN-81         2850                    10
     7788 SCOTT      ANALYST      7566 19-APR-87         3400                    20
     7839 KING       PRESIDENT         17-NOV-81         5400                    10
     7844 TURNER     SALESMAN     7698 08-SEP-81         1900         0          30
     7876 ADAMS      CLERK        7788 23-MAY-87         1500                    20

    EMPNO ENAME      JOB           MGR HIREDATE           SAL      COMM      DEPTNO
     7900 JAMES      CLERK        7698 03-DEC-81         1350                    30
     7902 FORD       ANALYST      7566 03-DEC-81         3400                    20
     7934 MILLER     CLERK        7782 23-JAN-82         1700                    10

14 rows selected.
```

```
/*Generate the explain plan for the above query*/
SQL> EXPLAIN PLAN FOR SELECT * FROM employees;

Explained.

/*Display the explain plan*/
SQL>SELECT * FROM TABLE(dbms_xplan.display);
```

```
PLAN_TABLE_OUTPUT
-----------------------------------------------------------------------------
Plan hash value: 1445457117

-----------------------------------------------------------------------------
| Id | Operation          | Name      | Rows | Bytes | Cost (%CPU)| Time     |
-----------------------------------------------------------------------------
|  0 | SELECT STATEMENT   |           |   14 |   532 |    3   (0)| 00:00:01 |
|  1 |  TABLE ACCESS FULL | EMPLOYEES |   14 |   532 |    3   (0)| 00:00:01 |
-----------------------------------------------------------------------------

8 rows selected.
```

We will take up the same scenario of employees where the employee often viewed other department's salaries and argued with their management. As a result, management took a heavy step by limiting the access in its host department only.

Assignment 1—implementing VPD using simple security policy

In our first assignment, we will see the implementation of a dynamic VPD policy on a user owned database table `employees`. The policy filters out only those employees who are working in department number 20:

1. Creating the policy function:

    Note the input parameters for the schema and object in the following policy function definition:

    ```
    /*Connect to the user*/
    Conn ORADEV/ORADEV
    Connected.

    /*Create the policy function*/
    CREATE OR REPLACE FUNCTION f_get_dept_predicate(p_schema
    varchar2,p_obj
    varchar2)
    RETURN VARCHAR2 IS
    BEGIN
      /*Specify the predicate clause*/
      RETURN 'deptno = 20';
    END;
    /

    Function created.
    ```

2. Creating the security policy:

The security policy can be created using the DBMS_RLS.ADD_POLICY subprogram. Notice that the table owner, the policy function owner, and policy owner is the same that is, ORADEV. However, they may be different from each other. This implies that a user A can implement a VPD policy P on a table T owned by a second user B1, using a policy function owned by a user B2. In such a case, the policy metadata is maintained by the user which owns the VPD protected table. Refer to the following code snippet:

```
/*Connect as ORADEV*/
SQL> conn ORADEV/ORADEV
Connected.

/*Add a policy*/
BEGIN
  DBMS_RLS.ADD_POLICY
  (
  object_schema => 'ORADEV',
  /*The object (table) owner*/
  object_name => 'EMPLOYEES',
  /*The object name to be protected*/
  policy_name => 'EMP_DEPT_20',
  /*The security policy name*/
  function_schema => 'ORADEV',
  /*The security policy function owner*/
  policy_function => 'F_GET_DEPT_PREDICATE',
  /*The policy function name*/
  statement_types => 'select, insert, update, delete'
  /*The statement types which are to be protected under the VPD
security
  scheme*/
  );
END;
/

PL/SQL procedure successfully completed.
```

3. Verifying the policy and observing the explain plan:

Query the employees table to verify the effect of the security policy:

```
SELECT * FROM employees;
```

EMPNO	ENAME	JOB	MGR	HIREDATE	SAL	COMM	DEPTNO
7369	SMITH	CLERK	7902	17-DEC-80	9200		20
7566	JONES	MANAGER	7839	02-APR-81	3375		20
7788	SCOTT	ANALYST	7566	19-APR-87	3400		20
7876	ADAMS	CLERK	7788	23-MAY-87	1500		20
7902	FORD	ANALYST	7566	03-DEC-81	3400		20

Generate the explain plan for the `SELECT` query on the VPD protected table and compare it with the one we generated before the implementation:

```
/*Generate the explain plan for the above SELECT query*/
SQL>EXPLAIN PLAN FOR SELECT * FROM employees;
Explained.

/*Display the explain plan*/
SQL>SELECT * FROM TABLE(dbms_xplan.display);
```

Refer to the following screenshot for the output of the previous code snippet:

```
PLAN_TABLE_OUTPUT
--------------------------------------------------------------------------------
Plan hash value: 1218979235
--------------------------------------------------------------------------------
| Id | Operation                    | Name                | Rows | Bytes | Cost (%CPU)| Time     |
--------------------------------------------------------------------------------
|  0 | SELECT STATEMENT             |                     |    5 |   190 |    2   (0)| 00:00:01 |
|  1 |  TABLE ACCESS BY INDEX ROWID | EMPLOYEES           |    5 |   190 |    2   (0)| 00:00:01 |
|* 2 |   INDEX RANGE SCAN           | IDX_EMPLOYEE_DEPTNO |    5 |       |    1   (0)| 00:00:01 |
--------------------------------------------------------------------------------

Predicate Information (identified by operation id):

PLAN_TABLE_OUTPUT
--------------------------------------------------------------------------------

   2 - access("DEPTNO"=20)

14 rows selected.
```

In the explain plan generated above, notice the `Predicate Information` section. It lists the policy function predicate output. It is because `employees` is a VPD protected table and the associated policy returns the predicate to filter the data. In addition, Oracle also uses the index on the predicate during query optimization. Notice the usage of index `IDX_EMPLOYEES_DEPTNO` in the above explain plan.

The Assignment 1 demonstration shows creation of a simple policy function and association with the `employees` table. The drawback of the `policy` function is its hardcoded predicate. Similar `policy` functions have to be created for every user from each department. It again sounds like a hectic job!

Assignment 2—implementing VPD using an application context

For the second demo, the last demonstration can be reset by dropping the security policy enforced upon the `employees` table. A policy can be dropped using `DBMS_RLS.DROP_POLICY`, as shown in the following code snippet:

```
/*Drop the policy EMP_DEPT_20*/
SQL>EXECUTE dbms_rls.drop_policy('ORADEV','EMPLOYEES','EMP_DEPT_20');

PL/SQL procedure successfully completed.
```

Let us now move further to create an application context and use it in the VPD policy implementation:

1. Creating an application context:

    An application context can be created by the DBA or a DBA can grant the CREATE ANY CONTEXT privilege to the user. We will go by the second one:

    ```
    /*Connect as DBA*/
    SQL> conn sys/system as sysdba
    Connected.

    /*Grant the privilege*/
    SQL> grant create any context to oradev;

    Grant succeeded.

    /*Connect as ORADEV*/
    SQL> conn ORADEV/ORADEV
    Connected.

    /*Create the context*/
    SQL> CREATE CONTEXT EMPLOYEES USING PKG_CONTEXTS;

    Context created.
    ```

2. Creating a trusted application package to set the context key value:

    A package can be created to assign the context key value for the newly created contexts:

    ```
    /*Connect as ORADEV*/
    SQL> conn ORADEV/ORADEV
    Connected.

    /*Create the package for setting the context*/
    CREATE OR REPLACE PACKAGE PKG_CONTEXTS IS
      /*Prototype the procedure to set the context*/
      PROCEDURE P_SET_CONTEXT (P_DEPT NUMBER);
    END;

    Package created.

    /*Create the Package body*/
      CREATE OR REPLACE PACKAGE BODY PKG_CONTEXTS IS

      /*Define the procedure to set the context*/
      PROCEDURE P_SET_CONTEXT (P_DEPT NUMBER)
      IS
      BEGIN
        /*Use DBMS_SESSION to set the content of DEPARTMENT
    namespace*/
    ```

```
        dbms_session.set_context(namespace => 'EMPLOYEES',
        attribute => 'DEPARTMENT' ,
        value     =>  P_DEPT);
    END;
END;
/

Package body created.
```

3. Creating a Logon trigger to set the context for the user and restrict the data access:

    A Logon is a system-level trigger which fires as soon as the user logs into the database. It will set the context for the entire user session:

    ```
    /*Connect as SYSDBA*/
    Conn sys/system as sysdba
    Connected.

    /*Create LOGON trigger to set the context as soon as a user logs
    in*/
    CREATE OR REPLACE TRIGGER ON_LOGON

    /*Specify the event of trigger firing as AFTER LOGON*/
    AFTER LOGON ON DATABASE
    BEGIN
      /*Invoke the policy function from the ORADEV user */
      ORADEV.PKG_CONTEXTS.P_SET_CONTEXT(20);
    END;
    /

    Trigger created.
    ```

    The working of the above Logon trigger can be verified. Disconnect and reconnect the session as ORADEV. Select the user defined context using SYS_CONTEXT built-in function for EMPLOYEES context:

    ```
    /*Connect as ORADEV*/
    SQL> conn ORADEV/ORADEV
    Connected.
    SQL> SELECT SYS_CONTEXT('EMPLOYEES','DEPARTMENT') FROM DUAL;
    SYS_CONTEXT('EMPLOYEES','DEPARTMENT')
    -----------------------------------------------------------
    20
    ```

4. Creating the policy function to get the predicate:

    The policy function can be created using the SYS_CONTEXT function:

    ```
    /*Connect as ORADEV*/
    SQL> conn ORADEV/ORADEV
    Connected.

    /*Create the policy function*/
    CREATE OR REPLACE FUNCTION f_get_dept_predicate(p_schema varchar2,
    p_obj varchar2)
    RETURN VARCHAR2 IS
    BEGIN
      /*Return the predicate using SYS_CONTEXT*/
      RETURN 'deptno = SYS_CONTEXT(''EMPLOYEES'', ''DEPARTMENT'')';
    END;
    /

    Function created.
    ```

5. Creating the security policy:

    ```
    /*Connect as ORADEV*/
    SQL> conn ORADEV/ORADEV
    Connected.
    BEGIN
    DBMS_RLS.ADD_POLICY
    (
    object_schema => 'ORADEV',
    object_name => 'EMPLOYEES',
    policy_name => 'EMP_DEPT_20',
    function_schema => 'ORADEV',
    policy_function => 'F_GET_DEPT_PREDICATE',
    statement_types => 'select, insert, update, delete'
    );
    END;
    /

    PL/SQL procedure successfully completed.
    ```

6. Verifying the working of VPD: Query the employees table to verify the
    working of the policy:

    ```
    SELECT * FROM employees;
    ```

EMPNO	ENAME	JOB	MGR	HIREDATE	SAL	COMM	DEPTNO
7369	SMITH	CLERK	7902	17-DEC-80	9200		20
7566	JONES	MANAGER	7839	02-APR-81	3375		20
7788	SCOTT	ANALYST	7566	19-APR-87	3400		20
7876	ADAMS	CLERK	7788	23-MAY-87	1500		20
7902	FORD	ANALYST	7566	03-DEC-81	3400		20

VPD policy metadata

The Oracle Server maintains the association information between the security policies and schema objects in data dictionary views. The data dictionaries available for this information is USER_DEPENDENCIES, ALL_DEPENDENCIES, and DBA_DEPENDENCIES. The structure of the dictionary view is as follows:

```
SQL> DESC USER_POLICIES

    Name                     Null?        Type
    -----------------------------------------------------
    OBJECT_NAME              NOT NULL     VARCHAR2(30)
    POLICY_GROUP             NOT NULL     VARCHAR2(30)
    POLICY_NAME              NOT NULL     VARCHAR2(30)
    PF_OWNER                 NOT NULL     VARCHAR2(30)
    PACKAGE                               VARCHAR2(30)
    FUNCTION                 NOT NULL     VARCHAR2(30)
    SEL                                   VARCHAR2(3)
    INS                                   VARCHAR2(3)
    UPD                                   VARCHAR2(3)
    DEL                                   VARCHAR2(3)
    IDX                                   VARCHAR2(3)
    CHK_OPTION                            VARCHAR2(3)
    ENABLE                                VARCHAR2(3)
    STATIC_POLICY                         VARCHAR2(3)
    POLICY_TYPE                           VARCHAR2(24)
    LONG_PREDICATE                        VARCHAR2(3)
```

The policy created above can be queried from the dictionary view as follows:

```
SQL> SELECT policy_name,
            Policy_type,
            Static_policy,
            function,
            pf_owner
FROM USER_POLICIES
/

POLICY_NAME      POLICY_TYPE      STA   FUNCTION                  PF_OWNER
---------------  ---------------  ---   ---------------------     ---------
EMP_DEPT_20      DYNAMIC          NO    F_GET_DEPT_PREDICATE      ORADEV
```

In addition to the policy object information, the user defined contexts are also maintained in the dictionary view [ALL | DBA]_CONTEXTS. The context EMPLOYEES created above for Assignment 2 can be queried as follows:

```
SQL> SELECT * FROM ALL_CONTEXT;

NAMESPACE        SCHEMA           PACKAGE
--------------   --------------   --------------------------
EMPLOYEES        ORADEV           PKG_CONTEXTS
```

Policy utilities—refresh and drop

Policy utility activities such as refreshing or dropping can be done through DBMS_RLS package subprograms. Refreshing a policy pushes an enabled VPD protocol to inherit the latest changes done to the policy and its dependents. Policy refresh is required when the underlying referenced objects of the policy undergo changes. So as to invalidate its dependent objects operationally during the policy refresh process, all the cached statements associated with the policy are parsed again.

Notice that a disabled VPD policy cannot be refreshed.

The subprogram requires the policy owner, the table or view name, and the policy name as the input parameters:

```
SQL> EXEC DBMS_RLS.REFRESH_POLICY('ORADEV','EMPLOYEES','EMP_DEPT_20');

PL/SQL procedure successfully completed.
```

Dropping a policy lifts the data restriction and full data is visible to all the users. Like REFRESH_POLICY, the dropping subprogram also requires the policy owner, the table or view name, and the policy name as input arguments:

```
SQL> EXEC DBMS_RLS.DROP_POLICY('ORADEV','EMPLOYEES','EMP_DEPT_20');

PL/SQL procedure successfully completed.
```

Summary

In the chapter, we learned an efficient security concept called Fine Grained Access Control. We started with the concept understanding and its components. Within the prescribed scope of the chapter, we had a walk-through demonstration on the VPD implementation with and without using the application contexts. Since VPD has been emerging as one of the promising security features, we will recommend further reading from the following links to touch other areas too:

- **Oracle documentation**: `http://docs.oracle.com/cd/B28359_01/ network.111/b28531/vpd.htm`

- **OTN Network**: `http://www.oracle.com/technetwork/database/ security/index-088277.html`

In the next chapter, we will handle one of the major application storage bottlenecks that is, storage of large objects. We will understand various large objects' data types and their management.

Practice exercise

1. Identify the correct statements about the working of Fine Grained Access Control:

   a. A table can have only one security policy.

   b. Different policies can be used to protect `SELECT`, `INSERT`, `UPDATE`, and `DELETE` statements on a table but not one.

   c. The policy function returns the predicate information as `WHERE <Column> = <Value>`.

   d. Once associated, the FGAC policy cannot be revoked from the table.

2. A security policy can be associated to group of objects by the DBA. State true or false.

   a. True

   b. False

3. Chose the correct statement about `DBMS_RLS`:

   a. `DBMS_RLS` is used only for Row Level Security policies.

   b. The package is owned by `SYS`.

   c. It can create/drop/refresh policies and create/drop policy groups.

   d. Using `DBMS_RLS` to set the policy degrades the application performance.

4. Identify the correct statements about the context of an application:

    a. A user who holds the CREATE CONTEXT privilege can create a context.

    b. It is owned by the user SYS.

    c. A user can check context metadata in USER_CONTEXTS.

    d. The trusted package associated with the context must exist before the context is created.

5. Arrange the sequence of VPD implementation using application contexts:

    i. Creating policy function.

    ii. Creating trusted package.

    iii. Creating and setting application contexts.

    iv. Associating a policy using DBMS_RLS.

    a. iii, ii, i, iv

    b. ii, iii, iv, i

    c. iii, iv, i, ii

    d. iv, i, ii, iii

6. All policies on different columns of the same table are collectively known as Policy groups.

    a. True

    b. False

7. Identify the correct statements about the Policy types.

    a. A shared static policy is an extension to the static policies where multiple static policies can be shared among multiple users.

    b. A shared static policy is an extension to the static policies where a single static policy can be shared among multiple objects.

    c. STATIC is the default policy type.

    d. DYNAMIC is the default policy type.

8. Pick the correct statement about the application contexts:

    a. Only a DBA can create a custom application context and add attributes under it.

    b. The DBA can modify all USERENV attributes.

    c. The package used for the context creation may or may not exist in the schema.

    d. Global contexts can be used by all the users on a server.

9. A policy of CONTEXT_SENSITIVE type executes the policy function once, every time the query is reparsed, if the local context has been changed.

    a. True

    b. False

10. Identify the cause of the following exception:

```
SQL>SELECT * FROM employees;
select * from employees
                *
ERROR at line 1:
ORA-28110: policy function or package ORADEV.F_JOB_POLICY
has error
```

    a. The policy function F_JOB_POLICY does not exist.

    b. The policy function F_JOB_POLICY has not been specified in DBMS_RLS. ADD_POLICY to add the policy on the employees table.

    c. The predicate returned by the policy function is not appropriate for this query.

    d. The VPD policy on the employees table is invalid and has errors.

6
Working with Large Objects

The challenge to manage information in a database has never been an iced cake. Besides the fundamental support to data integrity, security, and optimal storage mechanisms, the support to varied natures of data was equally challenging. With the growing demands of application development, the nature of large and unstructured data has been transformed from character based to binary based information.

Prior to the introduction of LOB data types in Oracle 8 Release, the LONG and LONG RAW data types used to serve as the storage type for large data. Numerous limitations associated with LONG data types and the need of a stable storage mechanism for unstructured data led to the evolution of LOB data types and set the stage for SecureFiles. While the character based large files are identified as CLOB, the unstructured binary files are treated as BLOB. Even the binary files which are OS location dependent can be stored in the database through a locator as BFILE data types in the Oracle database.

In this chapter, we shall understand the Oracle's support to large objects. Large objects can be a physical file in the system. It can be any regular file on the operating system such as document, media files, and so on. We will cover the LOB data type handling concept under the following topics:

- Introduction to the LOB data types
- Understanding the LOB data types
- Creating the LOB data types
- Managing the LOB data types
- Working with the CLOB, BLOB, and BFILE data types
- Migrating from LONG to LOB
- Temporary LOB data types
- Using temporary LOBs

Introduction to the LOB data types

Before the introduction of LOB data types, LONG and LONG RAW data types served as the storage types for large data. But soon the incompetency of the data types added the discomfort to the database developers and created an urgency for a stable data type. Some of the limitations of LONG and LONG RAW are as follows:

- A table can have only one LONG or LONG RAW column. Also, the data would always be stored inline with the record—thus dumping the same segment all the time.

- A LONG or LONG RAW column can store data only up to 2 GB.

- LONG data type can support sequential access of data. Besides, there are multiple restrictions associated with the usage of LONG data type. Limitations such as single column specification in a table and no possibility of indexing add to the compatibility concerns.

With the introduction of LOB data types in Oracle8*i*, the limitations of LONG and LONG RAW were overruled with multiple features. The LOB data types are CLOB, NCLOB, BLOB, and BFILE. These data types not only provide a stable storage philosophy of unstructured data in the database but also they can be accessed randomly. Let us examine some of the key features of LOB data types in Oracle 11*g*:

- They are capable to store up to 128 TB of semi structure and unstructured data.

- They can be stored in a separate segment LOBSEGMENT and can be optionally stored in a different tablespace too.

- They support the national character set.

- They have Oracle built-in package DBMS_LOB to perform LOB operations.

After the release of Oracle 11*g*, LOB data type has become a significant and proven member of the Oracle family. The earlier data types, LONG and LONG RAW, have been turned obsolete for development purposes. However, the data types still appear in dictionary views such as USER_VIEWS, USER_TRIGGERS, and USER_TAB_COLS to store free text data. Despite the proven capability of LOB data types, Oracle has retained the LONG and LONG RAW specifications in dictionary views.

Oracle 11*g* saw a major turnaround by boosting the storage mechanism of LOB in the form of SecureFiles. SecureFile is an advanced format of LOB storage which provides advanced compression, encryption, and de-duplication features. The new feature assures better storage, secure access mechanism, and better performance in comparison to its earlier format.

The LOB data type classification chart is as shown in the following diagram:

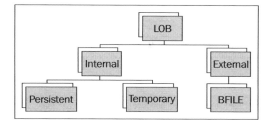

Let us understand the LOB classifications briefly.

Internal LOB

The LOB data which can be accessed from, or stored within the database, is internal to the database. A database column of one of the LOB data types (CLOB, NCLOB, or BLOB) is included in the table and a large object that is LOB value is stored in the database. A PL/SQL variable of the LOB data type can be accessed in a PL/SQL block. CLOB, NCLOB, and BLOB are internal LOB data types in Oracle. An internal LOB data type can be used to specify the data type of a column, or attribute of a user object type. In a PL/SQL block, internal LOB data types can be used as local memory variables.

An internal LOB can be Persistent or Temporary. The classification goes exactly with the name. The LOB data which is stored physically in the database tables is a persistent internal LOB. As it abides by the **ACID** (**Atomicity**, **Consistency**, **Isolation**, and **Durability**) properties, it can participate in data operations such as selection and transaction.

A temporary internal LOB is the one which is declared and accessed only within a PL/SQL block.

External LOB

When the large object is a heavy file, we use an external LOB data type to store only its locator's value and not actually the LOB data. The file still resides at the OS location and not physically in the database. External LOBs are supported by the data type BFILE. It is a read-only data type.

Since an external LOB follows only referential semantics to access an external object in the database, they cannot participate in database transactions. BFILE is a read-only data type where the external files can be accessed only in read mode and cannot be modified.

Understanding the LOB data types

As we came across the four LOB data types in Oracle, LOB structure can be split into its "What" and "Where" components. While LOB value answers to the "What' query, the LOB locator corresponds to the "Where" part. Together, they both make a complete structure of an LOB. Let us understand the LOB components.

LOB value and LOB locators

The LOB value is the actual large file to be loaded in the database. The LOB locator points to the location of this file on the system. It can be thought of as a pointer which references the system location of a file. A LOB locator is always stored inline with the table row irrespective of where the LOB value is stored. During insertion of the LOB data, the LOB column necessarily has the LOB locator component which points to the actual location of the LOB value in the system. The LOB value is always stored in the LOB segment which can be placed in the same or different tablespace.

For an internal LOB, the LOB segment has both the LOB locator and LOB value. The external LOB has only the LOB locator because the LOB value is not stored in the database but located externally on the OS.

BLOB or CLOB!

There are three types of internal LOB data types. They are briefly explained as follows:

- BLOB: It is a **Binary Large Object** data type. This data type is used to store binary large files such as PDFs, images, audios or videos, and so on. It is analogous to the LONG RAW data type which was used before the induction of LOB data types in Oracle.

- CLOB: This data type represents the **Character Large Object** data type which stores the single byte character data in a database character set format. It is compatible with the fixed length character set of the database. It is the data type complimentary to the LONG data type.

- NCLOB: It is similar to the CLOB data type with the compatibility difference that is, it can work for a variable width character set and the NLS settings of the database. Besides, it supports the storage of a multibyte character set data.

 Starting from Oracle 10*g*, Oracle can cast the CLOB data to the VARCHAR2 data implicitly.

BFILE

A BFILE data type column simply establishes and maintains the reference with the file which is located externally in the system. This implies that the BFILE value is always a NULL component for the BFILE data type column or attribute. Unlike the BFILE value, the BFILE locator always holds the pointer to the large file or the BFILE data. The file can be externally located on the operating system, hard drive, compact disks, or tape.

As the data held by this data type is read-only, it cannot participate in data operations or transactions. Now, a question rises that if I delete the BFILE data, will the external file also get deleted? No, it will not. Only the BFILE locator is dropped and de-referenced from the external file.

A BFILE locator must be secured to avoid unauthorized access. File location must be ensured at the server machine and a timeout must be set while reading a nonexistent BFILE data. Besides, some tasks can be performed at the OS file level. These tasks include access permissions, available space, and OS maximum file size to secure BFILEs.

Temporary LOBs

A PL/SQL variable of the CLOB or BLOB data type in a session act is considered as a temporary LOB. It is used to perform some LOB related operations and is placed in the temporary tablespace. If a temporary LOB is stored in the database as a column value, it becomes an internal LOB.

The temporary LOB must be freed once the related activities are over. Once it is freed, the corresponding LOB locator is marked invalid.

Creating LOB data types

Similar to other data types, table columns which are meant for the storage of large data must be declared as one of the LOB data types. This section focuses on the elementary step of LOB handling that is, creation of LOB columns.

Directories

Directory is a vital component in Oracle used to access an operating system file. It interfaces the location path as a directory object. The DBA creates it and grants read/write privileges to the concerned user.

A directory is a nonschema object and can be used as a security barrier for the files located on the server or the client. A directory can be created as per the following syntax:

```
CREATE DIRECTORY [DIRECTORY NAME] AS [OS LOCATION PATH]
```

Note that the directory creation does not validate the specified location on the system. This means that a directory can be created for a nonexistent path on the system.

For example, the CREATE DIRECTORY statement, as shown in the following code snippet, creates a directory for the path C:\Labs\:

```
/*Connect as SYSDBA*/
SQL> CONN sys/system AS SYSDBA
Connected.

/*Create directory for Labs folder located at the server machine*/
SQL> CREATE DIRECTORY MY_FIRST_DIR AS 'C:\Labs\';

Directory created.

/*Create directory for Labs folder located at the client machine
(ORCLClient)*/
SQL> CREATE DIRECTORY MY_CLIENT_DIR AS '\\ORCLClient\Labs\';

Directory created.
```

For the files located on the server, the actual path has to be specified in the CREATE DIRECTORY statement.

For the files which are located at the client machine, the CREATE DIRECTORY statement requires a relative access path as [\\Machine Name\File Location]. The directory path appears like a network path of the shared client location. The location must be shared with the server in read/write mode.

The access privileges on the directory can be granted using the GRANT command as follows:

```
SQL> GRANT READ, WRITE ON DIRECTORY MY_FIRST_DIR TO ORADEV;

Grant succeeded.
```

Directory metadata can be found under the DBA_DIRECTORIES and ALL_DIRECTORIES data dictionary views.

Creating LOB data type columns in a table

A table with a LOB data type column can be created, as shown in the following code snippet. The syntax demonstrates the creation of LOB data type columns prior to the release of Oracle 11*g*.

Note the highlighted LOB storage clause in the following code snippet:

```
CREATE TABLE <table name>
  (Column list)
  [LOB (<lobcol1> [, <lobcol2>...])
  STORE AS
  [<lob_segment_name>]
  (
    [TABLESPACE <tablespace_name>]
    [{ENABLE | DISABLE} STORAGE IN ROW]
    [CHUNK <chunk_size>]
    [PCTVERSION <version_number>]
    [ { CACHE | NO CACHE [{LOGGING | NOLOGGING}]| CACHE READS
    [{LOGGING |
        NOLOGGING}] }]
    [STORAGE {MINEXTENTS | MAXEXTENTS}]
    [INDEX [<lob_index_name>] [physical attributes] [<storage_for_LOB_
index>]
    ])]
```

Introduction of SecureFiles and BasicFiles in Oracle 11*g* brought slight manipulation in the above syntax. Now, the conventional LOB columns would be known as BasicFiles, while the columns which wish to pursue the latest LOB scheme would be declared as SecureFiles.

Check the new LOB specification clause in the following syntax,

```
[LOB (<lobcol1> [, <lobcol2>...])
STORE AS [BASICFILE | SECUREFILE]
  (LOB Storage parameters)
```

Let us highlight some of the facts in the previous syntax:

- **LOB storage clause**: The LOB storage clause is optional for LOB.
- LOB_SEGMENT_NAME: It can be specified for the LOB data type column in the table. The segment with the given name is created for the LOBSEGMENT segment type.
- TABLESPACE: It is used to reside target tablespace for the LOB data type column.

- ENABLE | DISABLE} STORAGE IN ROW: It ensures inline and out of the line storage of the LOB data type data in the table.

- CHUNK: It chunks size for the LOB data type data.

- CACHE, LOGGING: It Enables caching and logging options for the LOB data type data.

- STORAGE: It is used to provide extent specification for storage clause.

- INDEX: It is used to provide LOB index specification.

The EMP_LOB_DEMO table stores an employee ID, a document, and their image. Note the LOB segment specification, index specification, and the clause to specify the inline and out of the line storage in the following code snippet:

```
/*Create the table LOB_DEMO*/
CREATE TABLE EMP_LOB_DEMO
(
  EMPID NUMBER,
  DOC CLOB,
  IMAGE BLOB
)
LOB (DOC) --LOB storage clause for DOC
STORE AS LOBSEGMENT_DOC_CLOB
(
  CHUNK 4096
  CACHE
  STORAGE (MINEXTENTS 2)
  INDEX IDX_DOC_CLOB
)
LOB (IMAGE) --LOB storage clause for IMAGE
STORE AS LOBSEGMENT_IMG_BLOB
(
  ENABLE STORAGE IN ROW
  CHUNK 4096
  CACHE
  STORAGE (MINEXTENTS 2)
  INDEX IDX_IMAGE_BLOB
)
/

Table created.
```

LOB metadata is stored in the USER_LOBS dictionary view. Note that the LOB segment has been created for the particular LOB data type column in the table. The segments can even be queried in the USER_SEGMENTS dictionary view.

The following query selects the LOBs created in the table script shown in the previous code snippet:

```
/*Select LOB columns along with segment and index name*/
SQL> SELECT TABLE_NAME, COLUMN_NAME, SEGMENT_NAME, INDEX_NAME
FROM USER_LOBS
WHERE TABLE_NAME = 'EMP_LOB_DEMO'
/

TABLE_NAME     COLUMN_NAME    SEGMENT_NAME                    INDEX_NAME
------------   -------------  ------------------------------  -----------
----
EMP_LOB_DEMO DOC             LOBSEGMENT_DOC_CLOB             IDX_DOC_CLOB
EMP_LOB_DEMO IMAGE           LOBSEGMENT_IMG_BLOB             IDX_IMAGE_
BLOB

/*Select LOB segments to view the segment characteristics*/
SQL> SELECT segment_name,segment_type,segment_subtype,bytes,blocks
FROM USER_SEGMENTS
where segment_name in ('LOBSEGMENT_DOC_CLOB','LOBSEGMENT_IMG_BLOB');
```

SEGMENT_NAME	SEGMENT_TYPE	SEGMENT_SU	BYTES	BLOCKS
LOBSEGMENT_DOC_CLOB	LOBSEGMENT	ASSM	8388608	1024
LOBSEGMENT_IMG_BLOB	LOBSEGMENT	ASSM	2097152	256

Managing LOB data types

The LOB data management includes its interaction with the loading interface, data manipulation strategies, and selection of the LOB data. The section makes certain recommendations to manage internal LOBs, BFILEs, and temporary LOBs.

Managing internal LOBs

An internal LOB data type that is, a CLOB or BLOB data type column can be interacted through supported interfaces such as DBMS_LOB, JDBC, or OLE object structure. In PL/SQL, LOB data is majorly managed through the DBMS_LOB package which provides a wide variety of subprograms to populate the LOB data, manipulate it, and extract relevant information such as length, size, and so on.

Few of the recommendations to manage the internal LOB are as follows:

- The LOB column can be initialized as NULL using EMPTY_BLOB() or EMPTY_CLOB() functions.
- A CLOB can be populated through SQL or a text file loaded from a PL/SQL program. A BLOB should always be loaded through a PL/SQL block.
- Use of DBMS_LOB package is preferable for the LOB operations and activities.
- The LOB data can be modified using the UPDATE statement or DBMS_LOB subprograms.

Securing and managing BFILEs

A BFILE column is a LOB data type which has to be secured against malicious activities resulting from unauthorized access. The reason behind this is the external location of the file on the operating system or external hardware. Unauthorized access from PL/SQL can be ensured by regulating the access on the directory object. The privilege to write data at the directory location must be restricted only to authorized users, while other users should enjoy the read privilege only. The usage of a directory object prepares the database to take an additional layer of security for BFILEs after performing the varying security techniques from the external hardware. A file on the operating system can be secured against its access, nondesired manipulative activities, and file size restrictions at the operating system level.

Thereafter, once the BFILE data is populated in a fashion similar to internal LOBs, the BFILE operations and interactions are carried out by the DBMS_LOB package.

A user can open only a definite number of BFILEs in an active session. The session level static initialization parameter SESSION_MAX_OPEN_FILES governs the number of BFILEs to be opened in a session. Its default value is 10 and it resides in the spfile[DB].ora parameter specification file. Once this limit is reached, no more files can be opened in the session. The value of the parameter can be altered using the ALTER SESSION command.

The following example illustration modifies the parameter SESSION_MAX_OPEN_
FILES to 25:

```
/*Connect as SYSDBA*/
Conn sys/system as sysdba
Connected.
/*Alter the session to modify the maximum open files in a session*/
ALTER SESSION SET SESSION_MAX_OPEN_FILES = 25
/
Session altered.
```

Managing BFILEs is similar to that of internal LOBs. While the DBA takes care of
the security at the OS level and database level, the developer codes the programs
to interact with the file and populate its locator (rather BFILE locator) in the BFILE
column of a table. The DBA manages the file system on the operating system or
external hardware, creates the database directory object, and decides upon the
directory access. A BFILE column can be initialized using the BFILENAME function.
The BFILENAME function establishes a reference to the file at the specified physical
directory location. In simple terms, it returns the BFILE locator:

```
FUNCTION BFILENAME(directory IN VARCHAR2, filename IN VARCHAR2)
RETURN BFILE;
```

In the previous syntax, directory is a valid database directory name and filename
is a file located at the directory location. The function returns a BFILE locator
which can be simply assigned to a BFILE column in a table using INSERT/UPDATE
statement. Importantly, these external files are accessed in read-only mode through
BFILEs; as a result, files cannot be modified. Instead, the BFILE locator can be
modified to change the pointer to point to a different target.

Note that the same BFILENAME function is also used while populating an internal
LOB column from an external file.

The DBMS_LOB package—overview

DBMS_LOB is the built-in Oracle package which provides API level interface for LOB
operations. The package DBMS_LOB provides subprograms to query the LOB, sets the
operating status, performs the transactional activities, reads BFILEs, and so on.

Security model

The package is owned by SYSDBA. A DBA must grant an EXECUTE privilege to the
user which seeks the usage of LOB operations.

DBMS_LOB constants

The constants used by the DBMS_LOB package have been consolidated in the following table:

Constant	Definition
DBMS_LOB constants	
FILE_READONLY	CONSTANT BINARY_INTEGER := 0;
LOB_READONLY	CONSTANT BINARY_INTEGER := 0;
LOB_READWRITE	CONSTANT BINARY_INTEGER := 1;
LOBMAXSIZE	CONSTANT INTEGER := 18446744073709551615;
SESSION	CONSTANT PLS_INTEGER := 10;
CALL	CONSTANT PLS_INTEGER := 12;
DBMS_LOB option types	
OPT_COMPRESS	CONSTANT BINARY_INTEGER := 1;
OPT_ENCRYPT	CONSTANT BINARY_INTEGER := 2;
OPT_DEDUPLICATE	CONSTANT BINARY_INTEGER := 4;
DBMS_LOB option values	
COMPRESS_OFF	CONSTANT BINARY_INTEGER := 0;
COMPRESS_ON	CONSTANT BINARY_INTEGER := 1;
ENCRYPT_OFF	CONSTANT BINARY_INTEGER := 0;
ENCRYPT_ON	CONSTANT BINARY_INTEGER := 2;
DEDUPLICATE_OFF	CONSTANT BINARY_INTEGER := 0;
DEDUPLICATE_ON	CONSTANT PLS_INTEGER := 4;

DBMS_LOB data types

The list of data types used by the DBMS_LOB package is as follows:

Data type	Discription
BLOB	Source or destination binary LOB
RAW	Source or destination RAW buffer (used with BLOB)
CLOB	Source or destination character LOB (including NCLOB)
VARCHAR2	Source or destination character buffer (used with CLOB and NCLOB)
INTEGER	Specifies the size of a buffer or LOB, the offset into a LOB, or the amount to access
BFILE	Large, binary object stored outside the database

DBMS_LOB subprograms

The DBMS_LOB subprograms are listed in the following table:

Subprogram	Description
APPEND procedure	Appends the contents of the source LOB to the destination LOB
CLOSE procedure	Closes a previously opened internal or external LOB
COMPARE function	Compares two entire LOBs or parts of two LOBs
CONVERTTOBLOB procedure	Reads character data from a source CLOB or NCLOB instance, converts the character data to the specified character, writes the converted data to a destination BLOB instance in binary format, and returns the new offsets
CONVERTTOCLOB procedure	Takes a source BLOB instance, converts the binary data in the source instance to character data using the specified character, writes the character data to a destination CLOB or NCLOB instance, and returns the new offsets
COPY procedure	Copies all, or part, of the source LOB to the destination LOB
CREATETEMPORARY procedure	Creates a temporary BLOB or CLOB and its corresponding index in the user's default temporary tablespace
ERASE procedure	Erases entire or part of a LOB
FILECLOSE procedure	Closes the file
FILECLOSEALL procedure	Closes all previously opened files
FILEEXISTS function	Checks if the file exists on the server
FILEGETNAME procedure	Gets the directory object name and file name
FILEISOPEN function	Checks if the file was opened using the input BFILE locators
FILEOPEN procedure	Opens a BFILE
FRAGMENT_DELETE procedure	Deletes the data at the given offset for the given length from the LOB
FRAGMENT_INSERT procedure	Inserts the given data (limited to 32 KB) into the LOB at the given offset
FRAGMENT_MOVE procedure	Moves the amount of bytes (BLOB) or characters (CLOB/NCLOB) from the given offset to the new offset specified
FRAGMENT_REPLACE procedure	Replaces the data at the given offset with the given data (not to exceed 32 KB)
FREETEMPORARY procedure	Frees the temporary BLOB or CLOB in the default temporary tablespace

Subprogram	Description
GETCHUNKSIZE function	Returns the amount of space used in the LOB CHUNK to store the LOB value
GETLENGTH function	Gets the length of the LOB value
GETOPTIONS function	Obtains settings corresponding to the option_types field for a particular LOB
GET_STORAGE_LIMIT function	Returns the storage limit for LOBs in your database configuration
INSTR function	Returns the matching position of the nth occurrence of the pattern in the LOB
ISOPEN functions	Checks to see if the LOB was already opened using the input locator
ISTEMPORARY functions	Checks if the locator is pointing to a temporary LOB
LOADBLOBFROMFILE procedure	Loads BFILE data into an internal BLOB
LOADCLOBFROMFILE procedure	Loads BFILE data into an internal CLOB
LOADFROMFILE procedure	Loads BFILE data into an internal LOB
OPEN procedures	Opens a LOB (internal, external, or temporary) in the indicated mode
READ procedures	Reads data from the LOB starting at the specified offset
SETOPTIONS procedures	Enables CSCE features on a per-LOB basis, overriding the default LOB column settings
SUBSTR functions	Returns part of the LOB value starting at the specified offset
TRIM procedures	Trims the LOB value to the specified shorter length
WRITE procedures	Writes data to the LOB from a specified offset
WRITEAPPEND procedures	Writes a buffer at the end of a LOB

Rules and regulations

Here we shall discuss some of the basic validation rules for internal and external LOBs. These validations provide the usage guidelines while working with LOBs using the DBMS_LOB package.

Internal LOBs

Internal LOBs deal with character and binary data. The important validations for internal LOBs include the offset and LOB length. The usage guidelines are as follows:

- Length and offset value must be positive and definite. For CLOB, the values must be expressed as characters while for BLOB and BFILEs, the values must be expressed as bytes. By default, the offset value is 1.

- Numeric arguments such as `length`, `offset`, `newline`, `nth`, and `amount` must be a positive number not greater than LOBMAXSIZE (2^{64}).

- Subprograms with NULL inputs raise exceptions or return NULL output.

- Character function subprograms SUBSTR, INSTR, and COMPARE do not support regular expressions or character pattern matching in parameters.

- The LOB must be locked while querying to avoid simultaneous transactions on the same row.

BFILEs

External LOBs deal with externally located data. Most importantly, the file must exist physically at the location. The usage notes for external LOBs are as follows:

- BFILE locator is the mandatory component for all BFILE operations.

- The file must physically exist at the directory location pointed by the BFILE locator.

- Be reminded of the maximum open file limit in each session. In case of an abnormal termination of the program, the exception handler must close all the open BFILEs.

- Maximum buffer size is 32767 bytes.

Working with the CLOB, BLOB, and BFILE data types

By now, we have gathered enough understanding on the LOB data types. We will now see the handling of LOB data in PL/SQL. For illustration purposes, we will use the EMP_LOB_DEMO table, which has been created earlier.

Initializing LOB data type columns

As we learned earlier the LOB column in the table contains only the pointer (LOB locator), while the actual data is stored in the LOB segment. The LOB segment is a different storage area in the same or different tablespace.

For initialization of a LOB data type variable or column, Oracle provides two built-in constructor methods namely, EMPTY_CLOB() and EMPTY_BLOB(). These functions are supported in SQL as well as PL/SQL. The functions assign a default LOB locator to the CLOB and BLOB data type columns or variables. Let us check it out.

The PL/SQL block, shown in the following code snippet, declares a CLOB and BLOB variable and initializes them in the declarative section. However, the initialization can be made in the executable section also:

```
/*Start the PL/SQL block*/
DECLARE

/*Declare local variables of LOB types and initialize them with
corresponding constructor methods*/
  l_my_clob  CLOB := EMPTY_CLOB ();
  l_my_blob BLOB := EMPTY_BLOB ();
BEGIN
  NULL;
END;
/

PL/SQL procedure successfully completed.
```

A CLOB or BLOB type column can be created with its default value, as shown in the following code snippet:

```
/*Create the table with default initialization of LOB columns*/
CREATE TABLE dummy_lob
(
  my_clob CLOB DEFAULT EMPTY_CLOB(),
  my_blob BLOB DEFAULT EMPTY_BLOB()
)
/
Table created.
```

A table can be altered to add a column of CLOB or BLOB data type with its default value for the existing data. It is shown in the following code snippet:

```
/*Alter the table to add a column with default initialization*/
ALTER TABLE dummy_lob
ADD your_clob CLOB DEFAULT EMPTY_CLOB()
/
Table altered.
```

Inserting data into a LOB column

By using SQL, character data can be inserted only into a CLOB column. The BLOB column can only be initialized with a LOB locator using the EMPTY_BLOB() function. The reason is that BLOB is meant dedicatedly for a binary (or hexadecimal) data:

```
SQL> INSERT INTO EMP_LOB_DEMO
  VALUES
  (7900, 'I am the KING', EMPTY_BLOB());
1 row created.
SQL> COMMIT;
Commit complete.
SQL> SELECT * FROM emp_lob_demo;

    EMPID DOC                             IMAGE
---------- ----------------------------- ---------------------------
     7900 I am the KING
```

If character data is attempted for the BLOB column, Oracle raises the ORA-01465: invalid hex number exception.

Populating a LOB data type using an external file

Data from a system's text file can be loaded into CLOB using PL/SQL. Here, we will demonstrate populating of CLOB and BLOB columns from a system's text and image files. Observe the populating steps.

The application database maintains a directory object which points to the defined OS location. The OS location and the text file content is shown in the following screenshot. Note that we have two files:

- **LOB_data_file.txt**: The data has to be loaded into the CLOB column.
- **MyLogo.JPG**: The image file has to be loaded into the BLOB column.

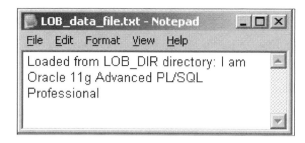

We will try to read the text file shown in the previous screenshot and load the character data in the EMP_LOB_DEMO table. The demonstration steps are as follows:

1. The DBA creates the directory for the defined OS location:

```
/*Connect as SYSDBA*/
Conn sys/system as SYSDBA
Connected.
/*Create directory LOB_DIR for the specified OS Location*/
SQL> CREATE DIRECTORY LOB_DIR AS 'C:\MyORCLFolders\';
Directory created.
```

2. The DBA grants read/write access on the directory to the ORADEV user:

```
/*Grant read and write privilege on the directory LOB_DIR to user
ORADEV*/
SQL> GRANT READ, WRITE ON DIRECTORY DEMO_DIR TO ORADEV;
Grant succeeded.
```

3. The PL/SQL block loads the two files into the table. Note the following observations from the PL/SQL program:

   - The PL/SQL variables L_SOURCE_CLOB and L_SOURCE_BLOB are assigned with the LOB locators using the BFILENAME function.
   - The temporary LOB columns are initialized with the EMPTY_CLOB() and EMPTY_BLOB() constructor methods.
   - DBMS_LOB.OPEN is used to open an external LOB in read-only mode.
   - DBMS_LOB.GETLENGTH is used to find the length of the external LOB.
   - The INSERT statement inserts the data and empty LOB locators returning into the temporary LOB variables.
   - DBMS_LOB.LODFROMFILE populates the external BFILE data to the temporary LOB variables.
   - The temporary LOB variables are updated in the EMP_LOB_DEMO table.
   - DBMS_LOB.CLOSE is used to close the external LOB.

Refer to the following code snippet:

```
/*Connect as ORADEV*/
Conn ORADEV/ORADEV
Connected.

/*Enable the SERVEROUTPUT to display the block messages*/
SET SERVEROUTPUT ON

/*Start the PL/SQL block*/
DECLARE

/*Declaring LOB locator for CLOB and BLOB*/
   L_SOURCE_CLOB BFILE := BFILENAME('LOB_DIR', 'LOB_data_file.
txt');
   L_SOURCE_BLOB BFILE := BFILENAME('LOB_DIR', 'MyLogo.JPG');

/*Declaring offset value for both LOB columns*/
   L_AMT_CLOB   INTEGER := 4000;
   L_AMT_BLOB   INTEGER := 4000;

/*Declaring temporary LOB columns for both LOB columns*/
   L_CLOB CLOB := EMPTY_CLOB();
   L_BLOB BLOB := EMPTY_BLOB();
BEGIN

/*Opening the LOB locator in read only mode*/
   DBMS_LOB.OPEN(L_SOURCE_CLOB, DBMS_LOB.LOB_READONLY);
   DBMS_LOB.OPEN(L_SOURCE_BLOB, DBMS_LOB.LOB_READONLY);

/*Calculating the length of LOB locator*/
   L_AMT_CLOB := DBMS_LOB.GETLENGTH(L_SOURCE_CLOB);
   L_AMT_BLOB := DBMS_LOB.GETLENGTH(L_SOURCE_BLOB);

/*Create the record into LOB_DEMO table with empty LOB instance in
both CLOB and BLOB. Fetch the LOB column values into temporary LOB
variables*/
   INSERT INTO emp_lob_demo
   VALUES (7369, EMPTY_CLOB, EMPTY_BLOB())
   RETURNING DOC,IMAGE INTO L_CLOB, L_BLOB;

/*Load the temporary LOBs with the LOB locator and object pointed
by them*/
   DBMS_OUTPUT.PUT_LINE('Inserting text file into database. . .');
   DBMS_LOB.LOADFROMFILE(L_CLOB, L_SOURCE_CLOB, L_AMT_CLOB);
   DBMS_OUTPUT.PUT_LINE('Populating CLOB data is over');
   DBMS_OUTPUT.PUT_LINE('Inserting Image file into database. . .');
   DBMS_LOB.LOADFROMFILE(L_BLOB, L_SOURCE_BLOB, L_AMT_BLOB);
   DBMS_OUTPUT.PUT_LINE('Populating BLOB data is over');
```

```
/*Close the LOB locators*/
  DBMS_LOB.CLOSE(L_SOURCE_CLOB);
  DBMS_LOB.CLOSE(L_SOURCE_BLOB);

/*Update the emp_lob_demo with the temporary LOB variable values*/
  UPDATE emp_lob_demo
  SET doc    = L_CLOB, image = L_BLOB
  WHERE empid = 7369;
END;
/

Inserting text file into database. . .
Populating CLOB data is over
Inserting Image file into database. . .
Populating BLOB data is over
PL/SQL procedure successfully completed.
```

4. The PL/SQL executes successfully and the data gets populated from the external files into the database. Let us fire a SELECT query on the table:

```
/*Query the table to verify the loading*/
SQL> SELECT * FROM emp_lob_demo
  WHERE empid = 7369;
```

EMPID	DOC	IMAGE
7369	Loaded from LOB_DIR directory: I am Oracle 11g Advanced PL/SQL Professional	FFD8FFE000104A464946000101010060006000000 FFDB0043000806060706050807070709090080A0C 140D0C0B0B0C1912130F141D1A1F1E1D1A1C1C20 242E2720222C231C1C2837292C30313434341F27

Note the data from the text file LOB_data_file.txt in the DOC (CLOB data type) column. The IMAGE (BLOB data type) column shows the hexadecimal code of the image MyLogo.JPG. The DOC_SIZE parameter corresponds to the size of the text file and IMAGE_SIZE corresponds to the size of the image file.

Let us check the size of the LOB data and compare with the actual counts:

```
/*Select the length of LOB column types*/
SQL> SELECT empid,
  DBMS_LOB.GETLENGTH(doc) doc_size,
```

```
DBMS_LOB.GETLENGTH(image) image_size
FROM emp_lob_demo
WHERE empid = 7369;

   EMPID    DOC_SIZE    IMAGE_SIZE
---------- ---------- ----------
    7369       75         11105
```

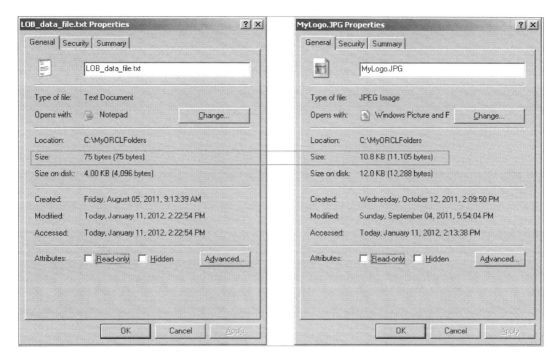

Selecting LOB data

In our above illustrations, we have already seen that the SELECT statement can read the CLOB data successfully. For the BLOB data, the hexadecimal value for the binary file appears:

```
SELECT empid, doc, image
FROM emp_lob_demo
/
```

```
EMPID DOC                                                     IMAGE
----- ------------------------------------------------------- -------------------------------------
 7900 I am the KING
 7369 Loaded from LOB_DIR directory: I am Oracle 11g Advanced FFD8FFE000104A46494600010101006000600000
      PL/SQL Professional                                     FFDB004300080606070605080707070908000A0C
                                                              140D0C0B0B0C1912130F141D1A1F1E1D1A1C1C20
                                                              242E2720222C231C1C2837292C30313434341F27
```

Similarly, in a PL/SQL block, the CLOB data can be fetched from the table:

```
/*Enable the SERVEROUTPUT to display block messages*/
SET SERVEROUT ON

/*Start the Pl/SQL block*/
DECLARE
l_lob_len NUMBER;

/*Cursor to select the data from emp_lob_demo table*/
CURSOR C IS
SELECT empid, doc, image
FROM emp_lob_demo;
BEGIN

  /*Iterate the cursor in the FOR loop*/
  FOR I IN C
  LOOP

    /*Get length of the CLOB column*/
    l_lob_len := DBMS_LOB.GETLENGTH(i.doc);

    /*Display the CLOB data*/
    DBMS_OUTPUT.PUT_LINE('Printing DOC for '|| i.empid||':
    '||DBMS_LOB.SUBSTR(i.doc, l_lob_len));
  END LOOP;
END;
/

Printing DOC for 7900: I am the KING
Printing DOC for 7369: Loaded from LOB_DIR directory: I am Oracle 11g
Advanced PL/SQL Professional
PL/SQL procedure successfully completed.
```

Modifying the LOB data

If the CLOB data is small, the CLOB data type column can be updated using the UPDATE statement. For example, we will try to update the DOC value for EMPID 7900 in the EMP_LOB_DEMO table:

```
/*Check the current value of CLOB column for EMPID 7900*/
SQL> SELECT doc FROM emp_lob_demo WHERE empid = 7900;
```

```
DOC
-----------------------------
I am the KING

/*Update the CLOB column for EMPID 7900*/
SQL> UPDATE emp_lob_demo
  SET doc = 'I am not a KING'
  WHERE empid = 7900;


1 row updated.

/*Verify the updated value of CLOB column for EMPID 7900*/
SQL> SELECT doc FROM emp_lob_demo WHERE empid = 7900;

DOC
-----------------------------
I am not a KING
```

The character data populated from an external file can also be updated. The changes will be in the external text file too. DBMS_LOB.WRITE and DBMS_LOB.WRITEAPPEND achieve the CLOB writing operations.

The PL/SQL block below selects the DOC column for EMPID 7369 in a local CLOB variable. It then appends a text to it and writes back in the text file corresponding to the LOB locator:

```
/*Start the PL/SQL block*/
DECLARE
  L_CLOB CLOB;
  L_WRITE_TXT VARCHAR2(50) := 'Write: Larry Ellison heads Oracle
Corp';
  L_APPEND_TXT VARCHAR2(50) := 'Append: Larry Ellison heads Oracle
Corp';
  L_BUFF_AMT NUMBER ;
  L_OFFSET INTEGER;
BEGIN

/*Selects the CLOB data in a local variable*/
  SELECT doc
  INTO l_clob
  FROM emp_lob_demo
  WHERE empid = 7369
  FOR UPDATE;
```

```
/*Calculate the offset pointer value*/
  L_OFFSET := DBMS_LOB.GETLENGTH(L_CLOB) + 115;

/*Calculate the buffer amount*/
  L_BUFF_AMT := LENGTH(L_WRITE_TXT);

/*Write the data into the CLOB locator*/
  DBMS_LOB.WRITE (L_CLOB, L_BUFF_AMT, L_OFFSET, L_WRITE_TXT);
  L_BUFF_AMT := LENGTH(L_APPEND_TXT);

/*Append the data into CLOB locator*/
  DBMS_LOB.WRITEAPPEND (L_CLOB, L_BUFF_AMT, L_APPEND_TXT);
END;
/


PL/SQL procedure successfully completed.
COMMIT;

Commit complete.
```

Delete LOB data

A row from a table which contains the LOB data can be deleted to remove the LOB data. If the scalar LOB data has to be removed, it is better to update the LOB column with an empty LOB locator through EMPTY_CLOB() or EMPTY_BLOB().

For example, the IMAGE column of the EMP_LOB_DEMO table for EMPID 7369 can be updated as follows:

```
UPDATE emp_lob_demo
SET image = EMPTY_BLOB ()
WHERE empid = 7369
/

1 row updated.
```

The same row could have been deleted but it would have also removed the DOC data.

Miscellaneous LOB notes

We will now overview certain LOB working and usage guidelines. We will understand few uncategorized and miscellaneous facts about LOB data types. In the development phases, it is necessary to understand the LOB column states and access,

LOB column states

A LOB column value in a table can exist in three states namely NULL, Empty, or Populated. The comparison between them is as follows:

LOB state	Locator exist	Value exist	LOB Length
NULL	No	No	Null
Empty	Yes	No	Zero
Populated	Yes	Yes	Definite value

Locking a row containing LOB

The row containing the LOB data must be selected using FOR UPDATE clause to prevent other users working on the same row. Once the row is locked, the LOB cannot be updated, modified, or replaced.

Opening and closing LOBs

The LOBs can be opened in read-only or read/write mode. The mode is specified using a DBMS_LOB subprogram.

In read-only mode, the LOB can only be selected but cannot be updated or modified until the LOB is closed and re-opened in write mode:

```
DBMS_LOB.OPEN(L_SOURCE_CLOB, DBMS_LOB.LOB_READONLY);
```

In read/write mode, a persistent LOB participates in database transactions. It defers the index maintenance on the LOB column until the mode is active.

```
DBMS_LOB.OPEN(L_SOURCE_CLOB, DBMS_LOB.LOB_READWRITE);
```

A LOB once opened in either of the modes, must be closed in the same session.

Accessing LOBs

Some key points to access LOB columns from the table are as follows:

- The character type LOBs (CLOB and NCLOB) follow the VARCHAR2 semantics for usage in SQL functions and with SQL operators. The semantics are supported and suggested up to 1 MB sized LOBs. The Oracle server performs implicit conversion of the first 4 KB data of CLOB data, when used in SQL; 32 KB of CLOB data, when used in PL/SQL.

- Concatenation, comparison, character functions, conversion functions, and aggregate functions are supported by LOB type columns. The functions such as INSTR, REPLACE, SUBSTR, CONCAT, TRIM, LTRIM, RTRIM, LOWER, UPPER, NLS_LOWER, NLS_UPPER, LPAD, and RPAD can be used well with character LOB columns.

- The LENGTH function is supported for all LOB types. The function DECODE works only for CLOB. The value returned by LENGTH function is the same as that returned by DBMS_LOB.GETLENGTH.

- The IS [NOT] NULL operator can be used with LOB columns in SQL. These operators check the NULL property of only the LOB locator.

- Following operations are not supported in SQL:
    - DISTINCT
    - ORDER BY clause
    - GROUP BY clause
    - SET operators except UNION ALL (UNION, MINUS, INTERSECT)
    - Join queries
    - CREATE INDEX

LOB restrictions

The LOB data type healed the drawbacks of the manual mechanism of large object storage. But there are a few restrictions as follows:

- LOB columns cannot behave as Primary Key.

- SQL Loader cannot recognize LOB column data as an argument input to the clause.

- In shared-server mode, a BFILE column does not support session migration.

Migrating from LONG to LOB

Starting from Oracle 10*g*, a LONG data is convertible to a LOB data in a table. This enhancement has enabled the migration of older data in LONG and LONG RAW columns to equivalent LOB data types in Oracle. The data in the LONG type column is mapped to CLOB or NCLOB data types and the data in the LONG RAW type columns is mapped to the BLOB data type. It can be achieved through the ALTER TABLE statement, where a LONG type column can be modified to the LOB type column:

```
ALTER TABLE [table name]
MODIFY [LONG type column] [LOB type (CLOB | BLOB)];
```

During migration, the Oracle server implicitly takes care of the data conversion and movement from the LONG to LOB data type. A LONG, LONG RAW, or VARCHAR2 type of data can be implicitly converted into CLOB or BLOB. Explicitly, the data can be converted using TO_CLOB() and TO_BLOB() converter functions. During migration, the nullity (NULL or NOT NULL) and default value is also carried away to the new columns. Let us follow an illustration which migrates a LONG type column to the CLOB type column:

```
/*Create a table with LONG type columns*/
CREATE TABLE i_am_old
(
   id NUMBER,
   doc LONG
)
/

Table created.

/*Insert the sample data in the columns*/
SQL> INSERT INTO i_am_old
   VALUES
   (10,'Oracle 8i');

1 row created.
SQL> INSERT INTO i_am_old
   VALUES
   (20,'Oracle 9i');

1 row created.
SQL> INSERT INTO i_am_old
   VALUES
   (30,'Oracle 10G');

1 row created.
SQL> INSERT INTO i_am_old
   VALUES
   (40,'Oracle 11G');

1 row created.
SQL> commit;

Commit complete.

/*View the current data in the table*/
SQL> select * from i_am_old;

        ID    DOC
---------- --------------------
        10    Oracle 8i
        20    Oracle 9i
        30    Oracle 10G
        40    Oracle 11G
```

```
/*Migrate the LONG to LOB. Oracle implicitly takes care of the data
conversion from LONG to CLOB*/
SQL> ALTER TABLE i_am_old MODIFY doc CLOB;

Table altered.

/*Describe the table to verify the migration*/
SQL> DESC I_AM_OLD

  Name              Null?     Type
  -------------------------------------
  ID                          NUMBER
  DOC                         CLOB

/*Re verify the data*/
SQL> select * from i_am_old;

        ID     DOC
  ---------- -------------------
        10     Oracle 8i
        20     Oracle 9i
        30     Oracle 10G
        40     Oracle 11G
```

Using temporary LOBs

Temporary LOBs provide a temporary solution to hold a LOB data in a limited scope—maximum up to a SESSION. It can be used in a PL/SQL block as a local variable. A temporary LOB created using the DBMS_LOB package resides in temporary tablespace. Note that neither the redo logs nor the rollback information is generated for it. For this reason, they yield better performance within a block.

A temporary LOB can be created as any of the internal LOBs, but cannot be initialized using empty LOB locator constructor methods (EMPTY_CLOB and EMPTY_BLOB). They can be a handy solution when manipulative operations are performed on the LOB type column in a PL/SQL block.

Temporary LOB operations

A temporary LOB allows most of the LOB operations such as create and update. A temporary LOB, being a temporary component, must be freed-up as soon as its related actions are over. The DBMS_LOB package provides the APIs to handle temporary LOB actions.

Managing temporary LOBs

The DBMS_LOB package offers certain subprograms to work with temporary
LOBs. DBMS_LOB.ISTEMPORARY checks whether the given LOB is temporary
or not. Syntactically, the overloaded subprogram is as follows:

```
DBMS_LOB.ISTEMPORARY (lob_loc IN BLOB)
   RETURN INTEGER;
DBMS_LOB.ISTEMPORARY (lob_loc IN CLOB CHARACTER SET ANY_CS)
   RETURN INTEGER;
```

In this syntax, LOB_LOC is the LOB locator. The LOB locator can be a CLOB or BLOB
type variable.

To create a temporary LOB, DBMS_LOB.CREATETEMPORARY can be used. It is, again, an
overloaded API which is shown in the following code snippet:

```
DBMS_LOB.CREATETEMPORARY
(
   lob_loc IN OUT NOCOPY BLOB,
   cache IN BOOLEAN,
   duration IN PLS_INTEGER := DBMS_LOB.SESSION
);
DBMS_LOB.CREATETEMPORARY
(
   lob_loc IN OUT NOCOPY CLOB CHARACTER SET ANY_CS,
   cache IN BOOLEAN,
   duration IN PLS_INTEGER := 10
);
```

Based on this syntax, let us understand a few facts:

- lob_loc: It is the LOB locator.
- cache: It is a Boolean parameter which determines whether the LOB should
  be in the buffer cache or not.
- duration: It specifies the life of the temporary LOB. It can be one of
  SESSION, TRANSACTION, or CALL. By default, the duration of a temporary
  LOB is SESSION.

DBMS_LOB.FREETEMPORARY frees the memory allocated for the temporary LOB. The
syntax for this subprogram is as follows:

```
DBMS_LOB.FREETEMPORARY (lob_loc  IN OUT  NOCOPY BLOB);
DBMS_LOB.FREETEMPORARY (lob_loc  IN OUT  NOCOPY CLOB CHARACTER SET
ANY_CS);
```

Validating, creating, and freeing a temporary LOB

Let us walkthrough a PL/SQL program to illustrate the usage of the temporary LOB subprograms. Observe the creation, validation, and release of the temporary LOB in the program:

```
/*Enable the SERVEROUT to display the block output*/
SET SERVEROUTPUT ON

/*Start the PL/SQL block*/
DECLARE
  L_TEMP_LOB CLOB;
  AMT NUMBER;
  OFFSET NUMBER := 5;
  L_WRITE VARCHAR2(100) := 'Oracle 8i introduced LOB types';
  L_APPEND VARCHAR2(100) := 'Oracle 11g introduced SecureFiles';
BEGIN

/*Create the temporary LOB*/
  DBMS_LOB.CREATETEMPORARY
  (
    lob_loc => L_TEMP_LOB,
    cache => true,
    dur => dbms_lob.session
  );

/*Verify the creation of temporary LOB*/
  IF (DBMS_LOB.ISTEMPORARY(L_TEMP_LOB) = 1) THEN
      DBMS_OUTPUT.PUT_LINE('Given LOB is a temporary LOB');
  ELSE
      DBMS_OUTPUT.PUT_LINE('Given LOB is a persistent LOB');
  END IF;

/*Open the temporary LOB is read write mode*/
  DBMS_LOB.OPEN
  (
    lob_loc => L_TEMP_LOB,
    open_mode => DBMS_LOB.LOB_READWRITE
  );

/*Write the sample data in the temporary LOB*/
  DBMS_LOB.WRITE
  (
    lob_loc => L_TEMP_LOB,
    amount  => LENGTH(L_WRITE),
```

```
    offset  => OFFSET,
    buffer  => L_WRITE );
  DBMS_OUTPUT.PUT_LINE
  (
    'Temporary LOB length after Write '||DBMS_LOB.GETLENGTH(L_TEMP_
LOB)
  );

/*Append the sample in the temporary LOB*/
  DBMS_LOB.WRITEAPPEND
  (
    lob_loc => L_TEMP_LOB,
    amount  => LENGTH(L_APPEND),
    buffer  => L_APPEND
  );
  DBMS_OUTPUT.PUT_LINE
  (
    'Temporary LOB length after Append '||DBMS_LOB.GETLENGTH(L_TEMP_
LOB)
  );

/*Display the complete content of the temporary LOB*/
  DBMS_OUTPUT.PUT_LINE
  (
    CHR(10)||'Temporary LOB Content: '
  );
  DBMS_OUTPUT.PUT_LINE
  (
    DBMS_LOB.SUBSTR
    (
      L_TEMP_LOB,DBMS_LOB.GETLENGTH
      (L_TEMP_LOB), 1
    )
  );
  DBMS_LOB.CLOSE(lob_loc => L_TEMP_LOB);
  DBMS_LOB.FREETEMPORARY(lob_loc => L_TEMP_LOB);
END;
/

Given LOB is a temporary LOB
Temporary LOB length after Write 34
Temporary LOB length after Append 67
Temporary LOB Content:
Oracle 8i introduced LOB typesOracle 11g introduced SecureFiles
PL/SQL procedure successfully completed.
```

Summary

In this chapter, we learned the handling of large objects in Oracle. We started with the need for a stable philosophy for large objects and understanding on the LOB data types in Oracle. We learned managing and working with internal and external LOBs with the help of illustrations and demonstrations. We wiped-up the chapter with a brief demonstration on working with temporary LOBs.

In the next chapter, we will see an enhanced version of LOB, SecureFiles, which has been released in Oracle 11*g*. We will see the archiving of an earlier LOB under BasicFiles and evolution of SecureFiles as a more promising framework to store large objects in the database.

Practice exercise

1. Internal LOBs can be used as attributes of a user-defined data type.

    a. True

    b. False

2. Internal LOBs cannot be passed as parameters to PL/SQL subprograms.

    a. True

    b. False

3. Internal LOBs can be stored in a tablespace that is different from the tablespace that stores the table containing the LOB column.

    a. True

    b. False

4. You issue the following command to create a table called LOB_STORE:

```
CREATE TABLE lob_store
(lob_id NUMBER(3),
photo BLOB DEFAULT EMPTY_CLOB(),
cv CLOB DEFAULT NULL,
ext_file BFILE DEFAULT NULL)
/
```

Identify the issue in the above script.

   a. The table is created successfully.

   b. It generates an error because a BLOB column cannot be initialized with EMPTY_CLOB().

   c. It generates an error because DEFAULT cannot be set to NULL for a CLOB column during table creation.

   d. It generates an error because DEFAULT cannot be set to NULL for a BFILE column during table creation.

5. Identify the correct statements about the initialization of LOBs.

   a. An internal LOB cannot be initialized in the CREATE TABLE statement.

   b. The BFILE column can be initialized with the EMPTY_BFILE() constructor.

   c. The EMPTY_CLOB() and EMPTY_BLOB() functions can be used to initialize both NULL and NOT NULL internal LOBs of CLOB and BLOB types.

   d. Initialization is a mandatory step for LOB type columns.

6. Which two statements are true about the FILEOPEN subprogram in the DBMS_LOB package?

   a. FILEOPEN can be used to open only internal LOBs.

   b. FILEOPEN can be used to open only external LOBs.

   c. FILEOPEN cannot be used to open temporary LOBs.

   d. FILEOPEN can be used to open internal and external LOBs.

7. Temporary LOBs can be shared among the users which are currently connected to the server.

   a. True

   b. False

8. Identify the correct statements about BFILEs.

   a. A BFILE column in a table must be initialized with a dummy locator.

   b. BFILEs cannot be used as attributes in an object type.

   c. The BFILE data type is a read-only data type.

   d. The external file still persists if the BFILE locator is deleted or modified.

9. Pick up the incorrect statements about the Temporary LOBs.

   a. It resides in the user's temporary tablespace.

   b. It can be used during LONG to LOB data type migration.

   c. It can be persistent for SESSION, TRANSACTION, or CALL.

   d. Temporary LOB of BFILE type can be created.

10. A table SAMPLE_DATA has the following structure:

```
Name Null? Type
-------------- -------- ---------
SD_ID NUMBER
SD_SOURCE BFILE
```

   You update a row in the table using UPDATE statement as follows:

```
UPDATE sample_data
SET sd_source = BFILENAME('SD_FILE', 'sample.pdf')
WHERE sd_id = 448;
```

   But you receive the error—ORA-22286: insufficient privileges—on file or directory to perform FILEOPEN.

   What could be the probable cause of the error?

   a. The directory SD_FILE does not exist.

   b. The file sample.pdf does not exist.

   c. The user does not have the READ privilege on the directory.

   d. The file sample.pdf is a read-only file.

11. Choose the correct statement regarding migration of the LONG column to LOB:

   a. Use DBMS_LOB.MIGRATE to migrate LONG column data to LOB column.

   b. Alter the table to modify LONG column type to LOB type.

   c. A LONG RAW column can be migrated to CLOB column.

   d. The ALTER TABLE...MODIFY statement doesn't allows manipulation of LOB storage parameters.

12. Choose the correct statement about the BFILENAME function:

   a. It checks the existence of external file and reads, if exists.

   b. It returns the LOB locator of the file which is located externally at the directory location.

   c. It can be used for operations on external LOBs only.

   d. The output of the BFILENAME function is one of the LOB data types.

13. Choose the correct option(s) for the usage of LOB data types in Oracle 11*g*:

   a. BasicFiles are advanced LOBs which assure enhanced security and performance.

   b. SecureFiles are advanced LOBs which assure enhanced security and performance.

   c. LOB columns created prior to Oracle 11*g* cannot be migrated to SecureFiles.

   d. Older LOBs would be retained as BasicFiles in Oracle 11*g*.

14. You create a table, MYLOB, using the following script:

```
create table MYLOB
   (id number,
     doc clob);
```

Choose the correct statements from the following options:

   a. The script runs successfully and the MYLOB table is created with system generated LOB segment and LOB index.

   b. The system generated LOB segment can be queried in the USER_SEGMENTS view just after the CREATE TABLE statement is run.

   c. The table and the LOB are created in the default tablespace of the user.

   d. The CREATE TABLE statement raises an error as the LOB storage clause is missing in the CREATE TABLE script.

7
Using SecureFile LOBs

Today, the application development has taken a new turn to catch up with the growing business. The application environments employ some of the best strategies to accommodate the varied nature of data. Surveys have revealed an astonishing estimation that the nonstructured data grows annually by 65 percent in a typical enterprise data-based application. This pace is accredited to the growing content digitization, boost up rich user experience, web based structures, and physical file storage requirements.

In the previous chapter, we learned the traditional storage of large objects in Oracle. Since its release in Oracle 8*i*, they have worked well and served at par with the systems' requirements until Oracle 10*g*. The earlier LOB storage philosophy was based on certain assumptions which by now, were transformed into limitations. These assumptions were as follows:

- Size of the large object was expected to be in MBs
- Large objects would be less transactional
- No Encryption support
- The uniform CHUNK size resulted in data fragmentation—hence the performance degrades
- No compatibility with Oracle RAC

Oracle 11*g* Release tried to cope up with the above limitations by evolving out a best in the world feature called SecureFiles. SecureFile is an enhanced implementation of traditional LOBs but with increased capability and secure data management. The chapter discusses about the SecureFile feature in Oracle 11*g* under the following topics.

- Introduction to SecureFiles
  - ° SecureFile LOB—understanding
  - ° SecureFile LOB features
- Working with SecureFiles
  - ° Enabling advanced features in SecureFiles
  - ° SecureFile metadata
- Migration from BasicFile to SecureFile
  - ° Online Redefinition method

Introduction to SecureFiles

Oracle 11*g* Release 1 introduced SecureFiles to recoup the limitations of conventional LOBs in Oracle. The special engineered implementation of SecureFiles enables enhanced performance, data security, and better storage optimization. The induction of SecureFiles does not mean the extinction of older LOBs, instead older LOBs still live with the name BasicFiles. The feature SecureFile has arrived as a superset of LOBs in Oracle. Consequently, older LOBs, alias BasicFiles, can be smoothly migrated to SecureFiles. Hereby, we shall refer to older LOBs as BasicFiles only:

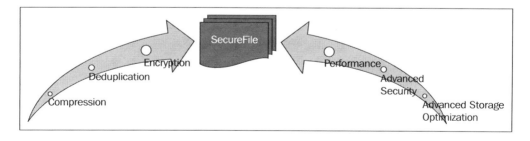

The SecureFile feature fuels up the database paradigms with advanced security and advanced storage options. A SecureFile can be independently enabled for transparent encryption, compression, and deduplication which contribute to its security and intelligence. The best part of SecureFiles is that, now no more different modeling strategies have to be adopted for structured data (relational) and nonstructured data (large objects). With SecureFiles, the application can manage relational and large object data under a single data model, single security model, and with uniform data management principles.

SecureFile LOB—an overview

The term SecureFile barely declares its objective that is, securing files within the database. Though storing files in the database was possible in earlier versions of Oracle too, the enhancement in Oracle 11*g* directs the focus to the enhanced storage scheme and packed security policy. Oracle 11*g* aims and works with a high level content management strategy to maintain the enterprise data. The enterprise data can come in a structured or unstructured form. This unification of data management architecture (rather re-architecture) has staged-up the storage platforms for large objects and relational data in the database. In this section, we will discuss certain architectural enhancements which build up SecureFiles for high performance, efficient storage, tight security, and convenient manageability:

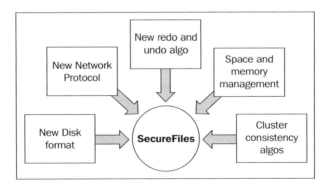

Architectural enhancements in SecureFiles

SecureFiles provide a wide infrastructure in the Oracle database to ensure secure storage of all enterprise content. Notice that it does not resolve any LOB failures but strengthens the storage mechanism of large objects in the Oracle database. This strength of SecureFiles lies in its architectural enhancements. Let us take a brief glance on the architectural components:

- **Write Gather Cache (WGC)**: A new cache memory component caches the SecureFile data up to 4 MB before writing the data on the disk. The cached data is flushed-off either during COMMIT operations or implicitly by the Oracle sever before the cache limit is reached. The WGC component is a part of the buffer cache. The WGC enhancement optimizes the space allocation of the LOB files inside the database (on the disk) and reduces the LOB write time by retaining it in the buffer.

[ A transaction uses only one WGC for all SecureFiles.]

- **Transformation management**: The LOB transformation features are ensured by the advanced compression and security options. The advanced compression option implements deduplication and compression features, while the advanced security option guarantees encryption of the LOB data.

- **Variable** CHUNK **size**: The fixed CHUNK size was a major drawback of BasicFiles. The uniform CHUNK size used to work well for smaller data but it failed for large sized files. Subject to the frequency of read operations, a large file can be downloaded multiple times and a small fixed CHUNK size could fragment the LOB data. SecureFiles uses variable CHUNK size (specified by the user) for storage and reading purposes of SecureFiles which internally allocates variable space on the disk depending on the file size.

- **Enhanced Inode and Space management**: SecureFiles could be staged only on **Automatic Segment Space Management (ASSM)** tablespaces. The Inode manager initiates the LOB data storage activity and requests the ondisk space to hold the data. Space management takes care of allocation and de-allocation of disk space. The Dynamic Space Manager intelligently handles the allocation operations. It can block an allocation for write operations or gathering up the space released from delete actions.

- **Prefetching**: The fact looks intelligent that the LOB data would be prefetched before the actual request has been made. This is made possible by maintaining the file access patterns for each file. Based upon the access frequency, the LOB data is fetched before the request. This intellectual upgrade improves performance of the read operation and avoids network congestion during read requests.

- **No LOB index and high water mark contention**: Unlike the participation of the LOB index in BasicFiles, SecureFiles do not have any index association for access navigation and space allocation operations. It might hit the performance in **online transaction processing (OLTP)** environments, but SecureFiles have eliminated such possibilities by cutting off the dependency on the LOB indexes. SecureFiles deploy the data blocks itself for the LOB operations.

  Similarly, if an LOB data is deleted, the freed space will be claimed by the Oracle server automatically. For this reason, SecureFiles are not impacted from the high water mark contention.

Besides the above architectural considerations, few enhancements were made regarding the transfer of the LOB data over the network channel. A new network protocol would now shoulder the responsibility of reading and writing the LOB data in bulk directly between the client and the server. In addition, the parameter specification list has been reduced by strengthening the internal implementation of the SecureFiles. The setting of FREELIST, FREELIST GROUPS, PCTVERSION, and FREEPOOLS is not required to make the SecureFiles an intelligent self-managed feature.

The following graphs compare the performance of the SecureFile against the BasicFile. In these graphs, the file size has been mapped against the Network Transfer Rate.

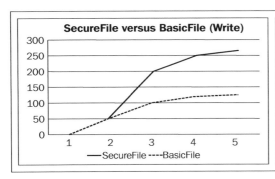 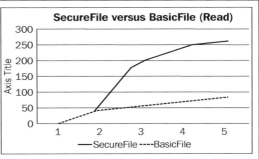

These graphs conclude that performance of write operations for large files can be improved by three times with SecureFiles. Similarly, the read performance of the LOB data can be raised by four times with SecureFiles.

SecureFile LOB features

Apart from the logical features, the practical features are as follows:

- SecureFiles are supported in Oracle versions in and above the compatibility 11.1 and offers wide range capabilities such as deduplication, compression, encryption, logging, and version maintenance as expected from a filesystem. Note that deduplication and compression features are the part of the licensed Oracle advanced compression option.

- SecureFiles support **Transparent Data Encryption** (TDE) which was not available with older LOBs. Note that the encryption feature is part of the licensed Oracle advanced security option.

- The SecureFile feature is governed by a system initialization parameter db_securefile. The admissible values of the parameter can be PERMITTED, ALWAYS, FORCE, NEVER, and IGNORE.

- SecureFiles can be created only on the ASSM tablespace. By default, Oracle 11*g* enables ASSM in all its tablespaces. Check the value of the column SEGMENT_SPACE_MANAGEMENT in DBA_TABLESPAES view to determine the type [AUTO | MANUAL] setting of a tablespace.

- Besides the basic logging options, LOGGING and NOLOGGING, a new logging level called FILESYSTEM_LIKE_LOGGING, has been introduced exclusively for SecureFile LOBs to log only metadata changes. The new logging level allows for the recovery of LOB segments during database failures.

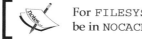 For FILESYSTEM_LIKE_LOGGING, SecureFile LOB must be in NOCACHE mode.

- Older LOBs, that is BasicFiles, can be migrated to SecureFiles using Online Redefinition or the Partition method. The SecureFile features cannot be imposed upon an existing database column or a partition.

- SecureFiles are easily accessible from client interfaces too (using JDBC/ODBC).

- SecureFiles can be integrated with XML DB, Oracle Spatial, Oracle Multimedia, and Oracle UCM.

Working with SecureFiles

Before discussing the implementation of advanced features in SecureFiles, we will see the creation of a SecureFile. The LOB clause makes the difference in the CREATE TABLE statement and decides whether the LOB has to behave as a BasicFile or SecureFile.

The interpreting behavior of the Oracle server depends upon a newly introduced parameter called db_securefile. It can accept the values as follows:

- PERMITTED: This value allows DBA to create SecureFiles in the system of appropriate compatibility that is 11.1 and higher. It is the default value setting for the db_securefile parameter.

- ALWAYS: Apart from normal SecureFiles, all BasicFiles on ASSM tablespaces are also treated as SecureFiles. But BasicFiles, which are created on a non-ASSM tablespace, are still BasicFiles.

- FORCE: All LOB columns (both with SecureFile and BasicFile specifications) are forced to be created as SecureFiles only. It does not allow any LOB column to be created on a non-ASSM tablespace.

- NEVER: This value restricts the creation of SecureFiles.

- IGNORE: It ignores the creation of SecureFiles. All LOB columns are created as BasicFiles.

The parameter can be set using ALTER [SYSTEM | SESSION] command. For new installations, the parameter must be set as ALWAYS, as shown in the following code snippet:

```
CONN sys/system as SYSDBA
Connected.
ALTER SYSTEM SET DB_SECUREFILE=ALWAYS
/
System altered
```

Similarly, in SESSION, the SecureFile feature can be enabled, as shown in the following code snippet:

```
ALTER SESSION SET DB_SECUREFILE=PERMITTED
/
```

Once the parameter is set, the Oracle server gets adapted to the appropriate behavior. The LOB clause in the CREATE TABLE statements has undergone the following modification:

```
LOB(COLUMN_NAME)
STORE AS [SECUREFILE | BASICFILE]
{STORAGE PARAMETERS [DUPLICATE | COMPRESS | ENCRYPTION]}
```

From the syntax you can see that there are three new parameters to explicitly define the intelligence level of the Oracle server. The advanced features such as compression, deduplication, and encryption has to be specified in the LOB storage clause. By default, the features are disabled.

The CREATE TABLE statement creates a table called EMP_LOB_SECFILE which includes an image and profile of an employee. Note the LOB specification as a SecureFile. By default, the LOB segments are staged at the default tablespace for the current user. However, a different ASSM-enabled tablespace can be specified against the LOB storage clause.

Let us first check the current settings of the db_securefile parameter at the database server:

```
/*Connect as sysdba*/
CONN sys/system as SYSDBA
Connected.
/*Check the current setting of db_securefile*/
show parameter db_securefile

NAME                                 TYPE         VALUE
------------------------------------ ------------ ------------
db_securefile                        string       PERMITTED
```

Execute the CREATE TABLE script in the ORADEV user:

```
/*Connect as ORADEV user*/
CONN ORADEV/ORADEV
Connected.
/*Create the table with SecureFile option*/
CREATE  TABLE EMP_LOB_SECFILE
(
  empid NUMBER,
  deptno NUMBER,
  image BLOB,
  profile CLOB
)
```

```
LOB(image) STORE AS SECUREFILE
LOB (profile) STORE AS SECUREFILE
/
Table created.
```

Now, let us see how the Oracle server maintains the SecureFile metadata.

SecureFile metadata

The SECUREFILE column in DBA_LOBS determines whether the LOB column is a SecureFile or BasicFile:

```
/*Connect as sysdba*/
CONN sys/system as SYSDBA
Connected.
/*Query the DBA_LOBS for the new table*/
SELECT
  column_name,
  segment_name,
  encrypt,
  compression,
  deduplication,
  securefile
FROM DBA_LOBS
WHERE table_name='EMP_LOB_SECFILE'
/
```

COLUMN_NAME	SEGMENT_NAME	ENCR	COMPRE	DEDUPLICATION	SEC
IMAGE	SYS_LOB0000080854C00003$$	NO	NO	NO	YES
PROFILE	SYS_LOB0000080854C00004$$	NO	NO	NO	YES

Now, the above segment can be queried in the DBA_SEGMENTS dictionary view as follows:

```
/*Connect as sysdba*/
CONN sys/system AS SYSDBA
Connected.
/*Query the segment view for SecureFile LOB segment*/
SELECT
  owner,
  segment_type,
  segment_subtype,
```

```
    tablespace_name
FROM DBA_SEGMENTS
WHERE segment_name='SYS_LOB0000080854C00004$$'
/


OWNER        SEGMENT_TYPE          SEGMENT_SU   TABLESPACE_NAME
----------   ------------------    ----------   ----------------
ORADEV       LOBSEGMENT            SECUREFILE   USERS
```

Note the value of the `segment_subtype` column in the view. It reflects the purpose behind the creation of a segment for a SecureFile. The `USERS` tablespace is the default ASSM-enabled tablespace of the `ORADEV` user. The violation of this rule raises the following exception:

```
ORA-43853: SECUREFILE lobs cannot be used in non-ASSM tablespace
"Tablespace_Name"
```

Besides the above dictionary views, SecureFile metadata for partitions can be queried from `DBA_PART_LOBS` and `DBA_LOB_PARTITIONS`.

The read/write operations on the SecureFile columns are exactly the same as described earlier. It involves creation of a database directory object, LOB locator, and LOB data. It has been already demonstrated in the last chapter.

Enabling advanced features in SecureFiles

As we learned earlier in this chapter, the SecureFiles implementation has been highly focused to raise storage and security levels. The transformation management features—deduplication, compression, and encryption—are exclusively available for SecureFiles. Thus, they get added-up to the database advanced compression and security features. Let us pick up these features individually, demonstrate their working, and learn their impacts.

Deduplication

With this feature enabled for the SecureFile, the Oracle server prevents the duplication of the LOB data in a table or a partition. The Intelligent LOB Manager in Oracle 11*g* maintains a unique secure hash for all the files. An incoming LOB data is checked against all the available secure hash codes. If the match is successful, the hash code reference is retained against the table row. Thus, multiple insert attempts of a single file in the database are detected and a single copy is stored in the database. On an unsuccessful match, the LOB data is stored on the disk.

The deduplication feature improves the write operations and demonstrates the optimized disk space management. Imagine that the performance boosts up when one has to make 10 copies of each of the available files in the database and there are no physical write operations on the disk. Refer to the following screenshot:

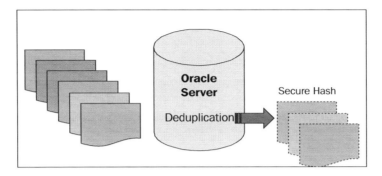

The feature can be enabled by including the DEDUPLICATE | KEEP_DUPLICATES keyword in the LOB storage clause. An existing SecureFile column can be modified to enable or disable the deduplication feature:

```
ALTER TABLE [TABLE NAME]
MODIFY LOB (COLUMN NAME)
(KEEP_DUPLICATES | DEDUPLICATE)
```

The DEDUPLICATE keyword enables the feature while KEEP_DUPLICATES disables it. Its working is transparent to the users. Let us enable the deduplication feature in the EMP_LOB_SECFILE table for the IMAGE column:

```
ALTER TABLE emp_lob_secfile
MODIFY LOB(image) (DEDUPLICATE)
/

Table altered.
```

Compression

The SecureFile compression feature introduces server-side compression of the unstructured data. Once again, like deduplication, the feature is a member of Oracle's advanced compression options. The Oracle server is intelligent enough to perceive the benefits of the SecureFile compression. If the impact can make a big difference in storage management, the LOB data is compressed. Otherwise, compression is disabled for the LOB data and is stored as actual. The compression feature brings in reduced I/O on the disk, minimal overhead of encryption, and redo generation.

Table compression plays no role in the SecureFile compression.

The compression feature can be enabled by specifying the COMPRESS [degree] during the SecureFile specification in the CREATE TABLE statement. Alternatively, an existing column can be modified using the ALTER TABLE statement as follows:

```
ALTER TABLE [TABLE NAME]
MODIFY LOB (COLUMN NAME)
(
    [COMPRESS {HIGH | MEDIUM | LOW} | NOCOMPRESS]
)
```

The COMPRESS keyword enables the server-side compression to use industry-standard compression algorithms. The compression degree [HIGH | MEDIUM] is responsible for latency in the data. MEDIUM is the default compression level. The NOCOMPRESS mode disables the feature for the upcoming LOB data.

The PROFILE column in EMP_LOB_SECFILE can be compressed at the highest degree as follows:

```
ALTER TABLE emp_lob_secfile
MODIFY LOB(profile) (COMPRESS HIGH)
/

Table altered.
```

Encryption

For the first time, large objects in the database can be encrypted under **transparent data encryption** (TDE) algorithm. The advanced security feature encrypts the data (at the block level), backup, and redo file on the disk. The database maintains the encryption keys which are independent of the applications. The SecureFile supports the following encryption algorithms:

- **3DES168**: Triple data encryption standard with 168 bit key size
- **AES128**: Advanced data encryption standard with 128 bit key size
- **AES192** (default): Advanced data encryption standard with 192 bit key size
- **AES256**: Advanced data encryption standard with 256 bit key size

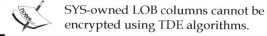 SYS-owned LOB columns cannot be encrypted using TDE algorithms.

A table can be altered to enable the encryption of a LOB column:

```
ALTER TABLE [TABLE NAME]
MODIFY LOB (COLUMN NAME)
(
   [ENCRYPT USING {ALGORITHM NAME} | DECRYPT]
)
OR
ALTER TABLE [TABLE NAME]
MODIFY
(
   Column_Name [ENCRYPT USING {ALGORITHM NAME} | DECRYPT]
)
```

The ENCRYPT keyword enables the encryption while the DECRYPT option disables it. A column can be encrypted only once.

The TDE algorithm is an encryption system which encrypts the column's value with a confidential key. An encrypted key can hold multiple encrypted columns of the same table. There exists a second level of security where the column keys are again encrypted with the database's master key. But note that none of the keys are stored in the database. They reside within an Oracle wallet. An encryption wallet has to be set as an external security module before enabling the feature for the LOB column. The steps to encrypt the SecureFiles in a system are as follows:

1. Creating a wallet directory:

    Create the wallet directory (C:\ExternalSecurity\Wallets\) to store the TDE wallet. The default wallet directory is $ORACLE_HOME\admin\ [global_db_name]\wallet\. Oracle manages the default wallet location implicitly. However, a new wallet working directory can be created to explicitly manage the wallet operations and encryption activities.

    It is the wallet location which is interpreted during the encryption process.

2. Editing the SQLNET.ora file:

    Add the ENCRYPTION_WALLET_LOCATION entry in the SQLNET.ora file. The SQLNET.ora file can be found at $ORACLE_HOME\network\admin\ directory. Take a backup and register the net setting, as shown in the following code snippet, for the encryption location. This step is required only if a nondefault wallet directory has been created.

The DIRECTORY parameter value must be set as the wallet directory path created in the step 1:

```
ENCRYPTION_WALLET_LOCATION=
(
  SOURCE=(METHOD=FILE)
  (
    METHOD_DATA= (DIRECTORY= <<Wallet location>>)
  )
)
```

3. Reloading the Listener using the RELOAD command to adopt the SQLNET changes:

```
C:\>LSNRCTL
LSNRCTL for 32-bit Windows: Version 11.2.0.1.0 - Production on 15-
JAN-2012 23:07:21
Copyright (c) 1991, 2010, Oracle.  All rights reserved.
Welcome to LSNRCTL, type "help" for information.
LSNRCTL> RELOAD
Connecting to (DESCRIPTION=(ADDRESS=(PROTOCOL=IPC)
(KEY=EXTPROC1521)))
The command completed successfully
LSNRCTL>
```

4. Logging in as SYSDBA to set the encryption key and its password:

    The ALTER SYSTEM command generates a new wallet at the wallet location. This command will also open the wallet by default and make it ready for use:

```
/*Connect as sysdba*/
CONN sys/system as SYSDBA
Connected.

/*Alter the SYSTEM to set the encryption key*/
ALTER system SET ENCRYPTION KEY IDENTIFIED BY "mywallets"
/

System altered.
```

Once the encryption key is set, the **ewallet.p12** file is generated in the **Wallets** directory. It results into generation of a new master key which is now the active master key. It resides within the wallet along with the earlier inactive master keys:

One can explicitly open the wallet using the following command:

```
/*Alter the SYSTEM to open the encryption wallet*/
ALTER system SET ENCRYPTION WALLET OPEN IDENTIFIED BY "mywallets"
/

System altered.
```

The wallet directory location and current status can be queried from V$ENCRYPTION_WALLET:

```
/*Connect as sysdba*/
Conn sys/system as sysdba
Connected.

/*Query the wallet information*/
SQL> SELECT *
  FROM v$encryption_wallet
/

WRL_TYPE    WRL_PARAMETER                                       STATUS
----------  --------------------------------------------------  ----------
file        C:\ExternalSecurity\Wallets                         OPEN
```

5. Altering the table to encrypt the SecureFile:

```
/*Connect to ORADEV user*/
Conn ORADEV/ORADEV
Connected
/*Alter the table to encrypt the IMAGE column*/
ALTER TABLE emp_lob_secfile
MODIFY
(
  image ENCRYPT USING 'AES192'
)
/

Table altered.
```

The encrypted columns can be verified by querying the Oracle data dictionary view USER_ENCRYPTED_COLUMNS:

```
/*Query the table to verify the encrypted column details*/
SQL> SELECT column_name, encryption_alg, salt
FROM USER_ENCRYPTED_COLUMNS
WHERE table_name='EMP_LOB_SECFILE';

COLUMN_NAME                      ENCRYPTION_ALG                SAL
-------------------------------- ----------------------------- ---
IMAGE                            AES 192 bits key              YES
```

The table carrying the encrypted column(columns) cannot participate in a conventional export or import process. But the data pump rescues the situation by supporting encrypted exports and imports.

Migration from BasicFiles to SecureFiles

The older LOBs are archived under the BasicFiles category. Note that they are not extinct or obsolete, but are less effective after the induction of the SecureFiles feature. A new system can adopt the SecureFiles as a new table or a new partition. What about the older data which follows costly implementation and has no security? It must inherit the new philosophy, so as to unify the system in terms of data security and management. For this reason, several migration techniques have been jotted-out to upgrade the BasicFile data to the SecureFile. We will briefly discuss these methods:

- **Online Redefinition method**: It is one of the highly recommended methods to move the BasicFile data. A table or a partition of a table can be redefined to achieve the migration from the BasicFile to the SecureFile. It is a secure and convenient method where the database remains up during the complete process.

- **Partition method**: Usually, this method is preferred in low prioritized environments where older LOB data can be axed for performance. The two migration strategies under this method are as follows:
    - **New SecureFile partition**: A new partition with SecureFile specifications can be added to a partitioned table so as to reap the feature benefits in future. Older partitions can still hold the LOB data as a BasicFile.
    - **Create a new partitioned table**: If the source table is a non partitioned one, a new partitioned table can be created with two partitions. The first partition holds the older LOB data as a BasicFile while the second partition holds the new LOB data as a SecureFile.

Within the scope of this chapter, we will discuss the Online Redefinition method.

Online Redefinition method

The Online Redefinition method is a highly preferred method for the BasicFile to the SecureFile migration. It employs the Oracle built-in package DBMS_REDEFINITION to achieve the purpose. While the redefinition process is alive, the advanced compression and security operations are carried out simultaneously during the process. Let us illustrate a case where we will move the BasicFile LOB data to SecureFiles.

During this process, we will create a new table with the desired configuration and specification (SecureFile and its advanced options). On the completion of this process, we can find our original table which has been redefined in synchronization with the new table. The table properties have been exchanged and the newly created table can now be dropped or retained for the backup options.

Pre-requisites of the Online Redefinition method:

- The Online Redefinition process requires free space on the disk (at least equal to the source table to be migrated).
- The original table (source) must have a primary key.
- The source and target tables must have the same structure.
- The target table should not have any indexes.

For demonstration, we will use a table READY_FOR_MIGRATION which stores a CLOB column in the BasicFile orientation. The following code snippet shows the structure and sample data in the table:

```
/*Table structure*/
SQL> DESC ready_for_migration

Name                    Null?       Type
-----------------       --------    -----------
ID                      NOT NULL    NUMBER
DOC                                 CLOB

/*Sample data*/
SQL> SELECT * FROM ready_for_migration;

        ID    DOC
----------    -------------
         1    Oracle 9i
         2    Oracle 10g
         3    Oracle 11g
```

The steps to migrate the LOB columns of the table READY_FOR_MIGRATION to SecureFiles are as follows:

1. Verifying the BasicFile nature of READY_FOR_MIGRATION:

```
/*Query the USER_LOBS view to check the status of LOB column*/
SELECT column_name, securefile
FROM user_lobs
WHERE table_name='READY_FOR_MIGRATION'
/

COLUMN_NAM     SEC
---------- -----
DOC            NO
```

2. Creating a table to support the migration activity:

   Now, let us migrate its data into our SecureFiles table TARGET_FOR_MIGRA-TION which has the same structure as the READY_FOR_MIGRATION table. Verify the SecureFile feature from the dictionary view:

```
/*Table structure*/
CREATE TABLE target_for_migration
(id NUMBER,
 doc CLOB)
 LOB(doc) STORE AS SECUREFILE
 /

Table created.

/*Query the USER_LOBS view to check the status of LOB column*/
SQL> SELECT column_name, securefile
     FROM user_lobs
     WHERE table_name='TARGET_FOR_MIGRATION';

COLUMN_NAM     SEC
---------- -----
DOC            YES
```

3. Starting the redefinition process using the DBMS_REDEFINITION package:

```
/*Login as SYSDBA*/
Conn sys/system as SYSDBA
Connected.

/*Start the PL/SQL block*/
DECLARE
L_ERROR PLS_INTEGER := 0;
BEGIN
```

```
/*Specify source and target tables for redefinition*/
  DBMS_REDEFINITION.START_REDEF_TABLE
  ('ORADEV', 'READY_FOR_MIGRATION', 'TARGET_FOR_MIGRATION',
  'id id,
  doc doc');

/*Specify source and target tables for copying the dependents*/
  DBMS_REDEFINITION.COPY_TABLE_DEPENDENTS
  ('ORADEV', 'READY_FOR_MIGRATION', 'TARGET_FOR_MIGRATION',1,
  true,true,true,false, L_ERROR);
  DBMS_OUTPUT.PUT_LINE('Errors := ' || TO_CHAR(L_ERROR));

/*Finish the redefinition process*/
  DBMS_REDEFINITION.FINISH_REDEF_TABLE
  ('ORADEV', 'READY_FOR_MIGRATION', 'TARGET_FOR_MIGRATION');
END;
/

PL/SQL procedure successfully completed.
```

Use `DBMS_REDEFINITION.ABORT_REDEF_TABLE` to abort the redefinition process of a table, if you encounter `ORA-23539: table "ORADEV"."READY_FOR_MIGRATION" currently being redefined` exception.

4. Verifying the `SECUREFILE` property for the `READY_FOR_MIGRATION` table:

```
/*Query the USER_LOBS view to check the status of LOB column*/
SQL> SELECT column_name, securefile
FROM USER_LOBS
WHERE TABLE_NAME='READY_FOR_MIGRATION'
/

COLUMN_NAME             SEC
-------------------- ---
DOC                     YES

/*Verify the data*/
SQL> SELECT * FROM READY_FOR_MIGRATION;
       ID   DOC
---------- -------------
        1   Oracle 9i
        2   Oracle 10g
        3   Oracle 11g
```

Now `READY_FOR_MIGRATION` has been migrated from the BasicFile to the SecureFile storage. The `TARGET_FOR_MIGRATION` table inherits the table properties from the original table during the redefinition. Its LOB columns now follow BasicFile orientation. Now, check the LOB column type in the table:

```
/*Query the USER_LOBS view to check the status of LOB column*/
SQL> SELECT column_name, securefile
FROM USER_LOBS
WHERE TABLE_NAME='TARGET_FOR_MIGRATION'
/

COLUMN_NAME              SEC
-------------------      ---
DOC                      NO
```

The Online Redefinition method is a verified and trusted method to migrate older LOB data to SecureFiles. It does not hamper the work in progress as the redefinition can be achieved while the table and database is online.

Summary

This chapter explained a new orientation of LOB handling in Oracle. It is introduced in Oracle 11*g* R1 and known as SecureFile. The chapter explained the concept and its architectural enhancements. We learned the working of SecureFiles and its advanced features. We understood the enabling of the compression, deduplication, and encryption features. Finally, we covered the migration of BasicFile LOBs to SecureFile LOBs to reap the benefits of a sparking feature.

Since implementation of a filesystem in the database is not limited with the introduction of Oracle SecureFiles, further reading should be continued to realize the strengths and application of SecureFiles. Implications of SecureFiles can be observed in RAC environments, information lifecycle management, **database filesystem (DBFS)**, and content management schemes. Further reading can be continued from the following links:

- http://www.oracle.com/technology/products/database/oracle11g/pdf/advanced-compression-whitepaper.pdf
- http://www.oracle.com/technology/obe/11gr1_db/datamgmt/securefile/securefile.htm
- http://www.oracle.com/technology/products/database/securefiles/index.html

In the next chapter, we will learn the compilation techniques in Oracle and multiple performance tuning tips.

Practice exercise

1. Which of the following are true statements about the SecureFiles?

    a. It requires ASSM-enabled tablespace.

    b. A BFILE type column in a table can be declared as SecureFiles.

    c. A SecureFile is not affected by the LOB index contention.

    d. SecureFiles use a new cache component of the buffer cache to hold the LOB data.

2. Identify the incorrect statement about the compression feature in SecureFiles.

    a. Compression might hit performance during the LOB write operation.

    b. Compression of SecureFiles is a part of the advanced compression feature in Oracle.

    c. Possible degrees of compression can be MEDIUM and HIGH.

    d. Oracle compresses all the LOB data at high priority, if the feature has been enabled for a SecureFile.

3. The compression feature can be enabled only for encrypted SecureFiles.

    a. True

    b. False

4. A compressed table having a SecureFile column will automatically enable compression for SecureFiles.

    a. True

    b. False

5. Identify the true statements about the deduplication feature of SecureFiles.

    a. KEEP_DUPLICATES is the default option.

    b. DEDUPLICATE retains one copy of the duplicate LOB data.

    c. The deduplication feature hits the performance in write operations as the server compares the secure hash code with the available hash codes before writing to the disk.

    d. Deduplication of files is performed on the basis of the filenames.

6. Pick the correct statement for the encryption feature in the SecureFile.

   a. SecureFile encryption keys are stored within the table.

   b. SecureFile encryption keys are stored within the database.

   c. SecureFile encryption keys are stored outside the database.

   d. Encryption algorithms cannot be modified for an encrypted SecureFile column.

7. Which of the following statements are true for the BasicFile to the SecureFile migration in oracle?

   a. BasicFile to the SecureFile migration can be done through data pump operation.

   b. Table redefinition is preferred as it does the migration with all the resources connected online.

   c. The DBMS_REDEFINITION package can migrate only one LOB column at a time.

   d. Unnecessary space consumption makes the redefinition process less preferable over partition method.

8
Compiling and Tuning to Improve Performance

The code compilation philosophy is one of the transparent activities in a programming language which latently influences a program's execution performance. Oracle 11*g* has introduced the real native compilation to cope with the bitter experiences of native and interpreted compilation techniques. Besides the compiler enhancement, Oracle 11*g* has introduced a new optimization level which brings terrific improvements in database performance by fueling up the optimizer's intelligence. Furthermore, the intra unit inlining feature applies an optimization level to assure logical gains in PL/SQL code performance by inlining local subprogram invocations in program calls. In this chapter, we will learn the best practices and recommendations to improvise upon the PL/SQL code performance. The topics to be covered in this chapter are as follows:

- Compiler enhancements
    - Native and interpreted compilation — background
    - Real native compilation in PL/SQL

- Tuning PL/SQL code
- Intra unit inlining
- Effect of `PLSQL_OPTIMIZE_LEVEL`
- `PRAGMA INLINE`

Native and interpreted compilation techniques

In basic terms, a language compiler converts the program code (in high level language) to a machine code (also known as M code or byte code), which can be understood by the machine runtime engine. Once the database is installed and ready for use, code compilation turns out to be a transparent activity to the users.

Until the release of Oracle9*i*, Oracle relied on an interpretable method of compilation of its database program units. A compiler in interpreted mode converts a PL/SQL program into machine code, stores in the database, and interprets upon its invocation. Oracle9*i* brought the revolutionary change in the compilation philosophy by introducing native compilation. But a question popped up amongst the DBAs and developers, "Is native compilation really more effective than an interpreted compilation?" An interpreted mode of compilation was not supported by RAC and backups.

It was the time when Oracle identified code compilation technique as a potential area of research and enhancement. Subsequently, Oracle 10*g* made underlying changes in native compilation with the use of C compiler. Native compilation now uses C compiler to convert the PL/SQL program into a C code, generates sharable library (DLL), and places them in the database catalog. In Oracle 10*g*, native compilation supports RAC environments. For database backups, the libraries are required to be mounted in a filesystem for the operating system utilities. The filesystem staging was being carried out with the help of the initialization parameters, PLSQL_NATIVE_LIBRARY_DIR and PLSQL_NATIVE_LIBRARY_SUBDIR_COUNT, which were set by the DBA. It was well-received but could not convincingly respond to the floating question.

Both the compilation processes follow almost similar paths but the major difference between the two is the code scanning. In the interpreted mode, the code scanning process is carried out during runtime, while in native mode it is carried out at the time of the compilation itself. This shifting of the code scanning process credits to the runtime performance of a natively compiled program unit by some extent, depending upon the code size and implementation. One cannot promise the performance of a natively compiled code over interpreted in all cases.

Note that the PL/SQL compilation has employed the services of C compiler to generate C code and link it to a sharable library module. Though the native compilation has been technically accepted, the reliability and reluctance with the C compiler (for which production databases have been reluctant to pay licenses) on production servers has daunted the users. In addition, maintenance of multiple compilation initialization parameters used to be a cumbersome job for DBAs.

Oracle 11*g* has reformed the native compilation as real native compilation with minimal settings.

Real native compilation

For the previously mentioned reasons, Oracle introduced real native compilation in Oracle 11*g*. The real native compilation technique compiles the PL/SQL program code directly into DLLs and stores the native machine code in the SYSTEM tablespace. In this way, the step where libraries are to be mounted on a filesystem has been bypassed. Whenever the program is invoked for the first time in a session, the corresponding machine code is placed in the shared memory. Thereafter, it can be readily invoked and used.

Let us examine the accomplishments of real native compilation:

- There is no dependency on C Compiler.
- Native byte code is stored in the SYSTEM tablespace.
- No sharable DLL is involved. So, no filesystem is required for DLL.
- Configuration works with a single parameter called PLSQL_CODE_TYPE [native/interpreted].
- In the INTERPRETED mode, the PL/SQL code is compiled to the equivalent byte code. At runtime, the PL/SQL interpreter engine executes them.
- In NATIVE mode, the PL/SQL code is compiled to the machine code. At runtime, the machine code is executed natively by the database server.
- Better runtime performance, two times faster than C native compilation. The interesting fact is that the selection of the compilation scheme depends upon the database development phase.
- Real native is used for PL/SQL codes. A program with an SQL statement might not yield the best performance but not the worst too.
- Real native compilation mode can be set at system level, session level, and object level. A natively compiled program unit can call an interpreted program and vice versa.

Selecting the appropriate compilation mode

The appropriate selection of the compilation mode is a crucial activity of a DBA. The question, "Native or interpreted?", hovers across the phases of the database development cycle which has to be intelligently handled by the administrator. The reason why this question pops up here is because of the demands at each stage. During the development phase, the program units are frequently debugged, compiled, and tested. Therefore, code compilation is expected to be fast. Program units compile faster in interpreted mode because the partially compiled code is interpreted at runtime. Similarly, during the post development stage, the program units are compiled and tested and it is the time to pay off the efforts in the development stage. Program unit execution is expected to be fast. Natively compiled units execute faster than those compiled in interpreted mode. Thus, native compilation mode is suitable for the post development stage.

Summarizing up this explanation, native mode aims to boost up the program execution time and interpreted mode raises the code compilation performance.

Usually, the setting can be made in the design phase and modified in the development stages. The active development stage of the database and the programmable logic are decisive for the selection of the exact compilation mode. For this reason, the compilation modes share intercompatibility—program units compiled in different compilation modes can exist together in a schema and invoke each other, as required. Since the compilation modes affect the execution time, these calls do not make any impact on the performance.

When to choose interpreted compilation mode?

The interpreted mode of compilation is preferred in the development stage of the database cycle. It is the stage where the program units are recompiled frequently to test various scenarios. Here, the strengths of a debugger are more desirable than the execution speed of a program. There might be cases to debug the code at optimization level 0 or 1, where native compilation is passive. The interpreted compilation mode is faster than the native mode compilation. Execution performance of a program can be raised through multiple code tuning techniques. In addition, interpreted mode mostly suits the programs which accommodate multiple SQL statements. The reason is accredited to the proportion of SQL to the interpretations. More number of SQL need more time for interpretation. Since native compilation does interpretation during runtime, it can adversely affect the performance.

When to choose native compilation mode?

The native mode of compilation is preferred when a step is out of the development stage where program compilation is quite rare. It is the stage when the user expects the program execution to be fast. The optimization level and compilation mode are expected to be fixed.

The native compilation mode is mainly for the PL/SQL program units which have computational or transformational logic. A program having plenty of SQL statements might reduce the performance in native mode because of the reason stated in the previous topic. For program units which do not require context switching across the SQL and PL/SQL engines, native compilation could make handy differences in performance.

Setting the compilation mode

The compilation method can be set using the PLSQL_CODE_TYPE parameter. The admissible values for the parameter are INTERPRETED and NATIVE. It can be set using the ALTER SYSTEM or ALTER SESSION statement.

At the Database level, the change is applied to the entire database and it is permenant:

```
ALTER SYSTEM SET PLSQL_CODE_TYPE = [NATIVE | INTERPRETED]
```

At the Session level, the change is applied to the database only for the current session:

```
ALTER SESSION SET PLSQL_CODE_TYPE = [NATIVE | INTERPRETED]
```

The DBA sets the compilation method to be followed in the database by setting the PLSQL_CODE_TYPE initialization parameter:

```
/*Connect as sysdba*/
Conn sys/system as SYSDBA
Connected.
/*Set the PLSQL_CODE_TYPE*/
ALTER SYSTEM SET PLSQL_CODE_TYPE = NATIVE
/

System altered.
```

Whenever the compilation method for the database or session is altered, the programs retain their compilation state until they are recompiled so as to inherit the latest compilation mode. Once they are recompiled, they adopt the current session compilation method.

Querying the compilation settings

Compilation settings can be queried from the data dictionary view [USER | DBA | ALL]_PLSQL_OBJECT_SETTINGS. The dictionary view contains the compilation settings by subprogram. The details include the subprogram TYPE, NAME, PLSQL_CODE_TYPE, and other object level initialization parameters. These parameters are shown in the following code snippet:

```
/*Connect as ORADEV user*/
Conn ORADEV/ORADEV
Connected.
/*Show structure of USER_PLSQL_OBJECT_SETTINGS*/
SQL> desc USER_PLSQL_OBJECT_SETTINGS
```

Name	Null?	Type
NAME	NOT NULL	VARCHAR2(30)
TYPE		VARCHAR2(12)
PLSQL_OPTIMIZE_LEVEL		NUMBER
PLSQL_CODE_TYPE		VARCHAR2(4000)
PLSQL_DEBUG		VARCHAR2(4000)
PLSQL_WARNINGS		VARCHAR2(4000)
NLS_LENGTH_SEMANTICS		VARCHAR2(4000)
PLSQL_CCFLAGS		VARCHAR2(4000)
PLSCOPE_SETTINGS		VARCHAR2(4000)

Let us now query the PLSQL_CODE_TYPE and PLSQL_OPTIMIZE_LEVEL values for the subprograms owned by the ORADEV user:

```
/*Query the compilation settings for ORADEV schema objects*/
SELECT name, type, plsql_code_type, plsql_optimize_level OPTIMIZE
FROM USER_PLSQL_OBJECT_SETTINGS
WHERE type in ('PROCEDURE', 'FUNCTION','PACKAGE','PACKAGE BODY')
/
```

NAME	TYPE	PLSQL_CODE	OPTIMIZE
P_TO_UPPER	PROCEDURE	NATIVE	2
P_SET_CONTEXT	PROCEDURE	NATIVE	2
P_EMP_LOCATION	PROCEDURE	NATIVE	2
PKG_CONTEXTS	PACKAGE BODY	NATIVE	2
PKG_CONTEXTS	PACKAGE	NATIVE	2
PKG_COMPUTEJAVACLASS	PACKAGE BODY	NATIVE	2
PKG_COMPUTEJAVACLASS	PACKAGE	NATIVE	2
F_LOWER	FUNCTION	NATIVE	2
F_GET_SUM	FUNCTION	NATIVE	2

F_GET_DOUBLE	FUNCTION	NATIVE	2
F_GET_DEPT_PREDICATE	FUNCTION	NATIVE	2
F_CONVERT_CASE	FUNCTION	NATIVE	2
F_COMPUTE_SUM	FUNCTION	NATIVE	2
F_CASE_CONVERT	FUNCTION	NATIVE	2
F_ADD	FUNCTION	NATIVE	2
ADD_JOB_HISTORY	PROCEDURE	NATIVE	1

```
17 rows selected.
```

Compiling a program unit for a native or interpreted compilation

In this section, we will illustrate how a program adopts the compilation mode at the object level which is different from the current session compilation mode. The steps are as follows:

1. Querying the current compilation mode of the session:

   ```
   /*Connect as sysdba*/
   Conn sys/system as sysdba
   Connected.
   /*Display current setting of parameter PLSQL_CODE_TYPE*/
   SHOW PARAMETER PLSQL_CODE_TYPE
   ```

NAME	TYPE	VALUE
plsql_code_type	string	INTERPRETED

2. Creating a sample function:

   The function is compiled as per the session's compilation scheme:

   ```
   /*Connect as ORADEV user*/
   SQL> CONN ORADEV/ORADEV
   Connected.
   /*Create a function*/
   SQL> CREATE OR REPLACE FUNCTION F_COMP_INT
     RETURN NUMBER
     IS
     BEGIN
       RETURN 1;
     END;
   /
   Function created.
   ```

3. Verifying the compilation mode used for the F_COMP_INT function:

   Yes, it is found correct as INTERPRETED:

   ```
   /*Query the compilation settings for the function F_COMP_INT*/
   SELECT name, type, plsql_code_type, plsql_optimize_level OPTIMIZE
   FROM USER_PLSQL_OBJECT_SETTINGS
   WHERE name = 'F_COMP_INT'
   /
   ```

NAME	TYPE	PLSQL_CODE_TYPE	OPTIMIZE
F_COMP_INT	FUNCTION	INTERPRETED	2

4. Recompiling the function and specifying the compilation mode:

   ```
   /*Connect as ORADEV*/
   Conn ORADEV/ORADEV
   Connected.
   /*Explicitly compile the function*/
   alter function f_comp_int compile plsql_code_type = NATIVE;

   Function altered.
   ```

5. Querying the compilation settings of the F_COMP_INT function:

   Note that it has been compiled in native mode:

   ```
   /*Query the current compilation settings for the function F_COMP_
   INT*/
   SELECT name, type, plsql_code_type, plsql_optimize_level OPTIMIZE
   FROM USER_PLSQL_OBJECT_SETTINGS
   WHERE name = 'F_COMP_INT'
   /
   ```

NAME	TYPE	PLSQL_CODE_TYPE	OPTIMIZE
F_COMP_INT	FUNCTION	NATIVE	2

Another way of modifying the compilation mode settings can be demonstrated by altering the session settings. Whenever a program unit is compiled, the preferred compilation settings go in the sequence of object, session, and then the database:

```
/*Connect as ORADEV user*/
SQL> conn ORADEV/ORADEV
Connected.
/*Alter the session to set compilation mode as NATIVE*/
SQL> ALTER SESSION SET PLSQL_CODE_TYPE='NATIVE'
/
```

```
Session altered.
/*Compile the procedure so as to inherit the current session
settings*/
SQL> ALTER FUNCTION F_COMP_INT COMPILE
/

Procedure altered.
/*Query the compilation settings for the function F_COMP_INT*/
SELECT name, type, plsql_code_type, plsql_optimize_level OPTIMIZE
FROM USER_PLSQL_OBJECT_SETTINGS
WHERE
name = 'F_COMP_INT'
/


NAME            TYPE          PLSQL_CODE_TYPE   OPTIMIZE
----------      ------------  ----------------  ------------
F_COMP_INT      FUNCTION      NATIVE                 2
```

Compiling the database for PL/SQL native compilation (NCOMP)

During database upgrades from lower versions to Oracle 11*g*, all the program units were required to be recompiled in **native compilation** (**NCOMP**) mode. Oracle provides a script called dbmsupgnv.sql to accomplish the task of compiling all program units in native compilation mode. Note that in case of database version upgrades, the upgraded scripts must be executed prior to dbmsupgnv.sql.

Here we will demonstrate the native recompilation of all program units. The steps of this process are as follows:

1. Shutting down the database:

   Ensure that all connections to the server are terminated and no new connections are established until the upgrade process is completed:

   ```
   /*Connect as SYSDBA*/
   SQL> conn sys/system as sysdba
   Connected.
   /*Shutdown*/
   SQL> shutdown immediate
   Database closed.
   Database dismounted.
   ORACLE instance shut down.
   ```

2. Setting `PLSQL_CODE_TYPE` as `NATIVE` for subsequent compilations:

```
plsql_code_type=native
```

This step is required to set the compilation scheme for the subsequent program units (after upgrade). It is not part of the database native recompilation process. Since, these days, most of the databases work with `spfile.ora` instead of `init.ora`, the setting of `PLSQL_CODE_TYPE` as `NATIVE` can also be done after the upgrade process is completed and the database is started normally. It can be done using the `ALTER SYSTEM` statement:

```
/*Alter the system to set the new compilation mode*/
SQL> ALTER SYSTEM SET PLSQL_CODE_TYPE=NATIVE SCOPE=SPFILE
/

System altered.
```

In addition, ensure that another initialization parameter called `PLSQL_OPTIMIZE_LEVEL` is set as 2 or higher. `PLSQL_OPTIMIZE_LEVEL` is an initialization parameter which enforces a level of optimization (out of an available four levels) to the PL/SQL optimizer and thus, manoeuvres the working profile of the compiler. This parameter was introduced in Oracle 10*g* and saw a major enhancement in Oracle 11*g*. We will discuss it later in this chapter.

3. Starting the database in the UPGRADE mode:

```
/*Startup in upgrade mode*/
SQL> startup upgrade
ORACLE instance started.
Total System Global Area   535662592 bytes
Fixed Size                   1375792 bytes
Variable Size              327156176 bytes
Database Buffers           201326592 bytes
Redo Buffers                 5804032 bytes
Database mounted.
Database opened.
```

Alternatively, the database can be started and mounted normally. Then, it can be opened in the UPGRADE mode as follows:

```
/*Open database in upgrade mode*/
ALTER DATABASE OPEN UPGRADE;
```

4. Executing the `dbmsupgnv.sql` script to recompile all the program units in Native mode:

```
/*Execute the recompilation script*/
SQL> @ORACLE_HOME\rdbms\admin\dbmsupgnv.sql
```

The script creates the native compilation package `sys.dbmsncdb` which provides two subprograms to perform interpreted or native compilation, as required. The `SETUP_FOR_NATIVE_COMPILE` suprogram sets the database for native compilation, while `SETUP_FOR_INTERPRETED_COMPILE` sets the database for interpreted compilation.

Furthermore, the script invalidates all PL/SQL procedures, functions, type bodies, triggers, and type body objects in the database and sets their settings to native.

5. Shutting down and restarting the database:

```
/*Shutdown and startup the database normally*/
SQL> shutdown immediate
Database closed.
Database dismounted.
ORACLE instance shut down.
SQL> startup
ORACLE instance started.
Total System Global Area   535662592 bytes
Fixed Size                   1375792 bytes
Variable Size              327156176 byteDatabase Buffers
201326592 bytes
Redo Buffers                 5804032 bytes
Database mounted.
Database opened.
```

6. Executing the `utlrp.sql` script to recompile invalid objects:

Before running the `utlrp.sql` script to recompile the invalid program units, make sure that no new connections are established with the servers. Cautiously, the session must be a restricted to single connection:

```
SQL> @ORACLE_HOME\rdbms\admin\utlrp.sql
```

The recompilation of the invalidated program units may take a longer time to complete, depending on the schema size. For large databases, the script execution may leave the system on hang for several hours to natively recompile all the program units. The invalidated objects can be queried from the USER_OBJECTS dictionary view. Ideally, the script should recompile all the invalidated program units, but if some objects are left out from the process, the `utlrp.sql` script can be rerun (until all the schema objects get validated).

The native compilation of all the program units can be verified using the SELECT query. In an ideal case, the query should show only the NATIVE value:

```
/*Select object count for each PLSQL_CODE_TYPE*/
SELECT plsql_code_type, count(*)
FROM user_plsql_object_settings
GROUP BY plsql_code_type
/
```

If the system requires moving back to the interpreted compilation scheme, the same steps must be followed, but the dbmsupgnv.sql script has to be replaced with dbmsupgin.sql.

Tuning PL/SQL code

Once the DBA configures the database for optimal performance, the code development plays an essential role in PL/SQL performance. Now, we will discuss certain areas of improvements. These improvements can be made during the development stage so as to avoid the nightmares later.

The tunable areas identified and covered in this section are as follows:

- **Avoiding implicit typecasting**: Identification of appropriate data type
- **Modularizing the programs**: Modular programming and effective code sampling shares the work load
- **Usage of bulk bind collections and the FORALL function** : Usage of the FORALL function and bulk bind collections optimize the bulk operations
- **Optimized conditional statements**: Conditional statements can be optimized by logically placing the conditions

Besides the above areas, there are several other areas where tuning can bring comprehensive changes in performance. There is an immense scope for tuning in the code which uses dynamic SQL, SQL queries in PL/SQL blocks, functions callable from SQL statements, and so on. However, from a certification preparation perspective, we will discuss the listed target areas which focus on improved code writing to improvise upon the code performance.

Comparing SQL and PL/SQL

We are well versed with the facts that SQL is a concrete trivial database interactive language, while PL/SQL is the procedural extension of SQL. Often, we debate on SQL in PL/SQL in terms of performance and embedding strategies. Here, we need to understand the specific strengths of each one of them. SQL is the best recognized language to interact with the database and perform data activities. Its procedural extension gives additional flexibility to deal with most of the real world problems in PL/SQL as a language. The SQL statements use the SQL engine for execution while PL/SQL hits the PL/SQL engine. When a SQL statement is encountered in a PL/SQL program, the context is switched from the PL/SQL engine to SQL engine. The context switching contributes to the performance degradation during the program executions. This implies that a greater number of SQL statements in a PL/SQL program can become hazardous for an application.

But, nevertheless, certain situations cannot be realized without the efficiencies of SQL. In such cases, SQL statements can be included in the PL/SQL program. In this regards, there are certain recommendations which are as follows:

- Avoid embedding of a SQL statement within iterative control structures in PL/SQL such as loops. A single SQL statement might work better in such cases.

- Transactions can be made through an API layer. An API or subroutine can be defined to handle transactions. SQL statements in an executable section can be procedurally enhanced as standalone procedures or a packaged subprogram.

Avoiding implicit data type conversion

The PL/SQL runtime engine can perform an implicit type conversion of values. For example, a numeric value can be assigned to a string variable but not vice versa. Similarly, a date value can be assigned to a string variable but not vice versa. This conversion depends on the compatibility matrix:

	Number	BINARY_INTEGER	BINARY_FLOAT	BINARY_DOUBLE	PLS_INTEGER	CHAR	NCHAR	VARCHAR2	NVARCHAR2	DATE	CLOB	NCLOB
NUMBER	■	✓	✓	✓	✓	✓	✓	✓	✓	X	X	X
BINARY_INTEGER	✓	■	✓	✓	✓	✓	✓	✓	✓	X	X	X
BINARY_FLOAT	✓	✓	■	✓	✓	✓	✓	✓	✓	X	X	X
BINARY_DOUBLE	✓	✓	✓	■	✓	✓	✓	✓	✓	X	X	X
PLS_INTEGER	✓	✓	✓	✓	■	✓	✓	✓	✓	X	X	X
CHAR	✓	✓	✓	✓	✓	■	✓	✓	✓	✓	✓	✓
NCHAR	✓	✓	✓	✓	✓	✓	■	✓	✓	✓	✓	✓
VARCHAR2	✓	✓	✓	✓	✓	✓	✓	■	✓	✓	✓	✓
NVARCHAR2	X	✓	✓	✓	X	✓	✓	✓	■	✓	X	✓
DATE	X	X	X	X	X	✓	✓	✓	✓	■	X	X
CLOB	X	X	X	X	X	✓	✓	✓	✓	X	■	✓
NCLOB	X	X	X	X	X	✓	✓	✓	✓	✓	✓	■

In the previous section, we learned that the Oracle server takes care of implicit type casting. The casting process adds up to its work load at the cost of performance. For this reason, a variable must belong to an appropriate data type to correctly accommodate the value which is assigned to it. Oracle also provides type cast built-in functions which can be used to help the optimizer to hint the type casting. Oracle provides TO_CHAR, TO_NUMBER, and TO_DATE to explicitly mark the conversion of a value.

Let us conduct a small illustration to check the effect of implicit type casting on the code's performance. The PL/SQL block, as shown in the following code snippet, declares a string variable and assigns a numeric value to it in a loop. Here, the Oracle server has to implicitly work upon the type conversion of the numeric value assigned to the string variable. The PLSQL_OPTIMIZE_LEVEL has been set to 1 to capture the precise results:

```
/*Set the PLSQL_OPTIMIZE_LEVEL to 1*/
ALTER SESSION SET PLSQL_OPTIMIZE_LEVEL = 1
/

Session altered.
/*Enable the SERVEROUTPUT to display block results*/
SET SERVEROUTPUT ON
/*Start the PL/SQL block*/
DECLARE
  L_STR VARCHAR2(10);
  L_COUNT NUMBER :=0;
BEGIN
/*Capture the system time before loop*/
  L_COUNT := DBMS_UTILITY.GET_TIME;
  /*Start a loop which assigns fixed numeric value to a local string
variable*/
  FOR I IN 1..1000000
  LOOP
    L_STR := 1;
  END LOOP;
/*Print the time consumed in the operations*/
  DBMS_OUTPUT.PUT_LINE('Time Consumed:'||TO_CHAR(DBMS_UTILITY.GET_TIME
-   L_COUNT));
END;
/

Time Consumed:17
PL/SQL procedure successfully completed.
```

Now, we will assign a string value to the string variable. Oracle has no extra activity except to assign the correct value type to the variable:

```
/*Enable the SERVEROUTPUT to display block results*/
SET SERVEROUTPUT ON
/*Start the PL/SQL block*/
DECLARE
  L_STR VARCHAR2(10);
  L_COUNT NUMBER :=0;
BEGIN
/*Capture the system time before loop*/
  L_COUNT := DBMS_UTILITY.GET_TIME;
  /*Start a loop which assigns fixed string value to a local string
variable*/
  FOR I IN 1..1000000
  LOOP
    L_STR := 'A';
  END LOOP;
/*Print the time consumed in the operations*/
  DBMS_OUTPUT.PUT_LINE('Time Consumed:'||TO_CHAR(DBMS_UTILITY.GET_TIME
-   L_COUNT));
END;
/

Time Consumed:6
PL/SQL procedure successfully completed.
```

Understanding the NOT NULL constraint

We often declare the NOT NULL variables in our program units to shield them against the NULL values in the program. Unknowingly, we pressurize the Oracle server to perform the additional NOT NULL test before each assignment of the particular variable. The overhead significantly affects the performance.

For testing a variable for nullity, Oracle follows a peculiar approach. The server assigns the result of an assignment statement to a temporary variable and checks this temporary variable for nullity. If it returns the true value, exception occurs and block terminates, otherwise the program control proceeds further. Therefore, a variable should never be declared with the NOT NULL constraint. Instead, it can be explicitly checked for nullity in the executable section whenever required. Let us check out how it is done.

You write a utility program in your application to add two numbers. You capture the sum of two numbers in a NOT NULL variable. Ensure that PLSQL_OPTIMIZE_LEVEL is set as 1 to yield clear results:

```
/*Set PLSQL_OPTIMIZE_LEVEL as 1*/
ALTER SESSION SET PLSQL_OPTIMIZE_LEVEL=1
/

Session altered.
/*Enable the SERVEROUTPUT to display block results*/
SET SERVEROUTPUT ON
/*Start the PL/SQL block*/
DECLARE
  L_NUM   NUMBER NOT NULL := 0;
  L_A NUMBER := 10;
  L_COUNT NUMBER;
BEGIN
/*Capture the start time*/
  L_COUNT := DBMS_UTILITY.GET_TIME;
/*Start the loop*/
  FOR I IN 1..1000000
  LOOP
    L_NUM := L_A + I;
  END LOOP;
/*Compute the time difference and display*/
  DBMS_OUTPUT.PUT_LINE('Time Consumed:'||TO_CHAR(DBMS_UTILITY.GET_TIME
-
  L_COUNT));
END;
/

Time Consumed:17
PL/SQL procedure successfully completed.
```

Alternatively, Oracle recommends the explicit handling of NOT NULL as follows:

```
/*Enable the SERVEROUTPUT to display block results*/
SET SERVEROUTPUT ON
/*Start the PL/SQL block*/
DECLARE
  L_NUM   NUMBER;
  L_A NUMBER := 10;
  L_COUNT NUMBER;
BEGIN
/*Capture the start time*/
  L_COUNT := DBMS_UTILITY.GET_TIME;
/*Start the loop*/
  FOR I IN 1..1000000
```

```
  LOOP
    L_NUM := L_A + I;
    IF L_NUM IS NULL THEN
      DBMS_OUTPUT.PUT_LINE('Result cannot be NULL');
      EXIT;
    END IF;
  END LOOP;
/*Compute the time difference and display*/
  DBMS_OUTPUT.PUT_LINE('Time Consumed:'||TO_CHAR(DBMS_UTILITY.GET_TIME
-
  L_COUNT));
END;
/

Time Consumed:12
PL/SQL procedure successfully completed.
```

Note that the time consumed in the second case is 30 percent less than the latter. The difference in the block execution timings illustrates the loss in performance due to the NOT NULL constraint. Similar observations can be made with the NOT NULL subtype of NUMBER that is, NATURALN (NOT NULL NATURAL), POSITIVEN (NOT NULL POSITIVE), and SIMPLE_INTEGER (NOT NULL PLS_INTEGER).

Using the PLS_INTEGER data type for arithmetic operations

The PLS_INTEGER data type, which hails from the number family, was introduced in Oracle 7 to speed up the intensive mathematical operations. It is the only data type which uses native machine arithmetic instead of the C arithmetic library. This makes it faster in arithmetic operations in program units. The 32 bit data type can store values in the range of -2147483648 to 2147483647.

Let us now undertake a case study where we will observe the difference in performance of arithmetic operations using NUMBER and PLS_INTEGER as the data type.

The following PL/SQL block performs addition in iteration:

```
/*Enable the SERVEROUTPUT to display block results*/
SET SERVEROUTPUT ON
/*Start the PL/SQL block*/
DECLARE
  L_NUM NUMBER := 0;
  L_ST_TIME NUMBER;
  L_END_TIME NUMBER;
BEGIN
```

```
/*Capture the start time*/
  L_ST_TIME := DBMS_UTILITY.GET_TIME();
/*Begin the loop to perform a mathematical calculation*/
  FOR I IN 1..100000000
  LOOP
/*The mathematical operation increments a variable by one*/
    L_NUM := L_NUM+1;
  END LOOP;
  L_END_TIME := DBMS_UTILITY.GET_TIME();
/*Display the time consumed*/
  DBMS_OUTPUT.PUT_LINE('Time taken by NUMBER:'||TO_CHAR(L_END_TIME -
L_ST_TIME));
END;
/
Time taken by NUMBER:643
PL/SQL procedure successfully completed.
```

The mathematical operation with the NUMBER data type consumes 643 ms. Now let us replace the NUMBER data type with the PLS_INTEGER data type:

```
/*Enable the SERVEROUTPUT to display block results*/
SET SERVEROUTPUT ON
/*Start the PL/SQL block*/
DECLARE
  L_PLS   PLS_INTEGER := 0;
  L_ST_TIME NUMBER;
  L_END_TIME NUMBER;
BEGIN
/*Capture the start time*/
  L_ST_TIME := DBMS_UTILITY.GET_TIME();
/*Begin the loop to perform a mathematical calculation*/
  FOR I IN 1..100000000
  LOOP
/*The mathematical operation increments a variable by one*/
    L_PLS := L_PLS+1;
  END LOOP;
/*Display the time consumed*/
  L_END_TIME := DBMS_UTILITY.GET_TIME();
  DBMS_OUTPUT.PUT_LINE('Time taken by PLS_INTEGER:'||TO_CHAR(L_END_
TIME -
  L_ST_TIME));
END;
/

Time taken by PLS_INTEGER:196
PL/SQL procedure successfully completed.
```

Note the execution time of the above block. It is almost one third of the execution carried out with the NUMBER data type. The demonstration makes it clear that the PLS_INTEGER data type rules the mathematical operations in PL/SQL.

Using a SIMPLE_INTEGER data type

Oracle 11*g* brings in the SIMPLE_INTEGER data type—a subtype of PLS_INTEGER which is of great use in applications and in the PL/SQL programming. We know it well that the range of the PLS_INTEGER data type is -2147483648 to 2147483647. Beyond its range, the PLS_INTEGER data type would raise the ORA-01426: numeric overflow exception.

The SIMPLE_INTEGER data type leaps a step forward to deal with the numeric overflow scenarios of PLS_INTEGER. The range is the same as that in PLS_INTEGER that is, -2147483648 to 2147483647. It restricts the NULL values and avoids overflow semantics.

 Since no overflow check is done for the SIMPLE_INTEGER data type, it might work faster than the PLS_INTEGER data type.

A small case study would justify the use of SIMPLE_INTEGER in PL/SQL programs. The following PL/SQL block declares a PLS_INTEGER variable and increments it by one. The numeric overflow exception is raised upon the second increment:

```
/*Enable the SERVEROUTPUT to display block results*/
SET SERVEROUTPUT ON
/*Start the PL/SQL block*/
DECLARE
/*Declare a variable of PLS_INTEGER type and initialize it with a
value nearing to its range*/
  l_pls PLS_INTEGER:= 2147483646;
BEGIN
/*Increment the variable by 1*/
  l_pls := l_pls +1;
  DBMS_OUTPUT.PUT_LINE('After 1st increment:'|| l_pls);
/*Re-increment the variable by 1*/
  l_pls := l_pls +1;
  DBMS_OUTPUT.PUT_LINE('After 2nd increment:'|| l_pls);
EXCEPTION
  WHEN OTHERS THEN
    DBMS_OUTPUT.PUT_LINE('Numeric Overflow exception occurred');
END;
/
```

```
After 1st increment:2147483647
Numeric Overflow exception occurred
PL/SQL procedure successfully completed.
```

Now, replace the data type in the preceding block with the SIMPLE_INTEGER data type and observe the output:

```
/*Enable the SERVEROUTPUT to display block results*/
SET SERVEROUTPUT ON
/*Start the PL/SQL block*/
DECLARE
  l_simple SIMPLE_INTEGER:= 2147483646;
BEGIN
/*Increment the variable by 1*/
  l_simple:= l_simple +1;
  DBMS_OUTPUT.PUT_LINE('After 1st increment:'|| l_simple);
/*Re-Increment the variable by 1*/
  l_simple:= l_simple +1;
  DBMS_OUTPUT.PUT_LINE('After 2nd increment:'|| l_simple);
EXCEPTION
  WHEN OTHERS THEN
    DBMS_OUTPUT.PUT_LINE('Numeric Overflow exception occurred');
END;
/

After 1st increment:2147483647
After 2nd increment:-2147483648
PL/SQL procedure successfully completed.
```

 SIMPLE_INTEGER is a NOT NULL data type. A variable of the SIMPLE_INTEGER data type must be initialized with a definite value at the time of declaration.

Modularizing the PL/SQL code

Modular programming is a way of designing and programming the development. It reduces the code redundancy by getting the executable sections cut-short, and promotes module reusability as they can be invoked from other PL/SQL blocks. The module can be a local subprogram in a PL/SQL block or a stored subprogram. It can be a packaged subprogram which can be used as many times as required in a database session.

Check the following example. The PL/SQL block fetches the details of all employees and displays the employees' names along with their working location. For location, a cursor has been declared which would query the DEPARTMENTS table for the input department number:

```
/*Enable the SERVEROUTPUT to display block results*/
SET SERVEROUTPUT ON
/*Start the PL/SQL block*/
DECLARE
/*Declare a cursor to select employee name and department*/
CURSOR c_emp IS
  SELECT ename, deptno
  FROM employees;
/*Declare a cursor to get the location of the department*/
CURSOR c_dept (p_dept NUMBER) IS
  SELECT loc
  FROM departments
  WHERE deptno = p_dept;
l_loc VARCHAR2(100);
BEGIN
/*Open cursor FOR loop*/
  FOR I IN c_emp
  LOOP
    OPEN c_dept(I.deptno);
    FETCH c_dept into l_loc;
    CLOSE c_dept;
/*Print the employee name and its location*/
    DBMS_OUTPUT.PUT_LINE ('Employee '||I.ename||' works in '||l_loc);
  END LOOP;
END;
/
```

The above programming involves much of code writing and also the code redundancy of getting through the cursor execution cycle. Let us see how we can modularize it to shorten the executable section of the block:

```
/*Enable the SERVEROUTPUT to display block results*/
SET SERVEROUTPUT ON
/*Start the PL/SQL block*/
DECLARE
CURSOR c_emp IS
  SELECT ename, deptno
  FROM employees;
/*Local function to get the department*/
FUNCTION F_GET_LOC (P_DEPTNO VARCHAR2)
```

```
RETURN VARCHAR2
IS
l_loc VARCHAR2(100);
BEGIN
  SELECT loc INTO l_loc
  FROM departments
  WHERE deptno = p_deptno;
  RETURN l_loc;
END F_GET_LOC;
BEGIN
/*Open the cursor FOR loop*/
  FOR I IN c_emp
  LOOP
/*Print the employee name and its location*/
    DBMS_OUTPUT.PUT_LINE ('Employee '||I.ename||' works in
    '||F_GET_LOC(I.deptno));
  END LOOP;
END;
/
```

The preceding block creates a local function which returns the location of the given employee.

Definition of the local subprograms must appear at the end in the declarative section. However, they can be prototyped along with other local variables. The concept of prototyping subprograms before their definition is known as **forward declaration**.

Using bulk binding

The bulk bind, as the name suggests, binds the multirecord data in a bulk. It is one of the most promising and efficient methods to reduce context switching between SQL and PL/SQL runtime engines. But, of course, the profit does not come without any investments. The load on the disk or the CPU usage increases with bulk operations.

Bulk bind can be implemented in two ways—BULK COLLECT and FORALL.

BULK COLLECT is used in the PL/SQL-embedded SELECT INTO statements to pull out a multirecord result set from the database in one single shot. Therefore, no cursors, no FOR loop construct, and no context switching is required except for the first time. It improves the code performance comprehensively by reducing the context switching and implementing data fetch as collections.

The usage goes as per the following syntax:

```
BEGIN
  SELECT <list of column(s)>
  BULK COLLECT INTO <collection variable to hold the data>
  FROM <table name>
  <WHERE conditions>
  <FOR UPDATE [NOWAIT | SKIP LOCKED]>
END;
```

BULK COLLECT can be used in:

- The SELECT INTO clause with the SELECT statement
- The RETURNING INTO clause with the UPDATE statement
- The FETCH INTO clause with an explicit cursor

 Prior to Oracle9*i*, BULK COLLECT could only be used with the static SQL statements but now it can be used with the dynamic SQL statements too.

FORALL is the bulk loop construct which is used to perform bulk transactions on a table. The most beneficial feature is that the loop would not exit abruptly if any single transaction out of the whole bulk fails. Instead, it stores all the raised exceptions in a bulk exception logger — BULK_EXCEPTIONS. The bulk exceptions can be taken-up and resolved separately under the EXCEPTION section. The only shortcoming is that only a single DML statement can be processed under the FORALL loop. Syntactically, the FORALL usage is as follows:

```
FORALL index IN
[
  lower_bound ... upper_bound |
  INDICES OF indexing_collection |
  VALUES OF indexing_collection
]
[SAVE EXCEPTIONS]
[DML statement]
```

In the preceding syntax, the DML statement can be INSERT, UPDAE, DELETE, or MERGE.

 Oracle 11*g* introduced support for MERGE with FORALL.

The following PL/SQL code uses BULK COLLECT to fetch the complete employee details (ID, name, department number, and salary):

```
/*Enable the SERVEROUTPUT to display block results*/
SET SERVEROUTPUT ON
/*Display the EMPLOYEES table structure*/
SQL> DESC EMPLOYEES

  Name                Null?        Type
  ----------------    --------     ------------
  EMPNO               NOT NULL     NUMBER(4)
  ENAME               NOT NULL     VARCHAR2(10)
  JOB                              VARCHAR2(9)
  MGR                              NUMBER(4)
  HIREDATE                         DATE
  SAL                              NUMBER(7,2)
  COMM                             NUMBER(7,2)
  DEPTNO                           NUMBER(2)
/*Start the PL/SQL block*/
DECLARE
/*Declare a record to include the required attributes */
  TYPE REC_EMP IS RECORD
  (
    EMPID EMPLOYEES.EMPNO%TYPE,
    ENAME EMPLOYEES.ENAME%TYPE,
    DEPT EMPLOYEES.DEPTNO%TYPE,
    SALARY EMPLOYEES.SAL%TYPE
  );
  TYPE T_EMP IS TABLE OF REC_EMP;
  L_EMP T_EMP;
BEGIN
/*FETCH cycle helps the reduce contact context switches*/
  SELECT empno, ename, deptno, sal
  BULK COLLECT INTO L_EMP
  FROM employees;
END;
/

PL/SQL procedure successfully completed.
```

> Few facts on BULK COLLECT:
>
> BULK COLLECT does not require the initialization of collection variables.
>
> The BULK COLLECT operation never raises the NO_DATA_FOUND exception. If no data is returned by the query, the collection variable contains no elements.

We will demonstrate the usage of FORALL in the following program only. We will try to update the salaries of all the employees and display the new salaries. Check it out in the following program:

```
/*Enable the SERVEROUTPUT to display block results*/
SET SERVEROUTPUT ON
/*Start the PL/SQL block*/
DECLARE
/*Declare a local record and a table of record to capture the values*/
  TYPE REC_EMP IS RECORD
  (
    EMPID EMPLOYEES.EMPNO%TYPE,
    ENAME EMPLOYEES.ENAME%TYPE,
    DEPT EMPLOYEES.DEPTNO%TYPE,
    SALARY EMPLOYEES.SAL%TYPE
  );
  TYPE T_EMP IS TABLE OF REC_EMP;
  L_EMP T_EMP := T_EMP();
  TYPE REC_EMP_UPD IS RECORD
  (
    ENAME EMPLOYEES.ENAME%TYPE,
    SAL EMPLOYEES.SAL%TYPE
  );
  TYPE T_EMP_UPD IS TABLE OF REC_EMP_UPD;
  L_EMP_UPD T_EMP_UPD;
BEGIN
/*Fetch the employee details in a local collection*/
  SELECT empno, ename, deptno, sal
  BULK COLLECT INTO L_EMP
  FROM employees;
/*Use FORALL to update the salary values. Note the use of RETURNING
INTO*/
  FORALL I IN L_EMP.FIRST..L_EMP.LAST
    UPDATE employees
    SET sal = L_EMP(I).SALARY + 1000
    WHERE empno = L_EMP(I).EMPID
    RETURNING ENAME, SAL BULK COLLECT INTO L_EMP_UPD;
/*Display the current data*/
  FOR I IN 1..L_EMP_UPD.COUNT
  LOOP
    DBMS_OUTPUT.PUT_LINE('New salary of '||L_EMP_UPD(I).ENAME||' is
    '||L_EMP_UPD(I).SAL);
  END LOOP;
END;
/
```

```
New salary of SMITH is 9800
New salary of ALLEN is 2600
New salary of WARD is 2250
New salary of JONES is 3975
New salary of MARTIN is 2250
New salary of BLAKE is 3850
New salary of CLARK is 3450
New salary of SCOTT is 4000
New salary of KING is 6000
New salary of TURNER is 2500
New salary of ADAMS is 2100
New salary of JAMES is 1950
New salary of FORD is 4000
New salary of MILLER is 2300

PL/SQL procedure successfully completed.
```

Using SAVE_EXCEPTIONS

Suppose you are asked to write a program to read 10,000 records from a legacy system and insert it into the database table. You fetch the records in a cursor, iterate the result set in the FOR loops, and insert the records one by one. If a data type mismatch occurs in the 2482nd record, exception occurs, control skips the rest of the loop, and the performed transaction is rolled back.

For such scenarios, Oracle provides the SAVE_EXCEPTIONS clause which is used with FORALL to restore the exceptions which are raised during the FORALL execution. The ongoing transactions are not affected by the exceptions raised. The defected records are skipped and are logged under the SQL%BULK_EXCEPTIONS pseudo column. If out of 5000 records, 13 records are defected, 4987 records are still inserted while 13 are logged in the SQL%BULK_EXCEPTIONS array structure with the cursor index.

The %BULK_EXCEPTIONS attribute maintains two fields — ERROR_INDEX and ERROR_CODE. ERROR_INDEX stores the defect record index where the exception was raised while ERROR_CODE records the exception message. %BULK_EXCEPTIONS.COUNT stores the count of exceptions raised during execution of the FORALL statement. Notice that the standard error code captured by the ERROR_CODE attribute is not prefixed with the hyphen (-) sign. Therefore, to fetch its equivalent error message, pass error code prefixed with a hyphen (-) sign to the SQLERRM function.

In the EMPLOYEES table, EMPNO is the primary key and NAME cannot be NULL. The following PL/SQL code declares the PL/SQL table which has a mix of fixed and NULL values. We shall try to update employee names with NULL through a program and store the defective records using SAVE_EXCEPTIONS:

```
/*Enable the SERVEROUTPUT to display block results*/
SET SERVEROUTPUT ON
/*Start the PL/SQL block*/
DECLARE
/*A local PL/SQL table holds the list of new names*/
  TYPE T_EMP IS TABLE OF VARCHAR2(100) ;
  L_EMP T_EMP := T_EMP('Smith','Adams',null,'King',null,'George');
  BULK_ERRORS EXCEPTION;
  PRAGMA EXCEPTION_INIT (BULK_ERRORS, -24381);
BEGIN
/*FORALL to update the employee names*/
FORALL I IN 1..L_EMP.COUNT
SAVE EXCEPTIONS
UPDATE EMPLOYEES
SET ENAME = L_EMP(I);
EXCEPTION
/*BULK_ERRORS exception handler*/
  WHEN BULK_ERRORS THEN
/*Display the errors occurred during BULK DML transaction*/
  FOR J IN 1..SQL%BULK_EXCEPTIONS.COUNT
  LOOP
  DBMS_OUTPUT.PUT_LINE(CHR(10));
  DBMS_OUTPUT.PUT_LINE('Error in UPDATE:
  '||SQL%BULK_EXCEPTIONS(J).ERROR_INDEX);
  DBMS_OUTPUT.PUT_LINE('Error Code is: '||sql%BULK_EXCEPTIONS(J).
ERROR_CODE);
  DBMS_OUTPUT.PUT_LINE('Error Message is: '||sqlerrm('-
  '||SQL%BULK_EXCEPTIONS(J).ERROR_CODE));
  END LOOP;
END;
/

Error in UPDATE: 3
Error Code is: 1407
Error Message is: ORA-01407: cannot update () to NULL
Error in UPDATE: 5
Error Code is: 1407
Error Message is: ORA-01407: cannot update () to NULL
PL/SQL procedure successfully completed.
```

Rephrasing the conditional control statements

Working on logical expressions for performance—sounds very ignored and rare, but true. Performance of logical expressions can be improved by properly framing the constructs. Though the conditional constructs are rarely attended areas in a PL/SQL code for performance, the evaluation of conditional statements can considerably affect code performance.

The evaluation of conditional statements such as IF THEN ELSE expression takes place from left to right. As soon as the result of the evaluating condition is derived, the control moves forward accordingly. Note that the OR condition is satisfied if any one of the operand is TRUE, while the AND condition is rejected if one of the operands is found FALSE. It is an important consideration which would help us to place the conditions in the logical condition.

Conditions with an OR logical operator

The OR logical operator requires any one of the operands to be true to return TRUE.

If one of the operands in the logical condition is more expected to be TRUE, it can be placed at the leftmost position. As soon as the condition is evaluated, it is set as TRUE and the PL/SQL engine would not move to execute other operands. This helps in performance boost up where large conditions are involved.

Conditions with an AND logical operator

The AND logical operator requires all of the operands to be true to return TRUE. One of the operands returning FALSE would make a complete condition to return FALSE.

If any one of the operands in the logical condition is expected to return FALSE, it must be placed at the leftmost position. During the condition's evaluation, once FALSE is confirmed, Oracle skips the further evaluation of the condition. Such operands placing can help the Oracle server to easily hip-hop through the programs.

If there are more than one mutual conditions possible, the IF THEN ELSIF structure can be used. Whichever IF (or ELSIF) condition is satisfied, the corresponding executable section is executed—the rest of the IF THEN braches are not evaluated.

Enabling intra unit inlining

In conventional programming terminology, the program body of an inline program is stored along with the program unit which references it. In context of Oracle subprograms, the term **inlining a subprogram** refers to the replacing of a subprogram call with the copy of an actual subprogram body itself. At major occasions, this activity cohesively demonstrates better performance and thus, reaps out better benefits along with modularity and call optimization.

Usually, when a program is executed, the PL/SQL engine searches for the program definition in the available objects' lists. It then validates the program, executes the body, and maintains the result in the stack frame. Later it substitutes the results in the calling program unit and proceeds for further execution. When an inline program is called from a program unit, the PL/SQL engine replaces the call statement with the copy of the program body. The copied program body works faster than the program call execution method because the latter step is skipped. Note that the Oracle optimizer is intelligent enough to decide upon a subprogram to be made inline or not. Performance gains are possible only if the inline subprogram body performs a small utility which is frequently used and is substitutable with its call.

Oracle recommends to inline the programs which perform static logic execution, less referential, and very frequently used in the application. An optimized and appropriate implementation of intra unit inlining feature can achieve 30-40 percent of a visible difference in performance of a database application system. The intra unit inlining can be traced from the session level warnings. Session level warnings can be turned on by setting the PLSQL_WARNINGS parameter to ENABLE:ALL.

The inlining can be enabled to achieve one of the following objectives:

- Strictly inline all the program calls at high priority
- Intelligent and appropriate inlining decided by Oracle optimizer
- Manually measure and analyze the subprograms for inlining

Oracle offers two methods of inlining implementation:

- Oracle initialization parameter, PLSQL_OPTIMIZE_LEVEL, offers transparent optimization
- Newly introduced PRAGMA INLINE allows explicit optimization through inlining

PLSQL_OPTIMIZE_LEVEL—the Oracle initialization parameter

Oracle 10*g* introduced the initialization parameter PLSQL_OPTIMIZE_LEVEL to set the working profile of the Oracle optimizer. The optimizer works in accordance with PLSQL_OPTIMIZE_LEVEL and checks for the removal of dead code, subprogram inlining, and construct optimization within the program.

A DBA sets the initialization parameter at the SYSTEM, SESSION, or OBJECT level. The current compilation setting of a program unit can be queried from the USER_PLSQL_OBJECT_SETTINGS dictionary view.

Prior to Oracle 11*g*'s release, the parameter could accommodate only three valid values that is, 0, 1, and 2. Oracle 11*g* introduced an additional optimization level—3. The default value of the parameter is 2. The compiler's effort is directly proportional to the parameter value—the higher the value, the greater the compiler's effort.

It can be set using the ALTER [SYSTEM | SESSION] command, as shown in the following block:

```
/*Connect to view the current parameter setting*/
Conn sys/system as SYSDBA
Connected.
/*Display current setting for PLSQL_OPTIMIZE_LEVEL*/
SQL> show parameter plsql_optimize_level

NAME                                 TYPE        VALUE
------------------------------------ ----------- -
plsql_optimize_level                 integer     2

/*Modify the setting for the current session*/
ALTER SESSION SET PLSQL_OPTIMIZE_LEVEL = 1
/

Session altered.
```

Let us check the behavior of the Oracle optimizer and its effect on the performance at different optimization levels.

Case 1—PLSQL_OPTIMIZE_LEVEL = 0

At this level, the optimizer is in the idle state. The optimizer does not effort in code optimization and it only maintains the evaluation order of the program unit.

Consider the following PL/SQL block which has two assignment statements and one computational statement inside a big loop:

```
/*Connect as ORADEV user*/
Conn ORADEV/ORADEV
Connected.
/*Alter the current session settings; set the PLSQL_OPTIMIZE_LEVEL to
0*/
ALTER SESSION SET PLSQL_OPTIMIZE_LEVEL = 0
/

Session altered.
/*Enable the serveroutput to display block output*/
SET SERVEROUTPUT ON
/*Start the PL/SQL block*/
DECLARE
  L_START_TIME NUMBER;
  L_END_TIME NUMBER;
  L_DEAD   NUMBER;
  L_ASN1 NUMBER;
  L_ASN2 NUMBER;
/*Declare a local function*/
  FUNCTION F_NUM (P_N NUMBER) RETURN NUMBER IS
  BEGIN
    RETURN P_N;
  END;
  BEGIN
/*Capture the start time*/
    L_START_TIME := DBMS_UTILITY.GET_TIME();
    FOR I IN 1..100000000
    LOOP
/*Perform dummy operations within the loop*/
      L_DEAD := 0;
      L_ASN1 := 1;
      L_ASN2 := F_NUM(I) + 1;
    END LOOP;
/*Capture the end time*/
    L_END_TIME := DBMS_UTILITY.GET_TIME();
/*Display the time consumed in the execution*/
    DBMS_OUTPUT.PUT_LINE('Execution time:'||TO_CHAR(L_END_TIME -
    L_START_TIME));
  END;
/

Execution time:4089
PL/SQL procedure successfully completed.
```

Case 2—PLSQL_OPTIMIZE_LEVEL = 1

At this level, the Oracle optimizer applies basic optimization techniques to a program unit. It ignores the redundant and irrelevant code from the program unit.

We will modify the parameter value to 1 and execute the last block again. Check the performance:

```
/*Connect as ORADEV user*/
Conn ORADEV/ORADEV
Connected.
/*Alter the current session settings; set the PLSQL_OPTIMIZE_LEVEL to
1*/
ALTER SESSION SET PLSQL_OPTIMIZE_LEVEL = 1
/

Session altered.
/*Enable the serveroutput to display block output*/
SET SERVEROUTPUT ON
/*Start the PL/SQL block*/
DECLARE
  L_START_TIME NUMBER;
  L_END_TIME NUMBER;
  L_DEAD  NUMBER;
  L_ASN1 NUMBER;
  L_ASN2 NUMBER;
/*Declare a local function*/
  FUNCTION F_NUM (P_N NUMBER) RETURN NUMBER IS
  BEGIN
    RETURN P_N;
  END;
  BEGIN
/*Capture the start time*/
    L_START_TIME := DBMS_UTILITY.GET_TIME();
    FOR I IN 1..100000000
    LOOP
/*Perform dummy operations within the loop*/
      L_DEAD := 0;
      L_ASN1 := 1;
      L_ASN2 := F_NUM(I) + 1;
    END LOOP;
/*Capture the end time*/
    L_END_TIME := DBMS_UTILITY.GET_TIME();
/*Display the time consumed in the execution*/
    DBMS_OUTPUT.PUT_LINE('Execution time:'||TO_CHAR(L_END_TIME -
    L_START_TIME));
```

```
   END;
/
```

```
Execution time:3001
PL/SQL procedure successfully completed.
```

The execution time has reduced by 30 percent when executed with optimization level 1. The reduction in the execution time is credited to the removal of dead code that is (L_DEAD := 0), it is not executed for the complete loop.

Case 3—PLSQL_OPTIMIZE_LEVEL = 2

This is the intelligent and standard optimization level of an optimizer, where it intelligently manages the code by refactoring it, separating out the dead code, and applying advanced techniques to restructure the code for best performance.

We will modify the parameter value again and check the performance:

```
/*Connect as ORADEV user*/
Conn ORADEV/ORADEV
Connected.
/*Alter the current session settings; set the PLSQL_OPTIMIZE_LEVEL to
2*/
ALTER SESSION SET PLSQL_OPTIMIZE_LEVEL = 2
/

Session altered.
/*Enable the serveroutput to display block output*/
SET SERVEROUTPUT ON
/*Start the PL/SQL block*/
DECLARE
  L_START_TIME NUMBER;
  L_END_TIME NUMBER;
  L_DEAD   NUMBER;
  L_ASN1 NUMBER;
  L_ASN2 NUMBER;
/*Declare a local function*/
  FUNCTION F_NUM (P_N NUMBER) RETURN NUMBER IS
  BEGIN
    RETURN P_N;
  END;
  BEGIN
/*Capture the start time*/
    L_START_TIME := DBMS_UTILITY.GET_TIME();
    FOR I IN 1..100000000
```

```
      LOOP
/*Perform dummy operations within the loop*/
      L_DEAD := 0;
      L_ASN1 := 1;
      L_ASN2 := F_NUM(I) + 1;
   END LOOP;
/*Capture the end time*/
   L_END_TIME := DBMS_UTILITY.GET_TIME();
/*Display the time consumed in the execution*/
   DBMS_OUTPUT.PUT_LINE('Execution time:'||TO_CHAR(L_END_TIME -
   L_START_TIME));
 END;
/

Execution time:2508
PL/SQL procedure successfully completed.
```

The code performance has been enhanced by 18 percent. The credit goes to the analytic behavior of our optimizer.

Case 4—PLSQL_OPTIMIZE_LEVEL = 3

It is a new level which got introduced in Oracle 11*g*. It performs strict optimization by inlining the local subprograms at high priority and immense code restructuring. It is used for instantaneous results in a session. Forced inlining of intra unit subprograms can be traced by enabling session level warnings:

```
/*Connect as ORADEV user*/
Conn ORADEV/ORADEV
Connected.
/*Alter the current session settings; set the PLSQL_OPTIMIZE_LEVEL to
2*/
ALTER SESSION SET PLSQL_OPTIMIZE_LEVEL = 3
/

Session altered.
/*Enable the serveroutput to display block output*/
SET SERVEROUTPUT ON
/*Start the PL/SQL block*/
DECLARE
  L_START_TIME NUMBER;
  L_END_TIME NUMBER;
  L_DEAD   NUMBER;
  L_ASN1 NUMBER;
  L_ASN2 NUMBER;
/*Declare a local function*/
  FUNCTION F_NUM (P_N NUMBER) RETURN NUMBER IS
```

```
   BEGIN
      RETURN P_N;
   END;
   BEGIN
/*Capture the start time*/
      L_START_TIME := DBMS_UTILITY.GET_TIME();
      FOR I IN 1..100000000
      LOOP
/*Perform dummy operations within the loop*/
         L_DEAD := 0;
         L_ASN1 := 1;
         L_ASN2 := F_NUM(I) + 1;
      END LOOP;
/*Capture the end time*/
      L_END_TIME := DBMS_UTILITY.GET_TIME();
/*Display the time consumed in the execution*/
      DBMS_OUTPUT.PUT_LINE('Execution time:'||TO_CHAR(L_END_TIME -
      L_START_TIME));
   END;
/
```

```
Execution time:1109
PL/SQL procedure successfully completed.
```

Amazed! It takes just half of the execution time taken in the last optimization setting. It is because it inlines all the calls of the local function F_NUM. Besides inlining, it evades the execution of the L_DEAD and L_ASN1 assignment statements. The results are baffling enough to justify the intelligence of the Oracle optimizer and its governance with a single knob that is, PLSQL_OPTIMIZE_LEVEL. The graph plots the preceding observations to show the performance gains with the optimizer level. When the optimization level is changed from 0 to 2, performance can be improved by nearly 40 percent:

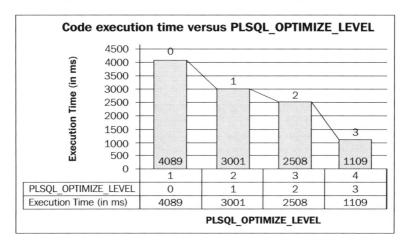

The optimization level degree 2 is the best suited for most of the database applications. Besides providing an intelligent optimization scheme, it keeps the scope for the developers to increase the degree of optimization by explicitly inlining the subprograms using PRAGMA INLINE. The optimization degree 3 performs the aggressive optimization and forced inlining which might not be required every time. However, it can be set at session level for quick illustrations.

PRAGMA INLINE

We learned the effect of the optimization level and subprogram inlining on the program performance. Once PLSQL_OPTIMIZER_LEVEL is set by the DBA, the optimization strategy is transparent to the end user. For this reason, Oracle introduced a pragma (PRAGMA INLINE) to authorize the user to explicitly inline a subprogram of its own choice. In the last section, we saw that PLSQL_OPTIMIZE_LEVEL 2 will prioritize the subprograms for inlining as per its own intelligence, while PLSQL_OPTIMIZE_LEVEL 3 will forcibly inline all the subprogram calls. While the latter setting might skip our expected subprogram, the latter setting might inline the expected subprogram along with the unnecessary inlining(inlinings).

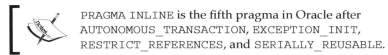

PRAGMA INLINE is the fifth pragma in Oracle after AUTONOMOUS_TRANSACTION, EXCEPTION_INIT, RESTRICT_REFERENCES, and SERIALLY_REUSABLE.

PRAGMA INLINE can be used with PLSQL_OPTIMIZER_LEVEL 2 and PLSQL_OPTIMIZER_LEVEL 3. When PLSQL_OPTIMIZE_LEVEL is set to 2, the pragma can be used to explicitly inline a subprogram call or explicitly avoid the inlining of a subprogram. When PLSQL_OPTIMIZE_LEVEL is set to 3, the pragma can only be used to avoid the inlining of a subprogram call.

PRAGMA INLINE has to be specified once, just before the subprogram call. The inlining effect would be persistent for all the subsequent calls to the subprogram, unless the effect is withdrawn. Syntactically, PRAGMA INLINE can be used as follows:

```
PRAGMA INLINE (subprogram name, [YES | NO]);
```

The effect of inlining can be confirmed through PL/SQL session level warnings. The warnings display the information messages at each stage of the intra unit inlining. The warnings can be enabled at the session level using PLSQL_WARNINGS.

Let us examine the effect of PRAGMA INLINE with a PL/SQL program. The PL/SQL procedure sums up the following series:

$(1*2) + (2*2) + (3*2) + \ldots + (n*2)$

The following program will demonstrate the usage of PRAGMA INLINE when the PLSQL_OPTIMIZE_LEVEL is set as 2:

```
/*Connect as ORADEV USER*/
Conn ORADEV/ORADEV
Connected.
ALTER SESSION SET PLSQL_OPTIMIZE_LEVEL=2
/

Session altered.
```

Note that a local subprogram DUBN calculates the sum of an index and candidate for intra inlining. It is called inside the procedure to sum up the series:

```
/*Enable the PLSQL_WARNINGS to capture the warnings*/
alter session set plsql_warnings = 'enable:all'
/

Session altered.
/*Create a procedure*/
CREATE OR REPLACE PROCEDURE P_SUM_SERIES(P_LIMIT NUMBER)
IS
  L_SERIES NUMBER := 0;
  L_ST_TIME NUMBER;
  L_END_TIME NUMBER;
/*Declare a local function which is candidate for inlining*/
  FUNCTION DUBN (P_NUM NUMBER) RETURN NUMBER IS
  BEGIN
    RETURN P_NUM * 2;
  END DUBN;
  BEGIN
/*Capture the start time*/
    L_ST_TIME := DBMS_UTILITY.GET_TIME();
/*Begin the loop for series calculation*/
    FOR J IN 1..P_LIMIT
    LOOP
/*Set inlining for the local subprogram*/
      PRAGMA INLINE (DUBN, 'YES');
      L_SERIES := L_SERIES + DUBN(J);
    END LOOP;
/*Capture end time*/
    L_END_TIME := DBMS_UTILITY.GET_TIME();
/*Display the time consumed with inlining of local function*/
    DBMS_OUTPUT.PUT_LINE('Execution time with inlining:'||TO_CHAR(L_
END_TIME -
    L_ST_TIME));
```

```
/*Repeat the steps with inlining off*/
   L_ST_TIME := DBMS_UTILITY.GET_TIME();
   FOR J IN 1..P_LIMIT
   LOOP
/*Set off inlining for the local function*/
     PRAGMA INLINE (DUBN, 'NO');
     L_SERIES := L_SERIES + DUBN(J);
   END LOOP;
   L_END_TIME := DBMS_UTILITY.GET_TIME();
   DBMS_OUTPUT.PUT_LINE('Execution time without inlining:'||TO_
CHAR(L_END_TIME
     - L_ST_TIME));
  END;
/

Procedure created.
```

Warnings for the procedure compiled in the preceding code snippet can be queried from the USER_ERRORS dictionary view:

```
/*Select the warnings for the procedure P_SUM_SERIES*/
SELECT line, text
FROM user_errors
WHERE name='P_SUM_SERIES'
/
LINE TEXT
---- ------------------------------------------------------------------
---------------------
   1 PLW-05018: unit P_SUM_SERIES omitted optional AUTHID clause;
default value
  DEFINER used
  22 PLW-06004: inlining of call of procedure 'DUBN' requested
  39 PLW-06008: call of procedure 'DUBN' will not be inlined
  22 PLW-06005: inlining of call of procedure 'DUBN' was done
```

Warnings confirm the subprogram inlining along with the line number where the request was made through PRAGMA INLINE and where it is actually done.

Now let us execute the P_SUM_SERIES procedure for a bigger value to observe the difference of subprogram inlining:

```
/*Executing the procedure with sample limit*/
SQL> EXEC P_SUM_SERIES (1000000);

Execution time with inlining:16
Execution time without inlining:28
PL/SQL procedure successfully completed.
```

Summary

In this chapter, we learned the effect of compilation settings on the application performance. We understood the difference between interpreted/native compilation modes and learned the real native compilation feature introduced in Oracle 11*g*. We covered the PL/SQL tuning recommendations supported with demonstrations. Towards the end, we saw the effect of the optimization level on code execution through illustrations, intra unit inlining feature, and usage of `PRAGMA INLINE` in programs to explicitly inline subprogram calls.

In the next chapter, we will cover one of the most talked about features of Oracle 11*g*. The feature is known as result caching which promises tremendous performance gains in database applications.

Practice exercise

1. Identify the nature of the program which is best suited for the interpreted mode of compilation.

   a. The program unit contains multiple SQL statements.

   b. The program unit has been just developed and is in debug stage.

   c. The program unit uses collections and bulk bind statements.

   d. The program unit is in production phase.

2. Choose the correct statements about the real native compilation mode in Oracle 11*g*;

   a. The compilation method uses C compiler to convert the program into the equivalent C code.

   b. The compilation method mounts the shared libraries through the `PLSQL_NATIVE_LIBRARY_DIR` and `PLSQL_NATIVE_LIBRARY_SUBDIR_COUNT` parameters.

   c. The compilation does not use C compiler but converts the program unit directly to the M code.

   d. The real native compilation is supported for RAC environments and participates in the backup recovery processes.

3. Determine the behavior of the PLSQL_OPTIMIZE_LEVEL optimizer when it has been set to 3.

   a. The optimizer would inline the programs which are necessary.

   b. The optimizer would inline all the programs irrespective of the gains.

   c. The optimizer would inline only those subprograms which have PRAGMA INLINE.

   d. The setting has no effect on inlining of subprograms.

4. Choose the correct statements about the compilation setting in Oracle:

   a. From Oracle 11*g*, the default value of PLSQL_CODE_TYPE is NATIVE.

   b. An object can be recompiled in a compilation mode different from the current database setting.

   c. During the database upgrade, PLSQL_CODE_TYPE must be modified in the instance pfile.

   d. In a real native compilation, the libraries generated are stored in a secured file system.

5. Identify the tuning tips in the following PL/SQL block:

```
DECLARE
CURSOR C IS
   SELECT ENAME, SAL, COMM
   FROM EMPLOYEES;
   L_COMM NUMBER;
   BEGIN
      FOR I IN C
      LOOP
         L_COMM := I.SAL + ((I.COMM/100) * (I.SAL * 12));
         DBMS_OUTPUT.PUT_LINE (I.ENAME||' earns '||L_COMM||' as
         commission');
      END LOOP;
   END;
/
```

   a. Use BULK COLLECT to select employee data.

   b. Declare L_COMM as NOT NULL.

   c. Use PLS_INTEGER for L_COMM.

   d. No tuning required.

6. Which of the statements are true about inlining in PL/SQL subprograms?

    a. The optimizer can inline only standalone stored functions.

    b. The optimizer can inline only locally declared subprograms.

    c. Inlining is always useful in performance irrespective of the size of the subprogram.

    d. The optimizer cannot identify any subprogram for inlining when the optimizer level is set at 0.

7. Examine the following code and determine the output:

```
DECLARE
  FUNCTION F_ADD (P_NUM NUMBER)
  RETURN NUMBER
  IS
  BEGIN
    RETURN P_NUM + 10;
  END;
  BEGIN
  FOR I IN 122..382
  LOOP
    PRAGMA INLINE (F_ADD,'YES');
    L_SUM := L_SUM + F_ADD (I);
  END LOOP;
  END;
/
```

    PLSQL_OPTIMIZE_LEVEL is set as 2.

    a. The local function F_ADD would not be called inline unless PLSQL_OPTIMIZE_LEVEL is set as 3.

    b. The local function F_ADD may be called inline because PLSQL_OPTIMIZE_LEVEL is set as 2.

    c. The local function F_ADD would be called inline because PRAGMA INLINE marks it for inline.

    d. Inlining cannot be done for locally declared subprograms.

8. The libraries generated from the real native compilation are stored in the SYSAUX tablespace.

    a. True

    b. False

9. Suggest the tuning considerations in the following PL/SQL block:

```
DECLARE
  L_SUM NATURALN := 0;
  L_ID VARCHAR2(10);
BEGIN
  L_ID := 256;
  L_SUM := L_ID * 1.5;
END;
```

   a. The data type of L_SUM can be changed to NATURAL and nullity can be verified in the executable section.

   b. L_SUM must not be initialized with zero.

   c. The multiple 1.5 must be assigned to a variable.

   d. L_ID must be of an appropriate data type such as NUMBER or PLS_INTEGER.

10. Identify the correct statements about PRAGMA INLINE.

   a. It is the fifth pragma in Oracle besides AUTONOMOUS_TRANSACTION, EXCEPTION_INIT, RESTRICT_REFERENCE, and SERIALLY_REUSABLE.

   b. It does not work for overloaded functions.

   c. It does not work for PLSQL_OPTIMIZE_LEVEL = 1.

   d. PRAGMA INLINE (<Function name>,'YES') is meaningless at PLSQL_OPTIMIZE_LEVEL = 3, because the optimizer inlines all the subprograms.

9
Caching to Improve Performance

Performance optimization is an immortal challenge in Oracle applications which demands sound essentials of a DBA and logical abilities of a developer. Every release of Oracle promises for new features to enhance the performance and scalability of an application.

In the last chapter, we saw the difference made by real native compilation and intra unit inlining. Another innovation was brought to notice in Oracle 11*g* and it was data caching. Data caching is a common feature to improvise upon the application performance. In the past, the architectural implementation of caching used to cache the data sets in the SGA buffer cache, but not the SQL with results. Oracle 11*g* presents a concrete effective feature which can restore the results in a dedicated component of SGA. It is not like the traditional features which boost performance but it is an alternate approach to yield better performance.

In simple terms, the result of an operation will be temporarily stored along with the operation specifications. Whenever the same operation would be repeated, instead of working out the whole operation again, system would directly return the previously stored result. We will cover the server result caching feature under the following topics:

- Introduction to result cache
    - ◦ SQL result cache
    - ◦ PL/SQL function result cache
    - ◦ OCI client result cache
- Configuring the database for the server result cache
    - ◦ The DBMS_RESULT_CACHE package

- Implementing result cache in SQL
  - ○ Manual result cache
  - ○ Automatic result cache

- Implementing result cache in PL/SQL

Introduction to result cache

The term cache is not new in the Oracle family. Prior to Oracle 11*g*, we have often heard of caching queries in SGA. Oracle 11*g* makes major enhancements in this area and evolves two new caching features namely, server result cache and client result cache.

Result cache allows the storage of result sets from a SQL query or PL/SQL function in a specific memory location, known as cache memory, along with the query specifications. Now, whenever the same SQL or the function (with the same specifications) is re-executed, the server picks up the result directly from the cache memory. The approach bypasses the SQL or function execution process—thus, saving a substantial amount of time. The server makes almost no effort in executing the SQL or PL/SQL function by employing cache memory for frequently executing queries and functions.

The specific memory location or cache memory is a new SGA memory component, dedicated for cached results. The query specification includes the SQL and the input values required in the WHERE clause predicates. Since the cached results are maintained at the server, they are sharable across the sessions connecting to the same server.

The result cache feature operates in two flavors as follows:

- Server-side result cache
  - ○ SQL result cache
  - ○ PL/SQL function result cache

- Client OCI result cache

Server-side result cache

The server-side result cache is used only for the SQL queries and PL/SQL functions. The feature can be enabled by setting newly inducted initialization parameters. The parameter description and their usage have been discussed later in this chapter. Once the cache configuration is completed at the server, results from SQL queries and PL/SQL functions can be held at the server. The cache configuration includes the setting of the cache mode, cache memory size, and cache result size. We will overview the configuration portion in the next section.

Oracle 11*g* segregates a new component of SGA known as **result cache**. It is part of a shared pool and the server allocates a small part of the shared pool to it before its size is explicitly allocated by the user. We will see how the explicit allocation of the cache memory size depends on the overall memory component structure, later in this chapter. Once the cache component is allocated, the **Automatic Memory Management (AMM)** feature internally manages the concurrency among the memory components.

The following diagram gives a rough demonstration of the new memory infrastructure in Oracle 11*g*:

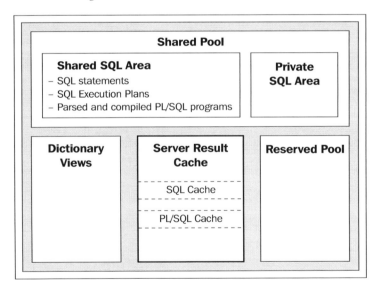

Let us briefly look over the SQL and PL/SQL result cache.

SQL query result cache

By the virtue of implementation of the server result cache, results of SQL queries can be cached under the cache component of the Oracle server memory infrastructure.

The results of a frequently used SQL can be cached using a RESULT_CACHE hint. When a SQL query with the RESULT_CACHE hint is executed on a cache configured server, the server caches the query results along with its signature. The next time when the same query is re-executed, the server finds the result in its cache and instantly produces the result to the user. The query execution process is completely ignored and, hence, the performance bar raises significantly. Data warehousing environments are the top rated beneficiaries from the feature. The server cache helps to distribute the workload of the server in parallel query executions. Oracle recommends caching the results of frequently used queries which are likely to take more time to fetch the results. Intelligent caching is preferable over forced caching.

The cached results get invalidated when the table is altered or the data contained is updated.

 The NO_RESULT_CACHE hint can be used to direct the server to ignore the caching for a SQL query.

PL/SQL function result cache

The PL/SQL result cache is the second component of the server-side result cache feature. The PL/SQL function can be marked for caching and it includes a new RESULT_CACHE clause in its header. During the first execution of the function, the server caches the results returned by the function along with the input parameters (if any). Next time, when the function is used again with the same parameters, the server picks up the result from the cache, instead of executing it again.

The results returned by the function can be retained in the server cache, until the function body has been recompiled or modified. Once the function definition undergoes logical or structural changes, all its earlier cached results are purged from the cache memory at the server. There is no additional configuration required for the PL/SQL cache, the server-side result cache configuration works for both SQL and PL/SQL.

Similar to the SQL result cache, the result cached for a PL/SQL function is also available across the active sessions of the database.

OCI client results cache

The caching feature allows OCI clients to fetch the result sets without accessing the database server memory but the result sets which are stored in the process (client's) memory are not. The process memory is enabled and configured at the database level and all OCI-based clients access it. Note that client result caching and database result caching are exclusive and independent methods of caching the data in memory.

Now, since the client results are cached into the client's memory cache component, it becomes easy for the OCI-based client to access their own cache memory instead of hitting the sever cache. If the required result set is found under the client cache, you save the execution time and SQL*net round trip time of the query.

 Besides the result caching options which work within a database, Oracle provides a database caching option known as **In Memory Database** (**IMDB**) cache option. The IMDB cache option allows the caching of data from the frequently used database tables which share referential integrity amongst them. The group of cached tables is known as **cache group**, while a collection of cache groups is known as **cache grid**.

Configuring the database for the server result cache

In this section, we will learn the configuration of the server-side result cache feature. Oracle 11*g* adds four new initialization parameters to DBA's basket to configure the caching feature on a database server. These parameters can be set at the database level and session level. Since these settings enable caching at the server side, results from both SQL and PL/SQL namespaces can be cached under the server cache.

The parameters are as follows:

- RESULT_CACHE_MODE: This parameter controls the caching operation by the server. The server operates the caching feature in three modes—AUTO, MANUAL, and FORCE. Check the server behavior in these modes. The result is held in the cache memory until it is flushed off explicitly. The cached results are invalidated when the result data is updated in the table or the table structure is altered.
  - AUTO: The server decides on its own whether the result of the SQL query has to be cached or not. The server takes the decision based on the query cost (as calculated by the optimizer) and the frequency of its usage.

- ○ MANUAL: The server caches the results of only the queries, which are specifically marked for the result cache using the RESULT_CACHE hint. It is the default operation mode of the server at the time of the installation. The mode of operation is sometimes referred as **manual result cache**.

- ○ FORCE: The server strictly caches the results of all possible SQL statements irrespective of the RESULT_CACHE hint specification in the query. Besides the queries with caching limitations, only the queries with the NO_RESULT_CACHE hint are ignored for caching. The caching feature in the FORCE mode is known as **automatic result cache**.

- RESULT_CACHE_MAX_SIZE: The parameter allocates the cache memory as part of the shared pool. It must have a definite value to enable the caching feature. Certain recommendations from Oracle to set this parameter are as follows:

  - ○ 0.25 percent of the MEMORY_TARGET parameter value.

  - ○ 0.5 percent of the SGA_TARGET parameter value.

  - ○ 1 percent of the SHARED_POOL_SIZE parameter value.

  - ○ In addition to the above recommendations, the cache memory size cannot go beyond 75 percent of the shared pool.

- RESULT_CACHE_MAX_RESULT: This parameter allocates the maximum size of a single result set in the cache memory. It is expressed as a percentage value of RESULT_CACHE_MAX_SIZE. It must be a positive integral value in the range of 0 to 100. By default, its value is 5 percent.

- RESULT_CACHE_REMOTE_EXPIRATION: This parameter defines the retention time of a result cached from a remote object. It is expressed in minutes and its value is zero, by default.

The above parameters can be set for a system or a session using the ALTER [SYSTEM | SESSION] command, as shown in the following code syntax:

```
ALTER SYSTEM SET [PARAMETER] = [VALUE]
```

Note that the session level setting enables the session level caching.

Suppose the server has MEMORY_TARGET of 812 MB. The DBA tries to set the cache mode as MANUAL, cache memory as 200 MB, and cache result size as 20 percent:

```
/*Connect to SYSDBA*/
Conn sys/system as SYSDBA
Connected.

/*Alter system to set cache mode*/
ALTER SYSTEM SET RESULT_CACHE_MODE = MANUAL
/
```

```
Session altered.

/*Alter system to set max cache size*/
ALTER SYSTEM SET RESULT_CACHE_MAX_SIZE = 200M
/

Session altered.

/*Alter system to set max cache results*/
ALTER SYSTEM SET RESULT_CACHE_MAX_RESULT = 20
/

Session altered.

/*Alter system to set cache result retention time*/
ALTER SYSTEM SET RESULT_CACHE_REMOTE_EXPIRATION = 100
/

Session altered.
```

The caching parameter settings can be queried from the V$PARAMETER dictionary view:

```
SELECT name, value
FROM v$parameter
WHERE name LIKE 'result_cache%'
/

NAME                               VALUE
------------------------------     -------------------
result_cache_mode                  MANUAL
result_cache_max_size              209715200
result_cache_max_result            100
result_cache_remote_expiration     100
```

In addition to the initialization parameters shown in the preceding code snippet, Oracle 11*g* keeps a server process RCBG for Oracle RAC systems. It is used to handle the messages generated by the server processes which are attached to the instances in Oracle RAC architecture:

```
/*Connect as DBA*/
Conn sys/system as sysdba
Connected.

/*Query the process details from V$BGPROCESS*/
SQL> SELECT NAME, DESCRIPTION
FROM V$BGPROCESS
WHERE NAME = 'RCBG'
/

NAME                 DESCRIPTION
-------------------- -----------------------------------
RCBG                 Result Cache: Background
```

The DBMS_RESULT_CACHE package

To coordinate the result cache activities at the server, Oracle 11*g* introduced a new built-in package DBMS_RESULT_CACHE. The package is owned by the SYS user. The package can be used to perform query result cache maintenance activities such as flushing, invalidating cache results dependent on an object, generating the memory report, and checking the cache status.

The public constants used in the package are as follows:

DBMS_RESULT_CACHE constants (reference: Oracle documentation)	
STATUS_BYPS	CONSTANT VARCHAR(10) := 'BYPASS';
STATUS_DISA	CONSTANT VARCHAR(10) := 'DISABLED';
STATUS_ENAB	CONSTANT VARCHAR(10) := 'ENABLED';
STATUS_SYNC	CONSTANT VARCHAR(10) := 'SYNC';

The subprograms used in the package are described in the following table:

DBMS_RESULT_CACHE subprograms (reference: Oracle documentation)	
BYPASS procedure	Sets the bypass mode for the result cache
FLUSH function and procedure	Attempts to remove all the objects from the result cache, and depending on the arguments retains or releases the memory and retains or clears the statistics
INVALIDATE functions and procedures	Invalidates all the result-set objects that are dependent upon the specified dependency object
INVALIDATE_OBJECT functions and procedures	Invalidates the specified result-set object(s)
MEMORY_REPORT procedure	Produces the memory usage report for the result cache
STATUS function	Checks the status of the result cache

For illustration, the cache memory report can be generated using the MEMORY_REPORT procedure, as shown in the following code snippet. Note that the cache size specifications are expressed as a percentage of shared pool:

```
/*Connect to sysdba*/
SQL> conn sys/system as sysdba
Connected.

/*Enable the serveroutput variable to display the block messages*/
SQL> SET SERVEROUTPUT ON
```

```
/*Generate the cache memory report*/
SQL> exec dbms_result_cache.memory_report
R e s u l t   C a c h e   M e m o r y   R e p o r t
[Parameters]
Block Size           = 1K bytes
Maximum Cache Size   = 200M bytes (200K blocks)
Maximum Result Size  = 40M bytes (40K blocks)
[Memory]
Total Memory = 9460 bytes [0.004% of the Shared Pool]
... Fixed Memory = 9460 bytes [0.004% of the Shared Pool]
... Dynamic Memory = 0 bytes [0.000% of the Shared Pool]

PL/SQL procedure successfully completed.
```

Since no results have been cached until now, the report shows 0 bytes for dynamic memory. The cache memory report, shown in the preceding code snippet, also serves as a confirmation for the feature being enabled successfully on the database server. In case the configuration is not proper, the memory report simply displays the following message:

```
SQL> EXEC dbms_result_cache.memory_report
R e s u l t   C a c h e   M e m o r y   R e p o r t
Cache is disabled.

PL/SQL procedure successfully completed.
```

We can check the current status of cache on the server by using the STATUS function as follows:

```
SQL> SELECT dbms_result_cache.status FROM DUAL
/

STATUS
-------------------------------------------------
ENABLED
```

Implementing the result cache in SQL

As we learned earlier, the database must be configured to enable server-side result caching. Let us now go through illustrations of the result cache in SQL.

Manual result cache

If the result cache operation mode is set as MANUAL, the caching feature is known as **manual result cache**. Here, the user has to explicitly specify the RESULT_CACHE hint in order to cache the query result. The Oracle server would not automatically cache any result set.

The `RESULT_CACHE_MODE` parameter can be set by the DBA to enable manual result caching:

```
/*Connect as SYSDBA*/
Conn sys/system as sysdba
Connected.

/*Set the parameter as Manual*/
ALTER SYSTEM SET RESULT_CACHE_MODE=MANUAL
/

System altered.
```

We will flush the cache memory and shared pool to clear all the earlier cached results:

```
/*Flush all the earlier cached results*/
SQL> EXEC DBMS_RESULT_CACHE.FLUSH
/

PL/SQL procedure successfully completed.

/*Flush the shared pool*/
SQL> alter system flush shared_pool
/

System altered.
```

Once the cache operation mode is set, the SQL query can be executed using the `RESULT_CACHE` optimizer hint. The hint instructs the server to cache the results of the particular query in the cache component of the memory:

```
/*Connect as ORADEV*/
Conn ORADEV/ORADEV
Connected.

/*Execute the query to get SMITH's salary*/
SQL> SELECT /*+RESULT_CACHE*/ sal
  FROM employees
  WHERE EMPNO = 7369
/

  SAL
------
  800
```

Generate the explain plan for the SQL query:

```
/*Generate the explain plan for the query*/
SQL> EXPLAIN PLAN FOR
  SELECT /*+RESULT_CACHE*/ sal
  FROM employees
```

```
    WHERE empno = 7369
/

Explained.
```

Query the explain plan from PLAN_TABLE:

```
/*Check the Explain plan*/
SQL> SELECT * FROM TABLE(DBMS_XPLAN.DISPLAY)
/
```

Refer to the following screenshot for the output of the preceding code block as follows:

```
PLAN_TABLE_OUTPUT
------------------------------------------------------------------------------------------
Plan hash value: 833960231
------------------------------------------------------------------------------------------
| Id  | Operation                    | Name                          | Rows  | Bytes | Cost (%CPU)| Time     |
------------------------------------------------------------------------------------------
|   0 | SELECT STATEMENT             |                               |     1 |     8 |     1   (0)| 00:00:01 |
|   1 |  RESULT CACHE                | 6jwjx7ap21w71g658hxt5vwng3    |       |       |            |          |
|   2 |   TABLE ACCESS BY INDEX ROWID| EMPLOYEES                     |     1 |     8 |     1   (0)| 00:00:01 |
|*  3 |    INDEX UNIQUE SCAN         | SYS_C0014587                  |     1 |       |     0   (0)| 00:00:01 |
------------------------------------------------------------------------------------------
```

Note the RESULT_CACHE operation in the explain plan. It implies that the Oracle server has stored the query results in the cache memory with the cache ID 6jwjx7ap21w71g658hxt5vwng3. The same cache ID would be used for the further re-execution of the same SQL.

In addition, we have a new section under PLAN_TABLE_OUTPUT as result cache information (identified by operation ID). This section represents the result cache metadata for this query. The result cache report contains the dependent tables information.

Automatic result cache

If the result cache operation mode is FORCE, the caching feature becomes automatic and the server strictly caches results of all the queries executed. The RESULT_CACHE hint is obsolete and ineffective at the time of automatic result caching. For any query (which is rarely executed), a NO_RESULT_CACHE hint can be specified to override the server operation mode and ignore the query results for caching.

Let us check out how it works:

```
/*Connect as sysdba*/
Conn sys/system as sysdba
Connected

/*Alter the system to set the new cache mode*/
ALTER SYSTEM SET RESULT_CACHE_MODE=FORCE
```

```
/

System altered.

/*Flush all the earlier cached results*/
SQL> EXEC DBMS_RESULT_CACHE.FLUSH
/

PL/SQL procedure successfully completed.

/*Flush the shared pool*/
SQL> alter system flush shared_pool
/

System altered.
```

Now, execute the same SQL query without the RESULT_CACHE hint:

```
/*Connect as USER*/
SQL> CONN ORADEV/ORADEV
Connected.

/*Execute the below SQL to generate the explain plan for the query*/
SQL> EXPLAIN PLAN FOR
  SELECT sal
  FROM employees
  WHERE empno=7369
/

Explained.

/*Query the Explain plan*/
SQL> SELECT * FROM TABLE(DBMS_XPLAN.DISPLAY)
/
```

Refer to the following screenshot for the output of the preceding code block:

The explain plan shows the RESULT_CACHE component and its cache ID in the cache memory. Note that no hint has been given in the SQL query, but Oracle caches the query results by virtue of its operation mode.

Result cache metadata

Oracle facilitates the monitoring of real-time cache information in the database through result cache dynamic performance views. These views are owned by SYS and content is always in synchronization with the latest database activities.

 Actual dynamic performance views are prefixed with V_$. Their public synonyms are prefixed with V$.

The following table enlists the result cache dynamic views along with their purpose:

Synonym	Purpose
V$RESULT_CACHE_STATISTICS	Records the server cache performance stats, including block count and create count values
V$RESULT_CACHE_MEMORY	Captures the server cache memory stats (in terms of blocks)
V$RESULT_CACHE_OBJECTS	Captures the cached result sets information including status
V$RESULT_CACHE_DEPENDENCY	Captures the dependencies of a result cache

Retrieve the cached result information. The dynamic view V$RESULT_CACHE_OBJECTS captures the information of the cached results. Some of the accomplishments of this view are as follows:

- A result in the cache memory stores the query result as the Result type and caches its dependent object information as the Dependency type.
- The results are cached by the user ID as their creator ID.
- The namespace (SQL or PL/SQL) associated with a cached result differentiates the caching from the two components of the server-side result cache.

The STATUS column determines the validity status of a cached result. The status of a cached result can be one of the following:

- NEW: An under construction cache result
- PUBLISHED: A cache result ready to be used
- INVALID; An invalid result due to data update or DDL on the dependent object
- EXPIRED: An expired cached result that is, the result which has crossed the expiration time

- BYPASS: The cached result has been marked for bypass and in bypass mode, the existing cached results are ignored in the query optimizations and new results are not cached

Out of the preceding status list, only the results with the PUBLISHED status are the healthiest ones to be used by other SQL queries:

```
/*Connect as SYSDBA*/
Conn sys/system as sysdba
Connected.

/*Query the User id of the ORADE user to query its cached results*/
SQL> SELECT user_id
  FROM dba_users
  WHERE username = 'ORADEV'
/

    USER_ID
----------
        97

/*Query the cached results*/
SQL> SELECT id, type, status, cache_id
  FROM V$RESULT_CACHE_OBJECTS
  WHERE CREATOR_UID = 97
/

  ID   TYPE         STATUS      CACHE_ID
  --- ----------  ---------  --------------------------------
  30   Dependency   Published   ORADEV.EMPLOYEES
  31   Result       Published   6jwjx7ap21w71g658hxt5vwng3

/*Query the SQL associated with the above cached results*/
SQL> SELECT id, name, namespace
  FROM V$RESULT_CACHE_OBJECTS
  WHERE cache_id = '6jwjx7ap21w71g658hxt5vwng3'
/
```

```
ID  NAME                                                              NAMES
--- -------------------------------------------------------------     -----
31 SELECT /*+RESULT CACHE*/ SAL FROM EMPLOYEES WHERE EMPNO=7369 SQL
```

Query result cache dependencies

The dependent objects of a given cache result can be queried from the dynamic performance V$RESULT_CACHE_DEPENDENCY. The RESULT_ID column of the view references the ID column of the Result type cache entries in V$RESULT_CACHE_OBJECTS:

```
/*Connect as SYSDBA*/
Conn sys/system as sysdba
Connected.

/*Query result cache dependencies for cache id 31*/
SQL> SELECT *
  FROM V$RESULT_CACHE_DEPENDENCY WHERE
  RESULT_ID = 31
/

 RESULT_ID   DEPEND_ID   OBJECT_NO
---------- ---------- ----------
        31          30       80571

/*Verify the dependent object in DBA_OBJECTS table*/
SQL> SELECT owner, object_name
  FROM dba_objects
  WHERE object_id = 80571
/

OWNER                           OBJECT_NAME
------------------------------ -------------------------------------
ORADEV                          EMPLOYEES
```

Cache memory statistics

The current cache memory statistics can be queried from the V$RESULT_CACHE_STATISTICS dynamic view. It gives the maximum block count and used block count information.

Create Count Success denotes the number of results which are successfully cached in the server result cache.

Find Count Value denotes the number of cached results which are successfully used in the repeated executions of the cached queries.

Refer to the following code snippet:

```
/*Cache result characteristics*/
SQL> SELECT *
  FROM V$RESULT_CACHE_STATISTICS
/

        ID    NAME                             VALUE
---------- ----------------------------- -----------
         1    Block Size (Bytes)               1024
         2    Block Count Maximum              204800
         3    Block Count Current              32
         4    Result Size Maximum (Blocks)     40960
         5    Create Count Success             1
         6    Create Count Failure             0
         7    Find Count                       0
         8    Invalidation Count               0
         9    Delete Count Invalid             0
        10    Delete Count Valid               0
        11    Hash Chain Length                1

11 rows selected.
```

Invalidation of SQL result cache

The result cached in the server cache gets invalidated if the dependent object gets invalidated or the data in the dependent tables gets updated. The result is still cached in the server cache but marked with the INVALID status.

First, we will generate a sample cache result at the server cache:

```
/*Connect as SYSDBA*/
CONN sys/system AS SYSDBA
Connected.

/*Flush the cache memory to clear the earlier cached results*/
EXEC DBMS_RESULT_CACHE.flush;
PL/SQL procedure successfully completed.

/*Flush the shared pool*/
SQL> alter system flush shared_pool
/

System altered.

/*Connect as ORADEV*/
Conn ORADEV/ORADEV
Connected.
```

```
/*Generate explain plan for a Query with result cache hint*/
Explain plan for select /*+result_cache*/ * from employees
/

Explained.

/*Check the PLAN_TABLE output*/
SELECT * FROM TABLE (DBMS_XPLAN.DISPLAY)
/
```

Refer to the following screenshot for the output of the preceding code block:

```
PLAN_TABLE_OUTPUT
-----------------------------------------------------------------------------------
Plan hash value: 1445457117
-----------------------------------------------------------------------------------
: Id : Operation          : Name                    : Rows : Bytes : Cost (%CPU): Time    :
-----------------------------------------------------------------------------------
:  0 : SELECT STATEMENT   :                         :  14  :  532  :   3   <0>: 00:00:01 :
:  1 :  RESULT CACHE      : 7j5z4u9hzff4036czuj67bwqnt :     :       :       :          :
:  2 :  TABLE ACCESS FULL : EMPLOYEES               :  14  :  532  :   3   <0>: 00:00:01 :
-----------------------------------------------------------------------------------
```

Now, the server contains a cached result with the cache ID
`7j5z4u9hzff4036czuj67bwqnt`. Verify it in the following code snippet:

```
/*Connect as SYSDBA*/
CONN sys/system AS SYSDBA
Connected.

/*Query the result cached at the server*/
SELECT id, type, status, namespace, cache_id
FROM V$RESULT_CACHE_OBJECTS
WHERE creator_uid = (SELECT user_id
  FROM DBA_USERS
  WHERE username='ORADEV')
/

    ID  TYPE        STATUS          NAMES  CACHE_ID
---------- ---------- -------------- ----- ----------------------------
     3  Dependency  Published              ORADEV.EMPLOYEES
     4  Result      Published       SQL    7j5z4u9hzff4036czuj67bwqnt
```

Now, we will update the salary of the employees:

```
/*Connect to ORADEV user*/
Conn ORADEV/ORADEV
Connected.

/*Update salary of employees in EMPLOYEES table*/
SQL> UPDATE employees
  SET sal = sal+100
```

```
/

14 rows updated.

/*Commit the transaction*/
SQL> commit;
Commit complete.
```

When we query the cached result in V$RESULT_CACHE_OBJECTS, the earlier cached results are found to be invalidated:

```
/*Connect as SYSDBA*/
Conn sys/system as sysdba
Connected.

/*Query the result cache objects view to check the INVALID status*/
SELECT id, type, status, namespace, cache_id
FROM V$RESULT_CACHE_OBJECTS
WHERE creator_uid = (SELECT user_id
  FROM DBA_USERS
  WHERE username='ORADEV')
/
```

```
      ID TYPE       STATUS          NAMES CACHE_ID
---------- ---------- --------------- ----- --------------------------
       3 Dependency Published             ORADEV.EMPLOYEES
       4 Result     Invalid         SQL   7j5z4u9hzff4036czuj67bwqnt
```

Displaying the result cache memory report

The cache memory report can be generated from the DBMS_RESULT_CACHE package using the MEMORY_REPORT procedure. The report displays the following details:

- A single block size
- Maximum cache memory available
- Maximum size of a cached result
- Used and unused portion of the cache memory
- Count of the cached results, invalidated results, and dependent objects

A sample cache memory report looks as follows:

```
/*Connect as SYSDBA*/
Conn sys/system as sysdba
Connected.
```

```
/*Enable the serveroutput variable to display the block messages*/
SQL> SET SERVEROUTPUT ON

/*Generate the cache memory report*/
SQL> EXEC DBMS_RESULT_CACHE.MEMORY_REPORT
Result    Cache    Memory    Report
[Parameters]
Block Size = 1K bytes
Maximum Cache Size = 200M bytes (200K blocks)
Maximum Result Size = 40M bytes (40K blocks)
[Memory]
Total Memory = 134992 bytes [0.062% of the Shared Pool]
Fixed Memory = 9460 bytes [0.004% of the Shared Pool]
Dynamic Memory = 125532 bytes [0.058% of the Shared Pool]
Overhead = 92764 bytes
Cache Memory = 32K bytes (32 blocks)
Unused Memory = 30 blocks
Used Memory = 2 blocks
Dependencies = 1 blocks (1 count)
Results = 1 blocks
SQL = 1 blocks (1 count)

PL/SQL procedure successfully completed.
```

Read consistency of the SQL result cache

While the server searches the cached result of a query, the query must ensure read consistency. The clauses given in the following list must hold true for the database to use the cache:

- In a session, if the table (whose earlier query results are cached) is under an uncommitted transaction, the database would not cache its results. The queries using the table fetch the result from the server cache until the transaction is committed and the cached result gets invalidated.

- For the query result to be reusable, the query must make use of flashback to specify the timeframe.

Limitation of SQL result cache

The result of a SQL query will not be cached if the SQL includes dictionary views, temporary tables, SYS-owned tables, sequences, pseudo columns (such as CURRVAL, NEXTVAL, SYSDATE, LEVEL, ROWNUM and so on), or non-deterministic PL/SQL functions.

Implementing result cache in PL/SQL

Result caching in PL/SQL is second component of server-side caching in Oracle 11*g*. As we discussed briefly in the first section, results of frequently used PL/SQL functions can be retained at the server cache. The PL/SQL result cache feature uses the same infrastructure as the server result cache. When a function marked for result cache is executed, its result is cached at the server cache along with the parameters. The server picks up the result from the cache memory, if the same function is executed with the same parameters. In this way, the server saves a handful of time by bypassing the execution of the function body every time it is invoked, resulting into enhanced performance. The function can be a standalone, packaged, or locally declared (in a subprogram, not in anonymous PL/SQL block) one.

However, the cached result gets invalidated when the function or its referencing tables undergo a structural change followed by recompilation. The cached result also sets to the invalid state when the data in any of the referencing tables is updated.

As a common property of the server-side result cache, the cached result remains available for all connected active sessions of the same database.

The RESULT_CACHE clause

The PL/SQL cache implementation and execution is similar to the RESULT_CACHE hint in SQL. The same hint appears as a keyword in the PL/SQL function definition. A function whose results are to be cached must include the RESULT_CACHE clause in its header. The clause asks the database to cache the results of the function with its actual arguments. Syntax of the new function header looks as follows:

```
CREATE OR REPLACE FUNCTION [FUNCTION NAME]
RETURN [Return data type]
   RESULT_CACHE
   RELIES ON [TABLE NAME] (optional)
AS
BEGIN
...
...
END;
```

The RELIES_ON clause was introduced in Oracle 11*g* Release 1. The clause was used to specify the dependent table or view names, whose state would affect the status of the cached result. The cached result would be invalidated if the data in these tables or views undergo DML transaction. But later, the concept was found redundant when databases were updated to take care of managing dependencies. Therefore, the enhancement was withdrawn by Oracle in its subsequent 11*g* R2 release. The removal of the RELIES_ON clause increased authenticity and capability of the server cache by wiping out chances of error due to dependency.

Once the server has been configured for caching, PL/SQL function results can be readily cached. Check the following illustration:

```
/*Connect as SYSDBA*/
Conn sys/system as sysdba
Connected.

/*Flush the cache memory to clear the earlier cached results*/
SQL> EXEC dbms_result_cache.flush;

PL/SQL procedure successfully completed.

/*Flush the shared pool*/
SQL> alter system flush shared_pool
/

System altered.
/*connect as ORADEV*/
Conn ORADEV /ORADEV
Connected.

/*Set the SERVEROUTPUT parameter on to display the results*/
SQL> SET SERVEROUTPUT ON

/*Create a function F_GET_SAL*/
CREATE OR REPLACE FUNCTION f_get_sal (P_EMPNO NUMBER)
RETURN NUMBER
RESULT_CACHE
IS
  l_sal NUMBER;
BEGIN
  DBMS_OUTPUT.PUT_LINE(' Function Body execution');
  SELECT sal
  INTO L_SAL
  FROM employees
  WHERE empno=P_EMPNO;
  RETURN l_sal;
END;
/

Function created.

/*Declare a local variable and execute the function*/
SQL> VARIABLE m_sal NUMBER;
```

```
SQL> EXEC :m_sal := f_get_sal (7900);
Function Body execution

PL/SQL procedure successfully completed.
SQL> PRINT m_sal
  M_SAL
  -------
   1050
```

As soon as the function is executed for an input argument, the server caches the function result for this parameter. Let us now investigate the server cache memory for the function result:

```
/*Connect as sysdba*/
Conn sys/system as sysdba
Connected.
/*Query the cached results*/
SELECT id,status,name, type, namespace
FROM v$result_cache_objects
WHERE creator_uid = (SELECT user_id
  FROM dba_users
  WHERE username='ORADEV')
/
```

Refer to the following screenshot for the output of the preceding code block:

The function result has been cached, along with the referenced object that is, the EMPLOYEES table. Next time, if the function is invoked with the same parameter 7900, the F_GET_SAL function would not be executed. In the following repeated execution of F_GET_SAL, note that the display message function body execution has not been printed. It is because the function result has been picked up from the server cache:

```
/*connect as ORADEV*/
Conn ORADEV /ORADEV

/*Enable the serveroutput variable to display the block messages*/
SQL> SET SERVEROUTPUT ON

/*Declare a bind variable to capture the function execution results*/
SQL> VARIABLE m_sal NUMBER;
SQL> EXEC :m_sal := f_get_sal (7900);

PL/SQL procedure successfully completed.
SQL> PRINT m_sal
    M_SAL
  ----------
    1050
```

For the parameter values different from the `7900`, server executes the `F_GET_SAL` function, returns and caches the result at the server. In the following function call for the argument `7844`, note that the display message from `dbms_output` has been printed. This implies that the function body has been executed once:

```
/*Enable the serveroutput variable to display the block messages*/
SQL> SET SERVEROUTPUT ON

/*Declare a bind variable to capture the function execution results*/
SQL> variable m_other_sal number;
SQL> EXEC :m_other_sal := f_get_sal (7844);
Function Body execution

PL/SQL procedure successfully completed.

/*Print the results*/
SQL> PRINT m_other_sal;

M_OTHER_SAL
-----------
       1600
```

The result from the above function execution for employee, if `7844` is cached and its information can be queried in the `V$RESULT_CACHE_OBJECTS` view, is as follows:

```
/*Connect to SYSDBA*/
Conn sys/system as sysdba
Connected.

/*Check the cached results*/
SELECT id, status, type, cache_id
FROM v$result_cache_objects
ORDER BY id
/

  ID   STATUS      TYPE        CACHE_ID
  ---  ---------   ----------  --------------------------------
   0   Published   Dependency  ORADEV.F_GET_SAL
   1   Published   Result      97wusxcnc35b3053yrt02j5qc7
   2   Published   Dependency  ORADEV.EMPLOYEES
   3   Published   Result      97wusxcnc35b3053yrt02j5qc7
```

The PL/SQL caching metadata is stored in the same way as it is done in the SQL result caching. The same type (`Result` and `Dependency`) and status (`New`, `Published`, `Invalid`, `Expired`, or `Bypass`) appear when querying the cached result information in `V$RESULT_CACHE_OBJECTS`. The dependent object information can be queried from `V$RESULT_CACHE_DEPENDENCY`. Once the function result is cached at the server, the counts in `V$RESULT_CACHE_STATISTICS` would get updated automatically.

Now, let us generate the cache memory report to verify the PL/SQL cache result entries. In the report, note the PL/SQL result's counts, which are cached under used memory:

```
/*Connect to SYSDBA*/
Conn sys/system as sysdba
Connected.

/*Enable the serveroutput variable to display the block messages*/
SQL> SET SERVEROUTPUT ON
SQL> exec dbms_result_cache.memory_report
R e s u l t    C a c h e    M e m o r y    R e p o r t
[Parameters]
Block Size         = 1K bytes
Maximum Cache Size  = 200M bytes (200K blocks)
Maximum Result Size = 100M bytes (100K blocks)
[Memory]
Total Memory = 140616 bytes [0.064% of the Shared Pool]
Fixed Memory = 9460 bytes [0.004% of the Shared Pool]
Dynamic Memory = 131156 bytes [0.060% of the Shared Pool]
Overhead = 98388 bytes
Cache Memory = 32K bytes (32 blocks)
Unused Memory = 28 blocks
Used Memory = 4 blocks
Dependencies = 2 blocks (2 count)
Results = 2 blocks
PLSQL   = 2 blocks (2 count)

PL/SQL procedure successfully completed.
```

Cross-session availability of cached results

Once again, by virtue of common features of the server-side cache, the function results cached in one session would be accessible in all the sessions. The reason for this is the function result which is cached in the SGA and SGA is available for all the sessions.

To be noted, PL/SQL function result caching works only if the formal parameters are passed by reference. This is one of the limitation of the result cache feature in PL/SQL.

Invalidation of PL/SQL result cache

The function result cache gets invalidated if the function or its referencing table undergo a DDL change (alter, modify, or recompilation). In addition, even if the data contained in any of the referencing table gets updated, the server purges the cached result.

Currently, we have two published cache results from the last demonstration:

```
/*Connect to DBA*/
Conn sys/system as sysdba
Connected.

/*Query the cached results*/
SELECT id, status, type, cache_id
FROM v$result_cache_objects
ORDER BY id
/

  ID STATUS       TYPE       CACHE_ID
 --- --------- ---------- --------------------------------
   0 Published    Dependency ORADEV.F_GET_SAL
   1 Published    Result     97wusxcnc35b3053yrt02j5qc7
   2 Published    Dependency ORADEV.EMPLOYEES
   3 Published    Result     97wusxcnc35b3053yrt02j5qc7
```

This time, without flushing the results, we will recompile the function to observe the effect on the cached results:

```
/*Connect to the ORADEV user*/
Conn ORADEV/ORADEV
Connected.

/*Compile the function*/
ALTER FUNCTION F_GET_SAL COMPILE
/

Function altered.
```

Now, when we check the cache object information in V$RESULT_CACHE_OBJECTS, the Published results will be invalidated:

```
/*Connect to SYSDBA*/
Conn sys/system as sysdba
Connected.

/*Query the cached results*/
SELECT id, status, type, cache_id
FROM v$result_cache_objects
ORDER BY id
/

  ID STATUS       TYPE       CACHE_ID
 --- --------- ---------- --------------------------------
   0 Published    Dependency ORADEV.F_GET_SAL
   1 Invalid      Result     97wusxcnc35b3053yrt02j5qc7
   2 Published    Dependency ORADEV.EMPLOYEES
   3 Invalid      Result     97wusxcnc35b3053yrt02j5qc7
```

The observation deduces that the cached result is highly sensitive to the changes occurring on the objects with which it shares direct and indirect dependencies.

Limitations of PL/SQL function result cache

The efficiencies and accomplishments of the server result cache are beyond doubts. However, in some exceptional cases the caching feature is automatically ignored by the database server. We will discuss certain limitations of the result caching feature in Oracle.

Argument and return type restrictions

The argument and return type limitations are as follows:

- Functions with pass by value parameters (OUT or IN OUT)
- Functions with CLOB, NCLOB, or BLOB arguments
- Functions with arguments of a user-defined object or collection type
- Function return type is LOB

Function structural restrictions

The function structural limitations are as follows:

- Functions which are created with its invoker's rights.
- The function declared locally in an anonymous PL/SQL block. Oracle raises the following PLS-00999 exception:

  ```
  PLS-00999: implementation restriction (may be temporary) RESULT_
  CACHE is disallowed on subprograms in anonymous blocks
  ```

  It appears as a temporary restriction and might be seen in the forthcoming releases. However, a function declared locally in a subprogram (procedure or function) can still be stored in the server cache.

- Pipelined table functions

Summary

In this chapter, we learned how server result caching can dramatically improve performance in SQL and PL/SQL applications. We understood the database configuration required to enable the caching feature at the server. We learned the SQL result caching and PL/SQL function result caching through demonstrations.

In the next chapter, we will learn the PL/SQL analysis steps and techniques.

Practice exercise

1. The initialization parameter settings for your database are as follows:

```
MEMORY_TARGET = 500M
RESULT_CACHE_MODE = MANUAL
RESULT_CACHE_MAX_SIZE = 0
```

You execute a query by using the RESULT_CACHE hint. Which statement is true in this scenario?

a. The query results are not stored in the cache because no memory is allocated for the result cache.

b. The query results are stored in the cache because Oracle implicitly manages the cache memory.

c. The query results are not stored in the cache because RESULT_CACHE_MODE is MANUAL.

d. The query results are stored in the cache automatically when RESULT_CACHE_MODE is MANUAL.

2. You set the following initialization parameter settings for your database:

```
MEMORY_TARGET = 500M
RESULT_CACHE_MODE = FORCE
RESULT_CACHE_MAX_SIZE = 200M
```

You execute the following query:

```
SELECT /*+RESULT_CACHE*/ ENAME, DEPTNO
FROM EMPLOYEES
WHERE EMPNO = 7844
/
```

Which of the following statements are true?

a. The query results are cached because the SQL uses the RESULT_CACHE hint.

b. The query results are cached because the result cache mode is FORCE.

c. The query results are not cached because the SQL uses the RESULT_CACHE hint.

d. The RESULT_CACHE hint is ignored when result cache mode is FORCE.

3. The cached query result becomes invalid when the data accessed by the query gets modified.

a. True

b. False

4. The SQL query result cache is persistent only for the current session.

a. True

b. False

5. Which of the following PL/SQL objects' results cannot be cached?

a. Standalone function

b. Procedure

c. A function local to a procedure

d. Packaged function

6. The RELIES_ON clause in the PL/SQL function result cache can be used to specify the dependent tables or views whose state would affect the cached result.

a. True

b. False

7. Server settings are as follows:

```
MEMORY_TARGET = 500M
RESULT_CACHE_MODE = FORCE
RESULT_CACHE_MAX_SIZE = 200M
```

Identify the SQL queries whose results cannot be cached by the server.

a. SELECT ename, sal FROM employees WHERE empno = 7900;

b. SELECT seq_empid.nextval FROM DUAL;

c. SELECT ename, sysdate, hiredate FROM employees;

d. SELECT dname, loc FROM departments WHERE deptno = 10;

8. Identify the correct statements about the PL/SQL function result cache.

   a. PL/SQL function result cache requires additional server configuration.

   b. PL/SQL function result cache cannot be operated on procedures.

   c. PL/SQL function result cache works with all categories of functions.

   d. PL/SQL function cache features can work with the function which take collection type arguments.

9. Identify the admissible value of the STATUS column in V$RESULT_CACHE_OBJECTS.

   a. PUBLISHED

   b. INVALID

   c. USED

   d. UNUSED

10. Choose the correct statement about the following sample cache memory statistics report:

ID	NAME	VALUE
1	Block Size (Bytes)	1024
2	Block Count Maximum	204800
3	Block Count Current	32
4	Result Size Maximum (Blocks)	40960
5	Create Count Success	1
6	Create Count Failure	0
7	Find Count	0
8	Invalidation Count	0
9	Delete Count Invalid	0
10	Delete Count Valid	0
11	Hash Chain Length	1

   a. Create Count Success is the count of successfully cached results.

   b. Find Count is the count of the successfully cached results found and used in the queries.

   c. Invalidation Count is the count of the invalidated cached results.

   d. Block Count Maximum is the static value of total blocks available in the cache memory.

10
Analyzing PL/SQL Code

Code writing and tuning is the first stage of application life cycle development. As this life cycle matures and grows, the maintenance of code base becomes mandatory for code analysis and forecasts. The code management strategy aims at code testing, tracing, profiling, and reporting the coding information. This chapter covers some recommended techniques to analyze PL/SQL code through Oracle-supplied resources such as data dictionary views, initialization parameters, and built-in packages. Within the scope of the chapter, we will cover the following topics:

- Tracing and generating reports on PL/SQL source code
- Reporting usage of identifiers in PL/SQL source code
- Extracting schema object definitions using DBMS_METADATA

Track coding information

Once the development stage of the code base is over, it might be required to track through the code for search operation or to extract some crucial information for analysis or maintenance purposes. Such scenarios do not require thorough line-by-line digging as might seem to be the case. The line-by-line or code-by-code approach not only eats up a lot of time and resource but also ends up in a huge effort with tiny result. For this reason, Oracle supplies a set of dictionary views which make the life of analysts easy. The Oracle-supplied dictionary views are proven metadata sources of Oracle to provide accurate and detailed end results. The dictionary views used for tracking PL/SQL code information are ALL_ARGUMENTS, ALL_OBJECTS, ALL_SOURCE, ALL_PROCEDURES, and ALL_DEPENDENCIES.

The following diagram lists the dictionary views along with a brief description. Note that only ALL_* views are listed in the chart but, nevertheless, the same purpose is achieved by the other [USER | DBA] flavors too:

ALL_ARGUMENTS	■ Stores information about member subprograms and its arguments for a PL/SQL subprogram
ALL_OBJECTS	■ Stores the objects created in the database
ALL_SOURCE	■ Stores the source code of the compilation and stores program units in a schema
ALL_PROCEDURES	■ Stores the package, procedure, and function information
ALL_DEPENDENCIES	■ Stores the dependencies of an object

When a schema object is compiled and created in the database, SYS-owned tables capture the relevant information about the PL/SQL object. Dictionary views are built on top of the SYS-owned tables to present the information in a meaningful way. These views exist in the following three flavors:

- USER: Contains metadata of the objects whose owner is the current user
- ALL: Contains metadata of the objects accessible by the current user
- DBA: Contains metadata of all objects

Dictionary views are accessed by prefixing their scope with the name. It is not mandatory that a view must exist in all three flavors. For example, the DBA_GLOBAL_CONTEXT view exists, but the USER_GLOBAL_CONTEXT and ALL_GLOBAL_CONTEXT views do not exist.

 All dictionary views along with their description can be queried from an Oracle-supplied view DICTIONARY.

Let us create a small procedure and a function to understand how the preceding dictionary views present meaningful metadata information. The P_PRINT_NAME procedure accepts a parameter and prints it in uppercase. A similar result is achieved by the F_GET_NAME function too:

```
/*Connect to ORADEV user*/
SQL> conn ORADEV/ORADEV
Connected.

/*Enable the serveroutput to display the error messages*/
SQL> SET SERVEROUTPUT ON

/*Create the procedure*/
SQL> CREATE OR REPLACE PROCEDURE p_print_name (p_name VARCHAR2)
   IS
     l_name VARCHAR2(255);
   BEGIN
/*Convert the input string case to upper*/
     l_name := UPPER(p_name);

/*Print the input string in upper case*/
     DBMS_OUTPUT.PUT_LINE(l_name);
   END;
/

Procedure created.

/*Create the function*/
SQL> create or replace function f_print_name (p_name varchar2)
   return VARCHAR2
   IS
   begin
/*Return the string in upper case*/
     return UPPER(p_name);
   END;
/

Function created.
```

[DBA | ALL | USER]_ARGUMENTS

Now, let us query each of the dictionary views to check the information collected by them. We will start with the USER_ARGUMENTS view. The view contains object properties such as the object ID, its name, its parent package name (if any), and argument information such as arguments of the subprogram, its sequence, data type, and parameter passing mode.

The structure of the view is as follows:

```
/*Print the structure of USER_ARGUMENTS*/
SQL> DESC USER_ARGUMENTS

 Name                        Null?      Type
 --------------------------  --------   ----------------
 OBJECT_NAME                            VARCHAR2(30)
 PACKAGE_NAME                           VARCHAR2(30)
 OBJECT_ID                   NOT NULL   NUMBER
 OVERLOAD                               VARCHAR2(40)
 SUBPROGRAM_ID                          NUMBER
 ARGUMENT_NAME                          VARCHAR2(30)
 POSITION                    NOT NULL   NUMBER
 SEQUENCE                    NOT NULL   NUMBER
 DATA_LEVEL                  NOT NULL   NUMBER
 DATA_TYPE                              VARCHAR2(30)
 DEFAULTED                              VARCHAR2(1)
 DEFAULT_VALUE                          LONG
 DEFAULT_LENGTH                         NUMBER
 IN_OUT                                 VARCHAR2(9)
 DATA_LENGTH                            NUMBER
 DATA_PRECISION                         NUMBER
 DATA_SCALE                             NUMBER
 RADIX                                  NUMBER
 CHARACTER_SET_NAME                     VARCHAR2(44)
 TYPE_OWNER                             VARCHAR2(30)
 TYPE_NAME                              VARCHAR2(30)
 TYPE_SUBNAME                           VARCHAR2(30)
 TYPE_LINK                              VARCHAR2(128)
 PLS_TYPE                               VARCHAR2(30)
 CHAR_LENGTH                            NUMBER
 CHAR_USED                              VARCHAR2(1)
```

The view columns can be described with comments using the DICT_COLUMNS dictionary view:

```
/*Query the view columns*/
SELECT column_name, comments
FROM dict_columns
WHERE table_name='USER_ARGUMENTS'
/
```

Refer to the following screenshot for the output:

```
COLUMN_NAME            COMMENTS
-------------------    -------------------------------------------------------
OBJECT_NAME            Procedure or function name
PACKAGE_NAME           Package name
OBJECT_ID              Object number of the object
OVERLOAD               Overload unique identifier
SUBPROGRAM_ID          Unique sub-program Identifier
ARGUMENT_NAME          Argument name
POSITION               Position in argument list, or null for function return value
SEQUENCE               Argument sequence, including all nesting levels
DATA_LEVEL             Nesting depth of argument for composite types
DATA_TYPE              Datatype of the argument
DEFAULTED              Is the argument defaulted?
DEFAULT_VALUE          Default value for the argument
DEFAULT_LENGTH         Length of default value for the argument
IN_OUT                 Argument direction (IN, OUT, or IN/OUT)
DATA_LENGTH            Length of the column in bytes
DATA_PRECISION         Length: decimal digits (NUMBER) or binary digits (FLOAT)
DATA_SCALE             Digits to right of decimal point in a number
RADIX                  Argument radix for a number
CHARACTER_SET_NAME     Character set name for the argument
TYPE_OWNER             Owner name for the argument type in case of object types
TYPE_NAME              Object name for the argument type in case of object types
TYPE_SUBNAME           Subordinate object name for the argument type in case of object types
TYPE_LINK              Database link name for the argument type in case of object types
PLS_TYPE               PL/SQL type name for numeric arguments
CHAR_LENGTH            Character limit for string datatypes
CHAR_USED              Is the byte limit (B) or char limit (C) official for this string?

26 rows selected.
```

The ARGUMENT_NAME view column denotes the actual argument name as given in the program header (DATA_LEVEL = 0). If it is NULL, it signifies the return type of the function to be in OUT mode (DATA_LEVEL = 0). For DATA_LEVEL > 0, the argument is of object type or composite data type.

> The USER_ARGUMENTS view contains only the argument name, type, passing mode, and default value. However, the view does not maintain any information about the NOCOPY hint, if used with the OUT or IN OUT arguments.

The argument contained in the P_PRINT_NAME procedure and the F_PRINT_NAME function can be queried from the view as shown in the following code snippet. Observe the record entry with the NULL argument name which denotes the return type of the function:

```
/*Query the arugment for the procedure P_PRINT_NAME*/
SELECT object_name, subprogram_id,argument_name, data_type, in_out
FROM user_arguments
WHERE object_name IN ('P_PRINT_NAME','F_PRINT_NAME')
/
```

```
OBJECT_NAME       SUBPROGRAM_ID   ARGUMENT   DATA_TYPE        IN_OUT
---------------   -------------   --------   --------------   ---------
F_PRINT_NAME      1               P_NAME     VARCHAR2         IN
F_PRINT_NAME      1                          VARCHAR2         OUT
P_PRINT_NAME      1               P_NAME     VARCHAR2         IN
```

[DBA | ALL | USER]_OBJECTS

The USER_OBJECTS view simply stores the metadata information of the schema objects. Apart from storing basic information such as the object ID, name, or creation timestamp, it collects the information about the object type, status, and namespace details.

The structure of the dictionary view looks as shown in the following code snippet:

```
/*Display the structure of USER_OBJECTS*/
SQL> DESC USER_OBJECTS

Name                     Null?      Type
----------------------   --------   ----------------
OBJECT_NAME                         VARCHAR2(128)
SUBOBJECT_NAME                      VARCHAR2(30)
OBJECT_ID                           NUMBER
DATA_OBJECT_ID                      NUMBER
OBJECT_TYPE                         VARCHAR2(19)
CREATED                             DATE
LAST_DDL_TIME                       DATE
TIMESTAMP                           VARCHAR2(19)
STATUS                              VARCHAR2(7)
TEMPORARY                           VARCHAR2(1)
GENERATED                           VARCHAR2(1)
SECONDARY                           VARCHAR2(1)
NAMESPACE                           NUMBER
EDITION_NAME                        VARCHAR2(30)
```

The view columns with comments can be queried from the DICT_COLUMNS view:

```
/*Query the view columns*/
SELECT column_name, comments
FROM dict_columns
WHERE table_name='USER_OBJECTS'
/
```

Refer to the following screenshot for the output:

```
COLUMN_NAME         COMMENTS
------------------  ---------------------------------------------------------------
OBJECT_NAME         Name of the object
SUBOBJECT_NAME      Name of the sub-object (for example, partititon)
OBJECT_ID           Object number of the object
DATA_OBJECT_ID      Object number of the segment which contains the object
OBJECT_TYPE         Type of the object
CREATED             Timestamp for the creation of the object
LAST_DDL_TIME       Timestamp for the last DDL change (including GRANT and REVOKE) to the object
TIMESTAMP           Timestamp for the specification of the object
STATUS              Status of the object
TEMPORARY           Can the current session only see data that it place in this object itself?
GENERATED           Was the name of this object system generated?
SECONDARY           Is this a secondary object created as part of icreate for domain indexes?
NAMESPACE           Namespace for the object
EDITION_NAME        Name of the edition in which the object is actual

14 rows selected.
```

In the preceding USER_OBJECTS view structure, it is important to understand the behavior of the date type columns — CREATED, LAST_DDL_TIME and TIMESTAMP. The CREATED column stores the fixed value as the date when the object was created for the first time. The LAST_DDL_TIME column stores the date when the object was recompiled last time. The TIMESTAMP column stores the date when the source code of the object was modified. If the object is recompiled, only the LAST_DDL_TIME column gets updated. But if the source code of the object undergoes a modification, both TIMESTAMP and LAST_DDL_TIME get updated.

The EDITION_NAME column stores the actual edition name of the object. Editions are non-schema objects which are used to maintain versions of schema objects. A new edition inherits all objects from the latest edition. Oracle 11*g* R2 brings in a mandatory default edition ORA$BASE for all databases. Further reading can be continued at Oracle documentation (http://docs.oracle.com/cd/E11882_01/appdev.112/e10471/adfns_editions.htm).

The object properties of the P_PRINT_NAME procedure, as schema objects, can be retrieved as follows:

```
/Query the object properties of P_PRINT_NAME*/
SELECT object_id, object_type, status,namespace
FROM user_objects
WHERE object_name='P_PRINT_NAME'
/

 OBJECT_ID OBJECT_TYPE          STATUS  NAMESPACE
---------- -------------------- ------- ----------
     81410 PROCEDURE            VALID   1
```

[DBA | ALL | USER]_SOURCE

The USER_SOURCE dictionary view should give you the complete source code for the object which you request. Here is the structure of the view:

```
/*Display the structure of USER_SOURCE*/
SQL> DESC USER_SOURCE

 Name                   Null?     Type
 ---------------------- --------- ---------
 NAME                             VARCHAR2(30)
 TYPE                             VARCHAR2(12)
 LINE                             NUMBER
 TEXT                             VARCHAR2(4000)
```

The columns of the USER_SOURCE view, along with their comments, can be queried from the DICT_COLUMNS view:

```
/*Query the view columns*/
SELECT column_name, comments
FROM dict_columns
WHERE table_name='USER_SOURCE'
/
```

```
COLUMN_NAME                   COMMENTS
----------------------------  ----------------------------------------------------------
NAME                          Name of the object
TYPE                          Type of the object: "TYPE", "TYPE BODY", "PROCEDURE", "FUNCTION",
                              "PACKAGE", "PACKAGE BODY", "LIBRARY" or "JAVA SOURCE"
LINE                          Line number of this line of source
TEXT                          Source text
```

The source code of the P_PRINT_NAME program unit can be queried as follows:

```
/*Query the source code of P_PRINT_NAME*/
SELECT *
FROM user_SOURCE
WHERE name='P_PRINT_NAME'
/
```

```
NAME               TYPE          LINE TEXT
-----------------  ----------    ---- ------------------------------------------
P_PRINT_NAME       PROCEDURE        1 PROCEDURE p_print_name (p_name VARCHAR2)
P_PRINT_NAME       PROCEDURE        2    IS
P_PRINT_NAME       PROCEDURE        3        l_name VARCHAR2(255);
P_PRINT_NAME       PROCEDURE        4    BEGIN
P_PRINT_NAME       PROCEDURE        5 /*Convert the input string case to upper*/
P_PRINT_NAME       PROCEDURE        6        l_name := UPPER(p_name);
P_PRINT_NAME       PROCEDURE        7 /*Print the input string in upper case*/
P_PRINT_NAME       PROCEDURE        8        DBMS_OUTPUT.PUT_LINE(l_name);
P_PRINT_NAME       PROCEDURE        9    END;

9 rows selected.
```

[DBA | ALL | USER]_PROCEDURES

The USER_PROCEDURES dictionary view stores the subprogram properties of an object. Unlike its name, it stores the details for a procedure, function, or packages contained in the database schema. The structure of the dictionary view looks as follows:

```
/*Display the structure of USER_PROCEDURES*/
SQL> DESC USER_PROCEDURES
  Name                         Null?      Type
  ---------------------------  --------   --------------
  OBJECT_NAME                             VARCHAR2(128)
  PROCEDURE_NAME                          VARCHAR2(30)
  OBJECT_ID                               NUMBER
  SUBPROGRAM_ID                           NUMBER
  OVERLOAD                                VARCHAR2(40)
  OBJECT_TYPE                             VARCHAR2(19)
  AGGREGATE                               VARCHAR2(3)
  PIPELINED                               VARCHAR2(3)
  IMPLTYPEOWNER                           VARCHAR2(30)
  IMPLTYPENAME                            VARCHAR2(30)
  PARALLEL                                VARCHAR2(3)
  INTERFACE                               VARCHAR2(3)
  DETERMINISTIC                           VARCHAR2(3)
  AUTHID                                  VARCHAR2(12)
```

The columns of the USER_PROCEDURES view can be queried from the DICT_COLUMNS view:

```
/*Query the view columns*/
SELECT column_name, comments
FROM dict_columns
WHERE table_name='USER_PROCEDURES'
/

COLUMN_NAME              COMMENTS
-----------------        --------------------------------------------------
------
OBJECT_NAME              Name of the object: top level
                             function/procedure/package/type/trigger name
PROCEDURE_NAME           Name of the package or type subprogram
OBJECT_ID                Object number of the object
SUBPROGRAM_ID            Unique sub-program identifier
OVERLOAD                 Overload unique identifier
OBJECT_TYPE              The typename of the object
```

```
AGGREGATE            Is it an aggregate function ?
PIPELINED            Is it a pipelined table function ?
IMPLTYPEOWNER        Name of the owner of the implementation type (if
any)
IMPLTYPENAME         Name of the implementation type (if any)
PARALLEL             Is the procedure parallel enabled ?
INTERFACE
DETERMINISTIC
AUTHID

14 rows selected.
```

From the above column description, it is important to understand a few columns such as IMPLTYPEOWNER, IMPLTYPENAME, and AUTHID. Implementation type and owner values interpret any object type association of the program. The AUTHID column shows the authorization holder during invocation—possible values can be DEFINER, if the program has to be invoked by its owner's rights, and CURRENT_USER, if the program has to be invoked by its invoker.

The procedural properties of the P_PRINT_NAME subprogram can be queried from the view as follows:

```
/*Query the subprogram properties of P_PRINT_NAME*/
select object_id,object_type, overload, authid
FROM user_procedures
WHERE object_name='P_PRINT_NAME'
/

  OBJECT_ID OBJECT_TYPE          OVERLOAD    AUTHID
---------- -------------------- ---------- ---------
     81410 PROCEDURE                        DEFINER
```

[DBA | ALL | USER]_DEPENDENCIES

The USER_DEPENDENCIES dictionary view reveals very important information about the dependencies shared by the object. In many cases, the dependency shared by an object is decisive over its validity status. The view contains the details of the objects which are referenced within the definition of a particular object:

```
/*Display the structure of USER_DEPENDENCIES*/
SQL> DESC USER_DEPENDENCIES
  Name                       Null?    Type
  ----------------------- -------- ------------
  NAME                    NOT NULL VARCHAR2(30)
  TYPE                             VARCHAR2(18)
```

```
REFERENCED_OWNER                    VARCHAR2(30)
REFERENCED_NAME                     VARCHAR2(64)
REFERENCED_TYPE                     VARCHAR2(18)
REFERENCED_LINK_NAME                VARCHAR2(128)
SCHEMAID                            NUMBER
DEPENDENCY_TYPE                     VARCHAR2(4)
```

The columns of the preceding view structure can be explained from the
DICT_COLUMNS view:

```
/*The view columns with comments*/
SELECT column_name, comments
FROM dict_columns
WHERE table_name='USER_DEPENDENCIES'
/
```

Refer to the following screenshot for the output:

```
COLUMN_NAME             COMMENTS
----------------------  ------------------------------------------------------------
NAME                    Name of the object
TYPE                    Type of the object
REFERENCED_OWNER        Owner of referenced object (remote owner if remote object)
REFERENCED_NAME         Name of referenced object
REFERENCED_TYPE         Type of referenced object
REFERENCED_LINK_NAME    Name of dblink if this is a remote object
SCHEMAID
DEPENDENCY_TYPE

8 rows selected.
```

The dependency shared by the P_PRINT_NAME procedure can be queried as per the
following query:

```
/*Query the dependent objects of P_PRINT_NAME*/
select type, referenced_owner, referenced_name, referenced_type
FROM user_dependencies
WHERE name='P_PRINT_NAME'
/
```

TYPE	REFERENCED_OWNER	REFERENCED_NAME	REFERENCED_TYPE
PROCEDURE	SYS	STANDARD	PACKAGE
PROCEDURE	SYS	DBMS_OUTPUT	PACKAGE
PROCEDURE	SYS	SYS_STUB_FOR_PURITY_ANALYSIS	PACKAGE

Using SQL Developer to find coding information

The object metadata information retrieved from the dictionary views is a conventional way to track code information. But these days, the IDE have been made self-sufficient to generate some vital predefined reports. The metadata information demonstrated in the last section using dictionary views can also be generated from SQL Developer. **SQL Developer** is a free UI based interactive IDE tool which boards multiple database utilities.

Here, we will demonstrate the tracking of code through SQL Developer:

1. Go to **View** | **Reports**:

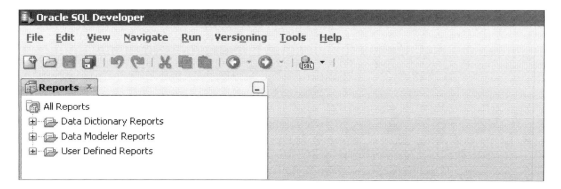

2. Go to **All Reports** | **Data Dictionary Reports** | **PLSQL**:
   - Under **PLSQL**, you find three options. These options are analogous to the dictionary views which we queried in the preceding section.
   - The **Program Unit Arguments** option queries the USER_ARGUMENTS dictionary view. The **Search Source Code** and **Unit Line Counts** options query the USER_SOURCE view.

○ When you click on any of the options for the first time, the following dialog box pops up. There you can select the connection, if you have multiple connections in your connect list:

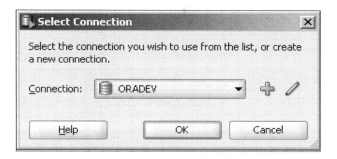

3. Once the connection is selected from the drop-down list, another dialog box appears and prompts for user inputs:

○ For **Program Unit Arguments**, the dialog asks for **Package** or **Program Unit Name**.

○ For **Search Source Code**, the dialog box asks for **PL/SQL Object Name** or **Text Search**.

○ For **Unit Line Counts**, there is no dialog box, as it generates the line count report for all the schema objects:

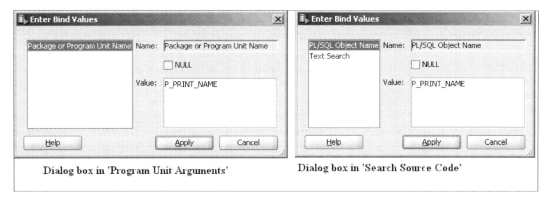

Dialog box in 'Program Unit Arguments'   Dialog box in 'Search Source Code'

4. We can demonstrate **Search Source Code** by providing P_PRINT_NAME as input:

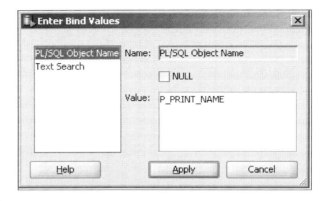

5. Click on **Apply** to generate the source code report:

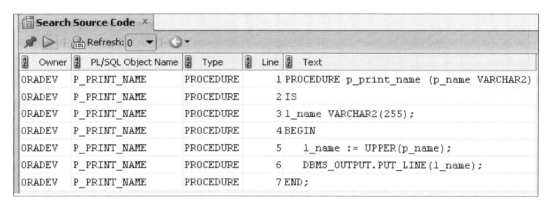

6. Demonstrate the generation of argument report from **Program Unit Arguments**:

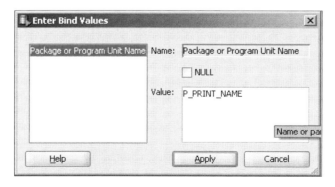

7. Click on the **Apply** button to generate the argument report for the given program unit:

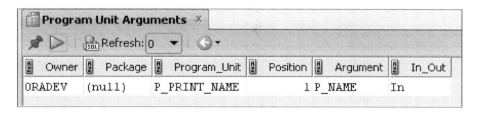

The DBMS_DESCRIBE package

The DBMS_DESCRIBE package is an Oracle built-in package which is used to gather information about the Oracle PL/SQL object—making it an essential Oracle data access component. It is owned by the SYS user, and all other users hitting the server, access its public synonym.

It contains only one subprogram that, is DESCRIBE_PROCEDURE.

The structure of the DESCRIBE_PROCEDURE subprogram is as follows:

```
DBMS_DESCRIBE.DESCRIBE_PROCEDURE(
    object_name                 IN   VARCHAR2,
    reserved1                   IN   VARCHAR2,
    reserved2                   IN   VARCHAR2,
    overload                    OUT  NUMBER_TABLE,
    position                    OUT  NUMBER_TABLE,
    level                       OUT  NUMBER_TABLE,
    argument_name               OUT  VARCHAR2_TABLE,
    datatype                    OUT  NUMBER_TABLE,
    default_value               OUT  NUMBER_TABLE,
    in_out                      OUT  NUMBER_TABLE,
    length                      OUT  NUMBER_TABLE,
    precision                   OUT  NUMBER_TABLE,
    scale                       OUT  NUMBER_TABLE,
    radix                       OUT  NUMBER_TABLE,
    spare                       OUT  NUMBER_TABLE
    include_string_constraints  OUT  BOOLEAN DEFAULT FALSE);
```

The DBMS_DESCRIBE procedure can extract the following information for a given procedure:

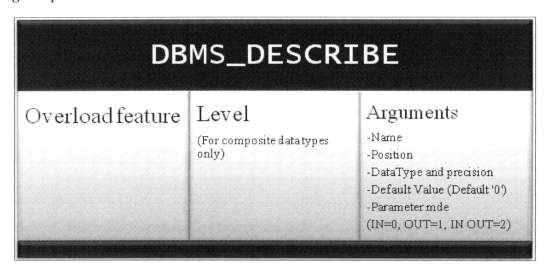

Note that the procedure accepts three IN mode parameters, one OUT parameter, and 12 OUT parameters of associative array type.

Two reserved parameters are the Reserved parameters and must be kept NULL. The remaining parameters are the OUT parameters of the Associative array type whose definition is as follows:

```
TYPE VARCHAR2_TABLE IS TABLE OF VARCHAR2(30)
   INDEX BY BINARY_INTEGER;
TYPE NUMBER_TABLE IS TABLE OF NUMBER
   INDEX BY BINARY_INTEGER;
```

For the P_PRINT_NAME procedure, the DBMS_DESCRIBE package works as follows:

```
/*Connect to ORADEV user*/
Conn ORADEV/ORADEV
Connected.

/*Enable the serveroutput to display the error messages*/
SET SERVEROUTPUT ON
DECLARE

/*Declare the local variable of DBMS_DESCRIBE associative array type*/
  v_overload DBMS_DESCRIBE.NUMBER_TABLE;
  v_position DBMS_DESCRIBE.NUMBER_TABLE;
  v_level DBMS_DESCRIBE.NUMBER_TABLE;
  v_arg_name DBMS_DESCRIBE.VARCHAR2_TABLE;
```

```
   v_datatype DBMS_DESCRIBE.NUMBER_TABLE;
   v_def_value DBMS_DESCRIBE.NUMBER_TABLE;
   v_in_out DBMS_DESCRIBE.NUMBER_TABLE;
   v_length DBMS_DESCRIBE.NUMBER_TABLE;
   v_precision DBMS_DESCRIBE.NUMBER_TABLE;
   v_scale DBMS_DESCRIBE.NUMBER_TABLE;
   v_radix DBMS_DESCRIBE.NUMBER_TABLE;
   v_spare DBMS_DESCRIBE.NUMBER_TABLE;
   BEGIN

/*Call the procedure DESCRIBE_PROCEDURE for P_PRINT_NAME*/
   DBMS_DESCRIBE.DESCRIBE_PROCEDURE
   (
     'P_PRINT_NAME',
     null, null,
     v_overload,
     v_position,
     v_level,
     v_arg_name,
     v_datatype,
     v_def_value,
     v_in_out,
     v_length,
     v_precision,
     v_scale,
     v_radix,
     v_spare,
     null
   );

/*Iterate the argument array V_ARG_NAME to list the argument details
of the object*/
   FOR i IN v_arg_name.FIRST .. v_arg_name.LAST
   LOOP

/*Check if the position if zero or not*/
     IF v_position(i) = 0 THEN

/*Zero position is reserved for RETURN types*/
       DBMS_OUTPUT.PUT('This is the RETURN data for the function: ');
       DBMS_OUTPUT.NEW_LINE;
     ELSE

/*Print the argument name*/
       DBMS_OUTPUT.PUT ('The argument name is: '||v_arg_name(i));
       DBMS_OUTPUT.NEW_LINE;
     END IF;

/*Display the position, type and mode of parameters*/
```

```
      DBMS_OUTPUT.PUT_LINE('The argument position is:'||v_
position(i));
      DBMS_OUTPUT.NEW_LINE;
      DBMS_OUTPUT.PUT_LINE('The argument datatype is:'||v_
datatype(i));
      DBMS_OUTPUT.NEW_LINE;
      DBMS_OUTPUT.PUT_LINE('The argument mode is:'||v_in_out(i));
      DBMS_OUTPUT.NEW_LINE;
    END LOOP;
  END;
/


The argument name is: P_NAME
The argument position is:1
The argument datatype is:1
The argument mode is:0
PL/SQL procedure successfully completed.
```

DBMS_UTILITY.FORMAT_CALL_STACK

We often encounter scenarios where subprogram calls have been extensively branched and nested among themselves. A subprogram can be called from multiple program units and it might be required to trace the complete invocation path.

The FORMAT_CALL_STACK function of the DBMS_UTILITY package is used to extract the current call stack as a formatted text string. The call stack contains the information about the sequential calls made from a program to another program. Every call, in the stack, is stored by the line number of the subprogram invocation.

Suppose a procedure P3 calls another procedure P2. P2 makes a call to another stored subprogram P1. Now, in P1, a call trace report can be embedded to see the call path:

```
/*Create the procedure P1*/
CREATE OR REPLACE PROCEDURE P1
IS
BEGIN
  dbms_output.put_line(substr(dbms_utility.format_call_Stack, 1,
255));
END;
/

Procedure created.

/*Create the procedure P2*/
CREATE OR REPLACE PROCEDURE P2
```

```
IS
BEGIN
/*Call procedure P1*/
  P1;
END;
/

Procedure created.

/*Create the procedure P3*/
CREATE OR REPLACE PROCEDURE P3
IS
BEGIN
/*Call procedure P2*/
  P2;
END;
/

Procedure created.

/*Enable the serveroutput to display the error messages*/
SET SERVEROUTPUT ON

/*Start a PL/SQL block to invoke P3*/
BEGIN
/*Call P3*/
  P3;
END;
/

----- PL/SQL Call Stack -----
  object      line   object
  handle    number   name
23D06844         4   procedure ORADEV.P1
23CEAD38         4   procedure ORADEV.P2
23EDCB38         4   procedure ORADEV.P3
23CF00CC         2   anonymous block
PL/SQL procedure successfully completed.
```

In the above output, the call stack shows the calls traversing from the anonymous block to procedure P1. Starting from the last, an anonymous block calls P3, which calls P2, and reaches P1. The call stack would appear different for different paths used to reach P1. If another procedure P4 calls P2, and hence P1, the call stack would show P4 in place of P3.

Tracking propagating exceptions in PL/SQL code

We are well versed in and aware of the propagation behavior of exceptions in PL/SQL. But locating the exact position from where the exception got raised has always been a cumbersome job for developers. After the failure of SQLERRM to truncate the error messages after 512 characters, FORMAT_ERROR_STACK is used to serve this purpose to some extent by presenting complete error messages up to 2000 characters, without truncation.

Oracle 10*g* Release 1 provides an error handling function under the DBMS_UTILITY package known as FORMAT_ERROR_BACKTRACE, to handle scenarios of exception propagation. The function produces a formatted string containing the stack of program unit information with line numbers. It helps developers to locate the exact program unit which has raised the exception.

Let us conduct a small case study where we will explicitly raise the exception in one program and try to access the same from another PL/SQL block.

The P_TRACE procedure declares a local exception and rises from the executable section:

```
/*Connect to ORADEV user*/
Conn ORADEV/ORADEV
Connected.

/*Create procedure P_TRACE*/
CREATE OR REPLACE PROCEDURE p_trace
IS
/*Declare a local user defined exception*/
  xlocal EXCEPTION;
BEGIN
/*Raise the local exception*/
  RAISE xlocal;
END;
/

Procedure created.
```

First, we will present the situation prior to the introduction of FORMAT_ERROR_ BACKTRACE in Oracle 10*g*:

```
/*Call P_TRACE in a PL/SQL anonymous block*/
BEGIN
  P_TRACE;
EXCEPTION
WHEN OTHERS then
```

```
/*Display the error message using SQLERRM*/
  DBMS_OUTPUT.PUT_LINE(sqlerrm);
END;
/

User-Defined Exception
PL/SQL procedure successfully completed.
```

Note that the block output does not clearly specify the defaulter program unit which caused the exception propagation. It is because SQLERRM logs only the last exception to occur.

Now, we will modify the same anonymous PL/SQL block and include FORMAT_ERROR_BACKTRACE to log the program unit which raises the exception:

```
/*Create the PL/SQL anonymous block*/
SQL> BEGIN
  P_TRACE;
  EXCEPTION
    WHEN OTHERS then
/*Print the error stack using FORMAT_ERROR_BACKTRACE*/
    DBMS_OUTPUT.PUT_LINE( DBMS_UTILITY.FORMAT_ERROR_BACKTRACE );
  END;
/
ORA-06512: at "ORADEV.P_TRACE", line 5
ORA-06512: at line 2
```

The output given by FORMAT_ERROR_BACKTRACE shows the name of the P_TRACE program unit along with the line number (5, in this case) which raises the exception. This error stack information expands as the nesting of calls increases. It helps to trace, debug, and log the correct information of the ongoing database activities and take appropriate action.

Determining identifier types and usages

All the local declarations of a program unit are categorized as **identifiers**. An identifier's declaration locates a memory on the server and keeps it busy until the program unit is executed or terminated. Redundant identifiers must be recognized within a program so as to restrict them from holding a chunk of memory for no operation.

Oracle provides a tool known as PL/Scope to monitor the activities of identifiers in a program. It is one of the new features in Oracle 11*g*.

The PL/Scope tool

The PL/Scope tool compiles and captures the information of the identifiers declared and used in a program. Once the feature is enabled, the language compiler filters out the identifier's information and stores it in a dictionary view called USER_IDENTIFIERS. An identifier is recognized by its name, type, and usage.

Let us examine some of the key features of the PL/Scope tool:

- Only unwrapped program units can use the PL/Scope tool.
- The feature can be enabled by setting a new initialization parameter called PLSCOPE_SETTINGS.
- The compiler stages the identifiers' information only in the SYSAUX tablespace. The feature remains deactivated if the SYSAUX tablespace is unavailable.
- The identifier information can be viewed in [DBA | ALL | USER]_IDENTIFIERS.
- The feature can be enabled for the whole database, for a session, or only for an object. It implies that a program can be compiled with different compilation parameters from the current session or database settings. The object level specification overrides the session or system level setting of the parameter.

PL/Scope brings great benefit to any large-size database application where developers frequently check the existence of an identifier so as to avoid redundancy. In addition, it can work as a PL/SQL IDE to build up a repository of all identifiers under multiple categories based on their type and usage.

The PL/Scope identifier collection

The PL/Scope feature can be enabled by setting a system parameter called PLSCOPE_SETTINGS. By default, the feature is disabled as the parameter value is IDENTIFIERS:NONE. The valid values for the parameters are NONE for disabled and ALL for enabled parameters.

A DBA can modify the value of the PLSCOPE_SETTINGS compilation parameter as IDENTIFIERS:ALL to enable the feature to collect the identifier information. Once the feature is activated at the required level, Oracle captures identifier information of all program units which are compiled henceforth.

Setting `PLSCOPE_SETTINGS` at system or session level:

```
ALTER [SYSTEM | SESSION]
SET PLSCOPE_SETTINGS = ['IDENTIFIERS:ALL' | 'IDENTIFIERS:NONE']
```

Setting `PLSCOPE_SETTINGS` at object level:

```
ALTER [PROGRAM NAME] COMPILE
PLSCOPE_SETTINGS = ['IDENTIFIERS:ALL' | 'IDENTIFIERS:NONE']
```

For illustration and demonstration purpose, we will keep the setting as
`IDENTIFIERS:ALL`. A DBA performs it as shown in the following code snippet:

```
/*Connect as sysdba*/
Conn sys/system as sysdba
Connected.

/*Modify the PLSCOPE_SETTTINGS*/
ALTER SYSTEM SET PLSCOPE_SETTINGS = 'IDENTIFIERS:ALL';
Session altered.

/*View the current setting of PLSCOPE_SETTINGS parameter*/
SELECT value
FROM v$parameter
WHERE name='plscope_settings'
/

VALUE
----------------
IDENTIFIERS:ALL
```

Another important aspect of PL/Scope is that it is stored only in the SYSAUX
tablespace. If the SYSAUX tablespace is unavailable, the feature remains in passive
state. Though the server does not raise any error message while logging, a warning
is raised:

```
/*Verify the PL/Scope occupancy in SYSAUX tablespace*/
SELECT occupant_desc, schema_name, space_usage_kbytes
FROM v$sysaux_occupants
WHERE occupant_name='PL/SCOPE'
/

OCCUPANT_DESC                       SCHEMA_NAME   SPACE_USAGE_KBYTES
-------------------------------     ------------  ------------------
PL/SQL Identifier Collection        SYS                         2496
```

The PL/Scope report

The PL/Scope report can be generated from the [DBA | ALL | USER]_IDENTIFIERS dictionary view. [DBA | ALL | USER] provides different flavors to the view as per the invoker's role:

```
/*Display the USER_IDENTIFIERS structure*/
SQL> desc USER_IDENTIFIERS
```

```
Name                    Null?      Type
----------------------- --------   ----------------
NAME                               VARCHAR2(30)
SIGNATURE                          VARCHAR2(32)
TYPE                               VARCHAR2(18)
OBJECT_NAME             NOT NULL   VARCHAR2(30)
OBJECT_TYPE                        VARCHAR2(13)
USAGE                              VARCHAR2(11)
USAGE_ID                           NUMBER
LINE                               NUMBER
COL                                NUMBER
USAGE_CONTEXT_ID                   NUMBER
```

Note the information captured for an identifier in the preceding USER_IDENTIFIERS description:

- SIGNATURE: The unique hash code of the identifier
- TYPE: The user defined type of the identifier (Variable, Cursor, Formal, and so on)
- OBJECT_NAME: The object name within which they are declared, assigned, or used
- OBJECT_TYPE: The type of the object using the identifier
- USAGE: The identifier action as CALL, ASSIGNMENT, DEFINITION, DECLARATION, or REFERENCE
- USAGE_ID: The unique key of the identifier usage
- LINE, COL: Exact location of the identifier in the program

Illustration

Let us now demonstrate the PL/Scope tool to capture identifier information of a program unit. The program unit is a function which declares a cursor and local variables to get the location of an input employee.

The current setting of PLSCOPE_SETTINGS is IDENTIFIERS:ALL:

```
/*Connect as ORADEV*/
Conn ORADEV/ORADEV
Connected.

/*Create the function*/
CREATE OR REPLACE FUNCTION F_GET_LOC (P_EMPNO NUMBER)
RETURN NUMBER
IS

/*Cursor select location for the given employee*/
CURSOR C_DEPT IS
  SELECT d.loc
  FROM employees e, departments d
  WHERE e.deptno = d.deptno
  AND e.empno = P_EMPNO;
  l_loc NUMBER;
BEGIN

/*Cursor is open and fetched into a local variable*/
  OPEN C_DEPT;
  FETCH C_DEPT INTO l_loc;
  CLOSE C_DEPT;

/*Location returned*/
  RETURN l_loc;
END;
/

Function created.
```

Generate the PL/Scope identifier report from the USER_IDENTIFIERS dictionary view:

```
/*Query the identifier information from the view*/
SELECT name, type, object_name, usage
FROM user_identifiers
WHERE object_name='F_GET_LOC'
/
```

NAME	TYPE	OBJECT_NAME	USAGE
L_LOC	VARIABLE	F_GET_LOC	REFERENCE
C_DEPT	CURSOR	F_GET_LOC	CALL
L_LOC	VARIABLE	F_GET_LOC	ASSIGNMENT
C_DEPT	CURSOR	F_GET_LOC	CALL
C_DEPT	CURSOR	F_GET_LOC	CALL
NUMBER	NUMBER DATATYPE	F_GET_LOC	REFERENCE
L_LOC	VARIABLE	F_GET_LOC	DECLARATION

P_EMPNO	FORMAL IN	F_GET_LOC	REFERENCE
C_DEPT	CURSOR	F_GET_LOC	DECLARATION
NUMBER	NUMBER DATATYPE	F_GET_LOC	REFERENCE
NUMBER	NUMBER DATATYPE	F_GET_LOC	REFERENCE
P_EMPNO	FORMAL IN	F_GET_LOC	DECLARATION
F_GET_LOC	FUNCTION	F_GET_LOC	DEFINITION
F_GET_LOC	FUNCTION	F_GET_LOC	DECLARATION

```
14 rows selected.
```

Assume that the database setting does not allow the capturing of identifiers' information—only this feature can be enabled for the selective program units. A program unit can be compiled as follows:

```
/*Alter the function with PLSCOPE_SETTINGS at object level*/
SQL> ALTER FUNCTION F_GET_LOC COMPILE PLSCOPE_
SETTINGS='IDENTIFIERS:ALL';


Function altered.
```

For better presentation purpose, you can generate the above output in report format:

```
/*Generate interactive report for identifiers*/
WITH v AS
(
  SELECT Line,
  Col,
  INITCAP(NAME) Name,
  LOWER(TYPE)   Type,
  LOWER(USAGE)  Usage,
  USAGE_ID, USAGE_CONTEXT_ID
  FROM USER_IDENTIFIERS
  WHERE Object_Name = 'F_GET_LOC'
  AND Object_Type = 'FUNCTION'
)
  SELECT LINE, RPAD(LPAD(' ', 2*(Level-1)) ||Name, 20, '.')||' '||
  RPAD(Type, 20)|| RPAD(Usage, 20)
  IDENTIFIER_USAGE_CONTEXTS
  FROM v
    START WITH USAGE_CONTEXT_ID = 0
    CONNECT BY PRIOR USAGE_ID = USAGE_CONTEXT_ID
    ORDER SIBLINGS BY Line, Col
/
```

Refer to the following screenshot for the output:

```
 LINE IDENTIFIER_USAGE_CONTEXTS
----- -----------------------------------------------------------------
    1 F_Get_Loc............ function          declaration
    1    F_Get_Loc......... function          definition
    1       P_Empno......... formal in         declaration
    1         Number........ number datatype   reference
    2       Varchar2........ character datatype reference
    5 C_Dept............. cursor            declaration
    9      P_Empno....... formal in         reference
   10 L_Loc............. variable          declaration
   10       Varchar2...... character datatype reference
   13 C_Dept.......... cursor            call
   14 C_Dept.......... cursor            call
   14       L_Loc.......... variable          assignment
   15 C_Dept.......... cursor            call
   17 L_Loc........... variable          reference

14 rows selected.
```

Applications of the PL/Scope report

The PL/Scope identifier report can achieve the following objectives:

- It searches all the identifiers declared in a schema (USAGE = 'DECLARATION').
  The SELECT query lists all identifiers declared in the schema as shown in the
  following screenshot:

```
/*List the identifiers declared in the current schema*/
SELECT NAME, SIGNATURE, TYPE
FROM USER_IDENTIFIERS
WHERE USAGE='DECLARATION'
ORDER BY OBJECT_TYPE, USAGE_ID
/
```

- It searches all identifiers of a specific type (BLOB, CURSOR, CONSTANT, and so
  on) used in a schema. The following SQL query lists all the cursors declared
  in the schema:

```
/*List the identifiers declared as CURSOR in the current schema*/
SELECT NAME, SIGNATURE, OBJECT_NAME, TYPE
FROM USER_IDENTIFIERS
WHERE USAGE='DECLARATION'
AND TYPE = 'CURSOR'
ORDER BY OBJECT_TYPE, USAGE_ID
/
```

- It searches all redundant identifiers within a program unit which are not referenced inside the executable section of the program:

```
/*List the redundant identifiers declared in the current schema*/
SELECT NAME, OBJECT_NAME, TYPE, SIGNATURE
FROM USER_IDENTIFIERS T
WHERE USAGE='DECLARATION'
AND NOT EXISTS (SELECT 1
  FROM USER_IDENTIFIERS
  WHERE SIGNATURE=T.SIGNATURE
  AND USAGE<>'DECLARATION')
/
```

- It determines the actions performed on an identifier in a program:

```
/*List the actions on a specific identifier in the schema*/
SELECT name, object_name, type, usage, line
FROM USER_IDENTIFIERS T
WHERE signature='C6DC4D2D5770696415F7EC524AFADAE4'
/
```

The DBMS_METADATA package

The DBMS_METADATA package was introduced in Oracle9*i*. It is a metadata API which is used to extract the definitions (DDL) of schema objects. The package was introduced to get rid of DDL exports, which used to produce poorly formatted DDL scripts. It is a powerful package which can generate DDL and retrieve relevant information associated with an object in XML (by default), or textual format. The package is owned by SYS while all other users work with its public synonym.

The package provides utilities to set the required formatting for the DDL, transforms, and parse items. Once the formatting settings start over, using transform handlers, the definition of an object can be retrieved as XML or text. It also provides the flexibility to execute DDL. Let us see some of the major features of DBMS_METADATA:

- Generate DDL through GET_DDL (GET_XML is its XML equivalent).
- Generate DDL for object dependencies through GET_DEPENDENT_DDL (GET_DEPENDENT_XML is its XML equivalent).
- Generate DDL for system grants on an object through GET_GRANTED_DDL (GET_GRANTED_XML is its XML equivalent).
- Manage and modify object definitions such as add column, drop column, rename table, manage partitions, indexes, and so on.

- Callable from the SELECT statements.

- DBMS_METADATA uses public synonyms of SYS-owned object and table types.

- Additional options have been added in the Oracle 10*g* release.

- Data pump (Oracle 10*g*) uses DBMS_METADATA to retrieve schema object DDLs.

DBMS_METADATA data types and subprograms

As referred to earlier, the DBMS_METADATA package uses the public synonyms of SYS-owned data structures. The following list shows SYS-owned object types:

- SYS.KU$_PARSED_ITEM: It is the object to capture the attributes of object metadata of a single object. The object structure looks as follows:

```
CREATE TYPE sys.ku$_parsed_item AS OBJECT
(
  item VARCHAR2(30),
  value VARCHAR2(4000),
  object_row NUMBER
)
```

ITEM, VALUE form the attribute name value pair for OBJECT_ROW.

- SYS.KU$_PARSED_ITEMS: It is a nested table of SYS.KU$PARSED_ITEM to hold the object metadata attributes for multiple objects.

- SYS.KU$_DDL: It is an object type to capture the DDL of an object along with its parsed item information. The object type structure looks as follows:

```
CREATE TYPE sys.ku$_ddl AS OBJECT
(
  ddlText CLOB,
  parsedItem sys.ku$_parsed_items
)
```

The parsed object information is stored in PARSEDITEM.

- SYS.KU$_DDLS: It is a nested table of SYS.KU$_DDL returned by the FETCH_DDL subprogram to hold the metadata of an object transformed into multiple DDL statements.

- SYS.KU$_MULTI_DDL: It is an object type to hold the DDL for an object in multiple transforms.

- SYS.KU$_MULTI_DDLS:It is a nested table of SYS.KU$_MULTI_DDL returned by the CONVERT subprogram.

- `SYS.KU$_ERRORLINE`: It is an object type to capture the error information. The object type structure is as follows:

```
CREATE TYPE sys.ku$_ErrorLine IS OBJECT
(
  errorNumber NUMBER,
  errorText VARCHAR2(2000)
)
/
```

- `SYS.KU$_ERRORLINES`: It is the nested table of the `SYS.KU$_ERRORLINE` object type to hold the bulk error information during extraction of each DDL statement.

- `SYS.KU$_SUBMITRESULT`: It is an object type to capture the complete error information incurred in a DDL statement. The object type structure is as follows:

```
CREATE TYPE sys.ku$_SubmitResult AS OBJECT
(
  ddl sys.ku$_ddl,
  errorLines sys.ku$_ErrorLines
)
/
```

- `SYS.KU$_SUBMITRESULTS`: It is a nested table of the `SYS.KU$_SUBMITRESULT` object type to hold multiple DDL statements and corresponding error information.

In the preceding list, `KU$_PARSED_ITEM` and `KU$_DDL` are the most frequently used object types of the package.

The following table lists the `DBMS_METADATA` subprograms (reference: Oracle documentation)

Subprogram	Remarks
`ADD_TRANSFORM` function	Specifies a transform that `FETCH_[XML	DDL	CLOB]` applies to the XML representation of the retrieved objects
`CLOSE` procedure	Invalidates the handle returned by `OPEN` and cleans up the associated state
`CONVERT` functions and procedures	Convert an XML document to DDL

Subprogram	Remarks
FETCH_ [XML | DDL | CLOB] functions and procedures	Return metadata for objects meeting the criteria established by OPEN, SET_FILTER, SET_COUNT, ADD_TRANSFORM, and so on
GET_ [XML | DDL | CLOB] functions	Fetch the metadata for a specified object as XML or DDL, using only a single call
GET_QUERY function	Returns the text of the queries that are used by FETCH_ [XML | DDL | CLOB]
OPEN function	Specifies the type of object to be retrieved, the version of its metadata, and the object model
OPENW function	Opens a write context
PUT function	Submits an XML document to the database
SET_COUNT procedure	Specifies the maximum number of objects to be retrieved in a single FETCH_ [XML | DDL | CLOB] call
SET_FILTER procedure	Specifies restrictions on the objects to be retrieved, for example, the object name or schema
SET_PARSE_ITEM procedure	Enables output parsing by specifying an object attribute to be parsed and returned
SET_TRANSFORM_PARAM and SET_REMAP_PARAM procedures	Specifiy parameters to the XSLT style sheets identified by transform_handle

Out of the preceding list, the subprograms can be segregated based on their work function and utilization:

Subprograms used to retrieve multiple objects from the database	Subprograms used to submit XML metadata to the database
ADD_TRANSFORM function	ADD_TRANSFORM function
CLOSE procedure 2	CLOSE procedure 2
FETCH_ [XML | DDL | CLOB] functions and procedures	CONVERT functions and procedures
GET_QUERY function	OPENW function
GET_ [XML | DDL | CLOB] functions	PUT function
OPEN function	SET_PARSE_ITEM procedure
SET_COUNT procedure	SET_TRANSFORM_PARAM and SET_REMAP_PARAM procedures

Subprograms used to retrieve multiple objects from the database	Subprograms used to submit XML metadata to the database
SET_FILTER procedure	
SET_PARSE_ITEM procedure	
SET_TRANSFORM_PARAM and SET_REMAP_PARAM procedures	

Parameter requirements

The parameter requirements for the DBMS_METADATA subprograms are as follows:

- Parameters are case sensitive
- Parameters cannot be passed by named notation, but by position only

The DBMS_METADATA transformation parameters and filters

As listed in the preceding API list, the SET_TRANSFORM_PARAM subprogram is used to format and control the DDL output. It is used for both retrieval and submission of metadata from or to the database. It is an overloaded procedure with the following syntax:

```
DBMS_METADATA.SET_TRANSFORM_PARAM
(
  transform_handle IN NUMBER,
  name IN VARCHAR2,
  value IN VARCHAR2,
  object_type IN VARCHAR2 DEFAULT NULL
);
DBMS_METADATA.SET_TRANSFORM_PARAM
(
  transform_handle IN NUMBER,
  name IN VARCHAR2,
  value IN BOOLEAN DEFAULT TRUE,
  object_type IN VARCHAR2 DEFAULT NULL
);
DBMS_METADATA.SET_TRANSFORM_PARAM
(
  transform_handle IN NUMBER,
  name IN VARCHAR2,
  value IN NUMBER,
  object_type IN VARCHAR2 DEFAULT NULL
);
```

From the preceding syntax:

- TRANSFORM_HANDLE: It is the handler, either from ADD_TRANSFORM, or a generic handler constant SESSION_TRANSFORM, to affect the whole session.
- NAME: It is the name of the parameter to be modified.
- VALUE: It is the transformed value.

Now, we will see some of the common sets of parameters applicable to all objects in a schema:

Parameter	Value	Meaning
PRETTY	TRUE | FALSE (default value is TRUE)	If TRUE, produces properly indented output
SQLTERMINATOR	TRUE | FALSE (default value is FALSE)	If TRUE, appends SQL terminator (; or /) after each DDL
DEFAULT	TRUE | FALSE	If TRUE, resets all parameters to their default state
INHERIT	TRUE | FALSE	If TRUE, inherits session level settings

For tables and views, the valid transform handlers are as follows:

Parameter	Value	Meaning
SEGMENT_ATTRIBUTES	TRUE | FALSE (default value is TRUE)	If TRUE, includes segment, tablespace, logging and physical attributes
STORAGE	TRUE | FALSE (default value is FALSE)	If TRUE, includes storage clause
TABLESPACE	TRUE | FALSE	If TRUE, includes tablespace specification
CONSTRAINTS	TRUE | FALSE	If TRUE, includes table constraints
REF_CONSTRAINTS	TRUE | FALSE	If TRUE, includes referential constraints
CONSTRAINTS_AS_ALTER	TRUE | FALSE	If TRUE, includes constraints in the ALTER TABLE statements
OID	TRUE | FALSE	If TRUE, includes the object table OID
SIZE_BYTE_KEYWORD	TRUE | FALSE	If TRUE, includes the BYTE keywords in string type column specifications
FORCE	TRUE | FALSE	If TRUE, creates view with the FORCE option

Filters can be imposed on the working schema objects by using the DBMS_METADATA. SET_FILTER procedure. It takes the metadata handle, filter name, and its value as input. It can be used to set include and exclude filters:

```
PROCEDURE set_filter(
handle     IN NUMBER,
name       IN VARCHAR2,
value      IN VARCHAR2|BOOLEAN|NUMBER,
object_type_path VARCHAR2
);
```

Some of the frequently used filters are schema, user, object dependencies, table data, tables, indexes, constraints, and so on. There are more than 70 filters available until Oracle 11*g*. It can be set as follows:

```
DBMS_METADATA.SET_FILTER(handle,'SCHEMA','ORADEV');
DBMS_METADATA.SET_FILTER(handle,'NAME','DEPARTMENTS');
```

Working with DBMS_METADATA—illustrations

We will illustrate the usage of browsing APIs of DBMS_METADATA.

Case 1—retrieve the metadata of a single object

DBMS_METADATA.GET_DDL can be called from the SELECT query:

```
/*Connect as ORADEV*/
Conn ORADEV/ORADEV
Connected.

/*Execute the DBMS_METADATA.GET_DDL to get the DDL for EMPLOYEES
table*/
SELECT dbms_metadata.get_ddl('TABLE','EMPLOYEES','ORADEV')
FROM DUAL
/
EMPLOYEE_DDL
  CREATE TABLE "ORADEV"."EMPLOYEES"
  (
    "EMPNO" NUMBER(4,0),
    "ENAME" VARCHAR2(10) NOT NULL ENABLE,
    "JOB" VARCHAR2(9),
    "MGR" NUMBER(4,0),
    "HIREDATE" DATE,
    "SAL" NUMBER(7,2),
    "COMM" NUMBER(7,2),
    "DEPTNO" NUMBER(2,0),
```

```
      PRIMARY KEY ("EMPNO")
      USING INDEX PCTFREE 10 INITRANS 2 MAXTRANS 255 COMPUTE STATISTICS
      (
        INITIAL 65536 NEXT 1048576 MINEXTENTS 1 MAXEXTENTS 2147483645
        PCTINCREASE 0 FREELISTS 1 FREELIST GROUPS 1 BUFFER_POOL DEFAULT
        FLASH_CACHE DEFAULT CELL_FLASH_CACHE DEFAULT
      )
      TABLESPACE "USERS"  ENABLE
  )
  SEGMENT CREATION IMMEDIATE
  PCTFREE 10 PCTUSED 40 INITRANS 1 MAXTRANS 255 NOCOMPRESS LOGGING
  STORAGE(INITIAL 65536 NEXT 1048576 MINEXTENTS 1 MAXEXTENTS
2147483645
  0 FREELISTS 1 FREELIST GROUPS 1 BUFFER_POOL DEFAULT FLASH_CACHE
DEFAULT
  CELL_FLASH_CACHE DEFAULT)
 TABLESPACE "USERS"
```

The same DDL generation can also be achieved through a generic function. The function F_DDL_TABLE takes a table name as input and fetches its DDL script. It returns the DDL script as CLOB. Since the transform handler opens only for the TABLE of ORADEV schema, DDL scripts can only be used for tables:

```
/*Create function to get DDL of a given table*/
CREATE OR REPLACE FUNCTION get_ddl_table (p_table_name varchar2)
RETURN CLOB IS
  l_hdl NUMBER;
  l_th NUMBER;
  l_doc CLOB;
  BEGIN
/*specify the OBJECT TYPE*/
    l_hdl := DBMS_METADATA.OPEN('TABLE');
/*use FILTERS to specify the objects desired*/
    DBMS_METADATA.SET_FILTER(l_hdl ,'SCHEMA','ORADEV');
    DBMS_METADATA.SET_FILTER(l_hdl ,'NAME',p_table_name);
/*request to be TRANSFORMED into creation DDL*/
    l_th := DBMS_METADATA.ADD_TRANSFORM(l_hdl,'DDL');
/*FETCH the object*/
    l_doc := DBMS_METADATA.FETCH_CLOB(l_hdl);
/*release resources*/
    DBMS_METADATA.CLOSE(l_hdl);

    RETURN l_doc;
  END;
/
Function created.
```

The above DDL scripts generated from the query and function comprise the storage clause, tablespace, and segment information, thus making them bulky and large. These clauses can be skipped by setting the transform handlers for the session. Before extracting the DDL, we will set the STORAGE, SEGMENT_ATTRIBUTES, PRETTY, SQLTERMINATOR, and REF_CONSTRAINTS handlers for the session transform handler.

```
/*Connect to ORADEV*/
Conn ORADEV/ORADEV
Connected.

/*Set transform handler for STORAGE*/
EXEC DBMS_METADATA.SET_TRANSFORM_PARAM (DBMS_METADATA.SESSION_
TRANSFORM,'STORAGE',false);

/*Set transform handler for SEGMENT_ATTRIBUTES*/
EXEC DBMS_METADATA.SET_TRANSFORM_PARAM (DBMS_METADATA.SESSION_
TRANSFORM,'SEGMENT_ATTRIBUTES',false);

/*Set transform handler for PRETTY*/
EXEC DBMS_METADATA.SET_TRANSFORM_PARAM
(DBMS_METADATA.SESSION_TRANSFORM,'PRETTY',true);

/*Set transform handler for SQLTERMINATOR*/
EXEC DBMS_METADATA.SET_TRANSFORM_PARAM( DBMS_METADATA.SESSION_TRANSFOR
M,'SQLTERMINATOR',true);

/*Set transform handler for REF_CONSTRAINTS*/
EXEC DBMS_METADATA.SET_TRANSFORM_PARAM(
DBMS_METADATA.SESSION_TRANSFORM,'REF_CONSTRAINTS',false);

/*Set transform handler for TABLESPACE*/
EXEC DBMS_METADATA.SET_TRANSFORM_PARAM( DBMS_METADATA.SESSION_
TRANSFORM,'TABLESPACE',false);

/*Set transform handler for SIZE_BYTE_KEYWORD*/
EXEC DBMS_METADATA.SET_TRANSFORM_PARAM(
DBMS_METADATA.SESSION_TRANSFORM,'SIZE_BYTE_KEYWORD',false);
```

Now, extracting the DDL script in a SELECT statement:

```
/*Generate the DDL for EMPLOYEES table*/
SELECT dbms_metadata.get_ddl('TABLE','EMPLOYEES','ORADEV') EMPLOYEE_
DDL
FROM dual;

EMPLOYEE_DDL
----------------
CREATE TABLE "ORADEV"."EMPLOYEES"
(
  "EMPNO" NUMBER(4,0),
  "ENAME" VARCHAR2(10) NOT NULL ENABLE,
  JOB" VARCHAR2(9),
```

```
"MGR" NUMBER(4,0),
"HIREDATE" DATE,
"SAL" NUMBER(7,2),
COMM" NUMBER(7,2),
"DEPTNO" NUMBER(2,0),
PRIMARY KEY ("EMPNO") ENABLE
) ;
```

Case 2—retrieve the object dependencies on the F_GET_LOC function

Refer to the following code snippet:

```
/*Retrieve object dependency for F_GET_LOC function*/
SELECT dbms_metadata.get_dependent_ddl
  ('OBJECT_GRANT','F_GET_LOC','ORADEV')OBJ_GRANTS
FROM DUAL;

OBJ_GRANTS
----------------
GRANT EXECUTE ON "ORADEV"."F_GET_LOC" TO "NANCY";
```

The output of the SELECT query shows that the ORADEV user has granted the EXECUTE privilege on the function F_GET_LOC to the NANCY user.

Case 3—retrieve system grants on the ORADEV schema

Refer to the following code snippet:

```
/*Retrieve system grants for the ORADEV user*/
SELECT dbms_metadata.get_granted_ddl
  ('SYSTEM_GRANT','ORADEV') SYS_GRANTS
FROM dual;

SYS_GRANTS
----------------------------------------------
  GRANT DEBUG ANY PROCEDURE TO "ORADEV";
  GRANT DEBUG CONNECT SESSION TO "ORADEV";
  GRANT CREATE ANY CONTEXT TO "ORADEV";
  GRANT CREATE LIBRARY TO "ORADEV";
  GRANT UNLIMITED TABLESPACE TO "ORADEV";
  GRANT CREATE SESSION TO "ORADEV";
```

Case 4—retrieve objects of function type in the ORADEV schema

It follows the same approach from Case 1 for tables owned by the ORADEV user. Here, we will create a generic function to retrieve the DDL of a given function:

```
/*Create the function to generate DDL of a given function*/
CREATE OR REPLACE FUNCTION F_GET_FUN_DDL (P_NAME VARCHAR2)
RETURN CLOB IS
  l_hdl   NUMBER;
  l_th    NUMBER;
  l_doc   CLOB;
  BEGIN
/*Open the transform handler*/
    l_hdl := DBMS_METADATA.OPEN ('FUNCTION');
/*Set filter for the schema and the function name*/
    DBMS_METADATA.SET_FILTER (l_HDL ,'SCHEMA','ORADEV');
    DBMS_METADATA.SET_FILTER (l_hdl ,'NAME',P_NAME);
/*Generate the DDL and fetch in a local CLOB variable*/
    l_th := DBMS_METADATA.ADD_TRANSFORM (l_hdl,'DDL');
    l_doc := DBMS_METADATA.FETCH_CLOB (l_hdl);
    DBMS_METADATA.CLOSE (l_hdl);
/*Return the DDL*/
    RETURN l_doc;
  END;
/

Function created
```

Testing the above function for the function F_GET_LOC:

```
/*Declare en environment variable*/
VARIABLE M_FUN_DDL clob;
/*Execute the function*/
EXEC :M_FUN_DDL := F_GET_FUN_DDL  ('F_GET_LOC');
/*Print the variable*/
PRINT M_FUN_DDL
  CREATE OR REPLACE FUNCTION "ORADEV"."F_GET_LOC" (P_EMPNO NUMBER)
  RETURN NUMBER
IS
CURSOR C_DEPT IS
  SELECT d.loc
  FROM employees e, departments d
  WHERE e.deptno = d.deptno
  AND e.empno = P_EMPNO;
  l_loc NUMBER;
  l_red number;
```

```
   L_BLUE NUMBER;
BEGIN
  OPEN C_DEPT;
  FETCH C_DEPT INTO l_loc;
  CLOSE C_DEPT;
  RETURN l_loc;
END;
```

Similarly, DDL scripts of all functions in a schema can be retrieved by holding all the functions in a cursor and iterating it to call the `F_GET_FUN_DDL` function.

Summary

In this chapter, we understood the usage of Oracle supplied packages and dictionary views to find the coding information. We got introduced to a new feature in Oracle 11*g*, the PL/Scope tool, and learned how to determine the usage of an identifier in the PL/SQL program. At the end of the chapter, we covered the `DBMS_METADATA` package and demonstrated the extraction of a schema object definition as XML or DDL using the package.

In the next chapter, we will overview the strategies of tracing and profiling in PL/SQL.

Practice exercise

1. Which of the following dictionary views is used to get information about the subprogram arguments?

    a. `ALL_OBJECTS`

    b. `ALL_ARGUMENTS`

    c. `ALL_DEPENDENCIES`

    d. `ALL_PROGRAMS`

2. The tablespace information on a database server:
    ```
    SELECT tablespace_name
    FROM DBA_TABLESPACES
    /

    TABLESPACE_NAME
    ----------------
    SYSTEM
    UNDOTBS1
    TEMP
    USERS
    EXAMPLE
    ```

You execute the following command in the session:

```
SQL> ALTER SESSION SET PLSCOPE_SETTINGS = 'IDENTIFIERS:ALL';
Session altered.
```

Identify the correct statements:

a. The identifier information would be captured by PL/Scope for the program created or compiled in the session.

b. The identifier information would not be captured by PL/Scope as IDENTIFIERS:ALL can be enabled only at the SYSTEM level.

c. The identifier information would be captured by PL/Scope only for the programs which are created in the session.

d. The identifier information would not be captured by PL/Scope since the SYSAUX tablespace is not available.

3. The parameters specified in DBMS_METADATA are case sensitive:

a. True

b. False

4. DBMS_UTILITY.FORMAT_CALL_STACK accomplishes which of the following objectives?

a. Captures exceptions in a PL/SQL block.

b. Prepares the stack of sequential calls.

c. Prepares the stack of execution actions.

d. Prepares the stack of block profiler.

5. Choose the accomplishments of the DBMS_METADATA package.

a. Generates a report of invalidated objects in a schema.

b. Generates DDL for a given or all object(s) in a schema.

c. Generates an object to table dependency report in a schema

d. Generates a report of object statistics in a schema

6. The PL/Scope tool can store the identifier data only in the USERS tablespace.

a. True

b. False

7. Which of the following are valid parameter values of SET_TRANSFORM_PARAM for tables?

a. STORAGE

b. FORCE

c. PRETTY

d. INHERIT

11
Profiling and Tracing PL/SQL Code

Now that we have stepped out of the code development stage, we are discussing best practices of code management and maintenance. In the last chapter, we walked through the strategies of code tracking, error tracking, and the PL/Scope tool for identifier tracking. We noticed that the PL/Scope tool does static code analysis. In this chapter, we are going to learn two important techniques for measuring code performance. The techniques are known as **tracing** and **profiling**. The primary goal of the code tracing and profiling techniques is to identify performance bottlenecks in the PL/SQL code and gather performance statistics at each execution step. We will discuss the tracing and profiling features in PL/SQL in the following topics:

- Tracing PL/SQL programs
  - The DBMS_TRACE package
  - Viewing trace information
- Profiling PL/SQL programs
  - The DBMS_HPROF package
  - The plshprof utility
  - Generating HTML profiler reports

Tracing the PL/SQL programs

Code tracing is an important technique to measure the code performance during runtime and identify the expensive areas in the code which can be worked upon to improve the performance. The tracing feature shows the code execution path followed by the server and reveals the time consumed at each step. Often developers assume tracing and debugging as one step, but both are distinctive features. Tracing is a one-time activity which analyses the complete code and prepares the platform for debugging. On the other hand, debugging is the bug identification and fixing activity where the trace report can be used to identify and work upon the problematic points.

Oracle offers multiple methods of tracing:

- DBMS_APPLICATION_INFO: The SET_MODULE and SET_ACTION subprograms can be used to register a specific action in a specific module.

- DBMS_TRACE: The Oracle built-in package allows tracing of PL/SQL subprograms, exceptions and SQL execution. The trace information is logged into SYS owned tracing tables (created by executing tracetab.sql).

- DBMS_SESSION and DBMS_MONITOR: The package can be employed in parallel to set the client ID and monitor the respective client ID. It is equivalent to a 10046 trace and logs the code diagnostics in a trace file.

- The trcsess and tkprof utilities: The trcsess utility merges multiple trace files in one and is usually deployed in shared server environments and parallel query sessions. The tkprof utility used to be a conventional tracing utility which generated readable output file. It was useful for large trace files and can also be used to load the trace information into a database.

Besides the methods mentioned in the preceding list, there are third-party tools from LOG4PLSQL and Quest which are used to trace the PL/SQL codes. A typical trace flow in a program is demonstrated in the following diagram:

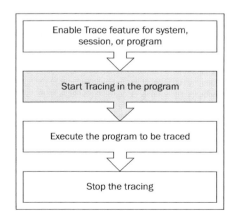

In this chapter, we will drill down the DBMS_TRACE package to demonstrate the tracing feature in PL/SQL. Further, we will learn the profiling strengths of DBMS_HPROF in PL/SQL.

The DBMS_TRACE package

DBMS_TRACE is a built-in package in Oracle to enable and disable tracing in sessions. As soon as a program is executed in a trace enabled session, the server captures and logs the information in trace log tables. The dbmspbt.sql and prvtpbt.sql table scripts are available in the database installation folder. The trace tables can be analysed to review the execution flow of the PL/SQL program and take decisions in accordance.

Installing DBMS_TRACE

If the DBMS_TRACE package is not installed at the server, it can be installed by running the following scripts from the database installation folder:

- $ORACLE_HOME\rdbms\admin\dbmspbt.sql: This script creates the DBMS_TRACE package specification
- $ORACLE_HOME\rdbms\admin\prvtpbt.plb: This script creates the DBMS_TRACE package body

The scripts must be executed as the SYS user and in the same order as mentioned.

DBMS_TRACE subprograms

The DBMS_TRACE subprograms deal with the setting of the trace, getting the trace information, and clearing the trace. While configuring the database for the trace, the trace level must be specified to signify the degree of tracing in the session. The trace level majorly deals with two levels. The first level traces all the events of an action while the other level traces only the actions from those program units which have been compiled with the debug and trace option.

The DBMS_TRACE constants are used for setting the trace level. Even the numeric values are available for all the constants, but still the constant names are used in the programs.

The summary of DBMS_TRACE constants is as follows (refer to the Oracle documentation for more details). Note that all constants are of the INTEGER type:

DBMS_TRACE constant	Default	Remarks
TRACE_ALL_CALLS	1	Traces all calls
TRACE_ENABLED_CALLS	2	Traces calls which are enabled for tracing
TRACE_ALL_EXCEPTIONS	4	Traces all exceptions
TRACE_ENABLED_EXCEPTIONS	8	Traces exceptions which are enabled for tracing
TRACE_ALL_SQL	32	Traces all SQL statements
TRACE_ENABLED_SQL	64	Traces SQL statements which are enabled for tracing
TRACE_ALL_LINES	128	Traces each line
TRACE_ENABLED_LINES	256	Traces lines which are enabled for tracing
TRACE_PAUSE	4096	Pauses tracing (controls tracing process)
TRACE_RESUME	8192	Resume tracing (controls tracing process)
TRACE_STOP	16384	Stops tracing (controls tracing process)
TRACE_LIMIT	16	Limits the trace information (controls tracing process)
TRACE_MINOR_VERSION	0	Administer tracing process
TRACE_MAJOR_VERSION	1	Administer tracing process
NO_TRACE_ADMINISTRATIVE	32768	Prevents tracing of administrative events such as: • PL/SQL Trace Tool started • Trace flags changed • PL/SQL Virtual Machine started • PL/SQL Virtual Machine stopped
NO_TRACE_HANDLED_EXCEPTIONS	65536	Prevents tracing of handled exceptions

The subprograms contained in the DBMS_TRACE package are as follows:

DBMS_TRACE subprogram	Remarks
CLEAR_PLSQL_TRACE procedure	Stops trace data dumping in session
GET_PLSQL_TRACE_LEVEL function	Gets the trace level
GET_PLSQL_TRACE_RUNNUMBER function	Gets the current sequence of execution of trace

DBMS_TRACE subprogram	Remarks
PLSQL_TRACE_VERSION procedure	Gets the version number of the trace package
SET_PLSQL_TRACE procedure	Starts tracing in the current session
COMMENT_PLSQL_TRACE procedure	Includes comment on the PL/SQL tracing
INTERNAL_VERSION_CHECK function	Has a value as 0, if the internal version check has not been done
LIMIT_PLSQL_TRACE procedure	Sets limit for the PL/SQL tracing
PAUSE_PLSQL_TRACE procedure	Pauses the PL/SQL tracing
RESUME_PLSQL_TRACE procedure	Resumes the PL/SQL tracing

In the preceding list, the key subprograms are:

- SET_PLSQL_TRACE: It kicks off the PL/SQL tracing session. For example, DBMS_TRACE.SET_PLSQL_TRACE (DBMS_TRACE.TRACE_ALL_SQL) traces all SQL in the program.
- CLEAR_PLSQL_TRACE: It stops the tracing session.

PLSQL_TRACE_VERSION returns the current trace version as the OUT parameter value.

 Trace level that controls the tracing process (stop, pause, resume, and limit) cannot be used in combination with other trace levels

The PLSQL_DEBUG parameter and the DEBUG option

As a prerequisite, a subprogram can be enabled for tracing only if it is compiled in the debug mode. The PLSQL_DEBUG parameter is used to enable a database, session, or a program for debugging. The compilation parameter can be set at SYSTEM, SESSION, or any specific program level. When set to TRUE, the program units are compiled in the interpreted mode for debug purpose. The Oracle server explicitly compiles the program in interpreted mode to use the strengths of a debugger. However, debugging of a natively compiled program unit is not yet supported in the Oracle database. For this reason, native compilation of program units is less preferable than interpreted mode during development.

```
ALTER [SYSTEM | SESSION] SET PLSSQL_DEBUG= [TRUE | FALSE]
```

The trace can be enabled at the subprogram level (not for anonymous blocks):

```
ALTER [Procedure | Function | Package] [Name]
COMPILE PLSQL_DEBUG= [TRUE | FALSE]
/

Or

ALTER [Procedure | Function | Package] [Name] COMPILE DEBUG [BODY]
/
```

Enabling tracing at the subprogram level is usually preferred to avoid dumping of huge volume of trace data.

> The PLSQL_DEBUG parameter has been devalued in Oracle 11*g*. When a subprogram is compiled with the PLSQL_DEBUG option set to TRUE in a warning enabled session, the server records the following two warnings:
>
> PLW-06015: parameter PLSQL_DEBUG is deprecated; use PLSQL_OPTIMIZE_LEVEL = 1
>
> PLW-06013: deprecated parameter PLSQL_DEBUG forces PLSQL_OPTIMIZE_LEVEL <= 1

Viewing the PL/SQL trace information

Oracle provides no built-in data dictionary view to query the trace session information. Instead, the trace information is logged into the trace tables. These trace tables can be created by running the $ORACLE_HOME\rdbms\admin\tracetab.sql script as SYS user. The script creates the following two tables:

* PLSQL_TRACE_RUNS: This table stores execution-specific information. The following structure shows that the table contains the trace header information such as RUNID and comments:

  ```
  /*Describe the PLSQL_TRACE_RUNS table structure*/
  SQL> DESC plsql_trace_runs
  ```

Name	Null?	Type
RUNID	NOT NULL	NUMBER
RUN_DATE		DATE
RUN_OWNER		VARCHAR2(31)
RUN_COMMENT		VARCHAR2(2047)
RUN_COMMENT1		VARCHAR2(2047)

RUN_END	DATE
RUN_FLAGS	VARCHAR2(2047)
RELATED_RUN	NUMBER
RUN_SYSTEM_INFO	VARCHAR2(2047)
SPARE1	VARCHAR2(256)

In the preceding table, RUNID is the unique run identifier which derives its value from a sequence, PLSQL_TRACE_RUNNUMBER. The RUN_DATE and RUN_END columns specify the start and end time of the run respectively. The RUN_SYSTEM_INFO and SPARE1 columns are the currently unused columns in the table.

- PLSQL_TRACE_EVENTS: This table displays accumulated results from trace executions and captures the detailed trace information:

```
/*Describe the PLSQL_TRACE_EVENTS table structure*/
SQL> desc plsql_trace_events
```

Name	Null?	Type
RUNID	NOT NULL	NUMBER
EVENT_SEQ	NOT NULL	NUMBER
EVENT_TIME		DATE
RELATED_EVENT		NUMBER
EVENT_KIND		NUMBER
EVENT_UNIT_DBLINK		VARCHAR2(4000)
EVENT_UNIT_OWNER		VARCHAR2(31)
EVENT_UNIT		VARCHAR2(31)
EVENT_UNIT_KIND		VARCHAR2(31)
EVENT_LINE		NUMBER
EVENT_PROC_NAME		VARCHAR2(31)
STACK_DEPTH		NUMBER
PROC_NAME		VARCHAR2(31)
PROC_DBLINK		VARCHAR2(4000)
PROC_OWNER		VARCHAR2(31)
PROC_UNIT		VARCHAR2(31)
PROC_UNIT_KIND		VARCHAR2(31)
PROC_LINE		NUMBER
PROC_PARAMS		VARCHAR2(2047)
ICD_INDEX		NUMBER
USER_EXCP		NUMBER
EXCP		NUMBER
EVENT_COMMENT		VARCHAR2(2047)
MODULE		VARCHAR2(4000)
ACTION		VARCHAR2(4000)
CLIENT_INFO		VARCHAR2(4000)

CLIENT_ID	VARCHAR2(4000)
ECID_ID	VARCHAR2(4000)
ECID_SEQ	NUMBER
CALLSTACK	CLOB
ERRORSTACK	CLOB

The following points can be noted about this table:

° The RUNID column references the RUNID column of the PLSQL_TRACE_RUNS table

° EVENT_SEQ is the unique event identifier within a single run

° The EVENT_UNIT, EVEN_UNIT_KIND, EVENT_UNIT_OWNER, and EVENT_LINE columns capture the program unit information (such as name, type, owner, and line number) which initiates the trace event

° The PROC_NAME, PROC_UNIT, PROC_UNIT_KIND, PROC_OWNER, and PROC_LINE columns capture the procedure information (such as name, type, owner, and line number) which is currently being traced

° The EXCP and USER_EXCP columns apply to the exceptions occurring during the trace

° The EVENT_COMMENT column gives user defined comment or the actual event description

° The MODULE, ACTION, CLIENT_INFO, CLIENT_ID, ECID_ID, and ECID_SEQ columns capture information about the session running on a SQL*Plus client

° The CALLSTACK and ERRORSTACK columns store the call stack information

Once the script has been executed, the DBA should create public synonyms for the tables and sequence in order to be accessed by all users.

```
/*Connect as SYSDBA*/
Conn sys/system as SYSDBA
Connected.

/*Create synonym for PLSQL_TRACE_RUNS*/
CREATE PUBLIC SYNONYM plsql_trace_runs FOR plsql_trace_runs
/

Synonym created.

/*Create synonym for PLSQL_TRACE_EVENTS*/
CREATE PUBLIC SYNONYM plsql_trace_events FOR plsql_trace_events
/
```

```
Synonym created.

/*Create synonym for PLSQL_TRACE_RUNNUMBER sequence*/
CREATE PUBLIC SYNONYM plsql_trace_runnumber FOR plsql_trace_
runnumber
/

Synonym created.

/*Grant privileges on the PLSQL_TRACE_RUNS*/
GRANT select, insert, update, delete ON plsql_trace_runs TO PUBLIC
/

Grant succeeded.

/*Grant privileges on the PLSQL_TRACE_EVENTS*/
GRANT select, insert, update, delete ON plsql_trace_events TO
PUBLIC
/

Grant succeeded.

/*Grant privileges on the PLSQL_TRACE_RUNNUMBER*/
GRANT select ON plsql_trace_runnumber TO PUBLIC
/

Grant succeeded.
```

Demonstrating the PL/SQL tracing

PL/SQL tracing is demonstrated in the following steps:

1. The F_GET_LOC function looks as follows (this function has been already created in the schema):

```
/*Connect as ORADEV user*/
Conn ORADEV/ORADEV
Connected.

/*Create the function*/
CREATE OR REPLACE FUNCTION F_GET_LOC (P_EMPNO NUMBER)
RETURN VARCHAR2
IS
```

```
/*Cursor select location for the given employee*/
CURSOR C_DEPT IS
  SELECT d.loc
  FROM employees e, departments d
  WHERE e.deptno = d.deptno
  AND e.empno = P_EMPNO;
l_loc VARCHAR2(100);

BEGIN
/*Cursor is open and fetched into a local variable*/
  OPEN C_DEPT;
  FETCH C_DEPT INTO l_loc;
  CLOSE C_DEPT;

/*Location returned*/
  RETURN l_loc;
END;
/

Function created.
```

We will trace the execution path for the preceding function.

2. Recompile the F_GET_LOC function for tracing:

```
/*Compile the function in debug mode*/
SQL> ALTER FUNCTION F_GET_LOC COMPILE DEBUG
/

Function altered.
```

3. Start the tracing session to trace all calls:

```
BEGIN
/*Enable tracing for all calls in the session*/
    DBMS_TRACE.SET_PLSQL_TRACE(DBMS_TRACE.TRACE_ALL_CALLS);
END;
/
```

 Specify additional trace levels using the + sign as:

```
DBMS_TRACE.SET_PLSQL_TRACE (tracelevel1 +
tracelevel2 ...)
```

4. Execute the function and capture the result into a bind variable:

```
/*Declare a SQLPLUS environment variable*/
SQL> VARIABLE M_LOC VARCHAR2(100);

/*Execute the function and assign the return output to the
variable*/
SQL> EXEC :M_LOC := F_GET_LOC (7369);

PL/SQL procedure successfully completed.

/*Print the variable*/
SQL> PRINT M_LOC

M_LOC
-----------------------------------------
DALLAS
```

5. Stop the trace session:

```
BEGIN
/*Stop the trace session*/
    DBMS_TRACE.CLEAR_PLSQL_TRACE;
END;
/
```

6. Query the trace log tables.

   Query the PLSQL_TRACE_RUNS table to retrieve the current RUNID:

```
/*Query the PLSQL_TRACE_RUNS table*/
SELECT runid, run_owner, run_date
FROM plsql_trace_runs
ORDER BY runid
/
```

RUNID	RUN_OWNER	RUN_DATE
1	ORADEV	29-JAN-12

Query the PLSQL_TRACE_EVENTS table to retrieve the trace events for the RU-NID as 1.

The highlighted portion shows the tracing of execution of the F_GET_LOC function. The trace events appearing before and after the highlighted portion represent the starting and stopping of the trace session.

```
/*Query the PLSQL_TRACE_EVENTS table*/
SELECT runid,
```

```
            event_comment,
            event_unit_owner,
            event_unit,
            event_unit_kind,
            event_line
FROM plsql_trace_events
WHERE runid = 1
ORDER BY event_seq
/
```

The output of the preceding query is shown in the following screenshot:

```
    RUNID EVENT_COMMENT                    EVENT_UNIT EVENT_UNIT    EVENT_UNIT_KIND    EVENT_LINE
 -------- -------------------------------- ---------- ------------- ------------------ ----------
        1 PL/SQL Trace Tool started
        1 Trace flags changed
        1 Return from procedure call       SYS        DBMS_TRACE    PACKAGE BODY               21
        1 Return from procedure call       SYS        DBMS_TRACE    PACKAGE BODY               76
        1 Return from procedure call       SYS        DBMS_TRACE    PACKAGE BODY               81
        1 PL/SQL Virtual Machine stopped
        1 PL/SQL Virtual Machine started              <anonymous>   ANONYMOUS BLOCK             0
        1 Procedure Call                              <anonymous>   ANONYMOUS BLOCK             1
        1 Procedure Call                   ORADEV     F_GET_LOC     FUNCTION                   13
        1 Return from procedure call       ORADEV     F_GET_LOC     FUNCTION                    9
        1 Return from procedure call       ORADEV     F_GET_LOC     FUNCTION                   18
        1 PL/SQL Virtual Machine stopped
        1 PL/SQL Virtual Machine started              <anonymous>   ANONYMOUS BLOCK             0
        1 Procedure Call                              <anonymous>   ANONYMOUS BLOCK             3
        1 Procedure Call                   SYS        DBMS_TRACE    PACKAGE BODY               94
        1 Procedure Call                   SYS        DBMS_TRACE    PACKAGE BODY               72
        1 Procedure Call                   SYS        DBMS_TRACE    PACKAGE BODY               66
        1 Return from procedure call       SYS        DBMS_TRACE    PACKAGE BODY               12
        1 Return from procedure call       SYS        DBMS_TRACE    PACKAGE BODY               67
        1 Procedure Call                   SYS        DBMS_TRACE    PACKAGE BODY               75
        1 PL/SQL trace stopped
21 rows selected.
```

The query output shows the F_GET_LOC function execution flow starting from the time the trace session started (EVENT_COMMENT = PL/SQL Trace Tool started) till the trace session was stopped (EVENT_COMMENT = PL/SQL trace stopped).

Profiling the PL/SQL programs

We just saw tracing capabilities in PL/SQL programs. It presents the execution flow of the program in an interactive format with clear comments at each stage. But it doesn't provide the execution statistics of the program which prevents the user from determining the performance of a program. The user never comes to know about the time consumed at each step or process.

Before the release of Oracle 11g, DBMS_PROFILER was used as the primary tool for profiling PL/SQL programs.

Oracle hierarchical profiler—the DBMS_HPROF package

Oracle introduced the PL/SQL hierarchical profiler in Oracle 11*g* release 1. The profiling was restructured as **hierarchical profiling**. The hierarchical profiling could profile even the subprogram calls made in the PL/SQL code. It fills the gap between tracing loopholes and the expectations of performance tracing. The hierarchical profiler creates the dynamic execution profile of a PL/SQL program. The efficiencies of the hierarchical profiler are as follows:

- Distinct reporting for SQL and PL/SQL time consumption.

- Reports count of distinct subprograms calls made in the PL/SQL code and the time spent with each subprogram call.

- Multiple interactive analytics reports in HTML format using the command line utility.

- More efficient than other tracing utilities and offers more powerful profiling than a conventional profiler. The conventional DBMS_PROFILER tracks the performance at a lower level (individual line of programs) while DBMS_HPROF tracks the cumulative performance of a program unit.

The DBMS_HPROF package implements hierarchical profiling. It is a SYS owned Oracle built-in package whose subprograms profile the PL/SQL code execution.

The PL/SQL hierarchical profiler consists of two subcomponents. The two components—**Data collector** and **Analyzer**—are indicative of the two-step hierarchical profiling process.

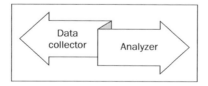

The Data collector component is the "worker" component which initiates the profiling process, collects all the raw profiler data from the PL/SQL code execution, and stops. The raw profiler data is dumped into a system-based text file for further analysis. In simple words, it stakes itself to prepare the stage for the Analyzer component.

The Analyzer component takes the raw profiler data and loads it into the profiler log tables. The effort of the component lies in understanding the raw profiler data and placing it correctly in the profiler tables. Conceptually, the Analyzer component lives the same life cycle as that of an **ETL** (**Extraction, Transformation**, and **Loading**) process.

The following table shows the DBMS_HPROF subprograms:

Subprogram	Description
ANALYZE function	Analyzes the raw profiler output and produces hierarchical profiler information in database tables
START_PROFILING procedure	Starts hierarchical profiler data collection in the user's session
STOP_PROFILING procedure	Stops profiler data collection in the user's session

In the preceding subprograms list, the START_PROFILING and STOP_PROFILING procedures come under the Data collector component while the subprogram ANALYZE is a sure selection under the Analyzer component.

The DBA must grant the EXECUTE privilege to the user who intends to perform profiling activity.

View profiler information

Similar to the trace log tables, Oracle 11*g* has facilitated the profiler with relational tables to log the analyzed profiler data. The profiler log tables can be created by running the $ORACLE_HOME\rdbms\admin\dbmshptab.sql script. On execution of this script, the following three tables are created:

- DBMSHP_RUNS: This table maintains the flat information about each command executed during profiling

- DBMSHP_FUNCTION_INFO: This table contains information about the profiled function

- DBMSHP_PARENT_CHILD_INFO: This table contains parent-child profiler information

The script execution might raise some exceptions which can be ignored for the first time. Once the script is executed and tables are created, the DBA must grant a SELECT privilege on these tables to the users.

Demonstrating the profiling of a PL/SQL program

The following steps demonstrate the profiling of a PL/SQL stored function, F_GET_LOC:

1. Create a directory to create a trace file for raw profiler data:

```
/*Connect as sysdba*/
Conn sys/system as sysdba
Connected.
```

```
/*Create directory where raw profiler data would be stored*/
SQL> CREATE DIRECTORY PROFILER_REP AS 'C:\PROFILER\'
/

Directory created.

/*Grant read, write privilege on the directory to ORADEV*/
SQL> GRANT READ, WRITE ON DIRECTORY PROFILER_REP TO ORADEV
/

Grant succeeded.

/*Grant execute privilege on DBMS_HPROF package to ORADEV*/
SQL> GRANT EXECUTE ON DBMS_HPROF TO ORADEV
/

Grant succeeded.

/*Grant SELECT privilege on DBMSHP_RUNS to ORADEV*/
SQL> GRANT select on DBMSHP_RUNS to ORADEV
/

Grant succeeded.

/*Grant SELECT privilege on DBMSHP_FUNCTION_INFO to ORADEV*/
SQL> GRANT select on DBMSHP_FUNCTION_INFO  to ORADEV
/

Grant succeeded.

/*Grant SELECT privilege on DBMSHP_PARENT_CHILD_INFO to ORADEV*/
SQL> GRANT select on DBMSHP_PARENT_CHILD_INFO  to ORADEV
/

Grant succeeded.
```

2. **Start the profiling:**

```
/*Connect to ORADEV*/
Conn ORADEV/ORADEV
Connected.

BEGIN
/*Start the profiling*/
/*Specify the directory and file name*/
```

```
      DBMS_HPROF.START_PROFILING ('PROFILER_REP', 'F_GET_LOC.TXT');
END;
/
```

```
PL/SQL procedure successfully completed.
```

 `max_depth` is the third parameter of the `START_PROFILING` subprogram which can be used to limit recursive subprogram calls. By default, it is `NULL`.

3. Execute the `F_GET_LOC` function:

```
/*Declare a SQLPLUS environment variable*/
SQL> VARIABLE M_LOC VARCHAR2(100);

/*Execute the function and assign the return output to the
variable*/
SQL> EXEC :M_LOC := F_GET_LOC (7369);

PL/SQL procedure successfully completed.

/*Print the variable*/
SQL> PRINT M_LOC

M_LOC
-----------------------------------------
DALLAS
```

4. Stop the profiling

```
BEGIN
/*Stop the profiling */
  DBMS_HPROF.STOP_PROFILING;
END;
/

PL/SQL procedure successfully completed.
```

5. Check the `PROFILER_REP` database directory. A text file, `F_GET_LOC.txt`, has been created with the raw profiler content. A small screen cast of the raw profiler data is as follows:

```
P#V PLSHPROF Internal Version 1.0
P#! PL/SQL Timer Started
P#C PLSQL."".""."__plsql_vm"
P#X 7
P#C PLSQL."".""."__anonymous_block"
```

```
P#X 695
P#C PLSQL."ORADEV"."F_GET_LOC"::8."F_GET_LOC"#762ba075453b8b0d #1
P#X 6
P#C PLSQL."ORADEV"."F_GET_LOC"::8."F_GET_LOC.C_
DEPT"#980980e97e42f8ec #5
P#X 15
P#C SQL."ORADEV"."F_GET_LOC"::8."__static_sql_exec_line6" #6
P#X 67083
...
...
```

From the preceding sample of raw profiler data, one can get clear indications for the following:

- Namespace distinction at each line as SQL or PLSQL
- Operations captured by the hierarchical profiler as follows:
  - `__anonymous_block` indicates anonymous block execution
  - `__dyn_sql_exec_lineline#` indicates dynamic SQL statement execution at line#
  - `__pkg_init` indicates PL/SQL package initialization
  - `__plsql_vm` indicates PL/SQL virtual machine call
  - `__sql_fetch_lineline#` indicates fetch operation at line#
  - `__static_sql_exec_lineline#` indicates static SQL execution at line#
- Each line starts with an encrypted indication as P#X, P#C. Let us briefly understand what they indicate:
  - `P#C` is the call event which indicates a subprogram call
  - `P#R` is the return event which indicates a "return" from a subprogram
  - `P#X` shows the time consumed between the two subprogram calls
  - `P#!` is the comment which appears in the analyzer's output

However, the raw profile doesn't appear to be a comprehensive one which can be interpreted fast and easily. This leads to the need for an analyzer which can translate the raw data into a meaningful form. The Analyzer component of HPROF can reform the raw profiler data into accessible form. The raw profiler text file would be interpreted and loaded into profiling log tables.

Note that until Step 5, the Data collector component of the hierarchical profiler was active. The raw profiler data has been collected and recorded in a text file.

6. Execute the ANALYZE subprogram to insert the data into profiler tables.

```
/*Connect as DBA*/
Conn sys/system as sysdba
Connected.

/*Start the PL/SQL block*/
DECLARE
  l_runid  NUMBER;
BEGIN

/*Invoke the analyzer API*/
  l_runid := DBMS_HPROF.analyze
                (location     => 'PROFILER_REP',
                 FILENAME     => 'F_GET_LOC.txt',
                 run_comment  => 'Analyzing the execution of F_
GET_LOC');

  DBMS_OUTPUT.put_line('l_runid=' || l_runid);
END;
/

PL/SQL procedure successfully completed
```

If profiling is enabled for a session and the trace file contains a huge volume of raw profiler data, you can analyze only selected subprograms by specifying the TRACE parameter in the ANALYZE API. The following example code snippet shows the usage of the TRACE parameter in the ANALYZER subprogram. The MULTIPLE_RAW_PROFILES.txt trace file contains raw profiler data from multiple profiles. But only the profiles of F_GET_SAL and F_GET_JOB can be analyzed as follows:

```
DECLARE
   l_runid NUMBER;
BEGIN
   l_runid:= dbms_hprof.analyze
           ( location=> 'PROFILER_REP',
             filename=> 'MULTIPLE_RAW_PROFILES.txt',
             trace => '"F_GET_SAL"."F_GET_JOB"'
);
end;
/
```

7. Query the profiling log tables

```
/*Query the DBMSHP_RUNS table*/
SELECT runid, total_elapsed_time,run_comment
FROM dbmshp_runs
ORDER BY runid
/


      RUNID TOTAL_ELAPSED_TIME RUN_COMMENT
---------- ------------------ -----------------------------------
          1             106407 Analyzing the execution of F_GET_LOC
```

In the preceding query result, note that TOTAL_ELAPSED_TIME is the total execution time (in micro seconds) for the procedure. The run comment appears as per the input given during analysis.

```
/*Query the DBMSHP_FUNCTION_INFO table*/
SELECT  runid, owner, module, type, function, namespace, function_
elapsed_time,calls
FROM dbmshp_function_info
WHERE runid = 1
```

The output of the preceding query is shown in the following screenshot:

RUNID	OWNER	MODULE	TYPE	FUNCTION	NAMESPAC	FUNCTION_ELAPSED_TIME	CALLS
1				__anonymous_block	PLSQL	772	2
1				__plsql_vm	PLSQL	23	2
1	ORADEV	F_GET_LOC	FUNCTION	F_GET_LOC	PLSQL	45	1
1	ORADEV	F_GET_LOC	FUNCTION	F_GET_LOC.C_DEPT	PLSQL	21	1
1	SYS	DBMS_HPROF	PACKAGE BODY	STOP_PROFILING	PLSQL	0	1
1	ORADEV	F_GET_LOC	FUNCTION	__sql_fetch_line14	SQL	38463	1
1	ORADEV	F_GET_LOC	FUNCTION	__static_sql_exec_line6	SQL	67083	1

7 rows selected.

Here, we see how the analyzer output clearly indicates the step-by-step execution profile of a PL/SQL program. It shows which engine (namespace) was employed on which call event along with the time consumed at each event.

The plshprof utility

The analyzer component simplifies much of the problem by interpreting the raw profiler data and loading it into the database tables. What more can one expect? But the services of hierarchical profiler don't end here. The correct analysis of the profiler data is as important as the interpretation of data. For this purpose, a command-line tool has been provided which can generate multiple reports in HTML format.

plshprof is a command-line utility which reads the raw profiler data and generates multiple HTML reports. Each report builds up and showcases a new frame of analysis and offers better statistical foresight to the user. The sixteen reports generated can be navigated from the main report page.

The `plshprof` utility can be executed as follows:

```
C:\Profiler path> plshprof —output [HTML FILE] [RAW PROFILER DATA]
```

Let us now generate the HTML report of the profiler data which we derived above:

C:\>cd profiler

C:\profiler>plshprof -output F_GET_LOC F_GET_LOC.TXT

PLSHPROF: Oracle Database 11g Enterprise Edition Release 11.2.0.1.0 - Production

[7 symbols processed]

[Report written to 'F_GET_LOC.html']

C:\profiler>

As soon as the `plshprof` utility process is over, the following HTML files are generated at the directory location:

- F_GET_LOC.html
- F_GET_LOC_2c.html
- F_GET_LOC_2f.html
- F_GET_LOC_2n.html
- F_GET_LOC_fn.html
- F_GET_LOC_md.html
- F_GET_LOC_mf.html
- F_GET_LOC_ms.html
- F_GET_LOC_nsc.html
- F_GET_LOC_nsf.html
- F_GET_LOC_nsp.html
- F_GET_LOC_pc.html
- F_GET_LOC_tc.html
- F_GET_LOC_td.html
- F_GET_LOC_tf.html
- F_GET_LOC_ts.html

Here, `F_GET_LOC.html` is the main index file which contains navigational links to all other reports. The main index page is shown in the following screenshot:

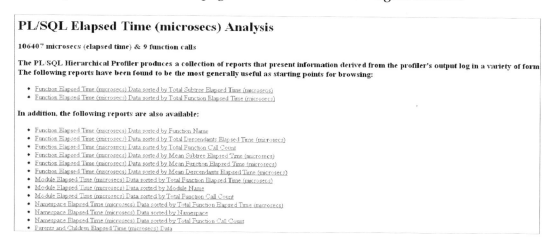

Sample reports

In this section, we will overview some important reports:

- **Function Elapsed Time (microsecs) Data sorted by Total Subtree Elapsed Time (microsecs)**: The report provides the flat view of raw profiler data. It includes total call count, self time, subtree time, and descendants of each function:

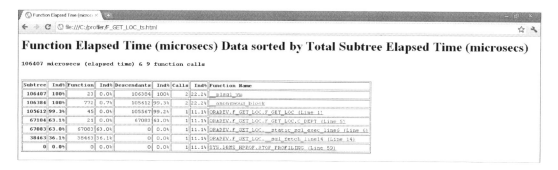

- **Function Elapsed Time (microsecs) Data sorted by Total Function Elapsed Time (microsecs)**: This is the module-level summary report which shows the total time spent in each module and the total calls to the functions in the module:

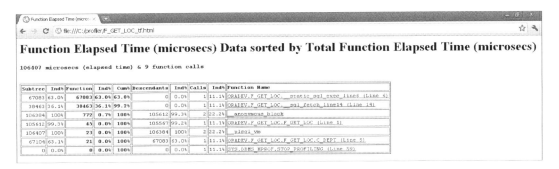

- **Namespace Elapsed Time (microsecs) Data sorted by Namespace**: This report provides the distribution of time spent by the PL/SQL engine and SQL engine separately. SQL and PLSQL are the two namespace categories available for a block. It is very useful in reducing the disk I/O and hence enhancing the block performance. The net sum of the distribution is always 100 percent:

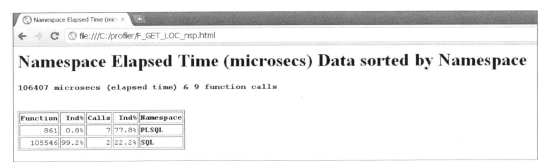

Likewise, other reports also reveal and present some important statistics for the PL/SQL code execution.

Summary

In this chapter, we learned the tracing and profiling features of Oracle 11*g*. While the tracing feature tracks the execution path of PL/SQL code, the profiling feature reports the time consumed at each subprogram call or line number. We demonstrated the implementation and analysis of tracing and profiling features.

In the next chapter, we will see how to identify vulnerable areas in a PL/SQL code and safeguard them against injective attacks.

Practice exercise

1. Which component of the PL/SQL hierarchical profiler uploads the result of profiling into database tables?

   a. The Profiler component

   b. The Analyzer component

   c. The shared library component

   d. The Data collector component

2. The `plshprof` utility is a SQL utility to generate a HTML profiler report from profiler tables in the database.

   a. True

   b. False

3. Suppose that you are using Oracle 11*g* Release 2 express edition and you issue the following command:

```
ALTER SESSION SET PLSQL_WARNINGS = 'ENABLE:ALL'
/
Session altered.
ALTER FUNCTION FUNC COMPILE PLSQL_DEBUG=TRUE
/
Function altered.
```

Determine the output of the following SELECT statement

```
SELECT * FROM USER_ERRORS
/
```

a. No output

b. PLW-06015: parameter PLSQL_DEBUG is deprecated; use
   PLSQL_OPTIMIZE_LEVEL = 1

c. PLW-06013: deprecated parameter PLSQL_DEBUG forces
   PLSQL_ OPTIMIZE_LEVEL <= 1

d. Both b and c

4. Identify the trace log tables:

   a. PLSQL_TRACE

   b. PLSQL_TRACE_ACTIONS

   c. PLSQL_TRACE_EVENTS

   d. PLSQL_TRACE_INFO

5. Identify the correct trace level combination from the following options

   a. DBMS_TRACE.SET_PLSQL_TRACE

      (DBMS_TRACE.TRACE_ALL_CALLS+DBMS_TRACE.TRACE_ALL_
      EXCEPTIONS);

   b. DBMS_TRACE.SET_PLSQL_TRACE

      (DBMS_TRACE.TRACE_ALL_SQL+DBMS_TRACE.TRACE_ALL_
      EXCEPTIONS);

   c. DBMS_TRACE.SET_PLSQL_TRACE

      (DBMS_TRACE.TRACE_ALL_LINES+DBMS_TRACE.TRACE_PAUSE);

   d. DBMS_TRACE.SET_PLSQL_TRACE

      (DBMS_TRACE.TRACE_ALL_EXCEPTIONS+DBMS_TRACE.TRACE_STOP);

6. From the following options, choose the correct statements about the
   plshprof utility:

   a. It is a command line utility.

   b. It generates the HTML reports from the raw profiler data.

   c. It is a SQL command to load the raw profiler data into profiler log tables.

   d. The utility was available with DBMS_PROFILER.

7. You issue the following command to analyze the profiler output:

```
begin
:r := dbms_hprof.analyze(
                   location=> 'DIR',
                   filename=> 'xyz.trc',
                   trace => '"FUNC1"."FUNC2"."FUNC3"'
);
end;
```

Choose the correct option:

a. The Analyzer component cannot trace multiple subprograms.

b. The Analyzer component can trace only text (.txt) files.

c. The Analyzer component analyzes the raw profiler data in xyz.trc and loads the data into profiler tables.

d. The trace file can contain profile information of only one subprogram.

8. The `max_depth` parameter specified the limit of recursive calls in `START_PROFILING`.

a. True

b. False

12

Safeguarding PL/SQL Code against SQL Injection Attacks

Oracle database is, undoubtedly, the uncrowned monarch of "Information Business" across the globe. Though it has narrowed the gap between the expectations and the potential, the question, "Is my information secure?" still hovers the DBMS philosophies. We often discuss the vectors of language strength, performance, storage, and data security. But code vulnerability and security share equal stake in data security. Nevertheless, the strength of SQL and PL/SQL is unquestionable, but vulnerable code writing might motivate a hacker to smuggle through the code and perform vicious manipulations in the data.

In this chapter, we will expand our bandwidth to understand PL/SQL code security. We will understand how "loose code writing" can encompass the code base injection and hence, the data. We will cover the following topics:

- SQL injection
  - ○ Introduction and understanding
- Immunizing SQL injection attacks
  - ○ Reducing the attack surface
  - ○ Avoiding dynamic SQL
  - ○ Using Bind argument
  - ○ Sanitizing inputs with DBMS_ASSERT
- Testing the code against the SQL injection flaws

SQL injection—an introduction

SQL injection is a database intrusion that occurs when an unauthorized "malicious" user hacks the PL/SQL code and draws unintended access to the database. Once the code has been cracked, the malicious user can pull out confidential information from the database. There can be many more hazardous consequences of code injection.

In 1998, Rain Forest Puppy (RFP) was the first to identify the "technology vulnerabilities" in his paper "NT Web Technology Vulnerabilities" for "Phrack 54". Later, the injective techniques were studied by many technology experts and evangelists to chalk out the best practices of code writing to dilute such acts. Till date, many application exploitation cases have been registered on account of code injection. For reference, check out `http://www.computerworld.com.au/index.php/id;683627551`. The applications working with personal information or financial data are more prone to injective attacks.

SQL injection—an overview

In the past, the reason for SQL injection was the vulnerability in the middleware— the layer which lies between the data and the client. Unfortunately, it victimizes most of the applications. The middleware layer acts as a communicating interface between the data and the client. The fact that the inputs received from the client acts as the hacker's weapon in major cases is undeniable. However, the code base can sustain such attacks and immunize any chances of SQL injection. Certain penetrable areas have been identified in PL/SQL code developments which can be improvised to safeguard the application against the smuggling attacks. The code sections which are best candidates of attack are:

- PL/SQL subprogram executed with owner's execution rights
- Dynamic SQL using direct inputs in the programs
- Non-sanitized inputs from the client

Hackers can employ a variety of techniques to hit upon penetrable code in an application. A serious injective attack can lead to the leakage of confidential information, unethical data manipulations, or even alteration in user access and the database state.

Let us check out a simple example of code injection.

The salary of an employee is highly confidential in an organization. Suppose a company's finance team uses a `P_DISPLAY_SAL` procedure to display the salary of all employees as a specific designation.

```
/*Connect to ORADEV user*/
Conn ORADEV/ORADEV
Connected.

/*Enable the SERVEROUTPUT to display the messages*/
SET SERVEROUTPUT ON

/*Create a procedure*/
CREATE OR REPLACE PROCEDURE P_GET_EMP_SAL (P_JOB VARCHAR2)
IS

/*Declare a ref cursor and local variables*/
  TYPE C IS REF CURSOR;
  CUR_EMP C;
  L_ENAME VARCHAR2(100);
  L_SAL NUMBER;
  L_STMT VARCHAR2(4000);

BEGIN

/*Open the ref cursor for a Dynamic SELECT statement*/
  L_STMT := 'SELECT ename, sal
             FROM employees
             WHERE JOB = '''||P_JOB||'''';
  OPEN CUR_EMP FOR L_STMT;
  LOOP

/*Fetch the result set and print the result set*/
  FETCH CUR_EMP INTO L_ENAME, L_SAL;
  EXIT WHEN CUR_EMP%NOTFOUND;
  DBMS_OUTPUT.PUT_LINE(RPAD(L_ENAME,6,' ')||'--'||L_SAL);
  END LOOP;

  CLOSE CUR_EMP;
END;
/

Procedure created.
```

The finance team uses the preceding procedure honestly to display the salaries of all salesmen as follows:

```
/*Testing the procedure for SALESMAN*/
EXEC P_GET_EMP_SAL ('SALESMAN')

ALLEN --2000
WARD  --1650
MARTIN--1650
TURNER--1900


PL/SQL procedure successfully completed.
```

Now, we will attack the code with a malicious input and pull out the salary details of all the employees:

```
/*Testing the procedure with malicious input*/
EXEC P_GET_EMP_SAL ('XXX'' OR ''1''=''1')

SMITH --9200
ALLEN --2000
WARD  --1650
JONES --3375
MARTIN--1650
BLAKE --3250
CLARK --2850
SCOTT --3400
KING  --5400
TURNER--1900
ADAMS --1500
JAMES --1350
FORD  --3400
MILLER--1700


PL/SQL procedure successfully completed.
```

Observe the impact of SQL injection. A hacker can get access to the salary information of all the employees in the organization. An unauthenticated string input is concatenated with a "Always True" condition for unintended execution of a dynamic SQL. Applications, where client input is required to invoke an Oracle subprogram, run a high risk of code injection.

Types of SQL injection attacks

Based on the injection attack type and its impact analysis, the SQL injection attack can be classified into two categories:

- **First-order attack**: When the code attack is done from the client inputs to alter the objective of the invoked Oracle subprogram, the degree of attack is "one". As an impact of the attack, the data may lose its confidentiality due to unauthorized access by the hacker.

- **Second-order attack**: When the attack performs a different activity from the ongoing system activity, the attack comes under second-order attack.

The categories in the preceding list are just a broad categorization of the hacker's activities. Apart from these categories, the hackers can employ different techniques "blindly", resulting in the malfunctioning of the application.

The following diagram branches the impacts of SQL injection:

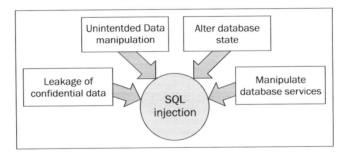

Preventing SQL injection attacks

SQL injection is a malicious practice, not a bug. Applications cannot be completely shielded against SQL injection but can be immunized against such acts. The code base development should take care to adopt the best practices which can evade the possibilities of code attack.

Let us briefly cover some of the precautionary measures which minimize injection attacks:

- **Avoid dynamic SQL**: Using dynamic SQL with "built up" inputs, they easily fell prey to injection attacks. Embedding dynamic SQLs within the programs must be avoided where static SQLs can be substituted. Static SQL must be used if all the query identifiers are known at the time of the code development. Otherwise, the dynamic SQL must use sanitized inputs or bind arguments to discourage the hackers from breaking through the code.

- **Monitor user privileges to reduce the attack surface**: A user must enjoy only the access for which he is authorized as per his role. Irrelevant and excess privileges must be revoked to reduce the access perimeter of a user.

  In addition, the PL/SQL subprograms must be invoked by the invoker's rights and not the owner's or the creator's rights.

- **Use bind arguments**: The dynamic SQLs seeking inputs must make use of the bind arguments. It is a highly recommended programming tip to reduce the injective attacks on the code. It reduces the possibility of breaking through the code by providing concatenated inputs. Besides shielding against the code attack, bind arguments also improve code performance. It is because the usage of bind variables in a query avoids hard parsing and it pushes the Oracle server to reuse the execution plans for the SQL queries.

- **Sanitize client inputs with DBMS_ASSERT**: The inputs from the client must be verified before using them in the program logic. The DBMS_ASSERT package provides niche subprograms to validate the inputs from the application layer.

Immunizing SQL injection attacks

We will discuss the ways to immunize code against SQL injection in detail. Besides the ways which are listed above, we will discuss some additional tricks too, to reduce SQL injection attacks.

Reducing the attack's surface

Reducing the attack's surface is one of the preventive measures that are proactively used to fight the SQL injection attacks. It aims to minimize the area of operation and visibility of the hackers by controlling the privileges and execution rights of a user on the accessible subprograms. The technique is helpful when a user plays a defined role in an application but is still bestowed with a lot more irrelevant privileges from the admin. The attack perimeter can be reduced by:

- Controlling the user privileges
- Creating the program units with invoker's rights

Controlling user privileges

The DBA must keep a hawk eye on the roles of the users in the application to prevent any malicious motivation. The availability of additional spare privileges might end up in misuse and, hence, might threaten the database security. The DBA must revoke irrelevant privileges from the user. For example, a user, UREP, plays the role of a report generator in a team. As per his role, he must have only the SELECT privilege on the tables; he should not have rights to perform any transaction. The DBA must revoke the DML privileges:

```
SQL> REVOKE INSERT, UPDATE, DELETE ON EMPLOYEES FROM UREP
/

Revoke succeeded.
```

Besides controlling the user privileges, the client-based application must intelligently handle the exposing of the database APIs and the required inputs. The end user interfaces must use only driving APIs which require user input. The user inputs should be treated with their actual data types instead of type casts.

Invoker's and definer's rights

As per the default behavior of Oracle, a subprogram is executed by its owner's or definer's rights.

Suppose a user A created a procedure P to insert sales data in the SALES table. The user A grants the EXECUTE privilege on procedure P to another user B, who has no such privilege to insert data into the SALES table. The user B executes the procedure P. Will it be executed successfully? Of course, it will execute because the user B executes the procedure P with its owner's rights which have the privilege to create sales data. This implies that the definers' rights not only offer subprogram execution privileges but also share privileges on the objects which are referenced inside the subprogram body.

This default behavior can become chaotic, if wrongly used. An attacker can get unauthorized access to an API, which can be used vindictively. In such cases, the subprogram invokers' rights must override the subprogram definers' rights. The AUTHID CURRENT_USER clause is used to override the invokers' rights over the definers' rights.

We will conduct a small case study to understand the fact that a user must invoke a non-owned subprogram at the cost of his owned rights.

We create a procedure to modify the default tablespace of a user in SYS. Note that only DBA has the privilege to modify the tablespace of a user. The following program has been created for demonstration purpose only:

```
/*Connect as SYSDBA*/
Conn sys/system as SYSDBA
Connected.

/*Enable the SERVEROUTPUT to display the messages*/
SET SERVEROUTPUT ON

/*Create the procedure to alter the tablespace*/
CREATE OR REPLACE PROCEDURE p_mod_tablespace
(P_USERNAME VARCHAR2 DEFAULT NULL,
 P_TABLESPACE VARCHAR2 DEFAULT NULL)
IS
  V_STMT VARCHAR2(500);
BEGIN

/*Dynamically alter the user to modify default tablespace*/
  V_STMT:='ALTER USER '||p_username ||
          ' default tablespace '|| P_TABLESPACE;

/*Execute the dynamic statement*/
  EXECUTE IMMEDIATE v_stmt;
END p_mod_tablespace;
/

Procedure created.
```

For demonstration purpose, the DBA grants the EXECUTE privilege on the procedure to the ORADEV user.

```
/*Grant execute on the procedure to ORADEV*/
SQL> GRANT execute ON p_mod_tablespace TO ORADEV
/

Grant succeeded.
```

Verify that the ORADEV user doesn't has sufficient privilege to modify the tablespace of a user:

```
/*Connect to ORADEV user*/
SQL> CONN ORADEV/ORADEV
Connected.
```

```
/*Verify the privileges of ORADEV user*/
SQL> ALTER USER nancy DEFAULT TABLESPACE system
/
ALTER USER NANCY DEFAULT TABLESPACE USERS
*
ERROR at line 1:
ORA-01031: insufficient privileges
```

The ORADEV user executes the P_MOD_TABLESPACE procedure for the preceding operation:

```
/*Connect to ORADEV user*/
Conn ORADEV/ORADEV
Connected.

/*Enable the SERVEROUTPUT to display the messages*/
SET SERVEROUTPUT ON

/*Execute the procedure to modify the default tablespace of user
NANCY*/
SQL> EXEC SYS.P_MOD_TABLESPACE ('NANCY','SYSTEM');

PL/SQL procedure successfully completed.
```

The procedure executed successfully because it uses the execution privileges of SYS, not of ORADEV. The ORADEV user enjoys only the invocation privilege.

Verify the change in the tablespace for the NANCY user

```
/*Connect as DBA*/
Conn sys/system as sysdba
Connected.

/*Check the default tablespace of NANCY*/
SELECT username, default_tablespace
FROM dba_users
WHERE username='NANCY'
/

USERNAME                        DEFAULT_TABLESPACE
------------------------------  -------------------
NANCY                           SYSTEM
```

Notice that a user can perform unauthorized activities as he executes the subprogram with the definer's rights. The DBA must realize the unintentional attacks resulting in the modification of important information.

Let us recreate the P_MOD_TABLESPACE procedure with the AUTHID CURRENT_USER option and repeat the steps:

```
/*Connect as SYSDBA*/
Conn sys/system as SYSDBA
Connected.

/*Enable the SERVEROUTPUT to display the messages*/
SET SERVEROUTPUT ON

/*Create the procedure to alter the tablespace*/
CREATE OR REPLACE PROCEDURE p_mod_tablespace
(P_USERNAME VARCHAR2 DEFAULT NULL,
 P_TABLESPACE VARCHAR2 DEFAULT NULL)
/*Specify the AUTHID CURRENT_USER clause*/
AUTHID CURRENT_USER
IS
  V_STMT VARCHAR2(500);
BEGIN

/*Dynamically alter the user to modify default tablespace*/
  V_STMT:='ALTER USER '||p_username ||
            ' default tablespace '|| P_TABLESPACE;

/*Execute the dynamic statement*/
  EXECUTE IMMEDIATE v_stmt;
END p_mod_tablespace;
/

Procedure created.
```

Now, the ORADEV user reconnects and invokes the procedure to revert back the tablespace changes in the last activity:

```
/*Connect to ORADEV user*/
Conn ORADEV/ORADEV
Connected.

/*Execute the procedure to modify tablespace of NANCY back to USERS*/
SQL> EXEC SYS.P_MOD_TABLESPACE ('NANCY','USERS');
BEGIN SYS.P_MOD_TABLESPACE ('NANCY','USERS'); END;

*
ERROR at line 1:
ORA-01031: insufficient privileges
ORA-06512: at "SYS.P_MOD_TABLESPACE", line 9
ORA-06512: at line 1
```

Now, the procedure execution fails as it is executed with the privileges of ORADEV and not of SYS. As ORADEV is a normal user, he cannot update the tablespace information for a user. Thus, the AUTHID CURRENT_USER clause can be used to minimize the chances of misusing the privileges.

Avoiding dynamic SQL

Dynamic SQL is the most vulnerable point identifiable in a PL/SQL program. A dynamically built up SELECT statement, which uses the parameter accepted by the subprogram, is an open invitation to attackers. In these scenarios, developers must predict and discover the scalability of the SQL query. If the query identifiers such as selected columns and table name are known at the runtime, static SQL must be encouraged. Dynamic SQL must come into the picture only when the complete SQL query has to be built up during runtime or dynamic DDL statements.

Static SQL statements in the PL/SQL program run rare threat of injection unless the attacker achieves code writing access. They are performance efficient also as they reduce the time consumed in identifier substitution and query building.

Let us observe the above recommendations in the following illustration.

The following P_SHOW_DEPT procedure accepts an employee ID and displays the corresponding department number:

```
/*Connect to ORADEV user*/
Conn ORADEV/ORADEV
Connected.

/*Enable the SERVEROUTPUT to display the messages*/
SET SERVEROUTPUT ON

/*Create the procedure*/
CREATE OR REPLACE PROCEDURE P_SHOW_DEPT
(P_ENAME VARCHAR2)
IS
    CUR SYS_REFCURSOR;
    l_ename VARCHAR2(100);
    l_deptno NUMBER;
BEGIN

/*Open ref cursor for a dynamic query using the input parameter*/
    OPEN CUR FOR 'SELECT ename, deptno
                    FROM employees
                    WHERE ename = '||P_ENAME;
```

```
    LOOP

/*Fetch and display the results*/
    FETCH CUR INTO l_ename, l_deptno;
    EXIT WHEN cur%notfound;
        DBMS_OUTPUT.PUT_LINE(RPAD(l_ename,6,' ') ||'--'|| l_deptno);
    END LOOP;
END;
/

Procedure created.

/*Testing the procedure*/
SQL> EXEC p_show_dept ('''KING''');
KING  --10

PL/SQL procedure successfully completed.
```

We will demonstrate how the objective of the procedure got changed due to the malicious inputs. The procedure was used to display the departments of employees but out of surprise, it can list the employees' salaries, too. The procedure input substituting an operand in the WHERE clause predicate is a clear threat to the data.

```
/*Invoking the procedure for a malicious input*/
EXEC P_SHOW_DEPT ('null UNION SELECT ENAME, SAL FROM EMPLOYEES');

ADAMS --1500
ALLEN --2000
BLAKE --3250
CLARK --2850
FORD  --3400
JAMES --1350
JONES --3375
KING  --5400
MARTIN--1650
MILLER--1700
SCOTT --3400
SMITH --9200
turner--1900
WARD  --1650

PL/SQL procedure successfully completed.
```

The preceding case demonstrates the vulnerability in dynamic SQLs. Leakage of confidential data!

Now as the query identifiers are already known in this case, we can replace the dynamic SQL by a static SQL. The P_SHOW_DEPT procedure can be rewritten as follows:

```
/*Create the procedure*/
CREATE OR REPLACE PROCEDURE P_SHOW_DEPT
(P_ENAME VARCHAR2)
IS
    CUR SYS_REFCURSOR;
    l_ename VARCHAR2(100);
    l_deptno NUMBER;
BEGIN
/*Open ref cursor for a static query using the input parameter*/
    OPEN CUR FOR SELECT ename, deptno
                 FROM employees
                 WHERE ename = P_ENAME;
    LOOP
/*Fetch and display the results*/
    FETCH CUR INTO l_ename, l_deptno;
    EXIT WHEN cur%notfound;
        DBMS_OUTPUT.PUT_LINE(RPAD(l_ename,6,' ') ||'--'|| l_deptno);
    END LOOP;
END;
/

Procedure created.

/*Testing the procedure*/
SQL> EXEC p_show_dept ('KING');
KING  --10

PL/SQL procedure successfully completed.
```

In the preceding code demonstration, notice that the query framing in a PL/SQL block minimizes the possibility of injection. In a dynamically framed SQL statement as a string, incoming parameters leave an open loop hole to the string where malicious inputs can flow in to deform the query. But static SQL queries use the input variables directly in the query predicates, which lowers down the probability of undesired deformation of the query. Now when we attempt to inject the procedure call again with the same input, the static SQL doesn't return any result, thus guarding the procedure against injective attacks.

```
/*Invoking the procedure for a malicious input*/
EXEC P_SHOW_DEPT ('null UNION SELECT ENAME, SAL FROM EMPLOYEES');

PL/SQL procedure successfully completed.
```

Another recommendation to immunize against attacks in dynamic SQLs is the usage of bind arguments. Dynamic SQLs must be implemented with bind arguments. We will see how to work with bind arguments in the next section.

Bind arguments

Bind arguments act as the placeholder in the dynamic SQL query. They can be substituted with actual arguments during query building at runtime. They minimize code injection attacks and yield good performance, too.

Dynamic SQL using concatenated inputs can substitute the concatenated parameter with a placeholder in the dynamic SQL or dynamic PL/SQL. At runtime, the placeholder can be replaced with an actual argument through the USING clause in the same positional order. Bind variables can successfully substitute the placeholders for the value operands in the WHERE clause.

Let us check the usage of bind arguments in our earlier example. We will recreate the P_SHOW_DEPT procedure using dynamic SQL and bind arguments. We will replace the parameter substitution in the dynamic SQL with a placeholder or bind variable (:bind).

```
/*Connect to ORADEV user*/
Conn ORADEV/ORADEV
Connected.

/*Enable the SERVEROUTPUT to display the messages*/
SET SERVEROUTPUT ON

/*Create the procedure*/
CREATE OR REPLACE PROCEDURE P_SHOW_DEPT
(P_ENAME VARCHAR2)
IS
   CUR SYS_REFCURSOR;
   l_ename VARCHAR2(100);
   l_deptno NUMBER;
BEGIN

/*Open ref cursor for a dynamic query using a bind variable*/
   OPEN CUR FOR 'SELECT ename, deptno
                 FROM employees
                 WHERE ename = :bind' USING P_ENAME;
   LOOP
```

```
/*Fetch and display the results*/
    FETCH CUR INTO l_ename, l_deptno;
    EXIT WHEN cur%notfound;
        DBMS_OUTPUT.PUT_LINE(l_ename ||'--'|| l_deptno);
    END LOOP;
END;
/


Procedure created.

/*Testing the procedure*/
SQL> EXEC p_show_dept ('KING');
KING--10


PL/SQL procedure successfully completed.
```

Now we will test the procedure against the malicious input:

```
/*Invoking the procedure for a malicious input*/
SQL> EXEC P_SHOW_DEPT ('null UNION SELECT ENAME, SAL FROM EMPLOYEES');

PL/SQL procedure successfully completed.
```

Once again, no result is returned. It is because the placeholder in the dynamic SQL substitutes a single string value. Here, a single string value is treated as null UNION SELECT ENAME, SAL FROM EMPLOYEES, which doesn't exists in the database.

Bind variables can be used as a placeholder in the dynamic SQL to substitute all types of inputs. It can be query identifiers such as columns or table names, keywords, and operands (like the one we just saw above). They are the preferred choice when the dynamic query uses the IN list or the LIKE operator.

As a limitation, bind arguments cannot substitute Oracle identifiers and keywords. Bind variables cannot be used in DDL statements and, also, they cannot substitute identifiers or keywords in a dynamic SELECT query.

Sanitizing inputs using DBMS_ASSERT

The inputs flowing from the client are another threat to code attacks. The string inputs to the dynamic SQL which do not use bind variables must be properly verified for purity and sanity before using them in the dynamic build of a SQL query. Frankly, it is the responsibility of both the client layer and middleware layer to authenticate the inputs. The client can programmatically perform the basic validation. A second layer check must be set up at the database side to sanitize the inputs supplied from the client.

Input sanitization becomes a mandatory activity when the dynamic SQL requires the substitution of Oracle identifiers.

The DBMS_ASSERT package

Oracle 10g release 2 introduced the DBMS_ASSERT package to sanitize the user inputs. The inputs from the application layer can be supplied to the DBMS_ASSERT subprograms and verified before they are employed in the program.

The DBMS_ASSERT package is owned by SYS and contains seven subprograms. These subprograms are listed in the following table:

Subprograms	Description
ENQUOTE_LITERAL function	Encloses a string literal within single quotes
ENQUOTE_NAME function	Encloses the input string in double quotes
NOOP functions	Overloaded function returns the value without any checking; does no operation
QUALIFIED_SQL_NAME function	Verifies that the input string is a qualified SQL name
SCHEMA_NAME function	Verifies that the input string is an existing schema name
SIMPLE_SQL_NAME function	Verifies that the input string is a simple SQL name
SQL_OBJECT_NAME function	Verifies that the input parameter string is a qualified SQL identifier of an existing SQL object

The most significant feature of DBMS_ASSERT is that most of its subprograms return the same input parameter as the output, after checking its properties. If the input fails expected "property", the VALUE_ERROR exception is raised.

Let us check the working of the subprograms.

The ENQUOTE_LITERAL subprogram can be used to sanitize the string inputs by enclosing them in single quotes. This function eliminates the possibility of leaking information by cladding an additional query using the UNION set operator:

```
/*Demonstrate the use of ENQUOTE_LITERAL*/
SELECT DBMS_ASSERT.ENQUOTE_LITERAL('KING')
FROM DUAL
/

DBMS_ASSERT.ENQUOTE_LITERAL('KING')
-----------------------------------
'KING'
```

The `ENQUOTE_NAME` can be used to enclose Oracle identifiers in double quotes and verify quoted identifiers.

```
/*Demonstrate the use of ENQUOTE_NAME*/
SELECT DBMS_ASSERT.ENQUOTE_NAME('KING')
FROM DUAL
/


DBMS_ASSERT.ENQUOTE_NAME('KING')
--------------------------------
"KING"
```

The `SCHEMA_NAME` function validates the current schema name. This eliminates the possibility of accessing other schema objects:

```
/*Demonstrate the use of SCHEMA_NAME*/
SELECT DBMS_ASSERT.SCHEMA_NAME('PLSQL')
from dual
/


SELECT DBMS_ASSERT.SCHEMA_NAME('PLSQL')
       *
ERROR at line 1:
ORA-44001: invalid schema
ORA-06512: at "SYS.DBMS_ASSERT", line 243


SELECT DBMS_ASSERT.SCHEMA_NAME('ORADEV')
from dual
/


DBMS_ASSERT.SCHEMA_NAME('ORADEV')
---------------------------------
ORADEV
```

Other subprograms—`SIMPLE_SQL_NAME` and `SQL_OBJECT_NAME`—are also of great relevance to validate the schema object names.

Identifier formatting and verification process

Oracle identifiers can be used in multiple contexts with different behaviors. This study is important to ensure the correct usage of an appropriate subprogram from a `DBMS_ASSERT` subprogram list. An identifier can be a quoted identifier, unquoted identifier, and a literal. All three contexts are entirely different from each other. Based on the context of the identifier in the scenario, the verification algorithm must be selected for sanitization.

We will check out for the identifier contexts. The different contexts are listed as follows:

- **Unquoted identifier**: This identifier obeys the naming convention of Oracle—it must begin with a letter followed by numbers or a set of defined special characters (_).

```
/*Use (employees) as unquoted identifier*/
SELECT * FROM employees
/
```

In the preceding query, the `employees` table acts as an unquoted identifier.

- **Quoted identifier**: It is enclosed with double quotes and follows no naming convention. It can start with a number (optionally) and can include any sort of characters.

```
/*Use (employees) as quoted identifier*/
SELECT * FROM "employees"
/
```

In the preceding query, the quoted identifier `"employees"` is different from the unquoted indentifier `employees`. Quoted identifiers can be used as a method of code attack.

- **Literal**: It can be any fixed value used in the SQL query.

```
/*Demonstrate a literal*/
SELECT * FROM employees WHERE ename = 'KING'
/
```

In the preceding query, `'KING'` is a literal.

```
/*Use (employees) as a literal*/
SELECT * FROM user_tables WHERE table_name='EMPLOYEES'
/
```

Note that the `EMPLOYEES` table (identifier) acts as a literal in the preceding query.

Appropriate usage of verification algorithm is necessary to ensure the sanity of the identifier. We saw that an identifier can be any of the following:

- **Basic**: This identifier is always an unquoted identifier. As the Basic identifier is built up of a defined set of characters, it requires less formatting and is deemed to be sanitized.

- **Simple**: This identifier may or may not be a quoted identifier. The `SIMPLE_SQL_NAME` function can be used to verify its purity and sanity. It checks only the admissible character sets and not the length of the identifier.

If the identifier is unquoted, the function checks for the naming convention as applied to Basic identifier (allowed character set is `A-Z`, `a-z`, `0-9`, `$`, `#`, and `_`).

If the identifier is quoted, it can include any character set within the double quotes.

Check out the following illustration:

```
/*Demonstrate verification algorithm for Simple identifier using
quoted identifier*/
SQL> select DBMS_ASSERT.SIMPLE_SQL_NAME('"1select"')
     from dual
     /


DBMS_ASSERT.SIMPLE_SQL_NAME('"1SELECT"')
-------------------------------------------------------
"1select"


/*Demonstrate verification algorithm for Simple identifier using
unquoted identifier*/
SQL> select DBMS_ASSERT.SIMPLE_SQL_NAME('1select')
     from dual
     /
select DBMS_ASSERT.SIMPLE_SQL_NAME('1select')
       *
ERROR at line 1:
ORA-44003: invalid SQL name
ORA-06512: at "SYS.DBMS_ASSERT", line 146
```

- **Qualified**: This identifier is mainly used for the sanity check of database links, but behaves in a similar way to simple SQL names in most of cases. It can include more than one simple SQL name as a schema name, object and a DB link, too. They can follow any one of the following syntax:

```
<local qualified name> ::= <simple name> {'.' <simple name>}
<database link name> ::= <local qualified name> ['@' <connection
string>]
<connection string> ::= <simple name>
<qualified name> ::= <local qualified name> ['@' <database link
name>]
```

Check out the difference between `SIMPLE_SQL_NAME` and `QUALIFIED_SQL_NAME` in the following illustration:

```
/*Demonstrate verification algorithm for Qualified SQL identifier
using SIMPLE_SQL_NAME*/
SQL> select dbms_assert.simple_sql_name('schema.obj@dblink')
```

```
      from dual
      /
select dbms_assert.simple_sql_name('schema.obj@dblink') from dual
      *
ERROR at line 1:
ORA-44003: invalid SQL name
ORA-06512: at "SYS.DBMS_ASSERT", line 146

/*Demonstrate verification algorithm for Qualified SQL identifier
using QUALIFIED_SQL_NAME*/
SQL> select dbms_assert.qualified_sql_name('schema.obj@dblink')
      from dual
      /

DBMS_ASSERT.QUALIFIED_SQL_NAME('SCHEMA.OBJ@DBLINK')
-----------------------------------------------------------------
schema.obj@dblink
```

The behavior of quoted and unquoted qualified SQL names remains same as we discussed earlier.

DBMS_ASSERT—usage guidelines

The best practices to use the DBMS_ASSERT validation package are as follows:

- Unnecessary uppercase conversion of identifiers must be avoided.

  ○ **Case 1**: The following statement is not the correct usage of basic unquoted identifiers:

  ```
  BAD_USAGE := sys.dbms_assert.SCHEMA_NAME(UPPER(MY_SCHEMA));
  ```

  As the SCHEMA_NAME function is case sensitive, the quoted inputs must be provided to check their sanity. Explicit transformation of the identifiers must be avoided to ensure the accuracy of the result. If the input schema name is not a valid schema, Oracle raises a ORA-44001: invalid schema exception.

  ○ **Case 2**: The following statement is a better practice to use the unquoted identifier:

  ```
  BETTER_USAGE := sys.dbms_assert.SCHEMA_NAME(MY_SCHEMA);
  ```

  ○ **Case 3**: The best way to avoid any possibility of bad input is demonstrated in the following statement. The schema name has been unquoted by setting off the ENQUOTE property:

  ```
  BEST_USAGE := sys.dbms_assert.ENQUOTE_NAME(
    sys.dbms_assert.SCHEMA_NAME(MY_SCHEMA),FALSE);
  ```

- Escape quotation marks when using ENQUOTE_NAME—avoid unnecessary quoting of identifiers when using ENQUOTE_NAME. Similarly, for ENQUOTE_LITERAL, single quotes in the input must be prevented. Note that ENQUOTE_NAME must be used with quoted identifiers only.

- NULL results from DBMS_ASSERT must be ignored. The subprograms SIMPLE_SQL_NAME, QUALIFIED_SQL_NAME, SCHEMA_NAME, and SQL_OBJECT_NAME sanitize the identifiers and the results returned are same as the input. Other subprograms such as NOOP, ENQUOTE_NAME and ENQUOTE_LITERAL can accept NULL values.

- Length validation check must be enforced in addition to the DBMS_ASSERT verification algorithms.

- Protect all injection prone parameters and code paths.

- The DBMS_ASSERT also exists as a public synonym; it is recommended to make all references to its subprograms by prefixing SYS which is the owning schema.

- Make use of DBMS_ASSERT specific exceptions to identify the actual exception raised by the bad inputs. The exceptions ORA44001 to ORA44004 are the DBMS_ASSERT exceptions:

  ○ ORA44001 stands for sys.dbms_assert.INVALID_SCHEMA_NAME

  ○ ORA44003 stands for sys.dbms_assert.INVALID_SQL_NAME

  ○ ORA44002 stands for sys.dbms_assert.INVALID_OBJECT_NAME

  ○ ORA44004 stands for sys.dbms_assert.QUALIFIED_SQL_NAME

DBMS_ASSERT—limitations

The DBMS_ASSERT package has certain limitations, as follows:

- No validation for TNS connection strings

- No validation for buffer overflow attacks

- It only checks the value property of an input value, it doesn't parse property of a value as a database identifier

- No validation for unprivileged access of objects

Testing the code for SQL injection flaws

Until now, we discussed the symptoms and remedies of SQL injection. We demonstrated the programming recommendations to mitigate the effects of code injections and smuggles. Assuring code quality and testing play a crucial role in taking preventive measures against hackers. Code testing resources must adopt a concrete strategy to discover and hit upon the code vulnerabilities before it invites an attacker to exploit the database. Now, we will discuss some of the testing considerations to test the code for SQL injection flaws.

Test strategy

A logical and effective test strategy must be employed to discover injection flaws. Of course, there is no magic practice to ooze out all flaws in the code.

The usual code reviews are part of static testing while testing the programs with sample data and inputs come under dynamic testing. These days, static testing has been absorbed into the development stage where developers, their peers and seniors review the code. Major syntactical errors, logical issues, code practices, and injection bugs can be traced at this level. The Dry Run concept can even check multiple scenarios and ensure bug-free application submission to the quality assurance team.

Reviewing the code

As a reviewer of the code, the first and foremost step is to check the attack surface. The code reviewer must measure the exposure of database programs in the client. In addition, he must check the privilege set available with the database users. Once these steps are passed with satisfaction, he must get into the code to search for key vulnerable areas.

In PL/SQL-based applications, always be careful to look for:

- Dynamic SQL build ups:
    - `EXECUTE IMMEDIATE`
    - `REF CURSOR` queries
    - `DBMS_SQL`
    - `DBMS_SYS_SQL`
- Check for appropriate usage of bind arguments
- Parameter input sanitization

Similarly, in Java or C client architecture, the reviewer must look for dynamic callable statement preparation.

Static code analysis

SQL injection attacks are mostly due to coding unawareness and dynamic SQLs. Therefore, static code analyzers cannot easily trace the application vulnerability. From the Oracle documentation, the term "Static Code Analysis" can be defined as follows:

> *Static code analysis is the analysis of computer software that is performed without executing programs built from that software. In most cases, the analysis is performed on some version of the source code and in other cases, some form of the object code. The term is usually applied to the analysis performed by an automated tool.*

It is advisable that such analysis tools should not be considered as the testing benchmark and confirmatory tools. Instead, they can be used for white box testing where the application is tested for smooth logical flow and program executions for different nature of input data.

Fuzz tools

Fuzz testing is similar to doing "Bungee jumping" with the code. It is rough testing, which is not based out on any logic, but meant to measure the security and scalability of the application. It measures the sustainable degree up of an application to the bad and malicious inputs. Without any preconception of the system or program behavior, it uses raw inputs to check the program semantics. The environment for fuzz testing tools can be made explicitly by modifying the context values and manipulating the test data.

The bugs reported in fuzz testing may not always be real threats to the application, but they can be a crucial clue to the vulnerability and injective attacks.

Generating test cases

The last and final call is the preparation of test cases. Though it is kept aside very often during the application development, test cases are a crucial stage to measure the strengths, robustness, and client input validation. Remember the following points:

- Each input from the client must be individually tested. All the remaining parameters should be kept unchanged while generating a test case for varied behavior of client input.

- The best way to test SQL injection is to provide junk data, concatenated string inputs, and many more.

- Test with varied nature of input; try with object names, identifiers, dummy names to arrive at a positive conclusion.

Summary

In the chapter, we learned a malicious hacking concept—SQL Injection. We understood the causes of code attack and its impact on the database. We covered the techniques to safeguard an application against the injective attacks through demonstrations and illustrations. At the end of the chapter, we discussed some of the testing considerations to hit the vulnerable areas in the code.

Practice exercise

1. Which method would you employ to immunize the PL/SQL code against SQL Injection attacks?

   a. Replace Dynamic SQLs with Static SQLs.

   b. Replace concatenated inputs in Dynamic SQL with binds arguments.

   c. Declare the PL/SQL program to be executed by its invoker's rights.

   d. Removing string type parameters from the procedure.

2. Use static SQL to avoid SQL injection when all Oracle identifiers are known at the time of code execution.

   a. True

   b. False

3. Choose the impact of SQL injection attacks:

   a. Malicious string inputs can extract confidential information.

   b. Unauthorized access can drop a database.

   c. It can insert ORDER data in EMPLOYEES table.

   d. A procedure executed with owners' (SYS) rights can change the password of a user.

4. Pick the correct strategies to fight against of SQL injection

   a. Sanitize the malicious inputs from the application layer with DBMS_ASSERT.

   b. Remove string concatenated inputs from the Oracle subprogram.

   c. Dynamic SQL should be removed from the stage.

   d. Execute a PL/SQL program with its creator's rights.

5. Statistical Code analysis provides an efficient technique to trace application vulnerability by using ideal and expected parameter values.

   a. True

   b. False

6. Fuzz tool technique is a harsh and rigorous format of testing which uses raw inputs and checks a program's sanctity.

   a. True

   b. False

7. Choose the accomplishments achieved by the DBMS_ASSERT package to prevent SQL injection?

   a. Enclose a given string in single quotes.

   b. Enclose a given string in double quotes.

   c. Verify a schema object name.

   d. Verify a SQL simple and qualified SQL identifier.

8. Identify the nature of a table name in the following SELECT statement
```
SELECT TOTAL
FROM "ORDERS"
WHERE ORD_ID = P_ORDID
/
```

   a. Unquoted identifier

   b. Quoted identifier

   c. Literal

   d. Placeholder

9. Which of the following DBMS_ASSERT subprogram modifies the input value?

   a. SIMPLE_SQL_NAME

   b. ENQUOTE_LITERAL

   c. QUALIFIED_SQL_NAME

   d. NOOP

10. The code reviews must identify certain vulnerable key areas for SQL Injection. Select the correct ones from the following list:

    a. DBMS_SQL

    b. BULK COLLECT

    c. EXECUTE IMMEDIATE

    d. REF CURSOR

11. The AUTHID CURRENT_USER clause achieves which of the following purposes?

    a. Code executes with invoker's rights.

    b. Code executes with current logged in user.

    c. Eliminates SQL injection vulnerability.

    d. Code executes with the creator's rights.

Answers to Practice Questions

Chapter 1, Overview of PL/SQL Programming Concepts

Question No.	Answer	Explanation
1	c	Currently, SQL Developer doesn't provide backup and recovery features. However, it can be done using a regular database export from SQL Developer.
2	a, c, and d	A function can be called from a SQL expression only if it doesn't hinder the database state and purity level.
3	a	The ALL_DEPENDENCIES dictionary view has been filtered by REFERENCED_TYPE and REFERENCED_OWNER for SYS owned tables and views.
4	c	The local variables are local to the block only. They cannot be referred outside their native PL/SQL block.
5	a, b, and d	An exception variable cannot be simply declared and used with RAISE_APPLICATION_ERROR. It has to be mapped to a self defined error number using PRAGMA EXCEPTION_INIT, and then raised through RAISE_APPLICATION_ERROR with an exception message.

Question No.	Answer	Explanation
6	a and b	A function must return a value using the RETURN statement while a procedure might return a value through the OUT parameters. Standalone subprograms (functions and procedures) cannot be overloaded. Only the subprograms declared in a package can be overloaded. Both procedures and functions can accept parameters in either of the two modes — pass by value and pass by reference.
7	c	For implicit cursors, the %FOUND attribute is set to TRUE, if the SQL statement fetches a minimum of one record.

Chapter 2, Designing PL/SQL Code

Question No.	Answer	Explanation
1	c	All the cursor attributes, except %ISOPEN, must be accessed within the cursor execution cycle. Once the cursor is closed, the cursor work area is flushed.
2	b and c	The use of cursor FOR loops prevents erratic coding. Fetching the cursor data into a record reduces the overhead of declaring block variables.
3	b	Implicit cursor attributes hold the value of the last executed SQL query. Therefore, it must be referenced just after the SQL query
4	a and b	Cursor variables can point to several cursor objects (cursor work area) in shared memory. Ref cursor types can be declared in a package specification.
5	a	A strong ref cursor must mandatorily have the RETURN type specification. The RETURN type can be a table record structure or a user-defined type.

Question No.	Answer	Explanation
6	a and b	Cursor variables can dynamically point to different work areas and, hence, different result sets. The biggest advantage of cursor variables is their ability to share the pointer variable amongst the client environments and other subprograms.
7	b	As the OPEN stage of cursor variables has to be explicitly specified, it cannot be opened with the cursor FOR loops.
8	a and d	A subtype inherits the complete table record structure and the NULL property of its columns.

Chapter 3, Using Collections

Question No.	Answer	Explanation
1	a and c	Associative arrays can have negative integer subscripts, positive integer subscripts and string subscripts. As associative arrays are treated as local arrays, initialization is not required for them.
2	c	Nested tables are an unbounded collection which can grow dynamically.
3	a	Varrays are always dense collections. Sparse varray doesn't exist.
4	c and d	BOOLEAN and NUMBER are not suitable index types for an associative array.
5	a and c	Yes, varray limit can be increased during runtime using the ALTER TABLE statement. If all the cells of a varray are populated with elements, LAST is equal to COUNT. This also holds true when the varray is empty.

Question No.	Answer	Explanation
6	b	The first DBMS_OUTPUT prints the first element from the default constructor. Once it is reassigned with a value in the executable section, the default values are overwritten.
7	a and c	Varrays are bounded collections which can accommodate data maximum up to the specified limit.
8	a, b, and c	EXISTS doesn't raises any exception.
		DELETE cannot be used with varrays.

Chapter 4, Using Advanced Interface Methods

Question No.	Answer	Explanation
1	a and c	The extproc process is a session specific process started by the Oracle listener and loads the shared library.
2	b	External procedure support was introduced in Oracle 8.
3	a	The PL/SQL wrapper containing the call specification is dependent on the database library object.
4	b	The TNS service ORACLR_CONNECTION_DATA connects to the listener with the SID_NAME in the CONNECT_DATA parameter.
5	b	The loadjava utility loads the Java class to a specified user in a database.
6	a	Java programs are directly supported by Oracle and do not use the extproc process.
7	c	The external function name is case sensitive. The PL/SQL wrapper must use it exactly in same case as specified in the external program.

Chapter 5, Implementing VPD with Fine Grained Access Control

Question No.	Answer	Explanation
1	c	The policy function returns the predicate as `<Column>=<Value>`.
2	b	The security policy can be associated to one and only one schema object.
3	b and c	The DBMS_RLS package is a SYS owned built in package whose public synonym is shared amongst the users. It is a useful package to work with policies and policy groups.
4	b	There is no such privilege as CREATE_ CONTEXT. It should be the CREATE ANY CONTEXT privilege. All context metadata is in either ALL_CONTEXTS or DBA_CONTEXTS.
5	a	Context creation followed by the creation of its trusted package. A policy function is created for the predicate and the security is attached for the protection.
6	b	Policy groups are created by the collection of policies under them.
7	b and d	Default policy type is Dynamic. Shared static policy is the one where a static policy can be shared by multiple database objects. In such cases, the column appearing in the predicate must exist in all the tables.
8	c and d	Either a DBA or a user with the DBA role can create and drop an application context. A DBA can modify certain USERENV attributes, but not all.
9	a	The predicate information returned by the policy function is retained in SGA until the query is reparsed. During the parse stage, the current context information is matched with the latest. If the value has been changed, Oracle synchs the context values; otherwise the old value is retained.
10	a	The applicable policy tries to access the F_JOB_POLICY policy function which doesn't exist in the ORADEV schema.

Chapter 6, Working with Large Objects

Question No.	Answer	Explanation
1	a	LOBs can appear as a database column or a user defined object type attribute.
2	b	LOB type parameters can exist.
3	a	LOB data greater than 4 K is stored out of line with the current row. Mandatorily, it's a different LOB segment which may or may not be in the same tablespace.
4	b	The BLOB column must be initialized with EMPTY_BLOB()
5	c	The constructor methods EMPTY_CLOB() and EMPTY_BLOB() are used to initialize NULL and NOT NULL LOB types.
6	b and c	FILEOPEN works only with BFILEs.
7	b	Temporary LOBs are session specific.
8	c and d	BFILE is a read-only type. The files accessed through the BFILE locator open in read-only mode. They cannot be manipulated in any way during the BFILE access.
9	b and d	Temporary LOB is always an internal LOB which is used for manipulative actions in the LOB columns within a block.
10	c	The user must have read/write privilege on the directory to access the files contained in it.
11	b	A LONG column can be migrated to a LOB column using the following syntax: ```\nALTER TABLE [<schema>.]<table_\nname>\n MODIFY (<long_column_name> {\nCLOB | BLOB | NCLOB }\n [DEFAULT <default_value>])\n[LOB_storage_clause]\n``` Note that a LONG column can be migrated to CLOB or NCLOB while a LONG RAW column can be modified to BLOB only.

Question No.	Answer	Explanation
12	b	The BFILENAME function is used to return the LOB locator of a file which is located externally. It can be used for internal LOBs as well as external LOBs.
13	b and d	SecureFile is a new feature in Oracle 11*g* to store large objects with enhanced security, storage, and performance. Older LOBs may still exist as BasicFiles and can be migrated to SecureFiles.
14	a and c	The CREATE TABLE script executes successfully. The table and LOB are created in the default user tablespace. Oracle implicitly generates the LOB segment and LOB index. However, the segments are not created until the data has been inserted in the table.

Chapter 7, Using SecureFile LOBs

Question No.	Answer	Explanation
1	a, c, and d	SecureFiles can reside only on ASSM tablespaces. They are free from LOB index contention and high water mark contention. Up to 4 MB, SecureFile LOB data can be cached under the WGC component of the buffer cache.
2	a and d	Being part of the advanced compression, compression in SecureFile doesn't affect performance. It is intelligently handled by the LOB manager to perceive the impact of compression on LOB data.
3	b	Compression, deduplication, and encryption are mutually exclusive features of a SecureFile.
4	b	Table compression has nothing to do with SecureFile compression.

Question No.	Answer	Explanation
5	a and b	KEEP_DUPLICATES is the default option. The feature doesn't affect performance as the secure hash matching is a transparent process in the server.
6	c and d	The encryption keys are stored in the wallet directory. An encrypted SecureFile column cannot be modified for the encryption algorithm.
7	b	Online redefinition works with materialized views to get the latest snapshot of the source table, so that the ongoing data changes are not lost during redefinition processes.

Chapter 8, Compiling and Tuning to Improve Performance

Question No.	Answer	Explanation
1	a and b	Interpreted compilation mode is preferred when a program unit is in development stage and involves SQL statement processing.
2	c and d	The Real Native compilation method removes the dependency on C compiler to generate DLL for the program unit. Instead, the native DLLs are stored in the database dictionary itself. As the DLLs are stored in the dictionary, they can be a part of the normal backup and recovery.
3	b	The PLSQL_OPTIMIZE_LEVEL value set to 3 strictly inlines all the subprograms at high priority.

Question No.	Answer	Explanation
4	b and c	The PLSQL_CODE_TYPE value specified during recompilation of a program overrides the current system or session settings. Its default value is INTERPRETED and it must be updated in the spfile instance after the database upgrade process. In real native mode, the libraries are stored in the SYSTEM tablespace.
5	a and c	Usage of BULK COLLECT can pull multi-row data from the database in a single attempt, thus reducing context switches. PLS_INTEGER is a preferred data type in arithmetic calculations.
6	d	Inlining of subprograms is only supported at optimization level greater than one.
7	b and c	The F_ADD local function would be called inline because its call has been marked inline using PRAGMA INLINE. It might also be considered for inlining as the PLSQL_OPTIMIZE_LEVEL value is 2.
8	b	The DLLs generated from the Real Native compilation are stored in the SYSTEM tablespace.
9	a and d	The NOT NULL data types add overhead to check every assignment for nullity. L_SUM must be declared as L_SUM NATURAL; Usage of appropriate data types to avoid implicit typecasting improves performance. L_ID must be declared as NUMBER.
10	a, c, and d	PRAGMA INLINE works for PLSQL_OPTIMIZE_LEVEL values 2 and 3. At level 1, the Oracle optimizer doesn't consider any subprogram for inlining. At level 3, all subprograms are strictly called for inline. However, inlining of a subprogram can be set off by specifying PRAGMA INLINE (<Function name>, 'NO').

Chapter 9, Caching to Improve Performance

Question No.	Answer	Explanation
1	a	The database server would cache the query results only when the user explicitly allocates the cache memory at the server and the caching feature is enabled. In the given scenario, caching is disabled as the value of the RESULT_CACHE_MAX_SIZE parameter is 0.
2	b and d	In automatic result caching, the RESULT_CACHE hint is ineffective as the server implicitly caches results of all SQL queries.
3	a	When the dependent table data gets updated, all the cached results get invalidated.
4	b	The cached results are stored at the server and are sharable across the sessions of the user.
5	b	PL/SQL result cache feature is operative only upon the functions which are declared as standalone or local to a stored subprogram or within a package.
6	a	The RELIES_ON clause has been deprecated in Oracle 11*g* R2.
7	b and c	The server doesn't cache the results of the queries which use sequence or any pseudo column (here SYSDATE).
8	b	PL/SQL function result cache works on server-side memory infrastructure which is the same for both SQL and PL/SQL. Only the results of functions can be cached at the server. The function must not be a pipelined one or the one declared with invoker's rights. It should accept parameters in the pass by reference mode of primitive data types only.
9	a and b	The valid values are PUBLISHED, NEW, INVALID, BYPASS, and EXPIRED.
10	a, b, c, and d	The V$RESULT_CACHE_STATISTICS dynamic performance view stores the latest cache memory statistics.

Chapter 10, Analyzing PL/SQL Code

Question No.	Answer	Explanation
1	b	The ALL_ARGUMENTS dictionary view captures the information about the subprogram arguments.
2	d	Server places the identifier information in the SYSAUX tablespace.
3	a	The parameter values used in the subprograms of the DBMS_METADATA package are case sensitive.
4	b	The FORMAT_CALL_STACK forms the stack of all program units traversed by the server.
5	b and c	The DBMS_METADATA package can generate reports for table grants, object dependencies and DDL of given objects in a schema.
6	b	The PL/Scope tool can store the identifier data in the SYSAUX tablespace only.
7	a and b	For tables and views, the DDL script can be extracted without a storage clause by setting the STORAGE parameter to FALSE. Similarly, views scripts can be made force free by setting the FORCE parameter to FALSE.

Chapter 11, Profiling and Tracing PL/SQL Code

Question No.	Answer	Explanation
1	b	The Analyzer component interprets the raw profiler data and loads into the database tables.
2	b	The plshprof is a command-line utility to generate HTML reports from raw profiler output.
3	d	The PLSQL_DEBUG parameter has been deprecated starting from Oracle 11*g*.

Question No.	Answer	Explanation
4	c	The `$ORACLE_HOME\rdbms\admin\tracetab.sql` script creates the trace log tables — `PLSQL_TRACE_RUNS` and `PLSQL_TRACE_EVENTS`.
5	c and d	The trace control levels cannot be used in combination with the other trace levels.
6	a and b	The `plshprof` utility is a command-line tool to convert raw profiler data into HTML reports.
7	c	The Analyzer component can trace multiple subprograms profiled into one trace file.
8	a	The `max_depth` parameter can be specified to limit the recursive levels in `START_PROFILING`.

Chapter 12, Safeguarding PL/SQL Code against SQL Injection Attacks

Question No.	Answer	Explanation
1	a, b, and c	Dynamic SQL is more prone to injective attacks. Static SQL must be preferred in major cases. In other cases, dynamic SQL must use bind variables.
2	a	If the SQL query identifiers are fixed for all the executions of a subprogram, static SQL can be used in the program.
3	a and d	SQL injection can lead to the leakage of confidential information and perform unauthorized activities.
4	a	The inputs from the application layer must be verified for purity before using in the application.
5	b	Statistical code analysis is used only for logical flow of the code but doesn't provide confirmation on the code vulnerability.

Question No.	Answer	Explanation
6	a	Fuzzing is a rough testing method to measure the resistivity and scalability of the program, which can discover the vulnerable areas of the code.
7	c and d	The DBMS_ASSERT.SQL_OBJECT_NAME subprogram validates the object contained in the current schema. The SIMPLE_SQL_NAME and QUALIFIED_SQL_NAME functions are used to verify the sanity of the SQL names.
8	b	The quoted identifier is used in queries enclosed within double quotes. Its meaning in the context is entirely different from the unquoted identifier.
9	b	ENQUOTE_LITERAL encloses a given string with single quotes.
10	a, c, and d	The Oracle keywords which implement dynamic SQL in the code are the most vulnerable areas in a PL/SQL code.
11	a and c	AUTHID CURRENT_USER eliminates the chances of SQL injection by executing a PL/SQL program with the rights of its invokers and not of the creator.

Index

B

BasicFiles
  migrating, to SecureFiles 220
BasicFiles to SecureFiles migration
  Online Redefinition method 220-224
  Partition method 220
BFILE 173
BFILE, DBMS_LOB data types 180
BFILENAME function 179
Binary Large Object. *See* **BLOB**
BLOB 172
BLOB, DBMS_LOB data types 180
bulk binding
  implementing 248, 249
  SAVE_EXCEPTIONS, using 252, 253
  using 249-251
BULK COLLECT
  about 249
  facts 250

C

cache 197, 270
cache grid 273
cache group 273
callback 123
callout 123
call specification 134
Character Large Object. *See* **CLOB**
CLOB 172
CLOSE procedure 181
code testing, for SQL injection flaws
  code, reviewing 386
  Fuzz testing 387
  static code analysis 387
  test case, generating 387
  test strategy 386
coding information
  [DBA | ALL | USER]_ARGUMENTS 301
  [DBA | ALL | USER]_DEPENDENCIES
    308, 309
  [DBA | ALL | USER]_OBJECTS 304, 305
  [DBA | ALL | USER]_PROCEDURES 307
  [DBA | ALL | USER]_SOURCE 306
  dictionary views 300
  finding, SQL developer used 310-319

  tracking 299-308
collection
  about 81, 103
  associative arrays, using 84
  categorizing 83
  characteristics 103, 104
  type structure 82
  initializing 115, 116
  nested tables, using 84
  non-persistent category 83
  overview 82
  persistent category 83
  type, selecting 84
  varrays, using 84
collection elements
  manipulating 113, 115
collection methods, PL/SQL
  about 105
  COUNT function 106
  DELETE function 112, 113
  EXISTS function 105, 106
  EXTEND function 109, 110
  FIRST function 108
  Last function 108
  LIMIT function 107
  NEXT function 109
  PRIOR function 109
  TRIM function 111
COLUMN_VALUE attribute 96
COMPARE function 181
compilation mode
  choosing 230
  interpreted compilation mode, choosing
    230
  native compilation mode, choosing 231
  setting 231
  setting, at database level 231
  setting, at session level 231
  settings, querying 232
compression feature 216
COMPRESS keyword 216
conditional control statements
  rephrasing 254
  rephrasing, AND logical operator used 254
  rephrasing, OR logical operator used 254
CONNECT_DATA parameter 127, 133

LONG data types
limitations 170
migrating to LOB 194
LONG RAW data types
limitations 170

M

machine code (bytecode) 228
manual result cache 274, 277

N

native compilation. *See* NCOMP
NCOMP
about 228, 235
program unit, comparing 233-235
nested table
about 84-89
creating, as database object 90, 91
DML operations 91
features 94-97
in PL/SQL 93, 94
using 84
versus associative arrays 104
versus varray 105
NOCACHE mode 210
non-persistent collection
associative array 83
NOOP functions 380
NOT NULL constraint 241-243

O

OCI client results cache 273
OID parameter 331
OLTP 209
Online Redefinition method
about 221
LOB columns, migrating 222, 223
pre-requisites 221
Online Transaction Processing. *See* OLTP
OPEN function 329
OPEN procedures 182
OPENW function 329
Oracle 11*g*
about 170
memory infrastructure diagram 271

Oracle Common Language Runtime.
See ORACLR
Oracle initialization parameter
enabling 256
PLSQL_OPTIMIZE_LEVELs 256-260
Oracle Net Configuration
about 125
LISTENER.ora 126-129
TNSNAMES.ora 125, 126
verifying 129, 130
Oracle-supplied packages
DBMS_ALERT 51
DBMS_HTTP 51
DBMS_LOCK 51
DBMS_OUTPUT 51
DBMS_SCHEDULER 51
DBMS_SESSION 51
packages 51
packages, categorizing 51, 52
reviewing 51
UTL_FILE 51
UTL_MAIL 51
Oracle Technology Network. *See* OTN
ORACLR 123
OR logical operator
using, for conditional control statements
rephrasing 254
OTN 15

P

packages
about 33
advantage 33
components, package body 34
components, package specification 33, 34
creating, syntax 34
parent table 89
partition method
about 220
new SecureFile partition 220
partitioned table, creating 220
performance optimization 269
persistent collection
nested table 84
Varray (variable-size array) 84
PGA 36

PUBLISHING

Thank you for buying
Oracle Advanced PL/SQL
Developer Professional Guide

About Packt Publishing

Packt, pronounced 'packed', published its first book "Mastering phpMyAdmin for Effective MySQL Management" in April 2004 and subsequently continued to specialize in publishing highly focused books on specific technologies and solutions.

Our books and publications share the experiences of your fellow IT professionals in adapting and customizing today's systems, applications, and frameworks. Our solution based books give you the knowledge and power to customize the software and technologies you're using to get the job done. Packt books are more specific and less general than the IT books you have seen in the past. Our unique business model allows us to bring you more focused information, giving you more of what you need to know, and less of what you don't.

Packt is a modern, yet unique publishing company, which focuses on producing quality, cutting-edge books for communities of developers, administrators, and newbies alike. For more information, please visit our website: www.packtpub.com.

About Packt Enterprise

In 2010, Packt launched two new brands, Packt Enterprise and Packt Open Source, in order to continue its focus on specialization. This book is part of the Packt Enterprise brand, home to books published on enterprise software – software created by major vendors, including (but not limited to) IBM, Microsoft and Oracle, often for use in other corporations. Its titles will offer information relevant to a range of users of this software, including administrators, developers, architects, and end users.

Writing for Packt

We welcome all inquiries from people who are interested in authoring. Book proposals should be sent to author@packtpub.com. If your book idea is still at an early stage and you would like to discuss it first before writing a formal book proposal, contact us; one of our commissioning editors will get in touch with you.

We're not just looking for published authors; if you have strong technical skills but no writing experience, our experienced editors can help you develop a writing career, or simply get some additional reward for your expertise.

OCA Oracle Database 11g: SQL Fundamentals I: A Real-World Certification Guide

Ace the 1Z0-051 SQL Fundamentals I exam, and become a successful DBA by learning how SQL concepts work in the real world

Steve Ries

OCA Oracle Database 11g: SQL Fundamentals I: A Real World Certification Guide (1ZO-051)

ISBN: 978-1-84968-364-7   Paperback: 460 pages

Ace the 1Z0-051 SQL Fundamentals I exam, and become a successful DBA by learning how SQL concepts work in the real world

1. Successfully clear the first stepping stone towards attaining the Oracle Certified Associate Certification on Oracle Database 11g

2. This book uses a real world example-driven approach that is easy to understand and makes engaging

3. Complete coverage of the prescribed syllabus

Oracle SQL Developer 2.1

Database design and development using this feature-rich, powerful, user-extensible interface

Sue Harper

Oracle SQL Developer 2.1

ISBN: 978-1-847196-26-2   Paperback: 496 pages

Database design and development using this feature-rich, powerful, user-extensible interface

1. Install, configure, customize, and manage your SQL Developer environment

2. Includes the latest features to enhance productivity and simplify database development

3. Covers reporting, testing, and debugging concepts

4. Meet the new powerful Data Modeling tool – Oracle SQL Developer Data Modeler

Please check **www.PacktPub.com** for information on our titles

Oracle Database 11gR2
Performance Tuning Cookbook

ISBN: 978-1-84968-260-2   Paperback: 542 pages

Over 80 recipes to help beginners achieve better performance from Oracle Database applications

1. Learn the right techniques to achieve best performance from the Oracle Database

2. Avoid common myths and pitfalls that slow down the database

3. Diagnose problems when they arise and employ tricks to prevent them

4. Explore various aspects that affect performance, from application design to system tuning

Getting Started with Oracle
Data Integrator 11g:
A Hands-On Tutorial

ISBN: 978-1-84968-068-4   Paperback: 450 pages

Combine high volume data movement, complex transformations and real-time data integration with the robust capabilities of ODI in this practical guide

1. Discover the comprehensive and sophisticated orchestration of data integration tasks made possible with ODI, including monitoring and error-management

2. Get to grips with the product architecture and building data integration processes with technologies including Oracle, Microsoft SQL Server and XML files

3. A comprehensive tutorial packed with tips, images and best practices

Please check **www.PacktPub.com** for information on our titles